AMERICAN LABOR IN A CHANGING WORLD ECONOMY

★ ★ ★ ★ ★ ★ ★ ★ ★

Carnegie Endowment for International Peace

edited by

Ward Morehouse

Published in cooperation with the Carnegie Endowment for International Peace

AMERICAN LABOR IN A CHANGING WORLD ECONOMY

PRAEGER PUBLISHERS
Praeger Special Studies

New York • London • Sydney • Toronto

Library of Congress Cataloging in Publication Data

Main entry under title:

American labor in a changing world economy.

1. Labor policy--United States. 2. International economics relations. 3. Industrial relations--United States. I. Morehouse, Ward, 1929- II. Carnegie Endowment for International Peace.

HD8072.A5135 331'.0973 78-15545

ISBN 0-03-045281-3

PRAEGER PUBLISHERS
PRAEGER SPECIAL STUDIES
383 Madison Avenue, New York, N.Y. 10017, U.S.A.

Published in the United States of America in 1978
by Praeger Publishers,
A Division of Holt, Rinehart and Winston, CBS, Inc.

0123456789 038 98765432

Printed in the United States of America

PREFACE

This is a book about jobs in a rapidly changing world economy. It explores the impact of international trade and foreign investment on jobs in the United States and in other countries. It examines the problems of establishing effective international fair labor standards and conducting meaningful collective bargaining with those extraordinary mobile giants known as multinational corporations. It looks at the dramatic changes in the international political and economic system brought about by the Organization of Petroleum Exporting Countries (OPEC) and their consequences for U.S. employment, the role of labor in Third World development and the meaning of new directions in North-South relations for American workers.

Two major themes stand out in the discussion of these issues. The first is that times have changed but that international economic policies affecting employment have not yet caught up with the times. Many of those involved in framing or influencing public policy in this arena are, in the eyes of their critics, burdened with old ideas and theories which do not fit the current reality.

The second theme is that the United States needs not so much a new set of international economic policies to cope with the changing times as it does a comprehensive and effective employment policy. A national employment policy would provide an integrating framework for coordinating tax policies on foreign and domestic investment and employment generation, tariffs and nontariff provisions affecting international trade, adjustment assistance and other labor market policies such as unemployment insurance and job training, and even international commodity and foreign aid policies which are having a growing impact on U.S. employment. Since the Carter administration has unveiled its energy program, it is time to go to work on framing a comprehensive, long-range national employment policy.

In other countries, productive and meaningful work is also a key issue. This is perhaps especially true in the developing countries, most of which, already saddled with high unemployment, are headed for an employment crisis of staggering proportions in the decade ahead. But more forthcoming U.S. policies on trade and aid abroad are politically out of the question at home as long as large numbers of Americans cannot find work. Therefore, the proper foundation for international economic policies which will promote employment in other countries is an effective national employment policy.

This book is an attempt to start up a dialogue, almost completely halted in recent years, between labor and those in government, the universities, foundations and the business community concerned with analyzing, formulating and influencing international economic policy. Readers should therefore keep in mind not only what is said but who is saying it. The result is not a weighty academic volume, even though some academics have contributed to it, but rather a wide ranging exchange of views, often expressed with urgency and intensity in plain and straightforward language. Such language is rarely encountered among "the occupants of think tanks and what Arthur Koestler has termed the 'call girls' who have learned papers and will travel to Aspen, Bellagio, Salzburg, Persepolis and other notorious sweatshops to ply their trade," to use the choice words of Lane Kirkland, Secretary-Treasurer of the AFL-CIO, in his contribution to this volume.

Dialogue does not necessarily lead to agreement, as is readily seen in the pages of this book. On some issues, those with contending views are 180 degrees apart, not even able to agree on the facts, let alone what should be done. But if participation in the dialogue is honest and serious, it can lead to a better understanding of the problem and of the views of those with a major stake in its solution. And on some issues it is possible to make out the shape, however dim, of a new consensus, with the principal parties within negotiable distance of one another.

This volume is based on a National Conference to Examine American Labor's Stake and Voice in a Changing World Economy, held in Portchester, New York, on December 14-16, 1976. It does not, however, purport to be a volume of proceedings of that conference. The presentations of some of those at the conference are not included here because their presentations did not fit naturally into the framework for this book. All of the contributions in the book have been revised, some substantially, since the conference. Nonetheless, the book would not have appeared if the conference had not been held, and the first round of acknowledgements should go to the American Federation of Labor-Congress of Industrial Organizations (AFL-CIO) and the following unions which cooperated in organizing the conference by taking part in its planning committee, encouraging key officials to attend, and in some cases, giving financial support as well:

AFL-CIO
Allied Industrial Workers, AFL-CIO
Amalgamated Clothing and Textile Workers, AFL-CIO
American Federation of State, County and Municipal Workers, AFL-CIO
American Federation of Teachers, AFL-CIO

Communications Workers, AFL-CIO
Industrial Union Department, AFL-CIO
International Association of Machinists and Aerospace
Workers, AFL-CIO
International Ladies' Garment Workers' Union, AFL-CIO
International Union of Electrical, Radio and Machine
Workers, AFL-CIO
United Auto Workers
Retail Clerks International Association, AFL-CIO
United Steelworkers, AFL-CIO

The three institutions sponsoring the conference—the Carnegie Endowment for International Peace, the New York State School of Industrial and Labor Relations of Cornell University, and the University of the State of New York, State Education Department—all provided time, manpower, and money. The Carnegie Endowment served as the conference secretariat and made available major funding. Generous financial support was also received from the Ford Foundation and the German Marshall Fund.

Much of the task of organizing the conference fell to three of us as the principal representatives of the sponsoring institutions—Betty Lall, Senior Extension Associate of the Cornell School of Industrial and Labor Relations, C. W. Maynes, then Secretary of the Carnegie Endowment and now Assistant Secretary of State for International Organization Affairs, and myself, then the Director of International Programs for the University of the State of New York. But the record should show that in the final, crucial months before the conference, the first two carried the main burden, and my agreeing to edit this book is in partial atonement of my delinquency during the conference preparatory period. Many others, too numerous to mention, including several devoted staff members of the Carnegie Endowment and the Cornell University School of Industrial and Labor Relations played important roles before and during the conference.

My work on this book has spanned half the world and involved two institutions which provided intellectual hospitality and vital logistic support: the Administrative Staff College of India in Hyderabad, where I was a visiting research fellow in the winter of 1977, and the Research Policy Program at the University of Lund in Sweden, where I was visiting professor during the 1976-1977 academic year. Alexandra C. Koppen, Kamal Raina, and R. K. Kapoor, the latter two on the staff of the University of the State of New York office in New Delhi, India, the Educational Resources Center, have all struggled with the voluminous correspondence and rapid typing of the manuscript essential in bringing out a volume with so many contributors in a timely fashion. Diane Bendahmane, the Carnegie Endowment's Assistant

Director of Publications, has also played an important role in making publication arrangements.

The final word of thanks must go to the contributors themselves. They have responded promptly to my requests for clarifications and revision, not always without prodding but responded nonetheless. And they have tolerated my surgical interventions in their manuscripts with remarkable equanimity and restraint. Indeed, it is only fair to note that in a few cases, my editorial interventions resulted in substantial condensation of some parts of the author's original text and expansion of other parts so that the version appearing here bears only limited resemblance to the original.

Some of the contributors occupied at the time of the conference or have since come to hold official government positions; in such instances, it should be assumed that the views expressed are their own and not necessarily those of the agencies with which they are associated. Furthermore, some critics of government policy have since moved to the other side of the table and are now actively engaged in trying to correct those abuses they previously criticized.

Abbreviated versions of several of the papers prior to their revision for publication in this volume were published immediately after the conference in order to share quickly with a wider audience some of the ideas and views presented at the conference. The January 1977 AFL-CIO American Federationist carried articles drawn from conference presentations by Lane Kirkland, Elizabeth R. Jager, Irving Brown, Ben Sharman and Stanley Ruttenberg. The winter 1977 issue of Foreign Policy carried excerpts from the presentations of Lane Kirkland, Peter Henle, Howard Samuel, Clas-Erik Odhner, Jack Berhman, Everett Kassalow and Shridath S. Ramphal. Brief excerpts from some of the papers just mentioned, as well as those by Daniel Mitchell, Herman Rebhan, William Walker and John Windmuller also appeared in the Monthly Labor Review of March 1977.

The labor movement's bottom line is jobs. This assertion is often made as though trade union officials were afflicted with a peculiar and parochial obsession. If the bottom line for corporate managers is profits and for political leaders in a democratic society, votes, then convention has it that labor leaders must be preoccupied with employment.

But jobs should be everybody's bottom line. For along with life itself and personal freedom, productive and meaningful work is one of the most basic human needs. The architects of American independence enshrined it as an inalienable right in their felicitous phrase, the pursuit of happiness. It is surely a critical test of the effectiveness of any economic and political system.

This book deals with the problem of providing productive and meaningful work in a changing international environment. Issues are involved which matter to all Americans, not just those in the labor movement. They also matter to workers everywhere else in the world. The issues are complex, the end result of alternative courses of action not always clear, and the choices therefore difficult. For far too long the interests of those who have the biggest stake in the choices being made have been left out. If this book helps in some measure to create a new calculus of decision-making on international economic policy which includes an honest search for answers to the question of who will pay for the choices made, it will have served its purpose.

Ward Morehouse

CONTENTS

LIST OF TABLES

Table		Page

LIST OF ABBREVIATIONS

ACP	African, Caribbean and Pacific Countries
AFL-CIO	American Federation of Labor-Congress of Industrial Organizations
AIEC	Association of Iron Ore Exporting Countries
CGT	Confederation General du Travail (General Confederation of Labor)
CIPEC	Intergovernmental Council of Copper Exporting Countries
DGB	German Federation of Trade Unions
DISC	Domestic International Sales Corporation
EC	European Community
EFTA	European Free Trade Association
EMF	European Metal Workers Federation
ETUC	European Trade Union Congress
FIET	International Federation of Commercial, Clerical and Technical Employees
GATT	General Agreement on Tariff and Trade
GNP	Gross National Product
GSP	Generalized Scheme of Preferences
IAM	International Association of Machinists and Aerospace Workers
ICFTU	International Confederation of Free Trade Unions
ICP	Integrated Commodity Program
ILO	International Labour Organisation
IMF	International Metalworkers Federation
IMF	International Monetary Fund
ITF	International Transport Workers Federation
ITS	International Trade Secretariats
LDC	Less Developed Countries
LO	Swedish Federation of Labor
m b/d	million barrels a day

MFN	Most Favored Nation
MNC	Multinational Corporation
NIEO	New International Economic Order
NTB	Nontariff barriers
OECD	Organisation for Economic Cooperation and Development
OPEC	Organization of Petroleum Exporting Countries
R&D	Research and Development
TEA	Trade Expansion Act
UNCTAD	United Nations Conference on Trade and Development
WCL	World Confederation of Labor
WFTU	World Federation of Trade Unions

PART I

TRADE AND JOBS

1

Promoting Economic Opportunity in a Changing World: Labor's Interests in Foreign Economic Policy

LANE KIRKLAND

LABOR'S VOICE IN WORLD ECONOMIC AFFAIRS

Among government policymakers, the occupants of think tanks, and what Arthur Koestler has termed the "call girls" who have learned papers and will travel to Aspen, Bellagio, Salzburg, Persepolis and other notorious sweatshops to ply their trade, the notion is epidemic that labor's voice in world economic affairs is simply an interference, producing regrettable distortions in the proper order of things. The premise seems to be that there is some higher and longer run interest to be served than the life span and well-being of plain people, no matter how numerous and sorely afflicted they are.

In those quarters, the only tolerable role for a labor union in such matters as trade policy is seen as one of torpid consent, of a blithe indifference to its own interests, and a benign neglect of the jobs and standards of its members. The unwelcome intrusion of labor's voice in protest is treated as the squall of a primitive infant impulse, to be stilled with a pabulum called Adjustment Assistance (which neither adjusts nor assists) while wiser heads get on with the world's business.

Labor does not, of course, accept that view of the matter. International economic and political issues are far too important and affect the lives of too many working people to be safely left in the hands of a tight incestuous breed of economists and diplomats.

We are not innocents or novices on the world scene. We have done our time in the field of international conflict; we have earned our scars and stripes; we have some perceptions born of experience, and we do mean to be heard.

The extent and nature of labor's work abroad is little known or understood by the public or the press, except for the revisionist historians of portside persuasion and the occasional diatribes by a variety of disinformation bureaus. Yet the AFL-CIO devotes a substantial part of its resources, attention, and manpower to overseas work. Through our international department and our free trade union institutes in Latin America, Asia, Africa, and our office in Europe, we maintain an extensive and experienced foreign service. Many of our affiliates are deeply involved in the work of the international trade secretariats, and, though sometimes strained or acrimonious, our bilateral relations with democratic trade union centers around the world are nevertheless active and important to us.

The political leaders and officials of many developing countries were trained in our trade union programs. They emerged from organizations that we helped to create and build, and enjoyed our support—and sometimes our refuge—in their struggles against colonialism and later persecution. They continue to visit us when in Washington, to seek our help on one matter or another or to rehash old times, to talk about when they were on the lam as well as their triumphs. I am sure many speak to us more frankly than they do to our embassies.

I recount these facts only to support an assertion that labor's voice belongs at the center of decision making rather than on the fringes, where decisions are simply talked about after they are made. Labor's aims, ideals, and interests parallel more broadly and closely the highest interests of the American people at large than does the voice of those who more frequently tip the scales of judgment.

JOBS, TRADE AND THE RIGHTS OF WORKERS

What are labor's interests? They embrace the preservation of economic opportunity for this and future generations of Americans, including the full range of human skills and talents vital to a strong, nonspecialized and nonelite society. Labor's interests emphasize the defense and expansion of human rights and human freedom. And they positively include the vigorous advocacy of a system of relations between labor and management whereby one confronts the other as an independent party rather than as a government agent, where neither embodies as well the army, the navy, the overt and secret police, the courts, not to mention the gulag and the madhouse.

Today we find our expression of those aims and interests widely labeled as "protectionism"—a pejorative term employed in haughty disregard of the value of the things we seek to protect or the cost of the ills that threaten them. Our critics recall with retroactive approval our long and often lonely support of reciprocal trade agreements and of other measures looking to the liberalization of international commerce. They will even sometimes acknowledge the fact that without labor's strong support, programs and appropriations for foreign aid would have long since expired.

Credit us then with some common sense. Concede us some knowledge of what is going on down there in the pit where people work and make their living, and where consequences are felt long before they enter the statistical abstracts or nudge against the strong inertia of theory at the service of powerful interests.

In assessing our past record, our present posture, and the position of those who champion the present order of things, I believe it is fair to ask: "Who really moved?" Distinguished and honorable men today cry "free trade" and there is no free trade. Every wind that blows from Geneva, or from Moscow, or Tokyo, or the capitals of the OPEC nations, or the bloc of 77, or from the Common Market, bears the tidings of rampant mercantilism.

They tell of cartels and monopolies, of government central trading corporations and purchasing missions exploiting—in secret—open commodities and markets, while we remain the only grain-exporting country in the world that does not protect its supplies and citizens through a governmental grain board. They spread the word of export subsidies, value-added tax gimmicks and remissions, subsidized credits, local "content" laws, rigged and manipulated exchange rates, and ever-rising barriers around the markets of nations and blocs of nations. They tell of joint ventures and barter agreements with state enterprises employing forced labor. They sing of tax havens and prostituted flags. They fly the Jolly Roger of industrial piracy and the bribery of corporations by nations through extravagant concessions and virtual gifts of land and labor to lure their plants. They tell of industrial "free" zones, fenced off from local markets, carved out as cut-rate export platforms.

I could extend this recitation with an endless litany of measures designed to tilt the scales of economic law to our disadvantage, but I will merely add the question: Are these things a spasm of the past, a temporary aberration of the present, or the running tide of the future? When labor resists these trends and practices, are we not more true to the precepts of free trade than are perhaps their apologists? One could argue with some force that, in this setting, labor generally is one of the last steadfast advocates of free trade. Free trade meaning the free movement of goods and products (not packaged industrial systems) according to where they can be made best and cheapest.

Our savings clauses would, however, cover the proposition that this freedom extends as well to the migration of people and ideas, and that the flow of trade should not encourage or reward the repression of human rights or the raw exploitation of human labor. We have never understood, incidentally, why the free movement of capital, plants, and technology promotes the cause of peace while insistence on the free movement of people and of the press aggravates international tensions.

MULTINATIONALS AND MERCANTILISM

As to those objects of our distemper, the multinational or supranational corporations, it is really rather futile to moralize. Is it not bootless and self-indulgent to deliver sermons against the great white shark which behaves according to its nature and pursues a blood-trail to the nearest red meat? Ask rather who spread the bait. There is the culprit.

On this score, I have found fewer romantic illusions current among the men of international business, at least in private discourse, than among their apologists in and around the Congress and academic institutions. Your authentic man of commerce is and ought to be embarrassed to disguise or disclaim what he regards as an entirely wholesome, natural and functional appetite for profit.

He does not—in his heart of hearts—believe that he was ordained to serve the world, but rather, to serve his corporate institution and its stockholders. The problem lies more with those who, by parliament and press, iconize him and hail him as the world's new redeemer.

The undershafts of industrial enterprise are not false to themselves or to any reasonably vigilant mark. After an officer of Chase Manhattan has inveighed in a public forum against the Communist threat to free enterprise, he will, in the corridors at recess, concede that the reason his firm established a branch at 1 Karl Marx Place in Moscow was to make a dollar, pure and simple.

A substantial man of commerce and industry may, when pressed, admit what kind of a house he is running. The confusion comes from the piano player who pretends not to know what is going on upstairs, or perhaps offers the opinion that it is a meeting of the Little Sisters of the Poor.

The mystique of the multinationals, as expounded by their apologists, does give rise to the kind of exasperation expressed, I believe, by Disraeli about Gladstone, when he exclaimed: "I don't mind that ace up his sleeve, but I do object to his behaving as though God put it there."

It is time to face the final paradox. These multinational enterprises which pursue license under the banner of free trade are in fact the spawn of mercantilism, the children of the protectionism of our "trading partners." By leaping the barriers—not with goods, but with industrial systems, technology, capital and all—they have gained shares in the vested interests those barriers defend, plus a subsidy from the injured American worker and taxpayer.

They have the best of both worlds. They have made a separate peace. They are not on our side in any struggle for the true liberalization of the terms of trade, and they ought not to be the favored instruments of public policy.

2

The Impact of International Trade on U.S. Employment

DANIEL J. B. MITCHELL

THE "JOB COUNTING" APPROACH TO LABOR AND TRADE

The impact of exports and imports on the American workforce has been a controversial issue during the past decade. Those most directly affected naturally protest if they feel that trade policy is detrimental to their economic welfare. Historically, trade policy has been particularly responsive to pressure from internal interests over import restrictions and tariffs. Future policy will certainly not be made in a vacuum without such pressures.

During the past decade many of the complaints about U.S. trade policy have come from organized labor. Unlike earlier complaints, concerned with the impact of imports on particular industries, organized labor now views current trade policies as harmful to the welfare of labor as a whole, or at least to wide segments of the labor force. This viewpoint has sparked the interest of labor and industry officials, academics and policymakers and has generated a flood of literature on the subject.[1]

Unfortunately, much of the literature has been preoccupied with the impact of foreign trade on the aggregate level of employment in the United States. This misleading approach could lead to incorrect policy assessments and prescriptions, particularly in the American position at the Tokyo Round of multilateral trade negotiations. The employment-related literature suggests that American interests would be best served by pursuing policies which would increase "employment creating" production for export and decrease "employment-destroying" imports. I will argue instead that the key variables to examine beyond the shortest of time horizons are not the overall effects of trade on creating or destroying jobs but those relating to the "composition" of employment and the character of exports and imports.

Data presented below suggest four general characteristics of the decade from 1965 to 1974.

1. During the late 1960s, imports grew less capital-intensive and more labor-intensive in relation to exports. During the early 1970s, the relative capital-intensity of exports and imports appeared to stabilize.

2. Imports tended to shift toward industries paying higher wages relative to the national average during 1965-74. This tendency was reflected in a shift toward industries employing fewer nonwhites, fewer older workers, and fewer workers with less than a high school education. Imports shifted toward industries with higher unionization rates in the earlier part of the period.

3. Although these categories of workers may have been adversely affected by shifts in imports, it must be remembered that in many respects exports and imports are more similar in production to each other than to the economy as a whole. The export and import labor forces use fewer minority, female, and production and nonsupervisory workers, are more highly paid and unionized, and are more likely to have workers with less than a high school education than the overall economy. Thus, attempts to benefit such workers by policies which restrict imports may be at least partially offset by the indirect effect of such policies in limiting exports.

4. Shifts in trade patterns during the decade may have had an adverse impact on labor compensation, especially in the earlier years. The aggregate impact had to be slight, however, because of the relatively small proportion of economic activity represented by exports and imports.

These general statements, of course, are based on past trends which may not continue into the future. In the next few years, special circumstances such as policies related to energy imports and agricultural exports may substantially change present American trade patterns.

The usual approach to the labor and trade issue has been to engage in "job counting." Essentially, this technique involves estimating the number of jobs which are embodied in exports and comparing this total with the number of jobs that would have been embodied in imports, had they been produced in the United States. It is usually assumed that if the net total is positive, trade is employment-creating and if it is negative, trade destroys jobs.

This approach is extremely misleading. If it is necessary to find a villain for unemployment, there are basically three choices: Congress, the President, and the Federal Reserve Board. Congress and the President control fiscal policy, that is, the expenditure and tax policies of the federal government. The Federal Reserve Board controls monetary policy, the extension or contraction of credit to the economy by the Federal Reserve banks, which in turn regulate the money supply. It is these policies, and not developments in particular sectors of the economy, which affect the overall level of economic activity and therefore unemployment.

Under certain circumstances increased imports and decreased exports can, of course, cause problems of structural unemployment. Detailed microlevel industry studies can estimate the impact of, say, a surge of imports in the shoe industry. (The Department of Labor has conducted such studies.) If imports rise by a certain percent over a given time period, the likely effect will be layoffs (adjusted for normal turnover) of so many thousand workers. The proportion of those workers unemployed after 6 months, 12 months or 18 months can then be calculated on the basis of mobility patterns of these workers.

THEORY AND SPECULATION ON THE LABOR INTENSITY OF INTERNATIONAL TRADE

International trade theory has long argued that the United States, as the world's most capital abundant country, should be exporting capital-intensive goods and importing labor-intensive goods. The Heckscher-Ohlin theory asserts that American "comparative advantage" lies in the production of goods using proportionately more of the factor the United States has in relative abundance.[2] Under the usual textbook assumptions of this theory, expansion of foreign trade would be adverse to labor because it would shift employment and production to capital-intensive industries and away from labor-intensive industries. The adverse effect would not be on unemployment totals but on income distribution. According to the theory, trade will tend to shift income from labor to capital and lower the real wage.

From a policy point of view, the Heckscher-Ohlin theory supports the proposition that policies affecting exports and imports must be considered in relation to the internal impact of these policies on income distribution. In particular, the theory suggests that restrictions on imports have the effect of shifting income toward labor, and away from profits and other forms of capital-based income. Organizations representing the interests of workers should, therefore, press for such restrictions, as organized labor is in fact now doing.

Many critical assumptions underlie the Heckscher-Ohlin theory. It is usually presented in the context of an economy producing only two goods under perfect competition—an export good and an import-competing good. Attempts to complicate the theory naturally lead to more qualified conclusions. The biggest blow to the Heckscher-Ohlin approach, however, has come not from further theoretical explorations but from empirical studies. During the 1940s and 1950s, the United

States was in fact exporting goods which were relatively labor-intensive compared with imports.

As late as 1965, this "paradox" still held. During the period 1965-1970, however, imports tended to become more labor intensive than exports. The phrase "tended to" must be stressed because the concept of capital or labor intensity is difficult to measure. One measure used for the concept, the ratio of depreciation to full time equivalent employment, indicated that imports had actually become absolutely more labor intensive than exports by 1970. Not all measures agreed on this absolute relationship, but the direction of the change, especially with regard to imports, was unambiguous.[3]

The period 1965-70 coincided with change in the attitude of labor's attitude toward trade as Heckscher-Ohlin would predict. In the early 1960s, labor supported the Kennedy administration's Trade Expansion Act which provided the authority to reduce tariffs within a framework of multilateral negotiations (the Kennedy Round).* By the end of the 1960s, labor opposed further tariff negotiations and supported limits on trade under the Burke-Hartke Bill.

The shift in the relative labor intensity of trade is subject to various interpretations. One is that in fact the old theory was right all along but that trade was distorted by the world wide restrictions imposed in the 1930s and after World War II. The Kennedy Round, by removing some of those restrictions, might have helped to restore the "natural" pattern. Another is that a technology gap, not envisioned in the theory, opened up between the United States and other countries in the 1940s and 1950s and happened to be especially wide in labor-intensive industries. The worldwide spread of technology in the 1960s, partly associated with the expansion of MNCs, might have tended to erode this advantage and permitted the theory to operate.

Other explanations, however, are also possible. For example, the United States was committed after World War II to a fixed exchange rate. Initially, the U.S. dollar seemed to be undervalued, the famous dollar shortage lasting until the latter part of the 1950s. During the 1960s the dollar showed progressive signs of overvaluation. In the latter part of the 1960s, the problem was aggravated by rising domestic inflation associated with the Vietnam War. In August 1971, the dollar was allowed to float. Although an attempt to establish a new and

---

*The Kennedy Round primarily affected goods traded between developed countries. However, exports from less-developed countries were also affected. See J. F. Finger, "Effects of the Kennedy Round Tariff Concessions on the Exports for Developing Countries," Economic Journal, 86, no. 341 (March 1976), pp. 87-95.

lower fixed exchange rate for the dollar was made later in that year, this attempt was abandoned by early 1973, and the world has been on floating exchange rates since then.

It could be that the fixed rates of the 1960s were responsible for the changing pattern of U.S. trade. For example, U.S. imports from Japan tend to be labor intensive and that Japanese imports expanded rapidly during 1965-1970. Since the yen was significantly undervalued, it might be argued that the growing labor-intensity of imports was a product of the fixed exchange rates.

To shed more light on these speculations, changes in the labor composition of trade occurring since 1970 should be examined. Ideally, it would be best to wait another few years before taking a look. Each year since 1970 has had its peculiarities. The dollar devaluation was accompanied by wage/price controls which created gaps between domestic and world prices, thus distorting normal export and import incentives. Controls were not removed until April 1974. Thus, 1974 should still exhibit some control effects, even though progressive decontrol began in 1973. Early 1974 was also distorted by a combination of the Arab oil embargo and the special controls on oil prices which jointly led to the gasoline shortage of that year. For these reasons, it is necessary to exercise caution and not establish 1970-1974 as a base from which to make long-term projections. But 1974 was the most recent year for which reasonably complete data were available for this study.

AN ANALYSIS OF THE LABOR COMPOSITION OF TRADE

The framework for this study is based in the role of the federal government in establishing overall target rates for economic activity and unemployment. While perfect fine tuning is not possible, aggregate demand policies are adjusted from time to time to try to keep the economy on course. (The advent of flexible exchange rates makes it easier for countries to pursue domestic economic goals.) In a modern economy such as that of the United States, the effect of the international sector is to alter the "composition" of industrial employment rather than the absolute total of employment.

To avoid similarity with the standard job counting literature, the figures on the labor content of U.S. trade presented here are in the form of ratios and proportions rather than absolute figures. In an earlier work I studied the composition effects of changing U.S. trade patterns during the period 1965-70.[4] In this paper, I examine changes through 1974. Because the 1974 figures are preliminary estimates, the results are subject to revision.

Three groups of variables related to U.S. exports and imports have been examined. The first is the labor-intensity of trade defined as the capital/labor ratio. The second is the demographic composition of the export and import labor forces through the characteristics of sex, race, age, education, unionization and type of occupation. (The export labor force refers to the labor embodied in U.S. exports; the import labor force refers to an estimate of the labor force which would have been embodied in imports had they been produced domestically.) Third, the wage compensation of the export and import labor forces is examined. Data generated from this examination of recent trends are presented in Tables 2.1-4 and some of the characteristics of U.S. exports and imports in Table 2.5.[5]

In many respects, exports and imports are more similar to each other than they are to the overall economy. This is not surprising since they are drawn primarily from agriculture, extraction and manufacturing and thus omit the service and distribution sectors. It is important to keep in mind the similarities between exports and imports because the two are both interconnected. For particular periods, exports may grow faster than imports or vice versa, but ultimately steps to restrict imports will tend to restrict exports. Thus a trade policy designed to improve job opportunities for a particular category of workers through import restrictions would tend to be at least partially self-defeating over time.

In general, exports and imports are using less of female workers, production and nonsupervisory workers and minority workers than is the overall economy. The export and import labor forces are more highly paid and unionized and more likely to have workers with less than a high school education. A slight tendency of both exports and imports to use more older workers (aged 50-64) relative to the national economy persists through 1965-1974. Exports and imports are both more capital-intensive as measured by the ratio of depreciation (capital consumption allowances) per full-time equivalent employee than the overall private sector. In terms of female workers, production and nonsupervisory workers, union workers, high school dropouts and nonwhite workers, exports have been relatively less intensive than imports.

The characteristics of U.S. exports and imports to Japan and Canada as the two leading trading partners are particularly important. A heavy concentration on agricultural exports to Japan tends to cut back on average pay levels and unionization rates embodied in those exports. Exports to Japan have also been persistently more capital-intensive than imports during 1965-1974. Exports to Canada by contrast have been less capital-intensive than imports over the same period.*

---

*Canadian and Japanese data for the categories and calculations

One of the findings of the earlier study was that exports were becoming more capital-intensive relative to imports during 1965-1970. According to Table 2.4, this trend ceased but did not reverse itself after 1970. The index of capital-intensity shows no change during 1970-1974. Underlying that result, however, are some industrial composition shifts. Within manufacturing trade the relative capital-intensity of exports and imports returned to roughly the 1965 level. Capital-intensive exports other than manufactured goods (mainly agricultural products) rose, tending to increase the relative capital-intensity of exports. On the import side increases in capital-intensive petroleum products had an offsetting effect, leaving the overall index unchanged. If petroleum products are excluded from the tabulations, the index continues to rise after 1970.

In terms of the trend toward greater capital intensity of exports, Japanese trade played little role after 1970, but the absolute reversal of the relative export and import capital-intensities by 1970 would not have taken place without inclusion of the Japanese data. Canadian exports became somewhat less capital-intensive relative to imports after 1970, so that the omission of Canada from the overall index produces a continually rising trend during 1965-1974. United States trade with Canada, however, is heavily affected by two-way trade in the automobile industry under a special duty-free arrangement which began in 1965. The automobile industry was especially hard hit by the gasoline shortage and the approaching recession in 1974. Thus the 1974 Canadian figures are likely to be distorted.

Both exports and imports tended to move toward higher-wage industries over the period 1965-1974. But for exports this movement occurred during the earlier part of the period while for imports it persisted. By 1974 the relative rate of compensation was about the same in both exports and imports, and unionization in exports was moving back to the levels of the mid-1960s while in imports it remained at the plateau reached in 1970. In relation to imports, exports became less unionized. The proportion of high school dropouts and minorities decreased in the import labor force throughout the period. Little trend was apparent on the export side, so that, compared with imports, the export labor force included relatively more of these groups by 1974.

---

in Tables 2.1-3 are given in Daniel J. B. Mitchell, "Trends in the Labor Content of American Trade: Revisited," Working Paper 2, UCLA Institute of Industrial Relations, October 1976. A study of an earlier period suggested that Canadian imports were more labor-intensive. See D. F. Wahl, "Capital and Labour Requirements for Canada's Foreign Trade," Canadian Journal of Economics and Political Science, 27, no. 3 (August 1961), pp. 349-358.

TABLE 2.1

Ratio of Export Value to Import Value, 1965-1974
(Percent)

World trade with United States	1965	1970	1974*
Per full-time equivalent employee (FTE):			
Depreciation PRE	93	106	106
Compensation T	109	106	98
Per Employee:			
Women workers T	84	77	85
Production workers[a] P	94	94	96
Older workers (50-64) T	97	98	101
Major union workers P	96	86	78
Union members T	86	84	73
Workers with less than 12 years education T	90	90	96
Nonwhite workers T	85	85	91
Average hourly earnings[a] P	106	105	99

Source: Compiled by the author.

TABLE 2.2

Ratio of Export Value to National Value, 1965-1974
(Percent)

World trade with United States	1965	1970	1974*
Per full-time equivalent employee (FTE):			
Depreciation PRE	141	135	130
Compensation T	108	114	115
Per Employee:			
Women workers T	57	56	60
Production workers[a] P	86	85	85
Older workers (50-64) T	105	103	103
Major union workers P	121	142	133
Union members T	131	146	124
Workers with less than 12 years education T	117	111	113
Nonwhite workers T	73	72	72
Average hourly earnings[a] P	102	106	105

Source: Compiled by the author.

TABLE 2.3

Ratio of Import Value to National Value, 1965-1974
(Percent)

World trade with United States	1965	1970	1974*
Per full-time equivalent employee (FTE):			
Depreciation PRE	151	128	123
Compensation T	99	107	117
Per Employee:			
Women workers T	68	72	70
Production workers[a] P	92	90	89
Older workers (50-64) T	108	105	102
Major union workers P	126	166	171
Union members T	151	173	170
Workers with less than 12 years education T	130	124	117
Nonwhite workers T	85	84	78
Average hourly earnings[a] P	96	101	106

Source: Compiled by the author.

TABLE 2.4

Depreciation Per Full-Time Equivalent Employee:
Exports as Percent of Imports

	1965	1970	1974*
All Trade[b]	93	106	106
excl. Japan	84	96	97
excl. Canada	96	109	113
excl. nonmanufacturing	93	106	91
excl. petroleum[c]	103	114	117

Source: Compiled by the author.

Notes

a. Production and nonsupervisory workers.
b. Excludes ordnance.
c. Excludes petroleum extraction and refining.
* Preliminary.
PRE = Private sector (excluding real estate).
T = Total economy.
P = Private sector.

TABLE 2.5

Labor Content of Total U.S. Trade,
Continuous Characteristics, 1965-1974

A. U.S. Exports Relative to Imports

Labor Force is:

less feminine
less using of production & nonsupervisory workers
less nonwhite
less unionized
less using of high school dropouts

B. U.S. Exports Relative to National Value

Labor Force is:

less feminine
less using of production & nonsupervisory workers
less nonwhite

but is:

more highly compensated
more unionized
more using of high school dropouts
slightly more aged

Exports are more

capital-intensive (less labor-intensive)

C. U.S. Imports Relative to National Value

Labor Force is:

less feminine
less using of production and nonsupervisory workers
less nonwhite

but is:

more highly compensated
more unionized
more using of high school dropouts
slightly more aged

Imports are more

capital-intensive (less labor-intensive)

Source: Compiled by the author.

The trend in imports relative to the overall national economy is worth emphasizing since movements in this area have been especially responsible for the demands by organized labor for import restrictions. Imports have shifted toward higher-paying industries over the entire 1965-1974 period. During the earlier part of that period, imports competing with relatively high-unionized industries grew rapidly. The result was that the import labor force came to contain a declining proportion of nonwhite, older, and high school dropout workers relative to the total labor force than it previously had. In volume terms, import growth slowed in the later part of the period, reflecting dollar devaluation and the recession, whereas export growth accelerated. As the economy recovers, imports will accelerate and the effect will more likely be concentrated in higher-paying industries.

Exports will also expand as the world economy recovers, but the pattern of export expansion is less clear. If substantial amounts of petrodollars are invested in the United States, this will tend to prop up the dollar exchange rate and promote an import surplus. The demand for U.S. agricultural exports can be volatile, depending on such factors as world weather and harvest conditions.

As noted, Canadian data tend to be heavily affected by the 1974 recession in automobiles. Imports from Japan have tended to shift away from products intensive in their use of female, minority, and high school dropout workers and more toward the heavy industry sectors characterized by high rates of unionization and pay. In fact imports from Japan seem to be becoming more like imports from Canada, a country with an economy similar to that of the United States. The high usage of female workers in the Japanese labor force which generates exports to the United States persists, nevertheless, because of products such as textiles.

THE COMPLEXITY OF CHOICE IN TRADE AND EMPLOYMENT POLICY

While the issues are quite complex, the preceding analysis should make clear that it is incorrect to blithely assume that expanding trade will necessarily benefit labor. Consider the capital-intensity issues. Trade theory suggests that if trade results in an expansion of capital-intensive industries and a decline in labor-intensive industries, real wages and labor's share of national income will suffer. The calculations for each of the three years 1965, 1970, and 1974, have shown that both exports and imports are capital-intensive relative to the overall private sector. This would suggest that over the long run, a move toward increased production for export would have an adverse effect on the real wage. But ironically so would a decrease in imports! Either adjustment would lead to more capital-intensive production which would be likely to exert downward pressure on real labor compensation.

These sorts of projections assume that future changes in trade would come mainly in the form of expanded volume across the board rather than selective expansions and contractions in particular industries. In fact the pattern of trade does change. During the latter part of the 1960s, the net effect of trade appears to have been adverse to labor. Import volume rose relative to export volume and imports became more labor-intensive. The net effect of trade (exports minus imports) was a "release" of labor which had to be absorbed elsewhere and some expansion of capital usage. Between 1970 and 1974, export volume expanded relative to import volume and relative capital intensity did not change very much. The net effect was some "absorption" of both labor and capital in the trade sector. Given the crudeness of the capital measure, it can only be said that the effect was ambiguous during the early 1970s. Thus it is not possible to dismiss the hypothesis of some worsening of labor's position since 1965.

It is important to note, however, that relative to the total economy, the overall trade sector is small. In 1974, merchandise exports were 6.9 percent of GNP and general imports were 7.1 percent. In particular, the income distribution effects between labor and nonlabor income are small.

The data presented above suggest that whatever adverse effects occurred were most visible in the late 1960s, the period encompassing a change in organized labor's attitude toward trade. After that time the trend was more obscure, perhaps contributing to the passage of the Trade Act of 1974, which the trade union movement generally regards as adverse to its interests.

International developments during 1970-1974, other than normal flows of exports and imports, may well have a greater impact on the "future" pattern of domestic production than the figures presented above. The oil embargo and the coalescence of the OPEC cartel has provoked demands for energy self-sufficiency. Similarly the discovery that U.S. and foreign food prices were linked through trade will probably lead to greater government involvement in agricultural trade. There are many unanswered questions concerning American trade relations with the Communist countries. In short, even if a clear trend in the labor content of trade had been established in the early 1970s, it is likely to be overwhelmed in the late 1970s and 1980s by these and other forces.

Foreign trade policy can never be conducted solely on the basis of the implications for international relations and without regard for the internal economic impact. Trade policy, moreover, has wider effects than those industries directly affected and may extend to broad groups within the labor force and even to the labor force as a whole. It can alter the "mix" of employment, although in the modern context it has little impact on "total" employment. And it can affect the distribution of income.

While trade policy cannot ignore these impacts, their magnitude is hard to estimate. Even so, policymakers should be cautious about bland assertions that trade benefits everyone. With any economic policy, there are gainers and losers, and trade policy is no exception. The complaints of organized labor cannot be dismissed out of hand. While the evidence is not yet conclusive, there could come a time when the impact of trade on the labor force will appear to be clearly adverse.

Finally, it must be noted that this study has ignored related issues for the sake of brevity. It is often argued that particular industries are vital for national defense and must be protected against import competition. Of course, this argument can be abused; the clothespin industry sought protection in the 1950's on the grounds of its contribution to the national defense.[6]

A more general and intangible argument is that a certain industrial "base" is in the national interest, and trade should not be permitted to erode it. This is an inherently difficult argument to assess. But it is one which scholars and policymakers should consider in the future. Is the whole of industry in some sense more vital than the sum of its parts?

Also related to the labor and trade issues is the program of "adjustment assistance" of unemployment benefits and training for workers injured by import competition. This program was established in 1962 and revamped and extended in 1974.[7] Adjustment assistance is supposed to be a method of coping with the structural unemployment problems which imports sometimes present, but its operation thus far is regarded by the organized labor movement as seriously flawed. A complete assessment of that program, along with other issues discussed here, should play a role in future trade policy.

NOTES

1. References to job-counting studies are given in Daniel J. B. Mitchell, Labor Aspects of American International Trade and Investment (Baltimore: Johns Hopkins University Press, 1976), p. 105, note 13. For related group of studies examining the employment growth of multinational firms, see Robert G. Hawkins, U.S. Multi-

national Investment in Manufacturing and Domestic Economic Performance (Washington: Center for Multinational Studies, 1972).

2. For further discussion, see Daniel J. B. Mitchell, Essays on Labor and International Trade (Los Angeles: UCLA Institute of Industrial Relations, 1970), pp. 5-16. See also David F. Burgess, "Tariffs and Income Distribution: Some Empirical Evidence for the United States," Journal of Political Economy, 84, no. 1 (February 1976), pp. 17-45.

3. For alternative measures see Daniel J. B. Mitchell, "Recent Changes in the Labor Content of U.S. International Trade," Industrial and Labor Relations Review, 28, no. 3 (April 1975), pp. 355-375.

4. Mitchell, "Recent Changes."

5. Details of the methodology and sources of data are given in Daniel J. B. Mitchell, "Trends in the Labor Content of American Trade: Revisited," Working Paper 2, UCLA Institute of Industrial Relations, October 1976.

6. Peter B. Kenen, Giant Among Nations (Chicago: Rand McNally, 1963), pp. 64-65.

7. Daniel J. B. Mitchell, "Trade-Related Inquiries and Adjustment Assistance," Industrial Relations Research Association Proceedings, December 1975, pp. 205-211.

3

Trade Adjustment Assistance for American Workers

PETER HENLE

ORIGINS OF TRADE ADJUSTMENT ASSISTANCE

The time is fast approaching for a searching reappraisal of trade adjustment assistance. The current program was enacted as part of the Trade Act of 1974, replacing somewhat similar provisions in the Trade Expansion Act of 1962 (TEA). Although the program is authorized until 1980, nothing prevents Congress from acting sooner to modify the program, and there are some indications that this is seriously being considered.

Unfortunately the brief period of operation of the new trade adjustment assistance program does not provide a full basis for such a reappraisal. This examination is thus only a preliminary account of how it has been working; it also raises some of the key issues involved in any comprehensive assessment of its current value.

In its broadest sense, trade adjustment assistance encompasses aid to workers adversely affected by the flow of imports, to their employers and to the communities in which they are located. My focus is on the program as its affects workers and on developments under the Trade Act of 1974. The history of the earlier adjustment program under the Trade Expansion Act is quite well known and needs only relatively brief mention here.

The original impetus for the adjustment assistance concept came from a minority report of the 1954 Commission on Foreign Economic Policy headed by Clarence Randall, formerly president of Inland Steel. The main issue before the Commission was whether U.S. policy should encourage further development of international trade. While the administration was favorably inclined, Congress was under substantial pressure from a number of industries adversely affected by competing imports. The Randall Commission supported further extension of trade and opposed any steps to facilitate "escape clause" actions, but it was the labor member of the commission, David

MacDonald, President of the United Steelworkers, who raised the possibility of approaching the problem in a third way. Rather than simply expanding trade or raising tariffs, he endorsed the principle of trade expansion but suggested that this be accompanied by a program of publicly financed special assistance to those adversely affected.

This proposal for trade adjustment assistance drew little support at that time, but in 1962 when Congress came to authorize what became known as the Kennedy Round of tariff negotiations, adjustment assistance became the focal point of considerable attention as it offered the legislators a convenient solution to a vexing problem: how to support trade expansion for what was considered to be benefits to the general public and at the same time respond to the pressures of constituents in such industries as pottery, glass, bicycles and clothing injured by the rising flow of competitive imports. Adjustment assistance thus became the touchstone for the passage of the legislation; in fact the AFL-CIO made it the price of their support for the trade expansion program. Not all the unions went along with the parent body, but by far the great majority did, including the larger industrial unions.

From such a promising start, the program went rapidly downhill. The major reasons were the criteria in the law for granting trade adjustments assistance, the elaborate administrative procedures for passing upon petitions for adjustment assistance and a reluctance, personal or official, among members of the Tariff Commission to utilize this new technique.

The procedures written into the law required findings by the Tariff Commission after extended investigation. The criteria for determining eligibility provided that the increase in imports causing the unemployment had to be, "in major part," the result of concessions granted in the trade agreements and that such increased imports had to be the "major factor" causing or threatening to cause the unemployment.

It is not surprising that until late 1969 no petition for worker adjustment assistance was approved by the Tariff Commission, when to these difficult requirements was added a natural reluctance by the Tariff Commission to take a step that might encourage more escape clause petitions for tariff relief. Eventually the logjam was broken as some of the concessions in the Kennedy Round led to unemployment in U.S. competing firms. By the end of 1974 when the program under the TEA ceased to exist, the Tariff Commission had acted upon 249 petitions, approving 50 of them (20 percent) involving 27,000 out of 110,000 workers. The chief industries in which such petitions were approved were women's shoes (17 petitions), electronic components (7) and radio, T.V. and related products (5). A total of close to 17,000 workers were represented by the petitions from these three industries.

By 1974 when time came to renew or recast the TEA, the international economic scene had become far more complicated. Imports to the U.S. were increasing, and in some sectors U.S. firms had lost or were losing entire markets. In some cases, U.S. multinational firms had become the importers to take advantage of lower costs, frequently in less developed countries. For some products such as textiles and apparel, U.S. business and labor had sufficient clout that the government—with their help—developed a series of import restriction agreements with producer countries that kept the level of U.S. imports from rising too sharply so that U.S. producers could maintain their share of particular markets.

Another development in the intervening years was the passage of the Automotive Products Trade Act of 1965 which implemented a special U.S.-Canada agreement providing for an unrestricted flow of both completely assembled autos and auto parts across the Canadian border. As part of that act, a broader program of adjustment assistance was included for adversely affected U.S. workers which avoided some of the pitfalls of the earlier TEA legislation.

ADJUSTMENT ASSISTANCE IN THE TRADE ACT OF 1974

In the 1973-74 debate over the trade legislation, organized labor was no longer interested in the adjustment assistance program. Their spokesmen argued that the international economic competition required an entirely new approach involving tax changes, curbs on multinational firms and other measures. This approach, embodied in the Burke-Hartke Bill, was too strong for most members of Congress. In the end Congress renewed the President's authority to negotiate trade agreements but added to this a broader, somewhat more simplified and expedited approach to trade adjustment assistance.

The new law built upon the provisions in the Automotive Products Trade Act. The Tariff Commission (renamed the International Trade Commission in the new law) was entirely bypassed and the Department of Labor assigned the task of investigating worker petitions for adjustment assistance within a sixty-day deadline. In addition to petitions by workers, petitions by any representative group for industry-wide import relief, reviewed by the International Trade Commission, can also lead to adjustment assistance programs for workers.

A major modification was a substantial change in the criteria set for approving worker adjustment petitions, dropping any required link to import concessions. The three new criteria are:

- A "significant number or proportion" of workers in the firm or subdivision must have become "totally or partially separated" (or threatened by such separation).
- Sales or production of such firm or subdivision must have "decreased absolutely."
- "Increases of imports of articles like or directly competitive with articles produced by such workers" must have "contributed importantly to such total or partial separation" of the employees concerned and to the decline in sales or production. In its report, the House Ways and Means Committee indicated that "contributed importantly" means "a cause which is important but not necessarily more important than any other cause."

The new law also broadened the benefits available to the affected worker to include the following:

- A basic weekly benefit of 70 percent of the worker's average weekly rate up to 100 percent of the average weekly wage in U.S. manufacturing for 52 weeks (except that workers enrolled in a training program and workers aged 60 or over at the time they become eligible for benefits can be given up to 78 weeks of benefits).
- Counseling, testing and placement services available from the U.S. Employment Service as well as training opportunities if suitable employment is not available.
- A relocation allowance for adversely affected workers if they have obtained suitable employment or an offer of such employment at another location within the United States (80 percent of family moving and transportation expenses plus a lump sum equal to three times the worker's average weekly earnings with a $500 maximum).
- A job search allowance to enable workers to travel to another part of the country in search of a job (80 percent of expenses incurred, also with a $500 maximum).

The benefit level, at 70 percent of average wages, is considerably above the typical unemployment insurance benefit paid under state law. (The Trade Act provides that federal funds pay only the difference in the two benefit levels.) The 52-week duration is double the typical 26-week period for unemployment insurance benefits, although during the recent recession federally legislated programs extended benefit duration up to 65 weeks. Neither relocation nor job search allowances are provided under the unemployment insurance program.

LABOR DEPARTMENT EXPERIENCE IN ADMINISTERING THE NEW LAW

Armed with the provisions in the 1974 Trade Act, the Department of Labor began in April 1975 to administer the new program. The procedures for certifying workers eligible for benefits require petitions from workers unemployed as a result of increased imports, an investigation by the Labor Department and a ruling within 60 days on the petition. If the petition is found to meet eligibility requirements of the new law, the case goes to the unemployment insurance agency in the state concerned to determine the specific individuals entitled to benefits according to the Labor Department certification. The state unemployment insurance agency locates the individuals, calculates the benefit amounts and writes the checks. The state employment service provides counseling, testing and job placement services and works out any needed relocation or job search allowances.

At first the Labor Department was able to keep within the statutory 60-day limitation for passing on petitions, but as the caseload increased, decisions were delayed beyond this limit. For the July-September 1976 quarter, only 6 percent of the decisions were reached within 60 days of filing, and over half the cases required more than 90 days, although the proportion of early decisions picked up markedly in the next quarter. Table 3.1 indicates quarter by quarter the extent to which the 60-day limit has been met.

The caseload has been increasing but somewhat erratically. A major increase occurred in the April-June quarter of 1976, was down to 155 petitions involving over 20,000 workers in the July-September period, and then shot up to 404 in the next quarter. Table 3.2 shows the caseload for each quarter, the proportion of petitions that have been denied and certified and the proportion of the quarterly caseload undecided at the end of the quarter.

A total of 1,538 cases were filed up to December 31, 1976, involving 462,000 workers. Of these 554 or roughly one-third of the petitions involving 235,000 workers have been certified as eligible for assistance. The industry with the largest number of workers approved for adjustment assistance is the automobile industry. Other industries with sizable groups of import-affected workers include apparel, leather, primary metals (steel), fabricated metal products and electrical and electronic equipment and supplies. Table 3.3 provides some industry statistics.

The older industrial states in the Mid-Atlantic and North Central regions have been hardest hit by import-affected unemployment. These regions, with 44 percent of manufacturing employment have 68 percent of the workers whose petitions have been certified. The states with

TABLE 3.1

Promptness of Labor Department Decision on Adjustment Assistance Petitions

Quarterly Period	Total Decisions	Interval Between Filing of Petition and Labor Department Decision			Percent of Cases Decided Within 60 Days
		0-60 days	60-90 days	90+ days	
1975					
April-June	19	19	-	-	100
July-September	86	83	3	-	97
October-December	130	46	81	3	35
1976					
January-March	193	21	116	56	11
April-June	301	37	119	145	12
July-September	185	12	78	95	6
October-December	191	67	75	49	35

Note: Cases withdrawn, terminated, or in process on September 30, 1976, are not included in the tabulations.

Source: Bureau of International Labor Affairs, U.S. Department of Labor.

TABLE 3.2

Disposition and Status of Petitions for Worker Adjustment Assistance

	1975		1976				Cumulative
	Apr.-Sept.	Oct.-Dec.	Jan.-March	Apr.-June	July-Sept.	Oct.-Dec.	Total Dec. 31, 1976
Total Filings							
Petitions	200	328	248	203	155	404	1,538
Workers	100,131	237,177	27,016	44,926	21,079	31,654	461,983
Total Considered							
Petitions	200	413	523	516	344	549	1,464
Workers	100,131	256,190	251,144	258,293	52,877	62,916	450,668
Certifications							
Petitions	59	64	116	119	77	116	551
Workers	34,849	16,412	23,847	74,703	11,333	21,883	183,026
Denials							
Petitions	46	66	74	187	107	74	554
Workers	41,651	15,236	10,809	149,533	9,379	8,168	234,776
In Process, at End of Period							
Petitions	95	283	333	210	160	359	359
Percent of Total Considered	47.5%	68.5%	63.7%	40.7%	46.5%	64.4%	—
Workers	23,631	224,542	216,488	34,057	32,260	32,866	32,866
Percent of Total Considered	23.6%	87.6%	86.2%	13.2%	60.8%	52.2%	—

Note: Date of filing is date at which the Department of Labor commenced its investigation of the petition. Total Considered excludes petitions terminated or withdrawn.

Source: Bureau of International Labor Affairs, U.S. Department of Labor.

TABLE 3.3

Disposition of Petitions for Worker Adjustment Assistance in Major Industries

Industry	1975		1976				Cumulative Total
	Apr.-Sept.	Oct.-Dec.	Jan.-March	Apr.-June	July-Sept.	Oct.-Dec.	Dec. 31, 1976
Apparel							
Certified:							
petitions	2	30	64	37	26	15	174
workers	900	7,596	9,435	14,947	1,902	2,657	37,437
Denied:							
petitions	2	36	33	22	19	9	121
workers	850	5,732	1,848	4,121	1,102	475	14,128
Shoes and Other Leather Products							
Certified:							
petitions	23	12	13	11	13	34	106
workers	5,211	2,005	2,707	---- 288 ----		6,374	16,585
Denied:							
petitions	9	1	0	3	13	19	45
workers	1,753	60	0	282	1,676	1,574	5,345
Primary Metals							
Certified:							
petitions	2	4	11	20	6	5	48
workers	716	2,665	4,170	8,526	1,803	520	18,400

Denied:							
petitions	0	3	3	21	9	3	39
workers	0	810	1,252	4,815	4,539	195	11,611
Fabricated Metal Products							
Certified:							
petitions	0	0	3	9	7	1	20
workers	0	0	365	11,472	1,273	240	13,350
Denied:							
petitions	2	2	2	34	16	6	62
workers	86	1,000	120	-- 27,828 --		355	29,389
Electrical and Electronic Equip. etc.							
Certified:							
petitions	14	7	6	13	6	4	50
workers	9,699	2,125	3,750	2,316	4,362	410	22,662
Denied:							
petitions	7	11	5	21	10	4	58
workers	4,620	4,435	994	21,993	1,268	110	33,420
Autos, Auto Parts, and Related Ind.							
Certified:							
petitions	8	4	3	17	2	1	35
workers	15,700	530	1,180	-- 29,332 --		4,200	40,942
Denied:							
petitions	10	1	6	54	3	6	80
workers	29,868	150	2,100	-- 79,829 --		1,025	112,972

Source: U.S. Department of Labor.

TABLE 3.4

Trade Adjustment Assistance Payments Data

Indicator	Cumulative Dec. 31, 1975	Jan.-March 1976	April-June 1976	July-Sept. 1976	Oct.-Dec. 1976	Cumulative Dec. 31, 1976
Applications	38,956	29,338	38,189	46,572	58,740	211,795
Applications Paid	18,095	21,425	18,864	46,766	33,033	138,183
Weeks Paid	334,817	573,153	598,436	1,631,983	748,809	3,887,198
Amount Paid (in $ thousands)	$15,112	$27,617	$30,072	$68,603	$42,027	$183,431
Average Weekly Amount	$45.0	$48.0	$50.0	$42.0	$56.0	$47.2
Average Amount per Claimant	$835	$1,289	$1,594	$1,467	$1,272	$1,327
Average Number of Weeks Paid	18.5	26.8	31.7	34.9	22.7	28.1

Source: U.S. Department of Labor.

the largest number of workers receiving adjustment assistance are Michigan, Pennsylvania and Ohio.

Once a petition has been certified, the state unemployment insurance agency must locate the eligible individuals since benefits can be paid only after the individual concerned has filed for his entitlement. By the end of December 1976 more than 211,000 workers had filed applications for adjustment assistance benefits with 138,000 receiving payments. The average weekly benefit amount was $47, paid for 28 weeks, with an average amount per claimant of $1,327. The total dollar amount paid in benefits was $183 million. For the fiscal year 1977 $240 million has been budgeted for an estimated 90,000 workers. (Table 4 gives details on benefit payments.)

Finally, state employment services become involved with any eligible applicant still unemployed. By the end of September 1976, new job applications growing out of the adjustment assistance program totaled over 21,000 with 1,720 job placements. Employment services had referred 1,184 individuals to training programs. The relocation and job search allowances had been utilized very sparingly, with only 65 relocations and 165 job searches approved for allowances. The training programs, relocation and job search allowances are financed by funds advanced under the Comprehensive Employment and Training Act (CETA).

OBSTACLES AND AMBIGUITIES IN ADMINISTERING ADJUSTMENT ASSISTANCE

This program for worker adjustment assistance is not easy to administer promptly and effectively. Interpreting ambiguous phrases in the statute in order to determine eligibility for benefits, and achieving coordination among three different agencies to deliver the benefits have both been difficult tasks.

A number of critical problems unforeseen by the lawmakers have arisen in reviewing petitions, forcing someone to decide in each case whether the circumstances met the criteria of the law.

1. Component parts of products. The law refers to increases of imports of articles "like or directly competitive with articles produced by such workers." In many cases a U.S. plan manufactures not a complete article, but rather only one part or possibly several components of an article. Are laid-off workers eligible if such a plant suffers a loss of business and has to lay off employees as a result of rising imports not of that component part but imports of the product as a whole? The Labor Department has been denying benefits to workers making parts where the import injury was caused by imports of the whole article.

2. Servicing industries and occupations. The law refers to workers who have been producing an "article." What happens, however, if increased imports have affected the employment not only of workers producing an article, but of workers supplying services in connection with the product? This has occurred, for example, with reference to individuals transporting automobiles from assembly lines to the retail sales agencies. Up to this point the Labor Department has ruled that only workers of manufacturing firms are eligible for adjustment assistance.

3. The one-year rule. The act specifically states that to be eligible for adjustment assistance, import-impacted workers must have lost their jobs within a one-year period prior to the filing of the workers' petition. The reasoning behind this provision is that the new law eases the filing requirements and speeds up the processing time so that one year should be ample to allow workers time to apply for benefits. In some situations, however, the filing of worker petitions has been delayed, most frequently in cases where an entire industry was petitioning for relief from imports. In these cases, when the petitions were finally filed and certified, the one-year rule kept a substantial number of workers from receiving adjustment assistance.

4. Switch to foreign operations. Some firms have shut down certain domestic operations, deciding to supply the domestic market by increasing their foreign operations or by starting a new plant outside the United States. Some firms have shut down a plant in the United States and physically removed the equipment from that plant to a location outside the United States planning to utilize it in a new plant to supply the U.S. market. However, the law is very specific that the unemployment must follow the increased imports, not the reverse, and in such situations the Department of Labor has denied adjustment assistance.

Problems have also arisen in the delivery of benefits.

1. Identifying eligible individuals. Generally this is a relatively simple task since the certification usually comprises all the employees in a given plant, but any time the certification is restricted to a specific part of a plant, difficulties are almost bound to arise. At the Motorola plant in Illinois, the imports affecting employment were judged to be imports of color T.V. sets, but the mix of plant operations did not permit the employer to separate out those who had been working on color T.V. sets from those working on black and white T.V. or radios. In other cases the problem of identification became quite involved as workers scheduled for layoff from the import-impacted operation exercised their right under the bargaining agreement to "bump" workers with less seniority in other departments.

2. Test for separation. To be eligible for benefits, the individual must have been working at the time of separation. This means,

for example, that if a plant should close because of imports, those on sick leave, disability, union duty or other type of excused absence will not qualify for benefits.

3. Promptness of benefits. Because of the many steps involved between the advent of the unemployment and the time when the check is written, a considerable delay is inevitable. Often by the time the typical beneficiary is identified and located, he is no longer unemployed. The Labor Department estimates that roughly 75-80 percent of the individuals concerned are back at work, most frequently at the specific firm from which he was laid off. Such rehiring has occurred either because normal turnover in the firm has created vacancies for which laid off employees are eligible or because improved business conditions have led to the rehiring of previously laid-off workers.

The Labor Department further estimates that another 10 percent of the workers have left the labor force, largely the older age group, leaving about 10 percent still unemployed at the time of the payment of adjustment assistance benefits. The relatively small proportion of these workers still unemployed helps to explain the very limited use that has been made of the training, relocation and job search provisions.

As time goes by, some of the early difficulties with the program have begun to work themselves out. The Labor Department staff has become more familiar with the new requirements. The state agencies have grown more cooperative, particularly when they are given additional funds for staff. Relocation and job search allowances, for example, are becoming a more acceptable tool in placing the eligible unemployed.

It is also worthwhile to note a significant change in attitude with the passage of time by the customers of the program. The unions, for example, were reluctant rather than enthusiastic supporters of trade adjustment assistance. However, once in operation with dollars to pass out to eligible recipients, such a program is bound to attract greater attention, with different groups of unemployed workers (or their unions) testing the water to see if they fit within the confines of eligibility. The result is a shift in attitude from a grudging acceptance of the program to an impatience because the program fails to meet all the demands placed upon it. This is one reason for the pressure on Congress to modify some provisions of the law.

ADJUSTMENT ASSISTANCE, UNEMPLOYMENT, AND INTERNATIONAL TRADE

From the standpoint of the administrators and the customers, the immediate problems facing this program tend to obscure the larger issue. In today's world, is trade adjustment assistance for workers a useful approach to dealing with unemployment resulting from the forces of international trade? This question cannot be easily answered, but some of the relevant issues can be identified.

International economic relationships between nations and between citizens of nations have changed drastically since the concept of trade adjustment assistance first originated. The flowering of multinational firms, not just in the United States but in Western Europe, certainly adds a new dimension to the forces of international trade. The flow of trade and capital across borders involves not simply firms of one country dealing with firms of another country, but dealings of many firms whose headquarters are in one country but whose operations are located throughout the globe. Decisions by firms regarding plant location, sources of raw materials and potential markets, carry far broader implications for trade and for employment throughout the world than similar decisions 15 or 20 years ago. In this kind of a world do the traditional advantages of international trade and capital flow still apply?

Is it possible to isolate those situations in which the international effects of trade constitute a major cause of unemployment? Searching for the root cause of a typical layoff situation can become quite complex, involving examination of shifting consumer demands, efficiency of business management and competitiveness of the firm's facilities and equipment. How accurate an answer can be obtained? The "cause" of anyone's unemployment looks quite different to the individual concerned, his foreman, the plant superintendent or the firm's chief cost accountant. Certainly the fact that under the current program such a large proportion of the beneficiaries return to their original employer suggests that for many of them the decline in the economy, rather than an increase in imports, was primarily responsible for their unemployment.

What is the justification for asserting that one type of unemployment deserves more extensive publicly supported assistance above and apart from any other type of unemployment? The traditional argument for trade adjustment assistance is that government policy caused the unemployment in the first place, so that the government should provide specific support programs above and beyond programs available to other unemployed. But this neglects the fact that many other types of government actions such as shifts in procurement, location of government agencies or support for research and development cause unemployment, sometimes quite damaging to particular groups of workers, without invoking any special assistance.

The United States is the only country providing special adjustment assistance for trade-impacted unemployment. Most of the Western European countries do not isolate this type of unemployment for special treatment. Instead they provide a broader program to minimize layoffs and provide assistance to all unemployed through various incentives to firms as well as training, relocation and income support benefits to the unemployed.

Finally, can an adjustment assistance program be devised to provide adjustment assistance to workers as they are laid off and not merely retroactive lump-sum payments to workers already reemployed at their old or at a new job? Certainly many difficulties have to be overcome if the assistance is to be available shortly after layoff.

These are not easy questions to answer; they make a strong case against trade adjustment assistance. On the other hand, both the administration and the Congress consider it imperative that for workers and employers in import-impacted industries an alternative or supplemental form of help be available to other forms of import relief such as quotas, higher tariffs and marketing agreements. In this view, adjustment assistance is a way of handling dislocations from trade as an internal U.S. matter, as opposed to taking action which might lead to international retaliatory action or otherwise jeopardize the fabric of international trade.

There is increasing recognition that in today's world, more workers' jobs can be in jeopardy from increasing imports. In a full employment economy, such dislocations, while unpleasant, might almost be welcome as a way of channeling resources to more productive industries. In an economy operating by fits and starts, the dislocations not only become more frequent but also more troublesome as more of those displaced cannot easily find alternative employment.

Increasingly, the line between adjustment assistance and basic unemployment insurance becomes blurred. The fact that a higher level of assistance is available to certain groups of unemployed workers starts to cause resentment. It is not necessarily recognized as a benefit to the more deserving. Eventually the pressures of operating a dual system of assistance to the unemployed will require reexamination of not just trade adjustment assistance but also the manner in which all the jobless are treated. Making some basic decisions of this character might ultimately prove to be the best way of developing an effective adjustment assistance program.

4

Labor and Multilateral Trade Negotiations: The Trade Act of 1974 and the Tokyo Round

HAROLD T. LAMAR

KEY ISSUES IN THE TOKYO ROUND OF TRADE NEGOTIATIONS

Three major issues lie behind the Tokyo Round of trade negotiations held in Geneva under the auspices of the General Agreement on Tariff and Trade (GATT).

1. Recognition, particularly among the industrialized countries, that the Kennedy Round results had been spun out and new impetus towards liberalization of trade barriers was needed with far greater emphasis on eliminating or bringing international discipline to nontariff distortions to trade.

2. Dissatisfaction on the part of most developing countries with the results of the Kennedy Round and firm resolve to obtain greater access to industrialized markets for exports from the developing countries through other means if the Tokyo Round negotiations did not offer real opportunities.

3. A strong feeling on the part of many interests in the United States that the international trading system was operating to the disadvantage of United States commercial and economic interests. Needless to say, other countries had complaints concerning U. S. trade practices, as well.

The Tokyo Declaration, as the charter for these negotiations, calls for expansion and ever greater liberalization of trade through the dismantling of trade obstacles and improvement of the framework for the conduct of world trade and recognizes that "added" benefits for the international trade of developing countries should be achieved by improving access for their products to industrialized countries. The specific means of reaching these overall goals include negotiations on tariffs and non tariff barriers, examination of multilateral safeguard (escape clause) system, and special negotiations in agriculture and tropical products. While the Tokyo Declaration thus reflected the various frustrations with the international trading system by such as nontariff barriers, trade of developing countries, agriculture and the "escape clause," the major theme was trade liberalization.

The United States agreed to the Tokyo Declaration in September 1973, while the legislation that ultimately became the Trade Act of 1974 was still being considered by the House Committee on Ways and Means. That act is the authorizing legislation for U.S. participation in the Tokyo Round negotiations, and no real U.S. negotiations could take place until the act was signed into law.

LABOR AND THE TRADE ACT OF 1974

Labor had little impact on the Trade Act of 1974. At the time the administration's trade reform bill was proposed, much of organized labor was supporting the Burke-Hartke bill. The latter bill dealt directly with labor's concerns with foreign trade and investment. The Burke-Hartke approach to labor's problems was the imposition of import quotas to assure U.S. producers of a stable share of the U.S. market, and amendments to trade and tax laws aimed at discouraging foreign operations by multinational corporations where U.S. jobs might be endangered.

The bill sponsored by labor was in sharp contrast to the broad legislation proposed by the administration. That legislation, which not only authorized the trade negotiations but also made a number of changes in trade law affecting the negotiations, contains several features of direct interest to labor. The procedural safeguards section of Title I, for example, includes a whole new process for assuring that advice on the negotiations from the private sector, including labor, will be formally recorded and taken into account.

The import relief provisions of the 1974 act were intended to make such relief much more accessible to injured industries and their workers. Congress overrode objections by the administration to improve the delivery of adjustment assistance to workers, firms and even communities impacted by increasing imports. Labor, perhaps disillusioned with the very concept of adjustment assistance which produced so few tangible benefits to workers under the TEA of 1962, made little attempt to influence the House Ways and Means Committee in shaping these provisions.

Labor spokesmen have long complained about the failure of the government to use the unfair trade practices statutes to protect U.S. producers and their workers against unfair competition in the U.S. market. The 1974 act improved administrative and judicial procedures under the Anti-Dumping Act and the countervailing duty and unfair import practices provisions of the Tariff Act of 1930, and the criteria and procedures for U.S. government response to problems faced by U.S. commercial interests in dealing with foreign import restrictions and export subsidies.

The provisions for relief from "fair" but injurious import competition in Title II and the relief from unfair trade practices provisions in Title III of the Trade Act aim at an overall reorientation of dealing with trade problems faced by U.S. producers which also affect U.S. employment. For more than a decade under the TEA of 1962, complaints from U.S. producing interests concerning both fair and unfair injurious imports went largely ignored, except when political considerations or latent congressional action provided solutions to unique competitive problems such as textiles in 1962 and steel in 1968. Whether these changes have resulted in any real improvement in the chances for the less "unique" producing interests and their workers for relief from injurious "fair" or unfair import competition remains to be seen.

Labor was generally opposed to the provisions of the 1974 act for tariff preferences to developing countries. In the consideration of these provisions by the House, however, no real effort was made by labor to suggest tightening up the provisions or to deleting them. Ironically, the duty-free entry of imports (for the most part manufactured goods) from developing countries made possible under the 1974 act was the one provision in the act above all others which epitomized labor's concern with developments in international trade.

The United States does not consider the GSP to be involved in the multilateral trade negotiations since it is a unilateral trade concession granted without reciprocity from the beneficiary countries. However, constant pressure is exerted by the developing countries on the developed countries to improve GSP and make it more secure. Imports of each product category from any beneficiary country are limited to $25 million, adjusted for increases in GNP. In addition, when its share of U.S. imports of a product category accounts for over 50 percent of total imports, eligible duty-free status is withdrawn from the beneficiary country for that product category. It is too early to assess the impact of GSP on U.S. employment.

There were several reasons for the lack of significant impact by organized labor in shaping the Trade Act of 1974. The two major preoccupations of the labor movement were the loss of jobs both through the operations of U.S. multinational firms and the failure of the U.S. government to act when imports were causing significant unemployment. Thus the main efforts of labor were in direct opposition to the legislation proposed by the administration which was backed by the liberal trade community of multinational corporation representatives, importer interests, consumers and public interest organizations. This group of interests was well organized and worked very closely with the administration in support of its proposal.

Labor spent a lot of its energy backing a losing cause in the Burke-Hartke bill, which encompassed both trade and tax policy. Even with broader public support for changes in the tax law Congress would have found it difficult to consider in one piece of legislation a major trade act and a major revision of tax rules on corporate income from overseas operation. Indeed, labor's insistence in changes in the tax law in the trade bill undoubtedly solidified opposition to labor's trade proposals.

During consideration of the Trade Act in the House Ways and Means Committee, labor strongly supported and lobbied hard for an amendment to the bill which provided for broad import quotas to be determined on the basis of an "equitable" market share. With the defeat of that amendment, labor in general made little or no effort to propose or pursue amendments to other aspects of the administration bill. The announced policy of the AFL-CIO was that no bill was better than the bill being developed in the committee. While labor's opposition to the bill was very clear, it did not engage in the normal day-to-day lobbying activity of proposing amendments and attempting to influence the general tenor of committee decisions which generally marks labor activity on measures of concern to workers.

This lack of involvement by labor was in sharp contrast to the activities of the liberal trade community. Work on specific issues and committee members were assigned to participants in an informal Trade Action Committee which met weekly or more often and constantly was in contact with committee members and staff as the committee moved through the mark-up of the bill. Such efforts were mostly in support of the administration's proposals and in opposition to amendments reducing the President's authority or flexibility to deal with problems of import competition.

Not until the trade bill moved out of the Senate Finance Committee to the floor of the Senate did labor representatives begin to make specific proposals for changing the provision of the bill to accommodate labor's concerns. By that time these efforts were too late. Labor was placed in a position of generally opposing any legislative action on a measure which had wide public support, on which the Congress had invested a great deal of time, and which was perceived as restoring a strong congressional voice in the development and execution of trade policy.

With the passage of the Trade Act of 1974, labor has not changed its basic position. Nor has there been any indication that trade policy officials are more attuned to labor's concerns with trade policy. Both government and labor, however, have an opportunity in the advisory committee procedure under the act to exchange views and address problems. Labor's willingness to participate fully in the advisory committees on the trade negotiations will be an important determinant of the job equation of international trade as reflected both in the trade negotiations and day-to-day developments in trade policy.

MULTILATERAL TRADE NEGOTIATIONS

The multilateral trade negotiations are at a crucial stage. The United States has put forward positions in most of the working groups under the Trade Negotiating Committee. The European Community (EC) and Japan have generally been less forthcoming, although the EC has been active on particular issues such as development of a new international customs valuation standard and adamant opposition to discussing agricultural problems except in the agriculture working group. Canada has offered positions in a number of working groups reflecting its importance as a raw material supplier and its relationship to the U.S. economy. The role of the developing countries in pressing for special and differential treatment is a constant theme. My own assessment of the potential impact of these negotiations on U.S. employment follows.

The United States has proposed a formula for tariff reductions which would utilize extensively the 60 percent tariff reduction authority of the 1974 Trade Act and maximize reduction of duties in the seven to fifteen percent range. (The U.S. formula is $y = 1.5x + 50$ percent where y is the percentage reduction up to a maximum of 60 percent and x is the current duty.) Other proposals by the EC, Japan and Switzerland, while providing for cuts higher than 60 percent in the very high range of duties, would result in a lower average reduction in tariffs among industrialized countries.

Other elements in the tariff negotiations include a multitude of requests by the developing countries, which are trying to protect the margin of preference between the existing rates of duty and the generalized scheme of preferences (GSP) rate. The desire of the developing countries to avoid erosion of their GSP margin of preference on a most-favored-nation (MFN) basis could play an important role in exceptions by developed countries, and in turn the extent of overall tariff reductions.

Any tariff reduction would be staged over an extended period, generally 10 years. Under current economic conditions, even major industrial countries are likely to end up excepting the more immediately import-vulnerable products from the full formula reductions. It is hard, therefore, to identify the net impact on U.S. employment of the tariff reductions being negotiated in the Tokyo Round.

Since the Tokyo Round negotiations were not finished in 1977, in spite of U.S. urging, tariff reductions are more likely to be tied in conditionally with other aspects of the negotiations. Under such circumstances there would be greater product coverage and deeper cuts as the breadth of the negotiations are maintained by greater negotiating effort. But wider and deeper tariff cuts will not necessarily have correspondingly greater impact on U.S. jobs because of all of the variables at work in the international market, floating exchange rates being one of the most obvious and important.

Developing countries have made specific requests for immediate improvements in market access to developed countries for tropical products, usually through tariff reductions. The response to these requests has been to propose tariff cuts on products which are not now on the GSP list or already eligible for duty-free treatment. The United States is the only industrialized country requesting that the developing countries benefiting from these make "contributions" by improving market access for its products of interest. The U.S. employment impact of tariff reductions under the tropical products' exercise is difficult to determine because of the staging of reductions and the limited product coverage involved.

The working group on nontariff measures includes subgroups on product standards, subsidies and countervailing duties, government procurement, quantitative restrictions and import licensing procedures, and customs matters. In the first three areas, the efforts are aimed at developing a separate international code of conduct with respect to country practices. The previous work on a draft product standards code completed by a GATT Committee has been further revised.

The subgroup on subsidies and countervailing duties has proceeded little beyond considering a U.S. proposal for a code to classify country practices on export subsidies in relation to the applicability of countervailing duties to counteract such subsidies. U.S. interest in minimizing foreign subsidies of exports requires a clear and consistent commitment, on the part of foreign countries to avoid trade-distorting subsidy practices, including enforcement procedures on those practices. At this time, the complex negotiations on an international code on subsidies and countervailing duties makes job impact assessment of such a code impossible. U.S. trade interests and the interests of labor certainly appear to lie on the side of an enforceable code.

Two of the working groups which directly involve a balance of U.S. trading interests, and therefore the impact of agreements on U.S. employment are the working groups on multilateral safeguards and on sectoral negotiations. In the Trade Act of 1974 the sectoral approach is assigned a high priority as a means of assuring that major industrial sectors will achieve full reciprocity in the negotiations. U.S. negotiators have thus far chosen to ignore congressional guidance on sector matters reflected in the act in favor of an overall negotiating strategy to reduce trade barriers across-the-board. Failure to assess the status of our major industrial sectors on the basis of their specific interests in the various aspects of the negotiations could result in loss of employment in some of our important industries.

The sectoral approach is not viewed as a viable procedure by most U. S. trade negotiators. This attitude is based on the fear that producers in particular sectors will oppose agreements expanding market access for imports and seek agreements which will maximize market access abroad. The resulting imbalance between "requests" and "offers" would minimize, it is argued, trade-offs between sectors. Thus, on an overall basis little trade liberalization would be possible.

Past negotiations, involving tariff concessions, for the most part have been assessed on an overall basis of trade coverage and depth of tariff cut. As tariff levels have been reduced, as nontariff barriers have increased in importance and as competition in industrial products has increased, the measurement of balance in trade negotiations has become both more difficult and more essential. When agreements are concluded and presented to the Congress, the President is required under the 1974 act to report on the advice he has received from the sector advisory committees and explain why he has not followed such advice. If trade liberalization is to be acceptable to producing sectors in the United States and to the Congress, the implications of all aspects of the negotiations, sector by sector, must be weighed carefully.

The President is required by the 1974 act to seek revision of article XIX of the GATT into a truly international safeguard procedure encompassing all forms of import restraints which countries use in response to injurious competition or threat of such competition. Most industrial countries when faced with the real or imagined necessity to restrain imports usually try through bilateral negotiations to reach an agreement with the exporting country to restrain its imports. Such actions call for no international review, and the agreements are made with little concern for the trade distortion effects of the "voluntary export restraint." The challenge of the working group on the multilateral safeguard system is to get all countries to adhere to a code of conduct under which all cases of restraint on imports into countries are reported and examined on the basis of internationally agreed-to criteria so that all countries are judged on the same basis.

With adequate stress in the negotiations on achieving equivalence of competitive opportunities for the major product sectors of American manufacturing, the employment impact of the overall negotiations should prove to be beneficial. However, the negotiations must be analyzed in terms of the specific competitive interests of each major manufacturing sector in order to take fully into account the consequences of the negotiations for the continued viability of the domestic production base and related employment.

Agreement on an international safeguard system in bringing discipline and uniform adherence to procedures for import restraints is essential to protect U. S. commercial interests. The rules must not preclude the United States from taking actions when justified by domestic import relief procedures. Quick action to avoid a threatened injury can often be more meaningful to remedying a competitive situation and less damaging to overall trade liberalization than full-scale formal import restraint action. In any event, the United States must have the flexibility to be responsive to industry and labor when temporary import restraints are demonstrably needed.

The Trade Act of 1974 also directs the President to seek adoption of international fair labor standards and of public petition and confrontation procedures in the GATT. Up to now little has been done by the Office of the Special Trade Representative in this connection. The American labor movement has long sought inclusion of fair labor standards in the GATT articles for two reasons. The first is to assure that trade injurious to importing countries does not result from the employment of labor under conditions and wages clearly substandard in the country from which the goods are being exported. The second purpose is to provide incentives for the distribution of the benefits of international trade on as wide a basis as possible within the exporting country.

Many trade policy observers are not enthusiastic about the changes for negotiating or implementing a code on international fair labor standards. It is often argued that developing countries would not be willing to afford yet another avenue for industrialized countries to reduce access to their markets. U. S. negotiators also point out that the United States would have to expend a great deal of negotiation credit both with the industrial trading partners and with the developing countries. They question the wisdom of such an effort in light of other important U. S. goals in the negotiations.

Such reasoning is based on preconceptions of responses without the benefit of a thorough research and analysis of the benefits of giving labor's role in international trade a positive focus. Labor, organized and unorganized, has as much long run interest in the rational allocation of resources as industry or government. Fair labor standards are as much a part of fair conditions of competition as pricing policies. Given the grave concerns of much of U. S. labor with international trade policy and given the goal of trade liberalization in achieving higher living standards in all countries, a concerted effort on international labor standards can be used imaginatively to establish common ground between developed and developing countries in the negotiations.

Since one of the aims of the multilateral trade negotiations in improving the trade posture of developing countries is to assist in their economic development, including improved living standards, measures to encourage a greater distribution of the returns from international trade would appear to be a sound means of achieving such a goal. Obviously, a code of international fair labor standards would not be a panacea for the problems faced by the American labor movement in terms of possible adverse job impact. It would, however, provide another international mechanism for the consideration of such impact and would at the same time assure the "ever greater liberalization of world trade and improvement in the standard of living and welfare of the people of the world," as provided in the Tokyo Declaration.

Sectoral considerations, a usable safeguard system, and provisions for fair international labor conditions are at least three aspects of the multilateral trade negotiations which require the special concern of the labor community if the Tokyo Round of trade negotiations is to provide a favorable climate of job opportunities in the United States.

OPENNESS AND FAIRNESS IN IMPLEMENTING TRADE POLICY

One other aspect of trade policy of special concern to American labor is the relative degree of openness and fairness with which various countries participating in world trade implement international agreements. In the United States, whenever a firm or industry is troubled by fair but seriously injurious import competition or by unfair practises, the statutory and regulatory procedures involve adversary and usually well-publicized proceedings. Almost without exception such petitions for relief from injurious imports are interpreted as requests for "protection." The number of law firms representing foreign exporters or U. S. importers before the U. S. Customs Service, the Customs Courts, the U. S. International Trade Commission, Congressional committees and other agencies has grown tremendously in recent years. The ability of such law firms to influence decisions has also grown as they have joined forces with the American liberal trade community made up of multinational corporations, retailers, public interest and consumer organizations.

The adversary and public nature of handling such trade disputes enhances the likelihood that the interests of all parties to the dispute will be considered, including the exporting country. If anything, since the label "protectionist" is a pejorative phrase, public pressure through press coverage and editorial comment often leans against the adversely affected U. S. industry and its workers.

Such public discussion of individual trade cases simply does not take place in other industrialized countries. Both in Western Europe and Japan administrative rulings affecting imports are not normally accompanied by adversary proceedings. Most countries have import licensing systems which may not have the purpose of holding down imports, but such licensing systems do lend themselves to manipulation from time to time in response to producer problems. In particular, Western European countries monitor sensitive imports and have special bilateral agreements or arrangements with Eastern European and developing countries providing specified import levels.

In contrast to the large customs and tariff bar representing importer or foreign exporter interest in the United States which skillfully makes use of the statutory and regulatory procedures involving possible action on import restraints, American export interests cannot avail themselves of such procedures abroad because the public procedures, including the right to appeal administrative rulings involving action on imports, are not usually available in other countries and the consumer-liberal trade oriented organizations have not yet developed to apply the kinds of pressures felt in the United States.

The openness of the U. S. system in reaching decisions on cases involving import restraint in contrast to the closed handling of such problems in other countries without opportunity for representation or appeal of the exporting country's interest poses a dilemma for the United States. Ultimately it affects the integrity of the agreements reached through multilateral trade negotiations and determines whether the benefits of further expansion of world trade are fairly distributed among all sectors of American society, including workers.

5

Implementing The Trade Act of 1974: A Trade Union Perspective

HOWARD D. SAMUEL

THE TOKYO ROUND AND TARIFF-CUTTING

It is no secret that organized labor strongly opposed most of the provisions of the Trade Act of 1974. Our experience has proved that our position in 1974, although it did not carry, was correct. Despite pious words that "the act would provide relief for American industry and workers suffering from increased imports. . . . " by President Ford when he signed the act in January, 1975, the act has been administered in a fashion to benefit those who profit from international trade rather than to protect those injured by trade.

The Trade Act of 1974 was conceived and is being administered in the spirit of a nineteenth-century attitude that all trade is beneficial and that more trade is more beneficial. There appears to be no understanding that unregulated trade, particularly when different nations play by different rules, can put many workers under severe disadvantage and have adverse effects on the economy as a whole. If we had spent the last two years in the embrace of a full employment economy, the damage might have been contained. Instead we have been struggling through the worst recession in 40 years, and the administration of the Trade Act has been making a bad situation worse.

The main thrust of the Trade Act was to provide legislative authorization to the United States to participate in the so-called Tokyo Round of trade negotiations. According to Title I of the act, the President "may proclaim" not only reduced tariffs, but "additional duties" as well. The tariff-cutting formula tabled by our negotiators a few months

---

Note: The author wanted this paper to stand as he prepared it for the conference in 1976. He felt that revising it, since he has subsequently joined the Carter administration, would be inappropriate.

ago, at the end of a lengthy and complex series of equations, comes out just as labor feared, proposing the maximum cuts the law permits.

One fails to find any recognition that certain industries would suffer severe disruption and unemployment as a result of tariff cuts or elimination of all regulation. As a matter of fact, the tariff-cutting formula was proposed without even prior public discussion of possible exempt industries. They apparently will be thrown into the soup at the end of the cooking. We recommended that the exceptions to tariff cuts be determined first. We were ignored. The result is that the United States has offered a formula to cut tariffs without knowing which tariffs will not be cut.

The same attitude appears to govern the administration of the act in respect to the GSP, the special tariff reductions made available to less developed countries (LDCs). Before knocking out tariffs on products imported from LDCs, the President is supposed to show "due regard" for the impact on U. S. industry. In at least one case—that of the leather apparel industry, where imports have been steadily climbing to a penetration level of 60 percent—the only "due regard" evident was for the diplomatic interests of the State Department. An appeal to remove leather apparel from the GSP list was filed in January, 1976. It took six months for the government to hold a hearing; another three months to come to a decision, which was to make another study and postpone final decision still further. The reason: the State Department is more interested in its relationships with certain Latin American nations than with U. S. jobs.

The attitude of U. S. negotiators toward the framework of the negotiations has been to look for trade-offs. Agricultural interests in this country, which are already profiting from the highest exports in history, are exerting major pressure to negotiate lower barriers in other markets. To accomplish such a goal, U. S. negotiators will have to reduce barriers on manufactured products in this country. This is fine for agriculture, but potentially disastrous to U.S. industry, which employs far more workers than does agriculture.

The act gives no license to this kind of trade-off, and in fact provides, to the extent feasible, for negotiations to take place sector by sector, to avoid drastic crossing over between product lines and clearly not to provide trade-offs between agriculture and industry. After almost two years of negotiations, the United States still has not committed itself to a broad-based sectoral approach despite the clear congressional directive to the Special Trade Representative to work with sector advisory groups to determine which sectors would lend themselves to sector negotiations. A lot of industries must still wait for the agricultural ax to fall.

The Ford administration responded to the provisions of Title I of the Trade Act by establishing a complex hierarchy of advisory committees. These range from the Advisory Committee for Trade Negotiations (whose members are subjected to an elaborate clearance procedure) to the Policy Advisory Committees and the Sector Advisory Committees for labor, industry and agriculture. It is a formidable structure, but if labor's experience is illustrative, it is largely a sham. The administration's policy makers have already made most of the major decisions, and the advisory committee sessions are largely "educational," to let us know what is on the calendar. Our views are solicited and ignored.

A few weeks after the proposed international standards and international subsidies codes were presented to the Labor Policy Advisory Committee, for example, its members read in the newspapers that the finished documents had already been put on the table in Geneva. That was uncommonly fast work—especially since labor had unanimously opposed the proposal. The same occurred several months later, for the administration's tariff-cutting formula. The officials who administered the advisory committees may have wondered why fewer advisors bothered to show up. There was no need to wonder; when advice was uniformly ignored, advisors tended to drift away.

UNFAIR TRADE PRACTICES AND ADJUSTMENT ASSISTANCE

The Trade Act of 1974 also promised some new ways of looking at unfair trade practices by other countries and extending relief to workers and industries hurt by such practices. But in the two years since the act was passed, the visible results demonstrate that although the language may have changed, nothing else has.

Take the escape clause. In 1975 when we were passing through a period of record-breaking unemployment and imports in many areas were still climbing, there were no findings of injury to any industry. To date, the International Trade Commission and the President have agreed to provide import relief to only one industry, specialty steel. The footwear industry received a unanimous ITC finding of injury, but the President threw it out, despite a long record of commitments by Ford administration leaders to support such a finding.

The record is equally bad on countervailing duty cases. Countervailing duty is supposed to be imposed on imported products which have benefitted by unfair subsidies. Of the 28 cases filed and decided since the act went into effect, only 6 resulted in the application of countervailing duties. In one case, the Secretary of the Treasury suspended a countervailing duty on handbags from Brazil on the vague promise of a reduction of export subsidies, in contravention of the intent of the Trade Act. Even worse, the trade negotiators are now trying to sell a new international countervailing duty formula, which would bring back the obligation to prove injury—a throwback to the pre-Trade Act period when countervailing duty was only a promise, never a reality.

Then there is adjustment assistance. Here is one area where at least some of the promise of the Trade Act has come true. The provisions of the new law are better than the old, and so far as our industry is concerned, they have been fairly administered. But adjustment assistance never was and never will be a meaningful answer to import-caused injury. It is a touch of mercurochrome to a gaping wound. In a period of high unemployment, which has been a chronic problem in recent years, adjustment assistance is a cynical approach to jobless workers, offering them not jobs but a few extra dollars of unemployment insurance.

The failure of adjustment assistance as a concept cannot be overemphasized. The textile and apparel industry was formerly a source of almost two and a half million jobs, the largest of any industry in the manufacturing sector. As those job opportunities gradually erode under the impact of rising imports, there is nothing to take their place. The workers who used to fill those jobs usually started without special skills or advanced education, and they will find it difficult to shift into another industry or sector.

How does adjustment assistance meet their problem? It means some additional income during the worker's search for a new job and the opportunity to enroll in a job training program. But that does not help much when there are already eight to ten million people looking for work and unable to find it. A few lucky unemployed textile and apparel workers may find jobs when they are displaced by imports. The average worker will join the ranks of the long-term unemployed—and adjustment assistance will soon be only a memory.

AN OPPORTUNITY FOR THE NEW ADMINISTRATION

A new administration is in the process of taking over from the old. There is not much it can do to change the provisions of the Trade Act of 1974, short of the difficult, lengthy and unlikely possibility of sponsoring new legislation. But there is much it can do in the way of interpreting the act in such a way to enhance job opportunities and to curb the destructive effects of unregulated trade.

We would hope, for example, that a new set of negotiators might entertain the possibility of looking at tariffs from the point of view of raising tariffs where job erosion is already taking place due to imports and would observe the law's dictates about sectoral negotiations both in the letter of the law as well as in its spirit.

We would hope that special provisions of the law, such as escape clause and countervailing duty, will be administered effectively and expeditiously to prevent the consequences they are supposed to prevent—unfair subsidies by exporting nations and disruption of domestic industry.

We would hope that the advisory commission structure will be retained but that the resulting advice be solicited equitably and received seriously and followed to the extent possible.

Most of all, we would hope that the new administration will not be bound by the shibboleths of the past and instead will take a look at international trade in the light of its consequences today, in the light of all the current factors, financial and technological, which have made a shambles of the trade theories of the past. International trade can contribute in an important way to our prosperity but only if it is subject to enlightened planning and discriminating management. Unregulated and unplanned, international trade will only serve to grease the skids toward long-term recession and unemployment.

6

Competition and Employment in International Trade

WILLIAM N. WALKER

THE U.S. ECONOMY IN A CHANGING WORLD

Generals are often accused of busily preparing for the last war rather than the next one. Many American interests affected by international trade, by no means limited to the American labor movement, seem to have prepared for the Tokyo Round of trade negotiations by fighting the Kennedy Round all over again. We live in a "changing" world economy. I emphasize the word "changing," because conditions which the United States faces in the international economic environment today are radically different from those which we confronted a decade ago at the end of the Kennedy Round of multilateral trade negotiations. These changing conditions represent an opportunity for American products and a strengthening of the U.S. advantage in trade liberalization.

The bargain we struck in that earlier negotiation has been roundly criticized by American farmers and American businessmen as well as by American working men. It is an enduring part of the conventional wisdom that the United States "lost" the Kennedy Round. I do not propose to replow that ground or to argue the merits or drawbacks of the results of that earlier effort.

What I do want to call attention to, however, is the economic environment which followed. By mid-1967 we were well launched into the Vietnam War-induced inflation of the late 1960s and headed toward the boom-and-bust cycle of the first half of the 1970s, culminating in the deep recession of a year ago, the effects of which still afflict the United States and other nations of the world. This is familiar material, but there are two parts of it that warrant emphasis. First, our economic distress was not caused by the Kennedy Round. That negotiation simply had the misfortune to conclude about the time disaster struck, and we should not make the mistake of asserting a causal relationship where there is only a coincidence in timing. Second, and even more important, during much of this period many American products were, in fact, unable to compete in international markets. Thus, our ability to export goods abroad was hampered, and our domestic industries were vulnerable to competition from imports. Under these circumstances concern about trade liberalization was well-merited. The deterioration in America's trade and monetary positions brought on by our noncompetitiveness was among the most pressing reasons for the series of sweeping economic reforms announced by President Nixon on August 15, 1971.

The legacy of America's inability to compete, which existed then has been accompanied in the last few years by unacceptably high rates of unemployment at home and sluggish economies abroad. For many Americans, and particularly for representatives of the American labor movement, the first priority has been to protect American jobs. Our ability to increase employment in export industries has been hampered because other economies have not yet recovered from the deep recession. Thus apprehensions about trade liberalization dating from this earlier period have not abated.

But I submit that current conditions cloak an unfolding era of renewed American economic strength with unparalleled opportunities for export growth and domestic competitiveness. The world is changing in a way that is opportune for Americans. The conditions which engulfed the U. S. economy a few years ago no longer exist. We can consequently approach issues of international trade less defensively and more confidently, surer of our ability to compete better both at home and abroad.

IMPROVING AMERICAN COMPETITIVENESS IN WORLD TRADE

Three elements in particular play an important role in this process. First, the American dollar is more competitive. At the close of the Kennedy Round, we were still subject to the Bretton Woods strict-parity regime, and the U. S. dollar by any measure was overvalued. U. S. export prices were thus too high to compete in foreign markets, and imports into the U. S. were priced too low. However, in 1971 currency values began to float relative to one another—to the sizable advantage of American goods. Since 1971, the dollar cost of the deutschmark, for example, has risen 53 percent, the Swiss franc has risen 74 percent, and the Japanese yen has risen 27 percent.[1] Certainly, on the basis of changed international currency values, American products are more competitive.

Second, the United States is more competitive because along with the foreign-currency depreciation of the dollar, we have controlled our rate of inflation better than nearly anyone else. Measured on a dollar basis, U. S. wholesale prices have increased the least among the industrialized Western economies since 1970. This is true despite the serious inflation we have suffered in the United States. U. S. wholesale prices have increased at an annual average of nine percent since 1970 while, on a dollar basis, wholesale prices in West Germany have risen by 14 percent, in France by 11 percent, in the United Kingdom by nine percent, and in Japan by 13 percent.[2] Thus prices of American goods have become more competitive in markets here and overseas.

Third, labor costs per unit of output have increased substantially more abroad than in the United States. Against an approximate overall increase in unit labor costs of 35 percent in the United States since 1970, the increase in West Germany has been in dollar terms, 111 percent, and in Japan 123 percent.[3] In 1965 the average compensation per manufacturing worker in the United States was several times that in other industrialized countries. Ten years later, Canada, Sweden, Belgium, Switzerland and West Germany have equal or higher average levels of compensation than the United States at current exchange rates, while the differential between the United States and other industrialized countries has shrunk drastically.[4] In terms of labor cost, American goods have become more competitive.

In all three of these vital areas—currency values, inflation and labor costs—the U. S. is doing better than most of our trading partners. The trends suggest this is no mere anomaly; they suggest instead fundamental structural advantages in the U. S. economy.

The improvement in the American competitive position is starting to be reflected in the growing importance of foreign trade in the U. S. economy. For most of the post-war period, and throughout the 1960s, exports constituted only about four percent of GNP. In the last two years, however, the export share of GNP has reached seven percent.[5] A recent study done at the Bureau of Labor Statistics has projected an even greater share of exports in the GNP over the next ten years.[6] Moreover, in terms of goods—leaving aside services, many of which are not exportable—the export share was 15 percent—practically double the eight percent average of the 1960s.[7] Thus, today approximately $1 of every $6 worth of goods produced in the United States is exported. Broken out by sector, approximately 25 percent of agricultural output is exported; and—important to industrial unions, approximately 15 percent of non-agricultural output is exported.[8]

In addition, greater U. S. competitiveness has already brought about major changes in world investment patterns. The United States is now a country that can attract job-creating investment, as evidenced by a number of European and Japanese automakers' plans to build plants in the United States. The recent decision by Volkswagen was one of the more dramatic demonstrations of confidence in America as a manufacturing base.

Just as the U. S. economy looks increasingly attractive to foreigners with money to invest, the idea of investing abroad is not so appealing as in the past to U. S. management. This is due not only to the economic considerations already mentioned, but also to a variety of political considerations in other parts of the world. There is increasing evidence of a trend away from overseas expansion of U. S.-based MNCs, and conversely, a trend toward expansion into the United States of foreign-based MNCs. Another aspect of these developments therefore is that the U. S. worker is more secure in his job because he is producing more goods at more advantageous prices than his foreign competitors.

PROTECTING U. S. EMPLOYMENT

I do not want to leave you, however, that the Government is content with this sort of macro-economic analysis. We are acutely aware of the differential impact of foreign trade in particular industries. In areas, especially hard hit areas such as textiles and apparel, however, successive U. S. administrations have taken the lead in negotiating international levels of protection. Recently the United States began a series of negotiations seeking extension of the so-called multifiber arrangement, a comprehensive international agreement covering textile trade. Similarly the United States is prepared to take action in escape-clause cases to safeguard industries against serious injury from imports, as in the specialty steel industry.

In addition, the Tokyo Round of multilateral trade negotiations in Geneva have been conducted with an eye to the impact of any agreements that may be reached on individual sectors of American industry. Our purpose is to take full account of the differing interests of different elements of the American economy with the goal of achieving as many specific sectoral negotiating objectives as possible. So trade liberalization is not simply an article of faith or a one-way street. There are occasions when defensive actions are warranted. Indeed, among the most noteworthy features of the Trade Act of 1974 are the procedural handles it offers for trying to make international trade fairer and imposing obligations on the government to deal with unfair foreign trade practices. So the Trade Act introduces a notion of balance—a stance which permits the United States to deal with aggressive trade policies by others and to take advantage of our own improved competitive capability.

The point of all this is to note the increased strength with which we face imports and the concern that is felt for the American labor movement's criticism of America's trade policy. The United States has a major stake in an expanding world economy. This is not just the narrow expression of a diplomatic shibboleth but a reflection of the fundamental interest of the American working man in a strong, secure and economically healthy world.

The American labor movement has been at the forefront of American post-war efforts to preserve freedom and to maintain a strong defense. Increasingly, the traditional geopolitical underpinnings of American foreign policy are being overshadowed by international economic issues—the challenge of OPEC oil policies and the awakening expectations of developing nations being only two of the more obvious examples. American interests and the well being of American workers are advanced by a healthy and prosperous world trading system. The American economy is in a position today as never before to allow its citizens to take advantage of a smoothly functioning world economic order. Americans can now get a fairer shake in the world economy. We can compete better. And the American working man has never shrunk from fair competition.

NOTES

1. U.S. Department of Commerce, Measures of Exchange Rate Change in the U.S. Dollar, April 1971-February 15, 1977, Washington: U.S. Government Printing Office (February 1977).

2. International Monetary Fund, International Financial Statistics (monthly), U.S. Department of Commerce, Business Conditions Digest, January 1977.

3. Organisation for Economic Cooperation and Development, Main Economic Indicators (monthly).

4. Citibank, Monthly Economic Letter, May 1976.

5. U.S. Council on International Economic Policy, International Economic Report of the President, Washington, U.S. Government Printing Office (January 1977), pp. 138, 150.

6. C. Bowman & T. Morlan, "Revised Projections of the U.S. Economy," Monthly Labor Review, 99, no. 3, March 1976.

7. Charles A. Waite and Joseph C. Wakefield, "Federal Fiscal Programs," Survey of Current Business 56, no. 2 (February 1976), pp. 16 ff.

8. U.S. Council of Economic Advisers, Economic Report of the President, U.S. Government Printing Office (January 1976), pp. 176, 178; International Economic Report of the President op. cit., p. 152.

7

Labor's Approach to World Trade

ELIZABETH R. JAGER

JOB LOSSES THROUGH WORLD TRADE

On jobs and trade, the AFL-CIO has been accurate throughout the 1970s in its diagnoses and prescriptions. Others have belatedly begun to acknowledge job losses from imports, economic impacts of dislocation from imports, economic impacts of dislocation from transfer of factories out of the United States and the problem of income distribution. These are now discussed seriously by some academic economists. Even the U. S. Department of Labor's so-called research studies show job losses from the impact of trade and foreign investment.[1]

But there is something much more far-reaching about jobs and trade. First, international trade has had a rapidly growing and changing impact on the United States and its work force. Even in the first three quarters of 1976, as the U. S. economy rocked in uncertain and inadequate recovery, imports rose 24.4 percent to $94.7 billion. Exports rose only seven percent to $83.3 billion.

These are import dollar values based on foreign prices plus cost, insurance and freight. They understate the impact. By any measure, imports have much more than a tiny impact on the U. S. economy. Between 1967 and 1974 imports as a share of U. S. output of farms, mines and factories more than doubled—from about 10 percent to over 25 percent in dollar value, according to the U. S. Department of Commerce.[2]

Exports have also taken an even larger share of U. S. output, which doubled in the same period. But the U. S. share of total world manufactured exports has declined from 21 percent in 1960 to about 15 percent in early 1976.[3]

The mismatch of exports and imports, both geared to different reporting systems, has cost jobs and production in virtually every manufacturing industry from aerospace to textiles.

Second, the United States loses jobs from investment outflows overseas, from the accelerating and unplanned transfer of technology and from exporting needed raw materials and intermediate products.

Third, while the above factors are important to consider in recognizing the shift to a "service" oriented economy, the fact is that in job terms, American service jobs and job opportunities have been exported for many years—in shipping, airlines, the general transportation field.

While U.S. trade experts and policy spokesmen point with pride to the rising volume of manufactured exports in the 1970s and the big dollar trade surplus in these manufactured dollar sales reports, the jobs involved have not demonstrated great gains. America is proud of her aircraft exports, for example, but American workers know that today there are fewer employees in aircraft than there were over 25 years ago. In addition to improvements in technology and productivity and shifts in the mix and demand in American industry, aircraft and capital equipment have begun to be imported into the United States. In addition, what usually happens in these big export sales is that foreign buyers demand and receive the right to "co-produce"—that is, to have their labor force make some portion of the airplane sold abroad. This is not an efficiency requirement; it is a political requirement. The American workforce pays the cost.

In the 1950s, the United States exported mostly products. In the 1960s, it exported standard auto and machinery factories. In the 1970s, it has been exporting factories with its newest technology, often even before such factories exist in the United States. These are direct job losses. But the U.S. economy is interdependent.

Losses in textile jobs affect jobs in textile machinery. Losses in factory jobs affect losses in service jobs and they also affect the tax base of both major cities like New York and tiny towns like Tazewell, Virginia. In a declining economy or in an area where new jobs are not developing, the fact that new plants are not being built affects the building trades and service workers of all kinds.

A rapidly growing, fully employed economy does not have the same trade and investment problems as an economy that is not. The United States should be ready as a nation to negotiate and cooperate with others. But international interdependence should include recognition that the United States has rights as well as responsibilities in international bargaining.

Government machinery, both national and international, guarantees that these industry and job losses should not happen. That is what the laws and treaties say. But that is not what has been happening. U.S. government machinery has not worked to the advantage of U.S. workers. The Trade Act of 1974, flawed in its conception, has been equally flawed in its implementation, as Howard Samuel has demonstrated.

Why does the government machinery not work? The policymakers, fearing the facts, fail to inform the U. S. public or its trading partners. Legal action is considered protectionist. According to the New York Times business pages, a plea for action by any industry or workers in the United States for help is a "time bomb." U. S. action, they claim, threatens diplomatic disaster and possibly the breakdown of all international relations. And both the news media and our State Department tell baldfaced lies about impacts on consumer prices.

THE MULTINATIONALS AND THE WELFARE OF AMERICAN WORKERS

Other countries have the good sense to recognize that the world has changed. The U. S. has absorbed enough imports from nations who have been shut out of other markets for those exporters to recognize the sincerity of U. S. labor's claims. We do not claim to be a desperately poor economy, but we see no reason to make ourselves so. The people who have lived through the last two years of worldwide recession know that the U. S. economy is not only the strongest but that it helps the most when it can. The free people of the world depend on that U. S. strength. A drop in this economy is a disaster for friends and foes alike.

But new actors—unseen hands dealing the cards at international tables—are now multinational enterprises, often with new found friends. Corporations, banks, state-owned institutions and even governments themselves now operate in and around the laws of every nation. They make up the rules as they go—joining free forces, and dictatorships, flirting with fascists, and consorting with Communists—all in the name of a quick buck or a power grab. They have no ideology or ideals. And they, unlike American workers, are suffering few ill effects from the current realities of world trade.

The U. S. -based multinationals are the only ones which get much attention in the world of nations. Others are scarcely noticed. The Soviet links to U. S. and western firms and to many other countries are seldom mentioned, for example. Yet this is a foreign operator with a multinational bank and lots of other operations in different countries. The effects of state-owned enterprises, either from free or controlled economies, are rarely examined.

Most countries have longstanding regulations about foreign investors, technology, capital and other flows. But now some multinationals have a new game. No government can control us, they say. So let the world government—the UN—set up a code to regulate us. How does a group of governments regulate a government-multinational?

Multinationals are the world's traders, shippers, banks, transferers of technology, capital and jobs. The United States has started to examine the impact, not only of the outflow of capital but also of the sudden in-rush of capital into the United States. The United States is the only large country in the world that does not have some form of adequate and up-to-date recordkeeping of these developments. The multinational maze is changing so rapidly that the U. S. government can recommend only that it will be glad to join others in finding answers. But America cannot afford to delay the necessary legislation at home, because this country is already behind the industrial policies of other countries. New tax, trade and technology policies are needed.

The United States is concerned because the current drift portends a nation without an economic future. Technology transfers are already disastrous, harming Americans and not helping many people elsewhere, so they should not be accelerated. The slogans and the propaganda about American labor are not providing answers. It is time for the multinationals to come out from behind their privileged board rooms and decide just what they are prepared to do for the people of this and other nations.

REALISM IN INTERNATIONAL ECONOMIC POLICY

Fair international investigations and international proposals could be helpful. But a UN proposal for a technology conference in 1979 cannot accomplish what the United States needs to do here at home. Nor can people in other countries be helped by policies that exempt the malefactors and punish the benefactors in this new international transfer.

The United States has long believed, and its trade unions still do, that the cause of freedom can be served only if people are free to seek their own destiny. Thus the kind of a chance people have is important, both in the United States and in other nations. Charity should not be confused with economic competition. Charity should not involve taking from the poor here to give to the poor abroad.

Just in the past, the United States imported from the world a total of $9. 8 billion in machinery and transport equipment in 1969. From developing countries the United States imported machinery worth about $400 million. In 1975, the United States imported $23. 5 billion in machinery from the world and $2. 6 billion from developing countries.[4] The imports have been rising faster and taking up a larger share of U. S. imports from developing countries in sophisticated electronic and mechanical equipment.

In other manufactured goods the record is even clearer. In 1969, the United States imported $12 billion in a category called "other manufactured goods" and in 1975, $23.9 billion from all the world. Imports from developing countries rose from $2.5 billion to $6.6 billion, with the imports valued at the foreign export price, which MNCs often set at a ridiculously low level.[5] This was during the worst economic downturn in our recent history when Americans were looking for jobs and America was losing parts of major industries.

The same kind of record could be shown for technology transfers, because many developing countries now have technology of the most advanced kind, brought to them by multinationals. The reason they deny it, of course, is because the measures of the capital flows and technology flows and job transfer fail to capture what multinational firms and organizations actually do. No clear measure is available. Naturally, the leaders of countries full of starving, depressed and oppressed people find it useful to blame the lack of technology transfer and the lack of investment from abroad. Naturally the outrageous operations of some multinationals in these countries add to the all-too-easy image.

The record shows that U.S. labor has been paying for the change in the world economy's high costs in jobs and production necessary for a growing economy. The record shows that government machinery—national and international—has not worked for the U.S. worker because our government has not acted. The record shows that government machinery, in fact, does not take into account the major actors on the world scene—the multinationals—which now seek the UN as a place to be governed, because they think they can avoid all supervision in that way. The record shows that the demands of the developing countries for access to our markets are false, because they have had such access all the while.

But the record also raises the new questions now coming from meetings of OPEC countries. What will happen to the world economy if the cartels of raw materials are extended, if the demands of tightly controlled and closed economies, often self-styled, but not at all "poor" countries, demand ever more technology? As Sheikh Yamani, the Saudi Arabian Oil Minister, said not long ago, "We want, one, your technology, and two, your markets. . . ."[6]

From all this, a few elementary facts should be recognized as the basis for realistic trade, tax, and technology policies. The United States cannot afford to be blackmailed into submission. Extortion is extortion in anybody's language. And appeasement is not the way to respond to extortion.

The United States cannot afford to let every industrialized nation that has a large population call itself "developing" and seek more handouts. Better living standards in the world have not been and will not be served merely by encouraging export markets for the products of oppressed labor from behind walls of countries with growth plans. Internal markets need to be developed and can be developed.

Vague talk about fair labor standards and healthy world growth and international interdependence will not substitute for action. We want fair labor standards at home as well as abroad. We do not want future goals to undermine current gains.

We live in a world of managed economies among friends and foes alike. We cannot continue to support a laissez-faire trade policy. The MNCs have amply demonstrated that they have a higher calling than the national interest of the United States. Therefore, the people of the United States must turn to their government to protect them in ways that only a government can.

NOTES

1. U.S. Department of Labor, Conference on Impact of International Trade and Investment on Employment, December 2-3, 1976, Washington, D.C., unpublished papers.

2. U.S. Department of Commerce, International Economic Indicator, December 1976, Table 49, "Ratios of Exports and Imports to GNP and of Exports to Production—Annual."

3. Ibid, p. 18, "Changes in Key Competitive Indicators," "Shares of Total World Exports," and "Shares of World Exports of Manufacturers."

4. U.S. Department of Commerce, Overseas Business Reports, October 1976, Table 3, "U.S. Imports of Principal Commodities from Major World Areas, 1969 to 1975," pp. 52-53.

5. U.S. Department of Commerce, ibid.

6. Sheikh Yamani, Urban C. Lehner, "Fuel-Short U.S. Firms are Eyeing Arab Lands as Sites for Factories," Wall Street Journal, January 7, 1974.

8

Jobs and Trade: A European Trade Unionist's View

CLAS-ERIK ODHNER

OPEC, BRETTON WOODS AND THE INTERNATIONAL TRADING SYSTEM

We cannot leave the development of trade and economic relations between countries to the free play of the present day "market forces," if we want to bring the big economic problems in the world today nearer to solution.

To save the free trading system with all its undisputed advantages from a protectionist flood, the apparent shortcomings have to be remedied in expanded and improved collaboration between governments. Here are six steps:

1. To create a more favorable environment for international trade, governments have to agree on the handling and financing of the unavoidable current account deficits, so that they do not, as at present, block the possibilities for economic expansion of many countries.

2. For the same purpose, the inflationary forces coming from the international markets have to be better controlled. Three urgent reforms are control of speculation in raw materials through creation of international buffer stocks, control of short-term capital movements (including the Euro-markets) to dampen swings in exchange rates, and control of the pricing policies of the multinational corporations (MNCs) to prevent unwarranted price increases due to oligopolistic market power.

3. Exchange rates have in the short run to be adjusted so as to contribute to an improved balance in trade between countries. In the medium term, industrial policy in surplus countries should aim at expanding employment in the tertiary sector, and in the deficit countries in expanding employment in the secondary sector. Such an adjustment should in itself lessen the pressure for protectionism.

4. International agreement between governments to limit the power and define the role of the multinational corporations must be at

the center of any program to reform international trade and the world economy.

5. The main objectives for industrial development in developing countries must be to expand production for their own markets, to provide for the basic needs of their own people, and to expand trade among themselves on the basis of a suitable division of labor between neighboring countries—instead of concentrating on exports to the rich countries. This will require substantially expanded and qualitatively improved development assistance from the rich countries.

6. The safeguard clause in GATT should be revised and a new social clause added to the treaty to protect labor and capital investment against temporary disturbances and permit reasonable time for adjustment.

The growing economic interdependence between countries has made it inevitable that national economic policies will be a subject of international negotiations. Such negotiations must be founded on full employment policies for the national economies, not only in words but also in deeds, if a progressive development of international trade and economic relations is to be achieved. The spectacular results of the 1950s and 1960s, in the field of international trade in the industrialized countries have been made possible mainly because of the high levels of employment.

Two events of lasting importance recently in international economic development have been the final collapse of the Bretton Woods' system of stable exchange rates and the OPEC action to increase oil prices, both occurring in 1973. The oil producing countries have presently a current surplus of around $50 billion, to which must be added the $15-20 billion surpluses of Japan, Germany, and some smaller European countries. The offsetting deficits are held mainly by the other Organisation for Economic Cooperation and Development (OECD) countries, developing countries, and Communist countries.[1]

The present exchange rates system of "managed floating," combined with an extremely high international liquidity of "oil money" in the hands of speculators, creates very great instability in the monetary and capital markets. In such a situation governments are afraid of giving birth to speculation against their currencies, seeing the fate of such countries as the United Kingdom and Italy. They are therefore trying to keep or create balance in their external relations through restrictive economic policies and concealed trade protection. But since the deficits have to be carried by someone, they are pushed around to the weakest countries, those least able to accommodate them. The disparities in the international economic system are thereby widened. The floating system is so distorted by government interventions and speculation, that the resulting exchange rates adjustments are not at all redirecting trade to improve balances in the way they theoretically were intended to do.

The differences in inflation rates are also creating big difficulties in international trade. It is unquestionably in the common interest of the trade unions that these differences should be diminished and the inflation rate cut, so as to stabilize trade and employment since the redistribution effect of inflation is always to the detriment of working people. Control of speculation and a buffer stock program for raw materials, control of short-term capital movements, and control of the pricing policies of the MNCs would greatly improve the conditions for the governments in managing stabilization policy between the Scylla of inflation and the Charybdis of unemployment.

European countries have a much greater stake in international trade. While foreign trade as a percentage of GNP is around eight percent in the United States, it is 15-25 percent in the larger European countries and 40-50 percent in some of the smaller ones. To counteract the potential instability in their economies they have formed a customs union in the EC of nine countries, including all the largest ones, and a free trade area for most of the remaining countries linked to that customs union. But even inside the EC, as long as there is no parallel monetary union, trade is subject to uncertainties such as different nontariff barriers (NTBs) and changes in the exchange rates.

EXCHANGE RATES, MULTINATIONALS, AND INTERNATIONAL TRADE

After two decades of quite stable international trade patterns, cost developments and competitiveness have varied widely between countries in the last five years or so.* It should be made quite clear that competitiveness does not entirely depend on cost. Technical developments of products, capacity and punctuality in deliveries, credits and a lot of other factors play an important role. This is the reason why reactions to price changes are mostly slow and incomplete, especially for manufactured products. In the last five years most governments have tried to solve their inflation, unemployment and deficit problems by promoting exports. But this is not a solution open to every country at the same time. Some have succeeded better than others.

During the 1950s and 1960s some of the big industrialized countries, notably Japan and Germany, expanded their manufacturing indus-

---

*This discussion is partly based on the International Confederation of Free Trade Unions program, "Economic Security and Social Justice," adopted at the Eleventh ICFTU World Congress, Mexico City, 1975, (Brussels: ICFTU, 1976).

tries with the protection of highly undervalued currencies in the Bretton Woods fixed exchange rates system, thus running high export surpluses against the rest of the world. For Japan it implied a very swift reduction of the population working in agriculture, from 30 percent of the total in 1960 to 13 percent in 1973, and a corresponding increase in industry. The population working in industry increased by around 50 percent in this period compared to a little more than 10 percent as an average for other OECD countries (6 percent for OECD-Europe). Internal demand for industrial products did not expand nearly to the same extent. Germany had a much larger share of its population working in manufacturing industry than is normal for a developed country, 50 percent as compared to 35 percent as an average for other OECD countries.[2]

This development was to a certain extent checked by the revaluation of currencies and the transition to a floating rates system at the beginning of this decade. In principle such a system should lead to a revaluation of the currencies of surplus countries and a devaluation of those of deficit countries until trade has changed to eliminate those surpluses and deficits. However, this would mean large unemployment in the surplus countries since their industrial structure cannot be changed in the short run. Neither are they likely to renounce the political strength that the economic surpluses give them.

The present exchange rate system is not free floating but highly "managed" floating. Governments intervene extensively in the monetary markets to keep their exchange rates at desired levels. The Japanese and German governments have continued to keep their currencies undervalued and thereby to score a considerable trade surplus. This surplus is to a certain extent used to pay for services, tourism and so on, but mainly for investments abroad and foreign lending. Their competition is severely felt in other industrialized countries.

In other industrialized countries, companies have preferred to establish and expand manufacturing production abroad instead of increasing exports. This applies especially to the United States but also to some of the smaller countries like the Netherlands, Sweden and Switzerland. There are several reasons why the companies in these countries have chosen another policy than in Japan and Germany. In the United States the main cause seems to have been the growing overvaluation of the dollar. For the smaller countries it was the necessity of getting behind trade barriers and the insufficient political backstopping governments of small countries are able to give to their exporters. There has been an interlacing of interests between MNCs and governments in many of their mother countries, which makes political support an important part of total MNC strategies.

The growing economic power of the MNCs has thus become a main economic and political issue, with which the trade unions are increasingly concerned.[3] The economic development of many countries, rich and poor, is becoming more and more dependent on decisions taken by the MNCs. The internationalization of investment, production and exchange cannot realistically be reversed. It has contributed considerably to the economic development in the postwar period. But steps must be taken to control the power of the MNCs and to make them accountable to the world community.

A code of conduct has been agreed on in the OECD in June this year. It is a very first step, but the code is too weak to have any real influence. The objective must be to arrive in a not too distant future at legally binding international conventions stating public accountability for the MNCs, enforcing basic social obligations, establishing control of foreign direct investments and takeovers, regulating restrictive business practices and oligopolistic pricing, providing rules for the taxation of MNCs, regulating the transfer of technology, and controlling short-term capital movements.

These developments have tended to create a rather rigid structural pattern of export, with the industrialized world divided into surplus and deficit countries. This has wide-ranging consequences for jobs and wages. In deficit countries trade unions come under increasing pressure to accept income policies as a means in redressing the national trade balance. But in the absence of any support through international coordination of the clearly incompatible national export objectives of the larger countries and the strategies of the MNCs, such policies have been largely unsuccessful.

THIRD WORLD COMMODITIES AND MANUFACTURES IN INTERNATIONAL TRADE

It should at last be clear to all countries and to all parties that although sudden and sharp price fluctuations may be in a few countries' short-term interest, the longer-term effects of repeated dislocations in the world economy from violent changes in commodity prices are in no country's interest. The answer to the seesaw of prices must, especially for Third World commodities, be found in commodity agreements which guarantee not only fair prices, but also continuous access to markets for producers and regular supplies for consumers. 55 percent of the world exports of basic commodities come from Western industrialized countries. Since few arrangements had been achieved mutually between consumers and producers, some raw material producers have tried to follow the example of the oil-producing countries and act unilaterally, thus far without much success.

As an alternative the Integrated Commodity Program has been launched by the so-called Group of 77 (now over 100 developing countries) in the United Nations Conference on Trade and Development (UNCTAD). This program, supported by the International Confederation of Free Trade Unions (ICFTU), has five basic elements: a system of international buffer stocks; a common fund for their financing, to which producing, consuming, and oil exporting countries, as well as international finance organizations, would contribute; a system of multilateral supply and purchase commitments; an improved system of compensatory financing; and a new emphasis on developing countries exporting their raw materials in processed rather than in crude form.

The only aid element in the agreement is the compensatory finance scheme which would stabilize the export earnings of countries exporting raw materials not suitable for stocking grants or loans. A scheme along these lines has in fact already been agreed upon under the Lome Convention of 1975 between the EC and 46 developing countries in Africa, the Caribbean and the Pacific (ACP) which contain about 10 percent of the population of the Third World. All industrial goods and 84 percent of processed agricultural goods of ACP countries enter the EC duty-free.

In the long run, however, export of manufactured products is more vital to developing countries to expand and more difficult for the industrialized to accept than export of commodities. At present, Third World countries have only seven percent of total world industrial production, and this share has not increased over the last decade. Restrictions on imports to industrialized countries have no doubt been a factor holding back their industrialization.

The call for a fairer and more equitable international "division of labor" in the UN's program of action for "a new international economic order" and in other resolutions, however, gives a misleading impression of the real problem and its solution. The proper role of industries in developing countries should surely not be only, or even mainly, to produce cheap export products with low-paid labor—such as textiles, shoes and chinaware—for the benefit of the people in the rich countries. It should be to produce goods for their own people more suitable to their needs. The term "division of labor" in fact gives the impression that the quantity of goods and labor the world requires is fixed and that this quantity can therefore only be divided up more equally, whereas what is really required is an expansion of employment and useful production everywhere.

The 1976 World Employment Conference organized by the International Labour Office, centered around the concept of "a basic needs strategy." The development efforts in the poor countries should be directed primarily toward providing the basic needs of food, clothing, shelter and public services of their population. This would be a very important redirection of development efforts in comparison to the present goal of indiscriminate economic expansion, since it implies a redistribution of incomes and wealth to cover the basic needs of the poorest among the people. Their industrial development should mainly be geared to this end. This certainly also implies an expansion of internal demand.

An expansion of trade among poor countries, especially among the smaller of them, could contribute considerably to reaching the new goals. The potentialities for a division of labor among these nations in manufacturing production is often much greater than between poor and rich countries. In fact, such trade would lead to a more balanced development of their economies and prevent an undue reliance on trade with industrialized countries with all the political problems this can pose.

Such a redirection of development policies would have important implications also for industrialized countries. If the developing countries should reduce their export efforts to the rich countries, and divert their interest towards their internal markets and towards exporting to their neighbors, their import requirements will have to be paid for in some other way. An obvious answer to such increased efforts from developing countries to implement a basic needs-strategy would be for the rich countries to enlarge their development assistance on a broad basis and reorient that assistance qualitatively toward support of a basic needs-strategy.

THE ROLE OF THE MULTINATIONALS

Even if such a policy should be successful, competition from low-wage imports will still be of great importance in industrialized countries. Thus agreement to reduce tariff and nontariff barriers in the Tokyo Round multilateral trade negotiations would also make significant contribution to increasing employment and production generally, by both enabling developing countries to sell more goods to the industrialized countries and to buy more goods from the industrialized world with the foreign exchange they have earned.

The MNCs have played an important role in expanding such exports to the rich countries. But they have been a mixed blessing to the developing countries to say the least. They are often located in industrial enclaves with little relationship to the rest of the economy. The recent creation of "free industrial zones" in such countries as Egypt, Senegal and South Korea, allows the MNCs to operate outside the laws and regulations of the host country. The companies established there are uninhibited by the ILO conventions and recommendations on working conditions, even if the host country should have ratified them.

In many countries the MNCs are creating a dichotomy between a modern sector using advanced technology and the traditional sector. They are upsetting the wage structure but nevertheless extracting in different ways big profits for the mother companies in the rich countries by selling their technology expensively and setting low transfer prices for the products and high prices for the supplies. A way to reduce the effects of this dichotomy would be for governments in developing countries to reach an agreement on levying a special tax on the MNCs in the modern sector to promote the development of the traditional sector. Unfortunately the competition to attract MNCs, despite all their drawbacks, is so strong among some developing countries that such an agreement does not seem realistic. And the rich countries are not offering the Third World any meaningful alternative for its industrialization.

THE IMPACT OF UNIONS ON CONSUMER AND PRODUCER INTERESTS IN INTERNATIONAL TRADE

In principle, the benefits of increased international trade should go to consumers in importing countries who are getting the products cheaper than if they were produced in their own country. The same applies indirectly when investment goods are imported, since production costs then are reduced. While market imperfections, restrictions and regulations of different kinds are nibbling at those benefits on the long way to the consumer, it is undeniable that a considerable part of the increase in living standards during the last century has been the result of an increased exchange between countries (as well as between regions within such a large market as the North American). Western Europe has in the last decade been reaping the same benefits from specialization and trade as the United States did before the First World War.

As is well known, consumers are in general politically weak, because people feel that their consumer function is much less important than their producer function. Producer interests always by far outweigh consumer interests on the same issue. Consumers' interests are spread over so many issues that the individual consumer is unable to give time and interest to a sufficient number of them to have a real impact on his economic situation. But when consumers' interests are concentrated on one large issue such as inflation, they can be quite powerful. A politician can rarely gain much by appealing to consumers' interests on trade issues because of the weak response, while the response to an appeal to a particular group of voters united by a common producer interest may be very powerful.

The situation for the consumer varies from country to country, depending among other things on the strength and the structure of the trade unions. The attitude to trade and to consumers' interests is certainly also influenced by the ideology of the unions. In countries with a high rate of organization, with unions covering all trades and professions and with a strong central organization, unions are apt to take the interest of all their members into account, that is, to sponsor the consumers' interest against the special producers' interest of some smaller member group. This is the case in the Scandinavian countries, which by tradition have been strongholds for free trade.

On the other hand, when the central labor organization is weak, as in the United Kingdom, powerful national unions can pursue their special producers' interests, often in collaboration with the employers. This gives a more protectionist character to the unions and possibly to the country. In the United States, with a very low overall rate of unionization concentrated in the manufacturing industry and a strong central organization, the attitude seems also to lean in a protectionist direction. The same appears to apply to Japan. When the rate of organization is low and the central organizations are weak and split into several movements, as in France and Italy, their influence becomes weak and commercial interests take over altogether, with strong protectionism as a result.

The following figures, calculated by Bela Balassa for 1970, show tariffs in percentages in the main industrialized countries. Little has happened since, with the exception that the United Kingdom has moved down to the EC level.[4]

1. Australia	16.2
2. Japan	16.1
3. Canada	16.0
4. United Kingdom	15.2
5. United States	11.5
6. EC (six countries)	11.0
7. Denmark	11.0
8. Norway	11.0
9. Sweden	6.6

The main opponents to free trade are quite naturally the companies producing goods inside the country in competition with imports, the workers in these companies, and their unions. But structural changes in industrialized countries such as technological innovations, changing living patterns, and tastes are more important reasons for opposition to free trade. There has nevertheless always been a tendency to put the blame on foreign competition because it is easy to understand and to gain allies against a foreign adversary.

Exports subsidized by the government of the exporting country pose a difficult problem in this connection. First, it should be said that foreign competitors are always accused of being subsidized as soon as competition bites. Proven cases are much fewer. But there is no doubt that large-scale government export subsidies of different kinds do exist. The customary reaction is certainly that this is unfair competition and that protectionist measures would be justified, a position supported by the GATT treaty.

In taking a detached view of export subsidies, however, it could be argued that consumers are benefited by cheaper imports. If domestic production is not very important or adjustment measures are inexpensive, this might be the most favorable solution, provided the export subsidies are estimated to last. The demand for protection of domestic production has to be weighed against four different factors:

1. The cost to the consumers. Even though it might be very small, not to say insignificant, to each consumer, it can become very significant to the economy as a whole in comparison to the producers' interests which demand protection.

2. There is always a risk of unfavorable long run structural effects arising from protective measures. The competitive unprofitability of domestic production might be small in the beginning but has a tendency to grow with time.

3. Protective measures always bring the risk of retaliation. Every government has to take into account that it might start a chain reaction of such measures if it introduces them itself. There is a difference between big and economically powerful nations and the small ones. The former can do many things with impunity that the latter do not dare.

4. Finally we have to take the developing countries' need to export into account. As already stated, increased development assistance from the rich countries should allow them to give more attention to their internal markets and to trade between themselves. But they will nevertheless always have a need to sell in the markets of the rich countries.

TRADE UNION ATTITUDES

Both conflicting solidarities and conflicting economic interests are at stake for the trade unions in international trade policies. If the four factors mentioned here are squarely weighed against demands for protection on an overall national level, the outcome will nearly always be for free trade, certainly in the small countries but mostly also in the larger ones. But workers in industries hurt by the foreign competition ask for union solidarity and offer their votes to politicians ready to support their claims for protection. They rightly think that they alone should not carry the burden of adjustment when the consumers at large are sharing the gains.

Workers question also, often rightly, whether their sacrifices really will benefit workers in the exporting countries. Workers in the industrialized countries cannot be expected to willingly accept greater trade liberalization either with developing or with other countries, unless their demand for sharing of the burden is effectively met and unless they know that their sacrifices really will benefit the poor workers in developing countries and not only the MNCs and other profiteers in those countries.

By and large the trade unions in Europe have supported the liberalization of trade and European economic integration, although it has meant and will still mean considerable changes in the industrial structure and adjustments to new jobs and new places.[5] Advantages to the workers as consumers by far outweigh the drawbacks of these changes. A fundamental precondition has also been that full employment has mostly been maintained. In the present situation of high unemployment, liberalization would probably not have been accepted by the unions.

PROTECTING WORKERS THROUGH ADJUSTMENT ASSISTANCE

European unions have been persistent in insisting on increased government and EC adjustment assistance for affected workers within the framework of an expanded and active labor market policy in order that the burden of adjustment should be carried more equally by the whole community. In this respect we are not at all satisfied with what has been achieved so far. To represent their interests at the regional level in the process of integration both in EC and the European Free Trade Association (EFTA) all the European national trade unions, socialist, Christian and communist, with the marked exception of CGT-France, have formed the European Trade Union Congress (ETUC).

The well warranted demands for solidarity by workers in affected industries can be met by a generous application of suitable adjustment policies, instead of protectionist measures. Changes in the industrial structure, whatever their causes, must not be left to the free play of market forces. In such cases the hardship suffered by workers in displaced industries can be severe, whatever the overall national gains will be. If this is allowed to happen, there will be a growing resistance of workers to development assistance generally and to Third World imports especially. This would be tragic and completely inexcusable, since governments are fully able to adopt adjustment policies which insure that the short-term costs of trade liberalization are borne equitably by the whole community and not just by those workers directly affected. On the contrary, we urgently need to strengthen the solidarity between workers in developed and developing countries as a major basis for a strongly needed expansion of the worldwide development cooperation.

The basic aim of adjustment policies should be to insure that workers who lose their jobs for whatever reason should be able to find new work, preferably in the same area in which they live. This means that governments must have a long term view of the way that industry and services should develop and must take into account for their planning such factors as growing foreign competition and technological change. If an industry or a firm is facing decline, then governments should plan, encourage and where necessary undertake the expansion of new activities to provide alternative employment.

Training, retraining, and labor market services in general should be strengthened to insure that workers are able to take on new jobs without undue difficulty. While looking for work or while being retrained, the living standards of workers and their families should be protected. If they have to move to find new employment, their moving costs should be met and assistance given with resettlement.

The justification of such a policy rests on economic as well as social grounds. Great flexibility in labor markets and expanded industrial planning will facilitate the attainment of growth targets with fewer bottlenecks and inflationary pressure in the growth areas. But it should be strongly emphasized that a precondition for a labor market policy effectively solving adjustment problems is an economic policy for full employment. There is no point in retraining or moving workers to new jobs if there are none. An expansion of services in the public sector such as education, health and care of the aged is urgently needed in almost all countries and provides ample opportunity for useful and productive employment. An active labor market policy involves working with selective economic measures, taking action where action is needed and avoiding the overheating effect of a more general stimulus in areas where capacity is already fully utilized.

SOCIAL AND SAFEGUARD CLAUSES IN THE GATT TREATY

There is another key factor in the willingness of workers to bear the burden of adjustment to imports from developing countries. Workers will resist trade liberalization and claim protection if they feel that the cost advantage of other countries is due to exploitation and that other workers will not benefit from a reduction in trade barriers which instead enrich multinational and other large companies established in such places as Hong Kong, Taiwan and Singapore or the new "free industrial zones," which transfer their profits to mother companies in the industrialized countries. For this reason, the ICFTU has proposed that a social clause should be added to the GATT treaty, not only obliging governments in industrialized countries to adopt anticipatory adjustment measures to protect their workers hurt by foreign competition but also obliging governments in developing countries to observe fair labor standards such as those laid down by ILO instruments.

The concept of fair labor standards has changed considerably over the two last decades. Fifteen to twenty years ago it generally meant that producers of imported products should pay the same wages as domestic producers of the same product. In this way trade unions in high wage countries could label all competing imports as unfair. This was certainly not a reasonable idea, and when trade unions became more aware of the problems in the developing countries the concept gradually changed. It now implies that governments and employers shall observe the ILO standards of working conditions, the right to organize and such things which are fundamental to any trade union activity.

Such a social clause seeks to minimize the potential resistance to international trade reform by guaranteeing the employment and income of those groups of workers affected by trade adjustment in the industrialized countries and by seeking to insure that the cost advantage enjoyed by the MNCs is not due to exploitation of the labor force in developing countries. On one important point it should be possible to reach agreement without much delay. To circumvent legislation concerning working conditions, MNCs sometimes move dangerous production methods to countries with less stringent legislation for workers' protection. This must be considered unfair competition and measures taken against the import of goods produced by such dangerous methods.

The safeguard clause of the GATT treaty (Article 19) needs to be substantially revised. The present clause allows countries to take action restricting imports if they are likely to "cause or threaten serious injury to domestic producers." It is up to the governments concerned to decide whether the clause is applicable. This makes it much easier for governments in large countries to invoke the clause than for governments in small ones. Furthermore, no obligation is placed on a country to introduce adjustment measures in the industry concerned, and there is no requirement to permit the orderly growth of offending imports at least in step with market growth. Nor is a government obliged to justify the form of protection adopted or to indicate how long it is intended to last.

More detailed principles for the use of safeguard actions have to be adopted. In particular, the trade effects on "employment" should be rated much more highly than the effects on "domestic producers." The basic aim should not be an unrealistic goal to prevent all restrictive measures, but instead to lay down workable principles governing emergency actions and to insure that there is effective consultation between countries concerned and international surveillance of measures adopted.

These proposals regarding social and safeguard clauses in GATT have, among other things, the merit of being agreed upon by all member unions of the ICFTU in both developed and developing countries.

THEORY AND REALITY IN FOREIGN TRADE

There has been a very strong expansion of international trade since the end of the Second World War, especially among industrialized countries. It has been based on the free trade ideology founded in turn in the traditional comparative advantage. GATT has been the international organization serving as a guardian of governments to see that they follow the principles of this theory. At the same time the character of trade has changed. The proportion of manufactured products in relation to commodities has increased sharply and so have internal deliveries between different parts of the same multinational companies. There are no accurate statistics for such deliveries, but they are estimated to approach one-third of total international trade. The technological content of trade is also growing, with contracts including not only goods but also know-how in planning, management, services, and so on. Technology and specialization have created a growing dependence for buyers on specific sellers.

All these changes have introduced new factors in international trade that greatly diminish the impact of clear-cut price competition. Many other factors are today determining the pattern of international trade, including political factors. This pattern also seems to have become much more rigid in its response to changes in competitive economic forces. The foundations for the free trade ideology are becoming increasingly less secure.

In the trade with developing countries on the other hand, the ideology of free trade has never really been applied except for unprocessed commodities. These countries have been faced with uncertain markets for such commodities because of violent swings in demand and speculation. For trade in processed and manufactured products developing countries have met a host of restrictions, severely limiting their exports to industrialized countries. With nominal tariffs increasing in relation to the degree of processing, the effective tariffs on processing itself have often become astronomical. The result of the efforts to reduce protectionism in the industrialized countries and improve their trade relations with the developing world has been very poor.

These policies of industrialized countries have severely disrupted both the agricultural and the industrial development of developing countries because they have been deprived of the means to pay for sufficient imports of necessary technology and investment goods for development and expansion. The industrialized countries have also been deprived of important export outlets. These restrictions on imports from developing countries also contributed to the increasing domination of their economies by the MNCs, interested primarily in pursuing their own interests rather than those of the host country.

So far nothing has been said about trade with state-trading countries with centrally planned economies. It defies theoretical treatment in the classical framework since relations between prices and costs of production are indeterminate. In any event, this trade represents a very small share of the total international trade.

The freedom of international trade developed by the Western industrialized countries during the last three decades has become an anarchical freedom, misused by multinational companies, speculators, other private interests, and often also governments irresponsibly exploiting workers and natural resources. This is not to deny that considerable advantages in rising living standards and in employment have also been reaped by consumers and workers. But the growing concentration of uncontrolled private power, often exercised in tacit understanding with governments, and uncoordinated interventions by governments in the system forced by political pressure, all too often cause serious malfunctioning of the free system. To save the free trading system with all its advantages from a protectionist flood, governments have to collaborate much more closely in order to mitigate its defects.

The theory of comparative advantage is a static theory concerned only with the present. The theory assumes total mobility of the factors of production—hence historical structures are of no importance—and it does not presume technological or other changes which necessitate planning for the future. When the theory was first conceived nearly 200 years ago this was perhaps more realistic than it is today. Investments in industrial production were much less important and less specialized and could more easily be adapted to changes in production. And the labor force was less skilled and could also change more easily. No one cared about the security of employment of the workers. And the governments did not have much ambition to guide the future industrial development of their countries.

Today in contrast, governments are under strong political pressure from trade unions and public opinion to secure employment in existing industries and regions in face of declining competitiveness. Governments are also convinced that success in industrial development is geared to the establishment and expansion of key "growth industries" in the technologically most advanced branches.

But the growing involvement of governments in the industrial development of their countries is not only or even mainly geared to the problems of international trade. They are taking an increasingly active part in the development of industry to solve regional imbalances, to foster special growth industries, to support Research and Development

(R & D) and so on. Many of these measures do, of course, influence the international competitiveness of the enterprises concerned.

Trade policy is still basically founded on the idea that there is a clear-cut borderline between free trade and protectionism and that profitability in export and import competing production is the same for the national economy as well as for the producing firm. The growing public involvement with increasingly selective measures in the development of national industries, however, creates a "gray zone" between free trade and protectionism and between the profitability for the producing company and for society as a whole. The extension of this "zone" varies between countries and industrial sectors, depending on the extent and character of government interventions and the transactions of the MNCs. Since these interventions mostly aim at strengthening export competitiveness, the goods in fact, are sold at subsidized prices.

Investments by governments, both in present production capacity and still more in the technologically advanced growth industries for the future are very substantial and the skills required are often very specialized. Governments have to judge their policy by the comparative advantage of the production being created over the whole economic lifetime of the assets and the special training of the workers. There is no market mechanism to deal with this situation. It often does not become much more than guesswork.

There is very little chance that governments will arrive at a correct assessment of their comparative advantage in the sense that it will lead to a sufficient but not excessive capacity in different industrial fields and thus to balanced trade. Some international coordination in sectors where investments are very heavy would therefore be of mutual advantage.

Such coordination would be in the interest of governments, and still more of workers and taxpayers, in order to avoid the creation of large overcapacity and the launching of prestigious and unprofitable projects in the growth industries, such as steel, computers, certain chemicals, and nuclear power.

NOTES

1. Organisation for Economic Cooperation and Development, Economic Outlook, July 1976. Foreign trade and current balances and effects of the latest oil-price increase have been added to these figures.

2. Organisation for Economic Co-operation and Development, Labor Force Statistics 1962-73 (Paris: OECD, 1975).

3. International Confederation of Free Trade Unions, Multinational Charter (Brussels: ICFTU World Congress Document, 1976).

4. Bela Balassa, "On Some Effects of Commercial Policy on International Trade, the Location of Production and Factor Movements" (The Nobel Symposium, Stockholm, 1976), mimeo.

5. John Dunning, "Trade, Location of Economic Activity and the MNE: A Search of an Eclectic Approach" (The Nobel Symposium, Stockholm, 1976), mimeo.

PART II

INVESTMENT AND EMPLOYMENT

9

Taxation and American Investment Abroad: The Interests of Workers and Investors

PEGGY B. MUSGRAVE

U. S. LABOR AND INVESTMENT ABROAD

It is only in the last 15 years or so that academics, policymakers and other students of foreign investment have begun to take a fresh and more critical look at the long-held assumption that the interests of foreign investors and of the nation as a whole necessarily coincide. This issue is so central that some attention to it is necessary before turning to the more specific question of taxation of investment abroad.

As an alternative to domestic investment, there is now a strong presumption that U. S. direct investment abroad, while in most cases helpful to the foreign host country and beneficial to the investor, is harmful to the interests of U. S. labor. Indeed, if carried too far, it is likely to reduce the level and growth of U. S. national income. *

The decision of multinational corporations to invest abroad rather than at home affects the interests of U. S. labor as workers, as consumers and as taxpayers.

As "workers", their employment and productivity may be affected adversely. With regard to employment, foreign investment under most reasonable assumptions leads to reduced plant and equipment expenditures at home to subsequent displacement of domestic production. Although the employment effects are apt in practice to be the most spectacular and visible when whole plants close down and the business moves abroad, the problem is essentially a transitional one of adjustment (albeit painful to labor) if compensatory monetary and fiscal policy is doing its work.

---

*I have developed this position at length in Peggy B. Musgrave, Direct Investment Abroad and the Multinationals: Effects on the United States Economy, Washington: U. S. Senate, Committee on Foreign Relations, Subcommittee on Multinational Corporations, August 1975 (Committee Print).

The less obvious and longer-run effects on labor productivity are in my view the more important. The loss of capital to the United States may be expected to result in a reduction in real wages. Although statistics are scarce and difficult to interpret, some 10 percent of U.S.-owned business fixed investment appears now to be in place abroad. In 1975, total capital expenditures of majority-owned foreign affiliates was $27 billion compared with business expenditures on new plant and equipment in the United States of $113 billion. For the 1970-75 period as a whole, foreign capital expenditures of U.S. business constituted some 17.3 percent of total (domestic plus foreign) such expenditures. For manufacturing industries, this percentage was 19 percent.[1] Put another way, if the foreign capital expenditures of majority-owned affiliates of U.S. corporations had been made in the United States, they might have raised the ratio of gross private fixed investment to GNP from the actual ratio of 12.2 percent to 13.8 percent. This estimate in fact underestimates the total effect since it excludes such investment attributable to U.S. shares in nonmajority owned foreign businesses, as well as inventory investment. (Effects on exports need not be considered here, where we deal with effects on the U.S. capital stock only.)

Although high, these rates of foreign investment relative to the size of the U.S. economy are nowhere near those experienced by the United Kingdom during its heyday of foreign investment in the decade or two prior to the First World War when Britain was annually exporting 75 to 90 percent of her current national savings. The contribution of this state of affairs to the subsequent economic decline of Great Britain has as yet not been adequately explored. Such a study might well carry lessons for the United States.

While many people stress the need for a higher rate of capital formation in the United States to raise the rate of growth of the economy and increase labor productivity (usually advocating lower business taxes and larger investment incentives to bring this about), curiously little mention is made of this everincreasing outflow of capital, stimulated as it is by tax advantages. How can we complain of a capital shortage when up to 20 percent of our national savings are annually being invested abroad?

As "consumers", American workers are affected if the capital outflow leads to a deterioration in the terms of trade through the displacement of U.S. exports by foreign-produced U.S.-type products or through capital outflow-induced exchange depreciation.[2] The question of whether foreign investment replaces export sales abroad has been the subject of long and heated debate. Business representatives have contended either that foreign investment is a necessary accompaniment to exports by providing supportive services and a conduit for market information, without which exports would be less than at present, or that export sales are inevitably destined for displacement by foreign competition which can only be met by moving U.S. production abroad.

With regard to the first point, some supportive foreign investments are probably necessary, but these could be primarily for marketing and servicing facilities. It is difficult to see why large investments in production facilities should be essential to sustain exports. As to the second argument, we need to ask whether U. S. capital movement abroad to displace foreign competitors is worth the cost to the U. S. economy in reduced capital formation and productivity. Such investment might, furthermore, have been made in import-substituting industries with favorable terms-of-trade effects.

The displacement of U. S. exports by foreign sales of U. S. affiliates abroad is almost inevitable, given the fact of their close similarity. Such sales have now reached a level 2.4 times the total value of U. S. exports, and have generally been growing at a faster pace than have U. S.-produced exports. The Domestic International Sales Corporation (DISC) tax provision was introduced in 1971 to provide the same tax advantages for exports as for foreign investment and has recently been extended on a modified incremental basis in the Tax Reform Act of 1976. The need for this measure is based on recognition by the administration and Congress that exports and sales by foreign affiliates of U. S. companies are in competition. The DISC tax provision which has resulted in an annual tax revenue loss approaching $2 billion, increases the burden on all taxpayers proportionately or diminishes government services. To the extent this revenue loss is reflected in lower export prices, furthermore, it means a deterioration in the U. S. terms of trade.

The argument that foreign investment which exploits lower-cost raw materials abroad serves not only the objective of more efficient resource allocation on a worldwide basis but also the interests of U. S. consumers does not always follow. As a timely example, consider U. S. investment in crude oil production abroad. Prior to the 1973 oil crisis, development and operating costs per barrel of heavy Arabian crude oil were about 10 cents, compared with perhaps $1.20 in the United States. Although the real resource cost of foreign oil was far lower and worldwide economic efficiency was served by investment in foreign oil, U. S. labor as workers, consumers and taxpayers would probably have been as well off if the investments had been made in the United States.

After adding 19 cents of royalties and 59 cents in taxes for foreign governments and allowing for transportation costs and a further substantial profit margin for the oil companies, the U. S. consumer was scarcely better off than if the U. S. oil resources had been drawn upon or alternative (and more costly) energy sources developed. The U. S. Treasury, moreover, was considerably worse off, since the high posted price for crude oil robbed it of tax revenue from profits at the refinery end and the foreign tax credit eliminated any tax share of crude oil profits. Indeed, because of transfer pricing manipulations, the oil companies were in a position to wipe out domestic profits with foreign loss offsets.

A third loss to labor is their loss as "taxpayers." Foreign investment (seen as a substitute for domestic investment) results in substantial revenue losses to the Treasury. Thus, in 1972 the United States collected an estimated 5 percent of the entire foreign income of more than $24 billion accruing to U. S. corporations in that year.[3] This revenue loss (the difference between the statutory rate of 48 percent in the United States and the 5 percent actually collected) was attributable to two factors—deferral of tax on foreign undistributed profits, and more importantly, the foreign tax credit for distributed earnings. The purpose of the latter is to ensure that the foreign investor pays only the higher of the U. S. or foreign rate by setting off the foreign tax against the U. S. tax liability on the same foreign income. These revenue losses must either be reflected in higher taxes paid on U. S. source income or in reduced levels of federal expenditures. In the former case, labor is likely to bear the major part of the burden since wages and salaries constitute some 85 percent of the individual income tax base.

On balance, the losses to U. S. labor arising from investment abroad are likely to outweigh the gains to investors, resulting in an overall national income loss.[4] It is also quite probable that with certain qualifications, substantial gains accrue to the foreign host country by way of larger tax revenues and real income of foreign labor. This raises the issue of U. S. investment in the less developed countries of the world. Should not American labor's position with respect to foreign investment be tempered by the desirability of transferring resources to the low-income countries of the world?

I believe that the United States and other high-income countries of the world should supply more capital and technical assistance to these impoverished lands. Yet putting heavy reliance on private investment for this purpose means that American labor must bear the major cost while capital enjoys the enlarged profits and various tax concessions provided for overseas investment. It seems reasonable for labor to take the position that aid to the LDCs should take the form not of tax concessions for private investment in these countries, but be primarily through a governmental capital transfer financed by all sectors of the American economy via the tax system.

Private investment in the developing countries, furthermore, is increasingly being criticized for its deficiencies as a mechanism for stimulating broadly based development. One reason for this is that much of such investment tends to be capital intensive with little capacity for expanding employment of the vast surplus labor force in these countries. Indeed, in promoting the adoption of such technologies, the effect may be counterproductive in view of the primary need to increase employment and spread the fruits of development to the mass of the population. Again governmental assistance is called for in developing the kinds of labor intensive technologies which are best suited to the needs of poor countries.

U. S. TRADE AND INVESTMENT IN THE WORLD ECONOMY

All these considerations imply that at the very least the United States should remove any preferential tax treatment now available to foreign investment. Business spokesmen, on the other hand, look at the matter from a different perspective. They generally argue that in order to maintain a U. S. share of foreign markets, they must move abroad to prevent foreign competitors from encroaching on that share. They further argue that in order to compete successfully with such foreign producers, U. S. investors abroad should pay no more tax than do their foreign competitors producing in the same country.

Relevant to the national interest, however, is the U. S. value-added share in world trade, not merely the share of sales of those products which carry the label of a U. S. company. The U. S. value-added share embodied in exports is many times the U. S. value-added component in sales by foreign affiliates of U. S. companies. There is no particular economic merit in maintaining a share of foreign markets with products the sale of which gives rise only to a small proportion of U. S. income, particularly when that share has to be preserved by revenue losses through tax incentives to invest abroad. Nor is there merit in enlarging the "U. S." share of foreign markets beyond that warranted on grounds of economic efficiency or national advantage.

Foreign investment and foreign sales can be expected to be somewhat less if such investment is taxed at U. S. rates than if taxed at lower foreign rates. But this surely does not imply that correction of the tax differential (for example through elimination of deferral) would strip foreign investment in full of its competitive capability. It would be made somewhat less profitable, and some marginal investments would not be made as a result. But that is as it should be, since if foreign and domestic investment are not taxed at the same effective rate there is likely to be over-investment abroad.

In fact, proceeding beyond considerations of world allocative efficiency to those of U. S. national advantage, an argument might well be made that in the future some restriction on foreign investment should be considered. Restrictions on trade and on capital flows are not the same thing and equally to be condemned. While free commodity and capital flows, with certain exceptions, are likely to promote the worldwide efficiency of resource use, important differences exist between the two, including their implications for the division of the economic gains both within and between countries. Taxation is certainly one element in the picture which greatly affects this division of gains.

Introduction of free commodity trade results in a rearrangement in the pattern of use of domestic resources, depending on the nature of foreign demand, and involves gains to some industries and losses to others. Introduction of free capital movement, however, results in a loss of capital resources to the domestic economy. Tax losses from foreign investment further strengthen the case for emphasizing free trade as a mechanism for achieving efficiency in world resource use.

Capital outflow is more likely to be detrimental to the interests of U. S. labor than is free commodity trade. A policy aimed at harmonizing national and world interests would do well to distinguish between these two issues. While I would generally oppose a restrictionist policy on trade, I am sympathetic to a policy of moderate restriction on foreign investment. U. S. policy has in the main, however, moved in the opposite direction—i. e., trade restriction combined with tax incentives to capital outflow.

USE OF TAXATION AS REGULATORY INSTRUMENT

The use of taxation as a policy device to modify the outflow of capital or otherwise to influence the behavior of multinational corporations is perfectly appropriate, if other regulatory measures are inferior on grounds of efficiency and effectiveness. There is, in fact, much to be said for the use of the tax instrument. Just as economists prefer tariffs to import quotas, and for very much the same reasons, an across-the-board penalty tax on foreign investment (or at least across-the-board removal of tax relief) is more preferable to a system of capital controls.

The foreign direct investment control program instituted by the United States in 1965 on a voluntary basis and in 1968 extended in mandatory form (but since terminated) was inefficient, ineffective, and inequitable. The program favored the large, already established foreign corporate investors, leaving them with enhanced profitability and market control. An overall tax surcharge on foreign profits, combined with the termination of deferral, would have been more equitable and effective. Since all investments would have been treated equally, moreover, the market adjustment would have tended to eliminate those investments of marginal profitability. Such a tax would have been similar in form and intent to the Interest Equalization Tax which had been applied to foreign portfolio investments. Advantages of this type of regulatory device are:

(1) it is non-discriminatory and therefore equitable among all foreign investments;

(2) it would limit foreign investments to the most profitable and therefore promote efficiency;

(3) it would generate additional tax revenue; and

(4) there would be less opportunity for investors to avoid and evade the restriction.

Other tax measures have been suggested recently to tip the tax scales in favor of investment in the domestic economy. These suggestions usually start with elimination of deferral. Tax reformers and most economists are generally agreed that the present U. S. system which permits the undistributed profits of foreign subsidiaries of U. S. corporations to escape U. S. taxation through deferral is defective and that, for both economic efficiency and taxpayer equity, such deferral should be terminated.

DEDUCTION AND CREDIT LIMITATION OF FOREIGN TAXES

Other suggestions and proposals which go beyond this minimal measure include deduction of foreign taxes. The pros and cons of converting the present treatment of foreign taxes, which allows them to be credited against (that is, subtracted from) the U. S. tax liability on foreign income, to one which only permits foreign taxes to be deducted from taxable income, in the same way as business costs are deductible, has been much discussed. Such a provision, in fact, reached the stage of a legislative proposal in the Burke-Hartke Bill which had wide support from organized labor. There are several arguments to be made in support of such a proposal. Accrual taxation provided for in the bill would close the inequitable tax loophole now open to foreign investment in the form of tax deferral. The deduction system would bring about a situation in which capital invested abroad would need to earn a rate of return sufficiently large that, after foreign tax, would be at least as great as the before-tax return on domestic investment.[5] In this way, the national return on foreign investment (that is, the return after foreign tax) would be no lower than the national return on investment at home (that is, the domestic return "before" domestic tax), and national efficiency would be met.

Other arguments for treating foreign taxes as deductions rather than credits include the consideration that foreign taxes on foreign investment would be treated for tax purposes as are state and local income taxes in the United States, that is, as deductions. This would make the system consistent and more equitable. In taxing foreign income on a net basis and defining taxable income net of foreign tax, most of the administrative complexities of the foreign tax credit could be avoided. Use of the deduction method, furthermore, would provide an incentive to foreign countries to lower their tax rates on U. S. investment, thus raising the national profitability of such investment to the U. S.

There are, however, strong disadvantages to the deduction method. The total (foreign and U. S.) tax burden would differ among investments in countries with differing tax rates. The total tax burden on U. S. investments abroad could also be unacceptably heavy, especially where foreign rates are high. These defects, it is to be noted, would be absent in the case of a uniform tax surcharge combined with a foreign tax credit.

Another tax measure to restrict investment abroad could take the form of a limitation placed on the foreign tax credit. For instance, the credit might be limited to some fraction of the foreign tax or to, say, the first specified number of percentage points of the foreign tax. Needless to say, such a system would include accrual taxation without deferral. Such an approach would be in keeping with the view that since the foreign tax credit represents a substantial sacrifice of tax revenue on the part of the U.S. Treasury, it is reasonable to impose limits on it. At present, that limit is the amount of U.S. tax on the same foreign income (without refund for the excess of the foreign over the U.S. rate), but there is no logical reason why that fraction might not be reduced from 100 percent to some lower figure. A credit limitation method would avoid certain disadvantages of the deduction method, such as large rate variations among countries of investment and confiscatory rates when the foreign tax rate is high.

REDUCED TAX ON DOMESTIC INVESTMENT

Too frequently, attempts and proposals to reduce or eliminate tax advantages to foreign investment or to swing the tax scales in favor of domestic investment have taken the form of giving the same or greater tax incentives to domestic investment. Indeed, this process has begun to take on the aspect of a worldwide tax competition for capital with a resulting erosion of taxation of capital income and loss of tax equity.

As an example of such a policy, the DISC tax provision was introduced in 1971, one purpose of which was to provide the same tax benefits to U.S.-produced exports as are available to foreign investment. DISC, in effect, extended deferral privileges to export profits. Although the effectiveness of DISC as an export incentive has been in dispute, it has been a major contributor to the attrition of the U.S. corporation income tax in recent years and has resulted in a revenue loss approaching $2 billion annually, with a large element of windfall gain to exporters. DISC, in turn, is thought to have triggered retaliatory corporate tax reductions in other countries, notably Canada.[6]

The extension and enlargement of the investment tax credit, which is limited to investment in domestic assets, has also been propounded as a means of redressing the tax balance in favor of domestic investment. In Britain, the 100 percent instant write-off provision recently introduced is limited to assets within the United Kingdom and likewise belongs in this category.

The recent attempt by the Ford administration to eliminate the U.S. withholding tax on portfolio investments by foreigners in the

United States (the exemption being limited to interest on bank deposits in the 1976 Tax Reform Act), must also be seen in the perspective of this tax competition for international capital.

INTEGRATION OF CORPORATION AND INDIVIDUAL INCOME TAXES

Much the most significant development in recent years, which can result in sharp changes in relative tax burdens on domestic and foreign investment, has been the trend towards integration of the corporation and personal income taxes. The general purpose of this change is to reduce or eliminate the so-called "double taxation" of corporate-source income to the shareholder, by effectively reducing or eliminating the corporation income tax and bringing all corporate profits into the individual income tax. If such integration is complete, corporate profits are then subject only to the individual income tax, as is the income of unincorporated business, with retained earnings imputed to the shareholder and the corporation tax acting only as a withholding tax subject to credit against the individual income tax.

If, on the other hand, as is more usual, the integration is only partial, only part of the corporate tax is "removed," or the integration is applied only to distributed earnings. In the latter case, integration is achieved either by imposing a lower corporate rate on distributed earnings (the dividends-paid credit or split-rate system) or by providing for a credit for part of the corporation tax against the income tax due on the shareholder's dividends (dividends-received credit system).

The European EC has decided to adopt the dividend-received credit system and already a number of countries follow an integrated system. West Germany has for long had a split-rate system but has now moved to the dividend-received credit form of integration. France now provides for a credit to the shareholder for 50 percent of the corporate profits tax and the United Kingdom allows a one-third credit. Canada introduced a one-quarter credit to shareholders of its corporate tax in 1971. In view of the broad political support for such a move, the United States will probably follow suit.

The principal motivation for such a change is individual taxpayer equity and efficiency of resource allocation in the domestic economy, combined with a stimulus to the overall rate of saving and investment. Integration of the income taxes may also be carried out so as to give strong relative tax advantage to domestic over foreign investment. This hinges on the question of whether the home country (country of residence, capital-exporting country) in adopting an integrated system allows crediting of the foreign corporation tax against its income tax applied to dividends paid out of foreign profits to domestic shareholders.

If credit is limited to the domestic corporate tax only, then foreign investment will be at a substantial tax disadvantage relative to domestic investment. It is to be noted in this connection that the dividends-received type of credit lends itself more readily to the crediting of foreign taxes than does the split-rate system.

Income tax integration may also have an impact on the host (capital importing) country's tax share in the profits earned by foreign investment within its own borders and in turn on tax incentives provided to foreign investment. If, for example, integration provides for the credit for corporate tax being extended to investors from abroad by way of a refund for tax on dividends paid abroad, and if, in turn those investors are taxed in their own countries of residence on foreign income with a foreign tax credit, the loss of revenue to the host country will simply be reflected in higher tax revenues to the home (residence) country without benefit to the investor. *

In a world in which some countries continue with a system of separate corporate and individual income taxes, while others apply varying degrees of integration coupled with different applications of the integration principle to foreign investment, investors are apt to find themselves confronted with a wide variety of tax treatments according to their choice of investment location. Spokesmen for MNCs have for long defended deferral and indeed urged full exemption for foreign-source income on the grounds that this would equalize their tax treatment with that of their competitors operating in the same foreign countries. Given the present pattern of widely disparate tax treatments arising from integration, it is very unlikely that such uniformity would result even under an exemption system. The present trend towards integrated income tax systems (and, with them, a diminution of the corporate tax) at least partly reflects the previously mentioned international tax competition for capital in a world in which capital has become increasingly mobile.

RECENT EFFORTS TO CHANGE TAXATION OF FOREIGN INVESTMENT

In view of the fact that attempts have been made to eliminate deferral for U. S. investment abroad since 1961 with little success, it seems unlikely that Congress would accept anything in the nature of an

---

*For a fuller discussion of this topic, see M. Sato and R. M. Bird, "International Aspects of the Taxation of Corporations and Shareholders," IMF Staff Papers, Washington: International Monetary Fund, July 1975.

across-the-board surtax on foreign investment income. The Interest Equalization Tax on foreign portfolio investment was introduced in response to a sharp and continuing deterioration in the U.S. balance of payments in the 1960s and has now been withdrawn. With more flexible exchange rates, it is unlikely that balance of payments considerations would prompt restrictive measures on capital outflow. Yet in view of the rapidly increasing demand for foreign exchange to finance the escalating energy needs of the United States, it may be time to scrutinize the performance of U.S. exports in the face of accumulating U.S. investment abroad. The future may well show that the U.S. export sector cannot generate the foreign exchange needed to cover these import needs while at the same time facing competition from and being displaced by the massive output and sales of U.S. direct investment abroad.[7]*

The estimated cost to the Treasury (in terms of foregone revenue) of deferral of U.S. tax on the undistributed earnings of foreign subsidiaries was $590 million in 1974.[8] The tax advantage to the U.S. investor of retaining earnings abroad exceeds this figure by the amount of foreign withholding taxes on dividends which would have to be paid on repatriation of the income. Inclusion of the latter would most likely more than double that figure. (The revenue gain estimate would have to allow for foreign losses which might well absorb part of the foreign income subject to U.S. tax.)

Although deferral as the major tax preference to foreign investment remains on the books, a beginning has been made in eliminating some of the more peripheral preferences. Limitations were placed on the use of the foreign tax credit for foreign oil and gas profits in 1975. The Tax Reform Act of 1976 included measures to close tax loopholes for foreign investors such as preferences to the so-called "less-developed-country corporations," to eliminate the Western Hemisphere Trade Corporation provision and the China Trade Act Corporation exemption, to reduce the role of foreign capital gains in raising foreign tax credit limits, to remove the per-country option for limitation of the foreign tax credit, and to provide for a foreign-loss recapture. These

---

*It should be noted in this connection that $1 invested in export production in the United States will generate many times the foreign exchange obtainable from $1 invested abroad for sales abroad. There should be a multiple return of foreign exchange to the export investment. The foreign investment involves a loss of foreign exchange due to the original investment but also a return of foreign income (after allowing for foreign tax and retentions abroad) which generally takes many years before the original capital outflow is returned.

reforms in combination might be expected to increase U.S. corporation tax revenues by perhaps $500 to $700 million, on the basis of present foreign income flows, which compares with actual tax collection of $1.2 billion on foreign income of U.S. corporations in 1972.

On the other hand, certain offsetting provisions were added in the act which tend to make the tax treatment of foreign income more favorable. Thus, the limitation on use of tax-deferred income for investment in U.S. property has been weakened, and the treatment of foreign-source shipping income and of U.S. investors doing business in the U.S. possessions has been liberalized.

Other nonstatutory preferences are also available to foreign investment, although they have had less attention from legislators. Prominent among them are the ability of foreign investing companies to manipulate their internal transfer prices to shift profits from high- to low-tax jurisdictions. Recent action by the Internal Revenue Service to specify the permissible allocation of overhead costs between the domestic parent and foreign affiliate has gone some way to limiting this preference. Another area which is replete with tax avoidance potential is the treatment of foreign exchange gains and losses experienced by foreign investors. With the increasing flexibility of exchange rates in recent years, this is an area of the tax law which calls for further study.[9]

It is also noteworthy that Congress chose to use the tax instrument to penalize companies transacting with those countries which are parties to the boycott of Israel. Deferral, the foreign tax credit and DISC concessions were all eliminated for those profits attributable to transactions with these countries. Foreign-source income used for bribery is also denied deferral of tax. While an extremely complicated and seemingly unenforceable set of provisions, it demonstrates how political considerations can generate swift action in areas where years of argument by tax reformers have yielded no results.

Thus we inch along the path of tax reform for foreign investment, with some steps backward as well as forward, leaving a trail of statutory complexities along the way.

INTERNATIONAL COMPARISONS OF TAXATION OF FOREIGN INVESTMENT

It has frequently been argued, particularly by business spokesmen, that the United States should seek to equalize the tax treatment of U.S. investors abroad with that afforded their foreign competitors. Apart from the impossibility of so doing for reasons given earlier, such an objective is incompatible with national goals of taxpayer equity and maximizing economic welfare for the greatest number of citizens.

Taxation of foreign income, whether individual or corporate, should equalize tax burdens between foreign and domestic investors, if it is to equalize anything. Equalizing tax treatment of U. S. investors abroad and those with whom they happen to share the same operating location has no particular virtue in terms of taxpayer equity. For the United States to merely copy the tax systems of foreign countries in order to increase the share of foreign markets by U. S. corporations operating abroad rather than at home, moreover, does not seem desirable.

Until recently, other capital-exporting countries were as generous in the tax treatment of their own foreign investors as was the United States of its foreign investment and in many cases more so. Thus Japan and the United Kingdom apply a global-type income tax as does the United States. They also allow deferral for undistributed foreign subsidiary profits. Other countries such as France, West Germany and the Netherlands exempt business income generated by direct investment abroad, although taxing remitted income from foreign portfolio investment.

The tax policies of these countries have recently become less favorable to foreign investment of their own residents than in the past. In particular, as many countries abroad adopt an integrated income tax system, they frequently do not allow the foreign corporation tax paid on foreign-source income to be credited against the individual income tax on the shareholders' dividends from that income in the same way as the domestic corporate tax is so credited. The United Kingdom advance corporation tax, for example, acts to restrict integration of the foreign corporation and domestic income taxes by imposing an additional tax, equivalent to the dividend credit, on distributions of foreign direct investment income. The recent tax change in the Federal Republic of Germany closely follows the British system. On the other hand, Canada permits the full 30 percent of net dividends to be credited against the shareholder's income tax whether or not the underlying corporation tax was paid to Canada. In this case, therefore, foreign investors are at no disadvantage relative to domestic investors.

It is also the case that some countries provide special tax incentives to investment in the developing countries on a selective basis. Thus West Germany allows a deferral of tax on any income, foreign or domestic, which is invested in specified developing countries, with a liberal recapture provision. Japan also provides certain such incentives, particularly generous in the case of foreign natural resource development. In the United States, it has generally been felt that deferral of tax on undistributed foreign earnings is an adequate incentive and, as noted earlier, the 1976 Tax Reform Act in fact eliminated some of those tax preferences that were directed at foreign investment in developing countries.

Another important issue arising with the spreading adoption of integrated income tax systems is whether the dividend credit is to be made available to nonresident investors. Thus far, such relief has not usually been so extended, although the United Kingdom and France offer some such benefits via tax treaty. The reason is that the tax collected on income earned by investors resident abroad is an important component of the gains to be derived from direct investment inflow. This argument has particular validity if investors are resident in countries which tax on a global basis with foreign tax credit (such as the United States) in which case such tax relief would merely be transferred to the foreign treasury without benefit or incentive to the foreign investor.

INTERNATIONAL TAX AGREEMENTS

A fairly extensive network of bilateral tax treaties already exists, although largely confined to the developed countries. Such treaties have achieved a good deal of uniformity in the international tax treatment of foreign investment, based as they usually are on the Model Tax Treaty format recommended by the OECD, as an extension of earlier recommendations by the League of Nations. In providing for reciprocal reductions in taxation of income accruing to nonresidents and arrangements to reduce the burden of double taxation, such treaties have redounded to the benefit of multinational corporations. The business world over the years has made a large contribution to the formulation of the Model Treaty, as, for instance, the International Chamber of Commerce in the League of Nations deliberations, and their imprint remains with the present typical treaty format. Just as in the context of domestic tax reform discussion, a broader representation of general taxpayer interest is desirable, so it is also at the international tax level.

The dominant objective of the OECD Model Treaty is to prevent, through the treaty mechanism, double taxation of foreign investment income which would act as an impediment to international capital flows. A further major objective is to restrict the tax share of the host country in the profits earned by nonresident investors. Without a full-scale discussion of the details of the OECD Model Tax Treaty[10] let me merely note a few shortcomings of its provisions.

1. It puts emphasis on "relief from double taxation," without attention to the problem of undertaxation of foreign investment. It gives no recognition to the importance of securing equal tax treatment of home and foreign investment in the residence country.

2. By applying the nondiscrimination principle to the corporation tax and the reciprocity principle to the withholding tax, the objective of

fair tax shares is not adequately met. Indeed, the Treaty for this and other reasons has never been attractive to the developing countries.*

3. Inadequate attention is given to the numerous problems arising from the allocation of the tax base among the various countries of source, transfer pricing and distribution of overhead costs and expenses among the various parts of the multinational corporation.

4. As it stands at present, the Treaty is not equipped to deal with the important new problems arising from the increasing adoption of integrated income tax systems.

5. Inadequate provision is made for cooperation between treaty partners in matters of tax administration and enforcement as they apply in particular to the multinational corporations.

The first step in reforming such international tax arrangements is to specify what the objectives and concerns of a multilateral tax treaty should be. Here are five:

1. To secure an evenhanded and nonarbitrary treatment of foreign investors by the host countries. This does not necessarily imply that such investors must be taxed at the same rates as are those countries' own domestic investors, but only that such taxes are applied in a nonarbitrary and predictable way.

2. To derive an agreed-upon system of tax share by the host country in the income earned by nonresident investors, taking into account all major taxes and not merely the withholding taxes as does the OECD Model. These tax shares might vary with the type of investment (e.g., natural resource vs. manufacturing) and the level of per capita income of the capital-importing country.

3. To establish a reasonable international division of tax base, apportioning taxable income among the countries in which the multinational corporations do business to avoid gaps and overlaps in taxing jurisdictions. To do this price rules and cost-allocation procedures will have to be formulated.

4. To set up rules preventing tax competition among the capital-importing countries for foreign capital, a problem which is especially acute for the less-developed countries and which requires an international agreement for its solution. Thus, countries might engage in regional tax compacts under which all investors from abroad would be

---

*There has been an effort in the United Nations to examine and modify the provisions of the OECD Model to make them more acceptable to the capital-importing developing countries. See Guidelines for Tax Treaties between Developed and Developing Countries (New York: Department of Economic and Social Affairs, United Nations, 1974).

taxed at a uniform rate. Alternatively, the capital-exporting countries might mutually agree to tax on a global basis, without deferral, providing a foreign tax credit in order to neutralize all competing incentives provided by the capital-importing countries.

5. To create a system of close cooperation between those countries in which the MNCs are resident and earn income, for purposes of exchange of information and tax enforcement with provision for arbitration by an outside panel in matters of dispute and eventually enforcement powers backed up by an international tax court. Bilateral treaties are not adequate to meet this purpose. Such an international tax agency would also determine the assignment of income of the multinationals among countries in which they do business and might handle tax collections on behalf of the member countries.

A system of this character would help to harmonize the competing interests of the capital-importing countries and bring about a more equitable taxation of those businesses which transact across international frontiers.

Beyond this, I believe that individual capital-exporting countries should be free to treat their foreign investment as they see fit, giving subsidies to it or restricting it by heavier taxation as their economic policies and particularly their own philosophies regarding the rate of saving and capital formation suggest. At the same time, when it comes to international tax agreements which affect the flow of international commodity trade, such as GATT, the United States should support those arrangements which seek to remove tax and tariff distortions and impediments to international trade.

Further into the future one could envisage a system which provides for an international tax code and collection agency. The ongoing discussions in connection with international laws of the sea to provide for taxation of those firms exploiting the international seabed property by a United Nations authority point the way. Given the complex and cosmopolitan nature of the large multinational corporation, an international tax administration for foreign investment may well be the only completely satisfactory solution.

NEED FOR BETTER INFORMATION ON MULTINATIONAL CORPORATIONS

Finally, the information available to individual governments on the status and operations of their own MNCs is woefully inadequate. Here are seven examples:

1. Statistical series covering important operating data of foreign affiliates is discontinuous, precluding satisfactory time-series analysis.

2. Tax data do not adequately separate foreign from domestic income or reveal such vital information as the amount of foreign losses written off against domestic income.

3. Foreign taxes paid are not adequately identified (that is as among profits and withholding taxes).

4. Quarterly data on such important variables as plant and equipment expenditures abroad are not available to enable current analysis of cyclical effects of such expenditures on the domestic economy.

5. Periodic surveys of foreign investment are rendered in large part unusable by the high degree of suppressed data for confidentiality reasons.

6. Numerous classification problems render the quality of data on foreign investment questionable and frequently noncomparable with corresponding domestic data.

7. The data are not provided in such a way to allow linking affiliates or groups of affiliates with their domestic parent companies, a necessary feature for studies on the behavior of foreign-investing firms.

The dearth of information makes economic analysis and policy-making based on that analysis very difficult. It is certainly time in the United States that fuller and better quality data be made available by mandatory reporting requirements on a systematic and regular basis. The privilege of operating abroad while at the same time deriving many of the advantages provided by the country of residence should also carry with it the requirement of full reporting of foreign activities. The United States is by no means worse off in this respect than other capital-exporting countries; in fact it is better supplied than most. However, much more needs to be done. It may well be that one of the functions of an international tax administration agency should be to collect and publish such material.

In the meantime, however, a U.S. government commission with inter-agency representation should be established to work out the details of a major new effort in data reporting by the MNCs. By operating abroad under foreign incorporation, the U.S. corporation can now largely escape the reporting obligations to which domestic operations are subject.* Very recently the Congress has responded to this need with the International Investment Survey Act of 1976. This act provides authority to the President to collect information on international investment and to provide analyses of such information to the Congress, the executive agencies, and the general public. This new authority was

---

*See my statement to the Subcommittee on Foreign Commerce and Tourism of the Senate Commerce Committee, February 27, 1976 for specific suggestions in this regard.

needed since the existing authority provided the Secretary of Commerce under the Bretton Woods Agreement is unsatisfactory and ambiguous. Hopefully the first step has been taken to remedy the problem by providing the data necessary for a proper assessment of the scope and effects of investment abroad and for the formulation of informed public policies.

NOTES

1. For recent data on U.S. investment abroad, see U.S. Department of Commerce, Survey of Current Business, March, May, and August 1976.

2. For a discussion of this aspect, see Wilson E. Schmidt, "U.S. Capital Export Policy: Backdoor Mercantilism," U.S. Taxation of American Business Abroad, Washington: American Enterprise Institute for Public Policy Research, Washington D.C., September 1975.

3. G.C. Hufbauer and J.R. Nunns, "Tax Payments and Tax Expenditures on International Investment and Employment," Columbia Journal of World Business, Summer 1975.

4. Musgrave, op. cit.

5. Peggy B. Musgrave, United States Taxation of Foreign Investment Income: Issues and Arguments, Cambridge: Harvard Law School, International Program in Taxation, 1969, p. 134.

6. Peggy B. Musgrave, "International Aspects of U.S. Tax Policy," 1973 Conference Report of the Canadian Tax Foundation, Montreal: 1974.

7. James A. Griffin, The Effect on U.S. Foreign Direct Investment of the Integration of the Corporate and Personal Income Taxes, Washington: U.S. Department of the Treasury, Office of Tax Analysis, OTA Paper 22, March 1974.

8. G.C. Hufbauer and J.R. Nunns, op. cit.

9. Peggy B. Musgrave, "Exchange Rate Aspects in the Taxation of Foreign Income," National Tax Journal, December 1975.

10. Peggy B. Musgrave, "The OECD Model Tax Treaty: Problems and Prospects," Columbia Journal of World Business, Summer 1975.

10

American Capitol, Taxes, and the Welfare of Workers

ARNOLD CANTOR

TAXES AND FOREIGN INVESTMENT

In today's world, those who still cling to the notion of a common identity of national interests and those of foreign investors are subscribing to a theory of global trickle down economics. This theory in effect says that the way to insure a healthy and happy population of sparrows is to see that the horses are well fed! We must not lose sight of the fact that the economic health and strength of the American society depends primarily and overwhelmingly on jobs and the purchasing power of those who work for a living. Wages and salaries account for two-thirds of this nation's personal income, and personal consumption expenditures represent two-thirds of the nation's total demand for goods and services.

Given today's job situation and the wide disparities in income shares between those who can save and invest, and those who must consume all or most all of their income, national policies further skewing the distribution of income toward large corporations and their stockholders and away from workers should be challenged and corrected. U. S. Commerce Department data show that the one percent of U. S. families with the largest personal income received 47 percent of the total income from dividends and owned 51 percent of the market value of stock. [1] This suggests that there is a significant difference in impact between dollars invested at home creating jobs and wages for American workers as well as profits, dividends, and capital gains, and the type and the distribution of income resulting from investment abroad.

The question of an alleged capital shortage in the United States surely needs closer examination when up to 20 percent of our national savings are annually being invested abroad. It is puzzling that those who continually call for more business tax incentives in the name of domestic capital formation and increased productivity ignore the fact that the tax structure now contributes to outflows of capital and domestic shortages. If they do recognize the fact, a policy is invariably proposed to correct the situation by lowering taxes for domestic operations rather than ending the tax advantages for overseas investment. This type of logic was the basis for enactment of the DISC provision in 1971. The Nixon Administration argued that since U. S. corporations producing abroad can defer their taxes, the same advantage should be given to firms producing at home for export.

There has been little evidence to demonstrate that the DISC provision has had any particular salutary effect on exports. But there is clear-cut evidence that somewhere between $1.5 to $2 billion annually is lost to the federal treasury and the great percentage of that revenue loss goes toward strengthening the balance sheets and cash flows of the largest U. S.-based multinationals.[2]

The process of redressing tax advantages through more tax advantages in the worldwide competition for capital, whatever may be happening in other countries, certainly has taken place in the United States. Twenty years ago, for example, the corporate income tax accounted for 28 percent of federal budget receipts; today it is only 14 percent.[3] An examination of the hearings and reports of the congressional tax-writing committees would reveal that most of the provisions contributing to this reduction in corporate taxes were in one way or another rationalized as improving our ability to compete abroad. The net result of such competition is to regress the tax structure generally, impede the ability of this nation to meet essential public investment needs including job creation programs, and further aggravate disparities in the distribution of income.

CAPITAL AND COMMODITY FLOWS

Another irony pertaining to the issue of capital formation should be noted. A major factor in the depth of the 1973-1975 recession and the failure of the subsequent "recovery" to gain any momentum has been the lack of domestic business spending on plants, machinery and equipment while the overseas spending of multinationals has continued on its merry way. During the 1974 and 1975 recession years for example, American companies' direct investment spending on foreign affiliates rose by respectively 14.6 percent and 12.1 percent. In contrast, for the same periods, business spending at home increased by 12 percent in 1974, and there was no increase between 1974 and 1975.[4]

According to December 1976 Commerce Department figures, moreover, domestic capital spending for 1976 will be only 7.5 percent above year-earlier levels (only 3 percent when adjusted for inflation). Surveys of planned expenditures for the first half of 1977 indicate an increase of only 4.1 percent above second half 1976 levels (only 3.2

percent increase in manufacturing). If inflation is taken into account, "the first half of 1977 would show virtually no change from the second half of 1976."[5] Yet planned increases in capital expenditures by majority-owned foreign affiliates in 1977 will be 8 percent higher than 1976, and in manufacturing, this increase is expected to be 15 percent.[6]

The two phenomena of commodity flows and capital flows are certainly different, and it is logical that U.S. tax policy should be used to regulate and limit capital flows. Implicit in the distinction between the two, however, is that there are worldwide, free and competitive markets and that all buyers and sellers are engaged in arms' length transactions. This is not the case. Other nations of the world, developed and underdeveloped, capitalist and Communist, have already created a world trade pattern deviating from any reasonable definition of free trade. And, so long as so much of what is euphemistically called "trade" can be more accurately described as intra-company transfers when multinational corporations produce abroad for sale to U.S. markets, the distinction between commodity flows and investment flows is at best quite blurred. Thus, I do not feel that we can meet national goals of employment, economic balance and necessary diversification through addressing ourselves solely to capital flows and ignoring the need to regulate imports and exports.

Within the context of regulating capital outflows through the tax structure, moreover, I feel Professor Musgrave's proposals are helpful but insufficient. The AFL-CIO has advocated elimination of DISC and deferral, as has Professor Musgrave, but we also feel that the tax credit should be eliminated and foreign income taxes allowed as a deduction. We do not advocate a tax policy which totally ignores the fact that U.S. companies are required to pay foreign taxes, but we see no reason why the tax burdens imposed by other countries should be given any consideration beyond a recognition that they represent a legitimate cost of doing business. They therefore should be permitted as an expense and deducted from otherwise taxable income just like other expenses incurred in the process of generating profits.

The current system of dollar-for-dollar U.S. tax credits for foreign taxes is in effect a form of no-strings revenue sharing, an open-ended, privately controlled transfer between the U.S. Treasury and the treasury of the foreign host government. It is another example whereby the private decisions of multinational corporations affect the disposition of billions of dollars which would otherwise be revenue for the U.S. government.

NOTES

1. U. S. Department of Commerce, "Stockownership in the U. S.: Characteristics and Trends," Survey of Current Business, U. S. Department of Commerce, 54, no. 11 (November 1974).

2. U. S. Department of the Treasury, "The Operation and Effect of the Domestic International Sales Corporation Legislation," 1973 Annual Report, U. S. Department of the Treasury (April 1975).

3. Executive Office of the President, "The Budget of the United States Government, Various Fiscal Years." Office of Management and Budget.

4. U. S. Department of Commerce, "U. S. Direct Investment Abroad in 1975," Survey of Current Business, U. S. Department of Commerce, 58, no. 8 (August 1976).

5. U. S. Department of Commerce, Bureau of Economic Analysis, NEWS, (December 6, 1976,) p. 1.

6. U. S. Department of Commerce, "U. S. Direct Investment Abroad in 1975," Survey of Current Business 58, no. 8 (August 1976).

11

Meeting Changing Economic Needs: Multinational Corporations, Employment, and Taxes

DONALD L. GUERTIN

THE IMPERATIVES OF BECOMING MULTINATIONAL

Companies become multinational because they see a market for their goods and services elsewhere in the world or because they need raw materials. Economic experience has proven that nations are better off if they do not try to produce all goods and services for themselves, even if they could. In the long run, they are better off if they specialize to some extent in a range of economic activities which they do best, produce a surplus of these and then trade for the other goods which they want and need, including raw materials. For this reason the economies of the world have become increasingly interdependent in the last few decades. Governments of both industrialized and nonindustrialized countries have deliberately encouraged this process.

Multinationals in the oil business are both producers of a raw material and manufacturers of gasoline, jet fuel, heating oil and hundreds of other usable products. Companies like Exxon are multinational by necessity, because nature has put most oil in countries which need far less oil than they have. For example, Saudi Arabia, with a population of around 5 million, is now producing more than 8 million barrels of crude oil daily, but consuming well under 100,000, or less than 1 percent. Japan consumes around 5 million barrels of crude oil a day, but produces virtually none. Europe also imports the great bulk of its oil, and even the United States now imports over 40 percent.

The oil industry must invest huge sums of money each year to explore for oil and to build and maintain wells, pipelines, tankers, refineries and petrochemical plants. Exxon, for example, invested more than $4 billion in 1975, and plans on investing $20 billion in the four-year period, 1977 to 1980, $10 billion of this in the United States.

Multinational companies tend to be technologically oriented, big marketers, large employers and relatively more profitable than purely domestic companies. They compete on a worldwide basis with other multinationals and often with local firms. They are concentrated in such industries as motor vehicles, drugs, metal products, chemicals, computers, machinery and virtually all raw materials. Of the U. S. multinationals less than two hundred account for the bulk of U. S. investment abroad.

ECONOMIC AND SOCIAL BENEFITS OF MULTINATIONALS

International investment is not a zero sum game. When a company invests abroad, it usually produces economic growth and a bigger pie, with benefits for all the parties concerned. Multinational companies are likely to be in businesses requiring large investments. This almost always means that the payback will take some time. They invest for the long term and for sound economic reasons, not to grab quick profits and run.

This primary role of the multinationals is to provide either goods or services. In doing this, they create jobs, both directly or indirectly through stimulating the development of support industries. Studies by the U. S. Commerce Department have shown that the rate of employment growth in U. S. MNCs was larger than the nation as a whole.[1] Studies by companies, notably Caterpillar and Union Carbide, have demonstrated the positive impact on U. S. employment of their foreign investments.[2]

MNCs also pay taxes, thereby helping governments fund social programs and services to improve the lives of their people. Exxon paid some $15 billion in income, excise, and other taxes in 1975, more than five time its profits; payments in the U. S. were $2. 3 billion.

The multinational oil companies play a key role in supplying the petroleum which the United States must have to keep its economy running. Over the past ten years, U. S. oil companies have been bringing home an average of at least $1 billion in foreign earnings each year. And as with other multinationals, the foreign affiliates of U. S. oil companies have been a big market for export of U. S. goods and services such as steel pipe, drill bits, computers, and engineering services; this amounted to $500 million in the case of Exxon in 1975. All this money flowing into the United States creates more jobs, provides more taxes to the U. S. government, and helps pay for our oil imports.

GOVERNMENT REGULATION OF THE MULTINATIONALS

It is sometimes argued that multinational companies owe their success to their ability to escape control by governments. Although a few may have tried, no multinational can survive by evading the laws or flouting the national goals of the countries where they operate.

Company wealth is often confused with political power. Corporate wealth consists mainly of fixed assets—in the oil industry, production facilities, pipelines, terminals, refineries, gasoline stations and so on. History has repeatedly shown how easily even the smallest country can impose controls on MNCs or even take over its assets.

What about bribery? A bribe or a kickback is a technique for trying to grab quick profits. As such, systematic bribery of governments is really at odds with the long-term profitability of a corporation. When the discovery comes, as it often does, it can poison the business climate for years. Corporate "political contributions" are a different matter. Although not legal in the United States, they are legal in many countries and are often expected as a matter of course. Such a system can, of course, invite abuses.

Business standards and government expectations vary from country to country, too, a situation that can seriously muddy the waters of international investment. This is one reason that in recent years we have seen more and more stress placed on achieving some intergovernmental agreement about the standards which should apply to MNCs.

One recent example is the Declaration on International Investment and Multinational Enterprises adopted in June 1976 by 23 member governments of the OECD.[3] The OECD code of conduct recognizes some sound principles. Governments as well as companies have responsibilities. Property should not be taken arbitrarily, and if taken, compensation should be prompt and adequate. Foreign companies should be treated as well as domestic companies, contracts should be respected and, in case of disputes, international arbitration should be employed.

While voluntary, the guidelines should carry great political and moral weight. They are drafted to allow some latitude of interpretation without violating the spirit of the whole. Their voluntary nature also avoids the difficult problems of trying to enforce them in countries having very different legal and social systems.

Turning to the issue of regulating U.S. MNCs through taxation, I want only to raise some questions about some of Professor Musgrave's assumptions in developing her arguments:

1. Is it reasonable to assume a dollar-for-dollar reduction in investments in plants and equipment in the United States if U.S. companies invest abroad?

2. Would all of the capital now invested abroad by U.S. companies be available for investment in the United States? Two-thirds of these funds are actually raised overseas, and there would be some cases in which foreign governments would restrict flow of these funds into the United States.

3. Would there be enough investment opportunities providing an adequate rate of return to invest these funds in the United States?

4. If the flow of investment funds into the United States were increased, would this drive rates of return in the United States down and rates of return in foreign countries up? Would this in turn stimulate investments of U. S. funds abroad through the purchase of stocks and bonds?

5. If U. S. companies confine their activities to the United States, would foreign corporations take over foreign markets and increase their positions significantly in raw material sectors abroad?

The issues involved in using tax policy to regulate foreign investment are extremely complex. If the implications of some of the proposed changes are not carefully examined, the results may be quite different than those intended and may have an adverse impact on U. S. economic welfare, including the capacity of our economy to provide jobs.

NOTES

1. U. S. Department of Commerce, The Multinational Corporation, Volume I, Studies in Foreign Investment (Washington: U. S. Government Printing Office, 1972), pp. 18-29.

2. Caterpillar Corporation, Statement to Committee on Ways and Means Regarding Tax Reform Proposals, (July 1975); Union Carbide Corporation, Union Carbide's International Investment Benefits the U. S. Economy (New York: Union Carbide, 1975), pp. 8-10.

3. Organisation for Economic Co-operation and Development, International Investment and Multinational Enterprise (Paris: OECD, 1976).

12

Foreign Investment, Employment, and Industrial Policies in a Changing International Environment

JACK N. BEHRMAN

THE COMPLEXITY OF THE ISSUES

The debate on the impact of foreign investment on employment has been joined in at least seven different ways:

1. The simplest and most straightforward is to look at the impact of foreign direct investment on U. S. jobs gained or lost by investment abroad. For this, one needs to know merely whether the number of jobs in the United States went up or down as the direct consequence of an overseas investment.

2. A more complex and indefinite analysis attempts to measure the net gain or loss of jobs in the situation which would have been obtained in the absence of no direct foreign investment. To make this analysis requires some information or assumptions regarding the exports of the investing company in the absence of the investment, and governmental policies to save jobs in the event of the investment. In addition, if the governmental policies restricted investment, reaction of foreign governments concerning investments in the United States and the possible loss of U. S. jobs resulting from a decline of inward foreign investment, would also need to be assessed.

3. The debate can also be joined on the loss of "specific" jobs in specific industrial sectors (or companies) and in specific geographic regions of the country. Adverse impacts in any of these specific categories might well be seen as highly unfavorable and inappropriate by those involved. The policy issue then is that of determining whether or not specific jobs need to be protected. It is not difficult to obtain information concerning the loss of specific jobs, but it is difficult (as illustrated by the lengthy hearings of the Tariff Commission on escape clause actions) to determine the cause of these job losses.

4. Matching some of the employment declines in the United States would be gains abroad in specific sectors and countries. U. S. policy might well support gains in some countries or sectors, while depoloring

gains in others. For example, if the increase in employment was in low-technology sectors in developing countries, even various labor groups might find the trade-off between U.S. employment and foreign employment acceptable. Therefore, the debate on the issues at this level requires analysis on the effects of investment on employment overseas.

5. If the analysis is to look at what would have occurred without the direct foreign investment, it must examine what other countries would be doing at the same time. We are confronted therefore, with the further complexity of determining what the European, Canadian, and Japanese investors would do in the absence of U.S. investment, or collaterally with it and the effects of these actions on the U.S. trade and employment.

6. Some of the debates have gone beyond the discussion of the level of employment in the United States to a concern for the nature of U.S. employment. If, for example, the loss of jobs in the United States was in low-technology industry and at the same time employment expanded significantly in high-technology industries, raising productivity and wages, and opening up markets abroad, there would be less objection to the effects of foreign direct investment. A further complication arises, therefore, in determining the relationship between employment in different sectors of the economy and the causal relationship between these and foreign direct investment.

7. A final complexity is introduced when the assessment extends to shifts in the location of employment within the United States. For example, if foreign investment shifted employment opportunities in the United States from low-technology to high-technology industries, and these were located in different regions of the country, employment shifts would also cause a movement of workers geographically. These shifts might exacerbate the problems of urban areas or alleviate them, depending on the location of industrial activity.

The issues raised in items 6 and 7 pose the question of whether or not there are possible social losses from the movement of employment even if there is no net loss in the numbers, as a result of foreign direct investment. Once again, analysis would have to be made of the pattern of employment both sectorally and regionally in the absence of foreign investment and comparison made with what occurred as a result of such foreign investment in order to be able to come to sound policy prescriptions.

The complexity of these issues makes it evident that the impact cannot be assessed solely quantitatively and that the remedies are not going to be applied "by the numbers." The numbers of jobs gained or lost, within specific skills, sectors, or regions, will not be the determining factor in the development of foreign investment policy by the U.S. government nor by foreign governments. The determining factor will be employment and investment policies at the microlevel (that is, governmental policies towards "specific" employment and investment decisions).

Policies toward both specific employment and foreign investment emerge from policies aimed at expanding specific industrial activity—as in the chemical, iron and steel, aircraft, or other industries—and from regional development policies aimed at creating employment in depressed areas or moving industry to labor rather than vice versa. There is naturally a tie between industrial policies and regional policies. Some industries are best set in certain regions, depending on the human and natural resources as well as the infrastructure available, and some regions would like to redesign their attractiveness to particular types of industry to raise the skill level.

All of these efforts are directed to changing the comparative advantages within a nation or region and should at least be consistent with the overall economic and social policies at the national level. National policy decisions can be supported by analysis of the impact on the numbers employed and skill levels. Grand decisions are not based on quantitative data, however, but on value judgments by political leadership of what is desirable for various segments of the population.*

Industrial policies, then, exercise the primary influence on the location of industrial activity, and thus on the number of jobs available in a particular community and the skill levels required. Each country has a different approach toward the location of industrial activity. This approach raised to the international level needs to be examined rather than the more simplistic one of the impact of foreign investment on employment. Once we focus on the broader issues, the remedies for the narrower issues will appear less difficult.

---

*The limitations on the quantitative analysis are pointed up by Jack Norman Schuman in these words: "The 'grand designs'—how much or which group from the population shall benefit—are value judgments. They are the expression of the personal commitment and perception of priorities of the policy maker. These are fundamental issues of choice with which no data system or analysis, however complete or sophisticated can ever cope." ("The Data Revolution: Its Policy Implications," Bulletin of the American Society for Information Science, February 1975, p. 12.)

LIMITATIONS OF EXISTING STUDIES OF FOREIGN INVESTMENT AND EMPLOYMENT

There have been a number of studies on the impact of foreign direct investment on employment both abroad and in the United States. Largely because of the inadequacy of the analytical models and even of the data, all of the descriptive studies provide an inconclusive basis for policy prescriptions. Arguments based on them to increase taxes on foreign investment or reduce outflows in other ways are, therefore, premature if not ill-considered. But even if the models were sound and the data complete, the policy prescription would not necessarily follow. Substantial questions of what action, if any, was desirable would remain.

A monumental investigation by the U.S. Tariff Commission in 1973 for the Senate Committee on Finance concluded that aggregate data were simply not adequate for the questions being raised concerning the impact of multinational firms on U.S. labor and that much more specific investigations would have to be made.

> Once again the important point brought out by this analysis is that the employment effects vary widely among industries. Even under the 'pessimistic' assumptions of the largest estimate of employment losses, there are a few industries in which gains appear nevertheless. Thus, in the case of employment effects as that of trade effects of MNC activity, final judgments can be made only on an industry-by-industry basis.[1]

In an effort to provide just such industry-specific evidence, Robert Stobaugh and others investigated the impact of nine different investments abroad on employment and balance of payments. They asked the question of what would have been the effect on employment in the absence of foreign investment. They found that the investments were made only after it was clear that alternative sources of production would exist in the foreign market and therefore that the market for U.S. exports would be lost. Even so, in specific cases, the level of employment by an auto company showed an estimated net contribution to U.S. employment in the firm of 659 man-years over a six-year period.[2] This study also concluded tentatively that "foreign investment by U.S. firms generates much larger exports of U.S.-made parts and components than would exist without such investment . . . . and results in a lower volume imports into the United States than would exist without such investment."[3]

In order to prove the case that foreign investment was harmful to U.S. employment, evidence would have to be found that exports dropped by more than they would have if the investment had not been made—and the evidence of the Stobaugh study is contrary to this. Further, it would have to be shown that domestic production would have remained the same or gone up from an investment of the same funds in the U. S. rather than abroad.

An examination of the sectors in which substantial investments are made abroad indicates that the alternatives of exports or domestic investment in the same industrial sector are not always available. In fact, if investments were not made overseas in some sectors, the market abroad simply could not be served, or, alternatively, U. S. imports of materials necessary for expanded domestic production would not be available.

The assumption of export displacement by foreign investment is unrealistic. Professor Musgrave, for example, assumes that the entire foreign direct investment could be turned inward and thereby reverse the unfavorable impact on labor. A look at the composition of U. S. foreign investment reveals that much of that investment simply could not be made internally without altering substantially the structure of the U. S. economy, for much of it brings in materials and semi-finished goods necessary for our continued production and export.

This point can be demonstrated by separating outstanding U. S. foreign investment in major categories over a recent three-year period.

	1972	1973	1974
		(Billions of dollars)	
Petroleum	24	27	30
Manufacturing	38	44	51
Other (service sector)	28	32	37
Total:	90	103	118

Source: U. S. Department of Commerce, Survey of Current Business, Washington, various issues.

These figures show that over 25 percent of the outstanding investment is in petroleum, which is supplied not only to the United States but to other countries. This investment raises the ability of the United States and other countries to produce and thereby the productivity of labor, as well as employment and wages. If the total product in Europe and the United States falls as a result of inadequate investment in petroleum resources around the world, there would be a decrease in demand for labor, reducing the returns to that factor.

Some of the investment in manufacturing is in processed resources and semi-finished inputs for U. S. industry—food products, primary metals, and paper pulp, which constitute 20 percent of total U. S. direct investment in manufacturing abroad. If these products were not offered in the world market, some of which flow back into the United States to support U. S. industry, total world demand and the demand for U. S. exports would be less, with the returns to labor falling consequently.

The investments in the service sector abroad—public utilities, transportation, financing, insurance, and so on—are in areas which simply cannot be served from the United States. They are not export-substituting in any sense, given the difficulties of moving the product across national boundaries or governmental limitations on foreign activities in their countries.

Of the total investment outstanding in the three years noted, therefore, only about 35 percent could have an export displacement impact. And the examples in Professor Stobaugh's studies indicate that even these did not always have the option of continuing to export. The companies studied showed a considerable reluctance on the part of management to jump overseas, rather responding tentatively and reluctantly to the pressures of competition abroad.

Even if there is an export displacement, the effect of U. S. investment overseas must be balanced against the favorable effects of foreign investment in to the United States on U. S. employment. The data on outstanding foreign investment in the United States in 1973 show that of the $26.5 billion, $7 billion was in the extractive sector, $8 billion in manufacturing, and $11.5 billion in the service sector. This total of $26.5 billion provides a substantial offset to the $35 billion of U. S. foreign direct investment in manufacturing, which conceivably could have displaced exports (under very doubtful assumptions). Of course, if this foreign investment in the United States displaced investment by American companies which would otherwise have increased their operations in the same areas, there is no net addition to U. S. employment. But, with unemployment, any investment in the U. S. is to labor's advantage.

If one looks at the displacement issue from the standpoint of actual sales by U. S. affiliates located abroad, we find considerable evidence that many of these sales could not have been made through direct exports. The following table shows sales abroad by majority-owned foreign affiliates of U. S. companies from 1969 to 1973.

	(Billions of dollars)				
	1969	1970	1971	1972	1973
Extraction	4	4	4	3	4
Petroleum	36	42	53	59	91
Manufacturing	68	78	91	108	141
Trade	18	22	25	30	39
Services	8	9	11	12	17
Total:	134	155	184	212	292

Source: U. S. Department of Commerce, Survey of Current Business, Washington, D. C. various issues.

Among these, it is quite clear much would not be substitutable by exports from the United States: for example, the minerals extracted from foreign mines, the petroleum, the commercial investments which facilitate U.S. exports (or draw on locally manufactured goods which are noncompetitive), and services supplied locally. Some of the goods sold through the trade sector could be conceivably exported from the United States, but the data indicates that between 35 and 50 percent of sales by these affiliates could not originate in the U.S. In addition, some of the U.S. manufacturers' foreign affiliate sales are semi-finished goods coming into the United States for further processing, particularly the paper and pulp investment in Canada. Therefore, even conceptually approximately 50 percent of the total sales of U.S. affiliates abroad are not substitutable by exports.

Of the rest, much would be stopped by the trade barriers in the developing countries and by competitive pressures in developed countries. If the developing countries removed their trade barriers they would have fantastically large balance-of-payment problems. During the years 1969-1973 the sales of U.S. affiliates in the developing countries amounted to $32, 35, 42, 48, and 74 billion, respectively. These countries could not have financed such voluminous imports. While sales by affiliates abroad may displace U.S. exports, this would occur in only insignificant amounts.

Even if a displacement effect could be established unequivocally, what should be done about it? Should the United States attempt to reduce foreign direct investment?—and if so, would there be a retaliation by other OECD members, thereby diminishing the contribution from that source to American employment?* Or should it seek to prevent imports back into the United States from foreign investment affiliates? If so, how should it select among the sectors to be restricted, since many of them add to U.S. production capabilities? Or, should the U.S. government select certain sectors to promote and others to prohibit foreign investment or technology transfers? The answers to any of

---

*The recent report to the Congress by the U.S. Department of Commerce on Foreign Direct Investment in the United States (Washington, April 1976) found a substantial increase in employment in the 100 firms studied as to their effects on employment in the United States. In 66 of these firms (about equally divided between start-ups and acquisitions), employment was increased at least 10 percent above that in the initial year; and in 53 of these companies current employment was 50 percent above that in the initial year. (Vol. 1, p. 133.)

these questions would move us a considerable distance toward the formulation of an industrial policy, which we will examine below.

Substantial evidence exists of a loss of specific employment in particular industries which have shifted production activities from the United States to overseas, but even here total employment increases in these same companies have partly offset the shift overseas. We need to know whether or not the workers displaced were reemployed in similar or other activities in the same company or industry. Stobaugh observes that:

> Perhaps the most important finding in our nine cases is that employment created in the United States as a result of U.S. foreign direct investment is of a higher skill level than exists on the average in U.S. manufacturing industries.[4]

In its study of the same aspects, the U.S. Tariff Commission concluded ". . . the MNCs appear on balance to have helped rather than hindered the expansion of U.S. trade in high technology goods."[5]

The evidence of employment loss from investment abroad on balance does not seem to be adverse, but even if it were, the reduction of foreign direct investment would not necessarily be advisable. Employment shifts occur continuously in a mobile economy such as ours, and the undesirable effects of prolonged unemployment can and should be rectified by macro policies to maintain the level of full employment, and by micro policies aimed at relocating industry, manpower training, and labor mobility. Increasing employment opportunities by moving industry rather than labor is desirable, and should be approached through industrial policy rather than foreign investment policy. In fact, it can be argued that if we were not now faced with high levels of unemployment, labor would have little objection to the size and direction of investment abroad. There might still be objections from specific sectors that were affected adversely, but the remedy should be found within the overall policies towards regional development and industrial expansion rather than focusing on foreign investment or technology transfers. To respond to arguments that are based essentially on mere numbers of jobs—without attention to their location and character—is unlikely to lead us in any useful direction on employment or investment policy.

Foreign investment and technology transfers are part of the wider problem of international industrial integration and should be treated within it. In turn, national industrial policies should be directed so as to form or coincide with international industrial policies. Unfortunately, this is not the case, but it is the issue on which we should focus our attention.

INDUSTRIAL POLICIES AND EMPLOYMENT

Industrial policies involve the selection of the industries to be developed within a particular country or region, the necessary infrastructure, and the specific location of that industry. Various countries such as Japan have adopted rather specific industrial policies, and the EC has discussed at length the desirability of establishing a regional industrial policy. Other countries such as Mexico have sought to develop such policies, and many states within the United States have established embryonic industrial policies to attract specific types of activities to specific locations within the state. Therefore, industrial policies can be discussed at three different levels—state (or provincial), national, and international. The problems and procedures are similar in all three, though the specific issues differ.

Within the United States the location of industry is determined primarily by management examining a variety of economic and market factors, modified by the various incentives provided by the state to attract industry and by some disincentives which may exist in regulations controlling the behavior of industry. Incentives take the form of loans, low rent sites, provision of plants, tax waivers, and manpower training. The disincentives might include a clean-air regulation which increases the cost to particular types of industry; this apparently is the concern of the representatives from Utah in the Congress over the present Clean Air Bill.

The states compete with each other for the attraction of industry, and there is no effort at coordinating these incentives. To do so would eliminate the attractiveness of one state over another. Nor is there any regional industrial policy from Washington which would provide a stimulus to industrial location in one region as compared to another, despite the fact that balanced growth might be much more desirable than the lopsided activities which have created substantial urban problems through population shifts.

This lack of coordination is acceptable to some extent because of the presumed mobility of labor, which permits it to move where industry is and therefore to equalize employment opportunities. Where mobility of labor does not exist, however, the ability of one state to attract industry from other states is seen by those states as inequitable. This generates pressure on Washington to formulate regional industrial policies in order to spread out industrial activity.

At the national level in the United States, there is no coherent and deliberate industrial policy, despite the fact that numerous policies effect industrial locations and the suitability of different types of industry among the regions of the country. Thus, there are policies towards transportation, urban development, housing, pollution, communication, model cities, education and manpower development, health, employment compensation, and welfare—all of which have impact on the attractiveness of different "locations" for industrial investment.

But in no one place are these different policies assessed in terms of their impact on industrial location. U.S. policy is oriented toward letting industry decide where to locate and then seeking to modify the ill effects. If, on the other hand, careful investigation of the impact of mobility on society (including the disturbance to the family, education of children. and the destruction of roots in the community) determined that the social costs were excessively high and that it would be desirable to adopt policies leading to greater stability of employment and family location, then it would become more important to move jobs to where the people were rather than people to where the jobs were.

Most countries have industrial policies without having consciously created these policies. Instead, they have directed their attention to tariff and trade policies in an effort to protect or generate particular industries on an ad hoc basis. They have imposed local content regulations to force investment in local industry. Many of the less developed countries have directed their industrial development through the process of import substitution—that is, identifying sectors in which there are substantial imports and then seeking to generate investment for local activity in that sector. More recently, LDCs have sought export-generating industry, again without a careful assessment of how this would fit into their total industrial development or even what overseas markets they could serve. Some countries such as South Korea have simply tried to develop infrastructure, hoping that it would attract a variety of industry and accelerate their development.

This lack of attention to the form of industrial development has resulted from the assumption that the signals of the free market would be adequate in determining what countries should produce what kinds of industrial products and trade with whom. In fact, of course, no country, not even the United States, has been willing wholly to accept the market as a decision-making mechanism. At the same time, most countries have avoided taking the logical next step of deciding what they want to do. Japan is an interesting exception along with Russia and China. Not even Mexico and India have gone so far, though they have taken initiatives in this direction. The Andean Group has also sought to institute an industrial policy through the special agreements, seeking to locate segments of fourteen different industrial sectors among the various members. Progress has been slow, but they have grasped the nettle of industrial policy.

At the international level, obviously no industrial policy exists, nor are there any agreed rules as to how industry should be selected or located throughout the world. The prior rules of the free market plus tariffs have been rejected. We are without an "ordering principle," and we do not even have an acceptable mechanism for determining a new principle within which to set the structure of industrial activity around the world. The developing countries are insisting on redeployment of industry from the advanced countries to the developing countries in order to redress the historical decisions of the advanced countries to locate industry within their own economies and use the colonial areas as sources for raw materials and markets. Appeals to free market criteria will not be acceptable since market criteria will continue to favor the location of industry where the largest markets are already and where infrastructure exists.

The inability of labor to move significantly across national boundaries introduces additional complications requiring mobility for industry—that is, moving jobs to people—if international imbalances are to be corrected. As the French have determined, it is probably less costly economically and certainly less disturbing socially and politically to move jobs to where the people are, rather than people to where the jobs are.

Until we have some internationally agreed upon rules, there will be continuous pulling and hauling on positions appearing more favorable to one country or another. Thus, the United States insisted on criteria of national treatment and limitations on incentives and disincentives to foreign investment in the recently promulgated OECD code of conduct for multinational corporations. This insistence fits with its own criteria of industrial location which are oriented towards free market signals. Canada, on the other hand, balked at the agreement on national treatment, seeking to have a stronger say in the selection and location of industry and particularly its ownership.

My own assessment is that we will gradually move into a difficult dialogue on the problems of industrialization, leading us to the formulation of new rules for the location of industrial activity among the advanced countries and between them and the developing world. To facilitate this development, former Secretary of State Kissinger has proposed the formation of an International Industrialization Institute at the private level, supported by government, business, foundations, and labor groups.

This institute would be an independent entity working with other organizations involved in industrial development, such as the UN Industrial Development Organization, UN Development Programme, OECD, ILO, and various national bodies,[6] to examine the problems of industrialization. Particular emphasis would be given to adjustments between the advanced and developing countries necessary to permit the latter to stimulate specific industries and to enter markets in the industrial countries. It would be able to advise governments on these adjustments as well as on the infrastructure needed to support different industrial sectors. Such an institute would also analyze the impact of shifting international patterns of industrial activity on employment in both the advanced and the developing countries.

The fundamental question underlying the need for industrial policies is "What kind of world economy do we wish to live in?" International economic policies of national governments continue to be predominately mercantilistic, reflecting a desire to diminish interference from abroad and to gain a greater share in the international distribution of benefits of economic growth. The drive to support national interests is modified by increasing pressures towards interdependence, as a result of technological advances and the need for greater efficiency in the use of scarce world resources. In responding to these pressures, national governments have undertaken ad hoc decision-making without a careful analysis of where they want to be in the decades ahead. They seek to protect individual sectors or companies, reflecting a "short run maximization" goal with little attention to long run goals. This approach results from paying attention to a few of the actors in the system rather than to all.[7]

The answer to the question of what kind of world economy we want requires attention to the interests of all of the major actors (with protection of minority interests as well), not just the interests of unionized labor or of business. Since decisions as to the selection and location of industrial activity affect people in all aspects of their life, including their relationship to their social, natural, and political environments, we must give consideration in our examination of industrial policies to these multiple facets.

Our approach, therefore, must be cooperative while at the same time retaining some of the advantages of competitive mechanisms. But competition requires acceptance of the rules and the results. Competition under free markets, given the present relative position of the players, is deemed unacceptable by most—in fact, by all under various circumstances. Similarly unacceptable is decision-making by the governmental bureaucracy which does not provide for adequate change of efficiency and innovation and is unnecessarily costly in its administration. Equally, determination of the goals and means of achievement by labor unions or management alone is unacceptable.

The degree and nature of cooperation that will be required will lead to new institutional forms of decision-making, with representation at least of labor, management, and government to assess the tradeoffs among local, national, and international interests. This assessment will be difficult, but in fact it is already done "implicitly" through ad hoc efforts at protection or at gaining greater benefits—e.g., voluntary quota agreements, escape clauses, content requirements, American selling price, subsidies, tax waivers, and so forth—giving special dispensation to specific industries or even companies.

These decisions do in fact constitute ad hoc industrial policies, but without an adequate assessment of where we want to go in creating a new international economic order and how to let others play the game and help set the rules. Since the past rules for the international economic order were not made with the participation of a large number of the countries which are now recognized as sovereign nations, these now insist on a reexamination and resetting of the rules, a logical extension of their being asked to play the international game.

In resetting the rules, the criteria of acceptability will certainly not be simply those of maximizing welfare for the world as a whole nor of maximizing market efficiency. Tradeoffs will have to be made among a number of goals including equitable sharing of benefits, innovation, mobility, stability, freedom, creativity, growth, community orientations, environmental protection, and conservation of resources.[8] Once this is done, the demand by any one group that its interests be cared for can be set within these broader determinations. We must recognize that all parties have a stake in cooperative means of achieving rewarding employment throughout the world and in having a voice in the decision-making process.

It is unlikely that governments will bring together all those who have a legitimate voice in the problems discussed here, although obviously governments must be involved. Initiatives should also be taken by both labor and business to meet on a continuing basis in small groups to focus on concrete issues and come to some broad agreement—or at least agreement to disagree on certain aspects. There is too much talking to ourselves or speaking "for the record" and too little attempt to understand the position of others so as to reach mutually agreeable accommodations. New institutional ties must be formed among the various parties to replace the adversary attitudes of the past. We need now more than ever cooperative efforts to determine acceptable tradeoffs on the difficult problems generated by changing patterns of industrialization and employment throughout the world.

NOTES

1. U.S. Senate Committee on Finance, Implications of Multinational Firms for World Trade and Investment and for U.S. Trade and Labor, Washington: February 1973 (Committee Print), p. 7.

2. Robert B. Stobaugh, Nine Investments Abroad and Their Impact at Home, Cambridge: Harvard University, Graduate School of Business Administration, 1976, p. 34.

3. Ibid., p. 210.

4. Ibid., p. 16.

5. Ibid., p. 11.

6. For details on the Institute see Meeting the Challenge of Industrialization (Washington, National Academy of Sciences, 1973).

7. Jack N. Behrman, "Actors and Factors in Policy Decisions on a Foreign Direct Investment," World Development, 2, 1974, pp. 1-14.

8. Jack N. Behrman, Toward a New International Economic Order, (Paris: The Atlantic Institute, 1974).

13

Prospects for American Manufacturers and Workers in a Rentier Economy

GUS TYLER

MULTINATIONALS AND THE MYTH OF COMPARATIVE ADVANTAGE

The growing dominance of the global corporation over the international creation and flow of goods and capital makes classic discussion of "free trade" versus "protectionism" an empty echo without relevance to the real problems of our times. The classic free trade position proposed to let each country do what it can do best, trading its output with other countries that were also exploiting their "comparative advantages." This "theory of comparative advantage," as Robert d'A Shaw pointed out in the Columbia Journal of World Business, "assumes full employment in trading countries and also assumes that the factors of production are not transferred across national boundaries."

Neither of these classic assumptions is valid today. There is no full employment. And if there were, the factors of production are no longer confined to national boundaries, precisely because of the rise of the multinational corporation.

Consider each factor of production that might give the United States a "comparative advantage." We have loads of capital, but this can be and is exported around the world.

In 1969, some 3,400 United States firms with overseas operations involving an investment of $71 billion turned out more than $200 billion in goods, while U.S. exports ran to about one-fifth that sum. Since 1969 our overseas investments have galloped along.

We have an edge in technology, but much of our comparative advantage is sent abroad. A 1973 staff report to the Senate Committee on Finance states that "exports of technology [from America] outweigh imports by a factor of ten to one."

We have entrepreneurial know-how, but we export this by sending our managers overseas or by training foreign managers here. We have skilled labor, but so do other industrial nations. We have raw materials. But if we had to rely for our strength on those raw materials that were exclusively ours, we would find that we were not faring much better than South Africa, Argentina, Australia or Saudi Arabia.

The world of the 1970s is not the world of the 1950s, with its Marshall Plan or Point Four program. Just as the world economy has changed in the last half century, so too has America's role in the world changed in the last generation.

The assumptions of American economic policy internationally after World War II were that America must give blood to restore a bleeding world and that to do so was in our long range interest, both economically and politically. We were able to pursue this policy with minimal pain to ourselves. The war had wrecked the productive plant of many nations. The United States dominated the world manufacturing scene easily. Much of the money we gave away came back to us in the form of purchases of American machinery and commodities.

By the 1960s, however, our role had changed. Europe and Japan were no longer weak and bleeding economies about to collapse. Both the European Common Market and Japan viewed themselves as America's prime competitors. While continuing to count on America's market as an outlet, they made it increasingly difficult for America to get into their market.

As we moved into the 1970s, the United States found itself to be an island of free trade (if that word still has any meaning) in a sea of protectionism. Europe, Japan, Australia, Brazil, Argentina and of course the Communist countries were all "closed" markets when compared with our relative openness. Our changed position became apparent when, in the early 1970s, the balance of trade turned against us.

The multinationals contributed to this turn of trade balance against the United States. Once they encountered difficulty in penetrating tariff and nontariff barriers in other countries, they hopped the barriers by opening up foreign facilities. Since they had a hard time exporting their product, they exported their production. Located in these "protected" markets, American multinationals could live in the best of all possible worlds, enjoying the advantages of "protectionism" abroad while taking advantage of the "open" market in the United States.

By these policies, our multinationals also helped weaken America's position whenever we asked for a mutual lowering of tariff and nontariff barriers. Why should Brazil lower its tariff, when it knew that its high tariff would entice American multinationals to open plants in Brazil?

This turning of the trade balance against the United States was more than so much red ink on the nation's ledger. As imports rose, American workers lost jobs to low wage competitors. As multinationals shifted production from Memphis to Hong Kong, American workers found themselves jobless.

Consequently, American labor was compelled to seek remedies through control of commodity imports and capital exports by multinationals. Labor's stand is not just another of those grievances that unions are supposed to voice because some dues paying members are momentarily discomforted. What is at stake is the future of the American economy. The unions have been first in raising these crucial questions, because working people and the organizations representing them are the first to experience the coming crisis.

Multinationals are usually classified as corporations with wholly owned subsidiaries overseas. This is a highly limited view of multinational operations. Some American corporations operate through joint ventures while others hold large blocs of shares in foreign firms and still others grant licenses or franchises.

One of the least noted operations is the "contracting" out of work to foreign producers. This is most common in the LDCs carrying on labor intensive production. In the shoe industry, for instance, reported Fortune in March 1973, "a U. S. importer pays for the entire output of a foreign plant before the shoes are produced." Norman Hinerfeld, executive vice-president of Kayser-Roth, stated in 1972 that "50 percent of all apparel currently imported into the United States is brought in by apparel manufacturers rather than by retailers and wholesalers." Thus, American distributors, importers or manufacturers use overseas producers in the same way that some giant American retail chains use their "captive" suppliers.

LAYING THE FOUNDATION FOR A RENTIER ECONOMY

If America loses its manufacturing under the double assault of commodity imports and job exports, what shall we substitute as the backbone of our economy? A school of economists who are not worried about our loss of manufacturing propose that we become a rentier economy.

A rentier economy is one that lives on its investments. It does not depend primarily on making and selling things but by clipping its coupons. In the summer of 1971, Brookings Institution economist Lawrence B. Krause described an America that was already on the way to becoming a rentier economy. "American companies for many years have been investing substantial sums abroad, primarily by direct investments. These investments are now yielding large dividend and interest returns to their parents (representing a net of $5.8 billion in 1969)," he wrote in Foreign Policy, "and such returns are likely to grow substantially during the decade of the 1970s."

As Krause forecast, overseas investments continued to rise. A 1972 U. S. Department of Commerce study showed that the top 298 multinational corporations in the United States earned 40 percent of their net profits outside our borders. The chemical industry had about 33 percent of its total assets abroad; the consumer-goods industry about 40 percent; the electrical industry an incredible 75 percent; the pharmaceutical industry about one-third of its assets. By 1973, the seven largest banks in the United States were drawing 40 percent of the total profits from abroad, rising from 23 percent only two years earlier.

U. S. investment overseas amounted to more than $100 billion in 1973. (There is, of course, some reverse flow but as of 1973, foreign investments in the United States were only about 40 percent of American investments abroad.) Our net inflow of earnings on investments was $7.4 billion. Capital has been pouring into other countries for several reasons. When a multinational corporation carries on overseas production, its product can then be sold in a protected market. Hence, both prices and profits are artificially high.

Often the host country offers inducements to entice American investment such as remission of income and other taxes and of import duties on materials and machinery used in producing goods for export. Other inducements may include subsidies for new plant construction through low interest rates or government financing, provision of working capital or joint investment and preferential treatment in getting foreign exchange for exports.

Once implanted overseas, American multinationals turn around to use their foreign base as a launching platform to export to the United States. Between 1966 and 1970, the 298 multinationals covered by the Commerce Department study showed a 52.9 percent increase in sales to the countries in which they were located, but a whopping 129.4 percent rise in their sales to the United States.

In many countries, American companies find they can get cheap labor and child labor; do not have to pay minimum wages, workers' compensation, unemployment insurance or social security; and do not have to observe occupational, safety and health legislation or environmental standards, or maintain fair hiring practices. Hence, so long as America maintains a relatively open door policy for commodities flooding into this country from abroad and an open handed policy in allowing American companies to export capital and technology, it is profitable for U. S.-based global corporations to do their manufacturing in other lands—the financial basis for a rentier economy.

A key problem for the United States in a rentier economy is how other countries will get the necessary money to pay us, the rentier. If we just keep drawing their funds from them in the form of interest on our investments, we will ultimately exhaust their ability to pay us. Krause offers a direct solution. "Larger trade surpluses by other countries will be required to make possible these payments," he explains. We must consciously create an unfavorable balance of trade for the United States.

The items we are most likely to import will be wares from factories rather than farms. At present, the United States is the world's greatest exporter of agricultural products. While we do import fuels (oil), we are likely to be less dependent in the years ahead as we find alternate sources of energy. Hence, the commodities we import will be mostly manufactured wares.

Under ideal circumstances, international trade need not result in foreign products displacing American-made goods and American workers. Theoretically, we could sell as much as we buy—exchanging our output for the equal output of other nations. But, by its very nature, the rentier system disallows such an equilibrium, requiring an unfavorable trade balance for America so that other nations may gather surpluses with which to pay interest and dividends to American rentiers. Hence loss of manufacturing and manufacturing jobs are inherent in a rentier economy.

EMPLOYMENT IN A RENTIER ECONOMY

The next question is what happens to the 20 million workers currently employed in American factories? The answer of those who envision the rentier economy is that those displaced from manufacturing will find employment in the new system. But will they? A rentier economy is, by its very nature, no great employer. Those who live by it require few busy hands, since the primary operation is placing money abroad and then reaping the returns from the investment. That operation employs few workers.

Proponents of the rentier economy suggest another source of employment: research and development for corporations that will then make the results available to other countries for their lease or purchase. The United States would be the great inventor and innovator for the planet. This notion, however, stands on two infirm legs. Even if we were to assume this presumptuous role, the number of people engaged in such work would be necessarily limited, as it is today. Beyond that, however, we are very likely to lose this role, first because without our own industries we would find it difficult, if not impossible, to put our ideas to a valid test, and secondly, with their own growing industries and know-how, other nations would soon develop their own scientists and engineers.

In theory, the income that pours into the coffers of the American corporations will drip down to the people below. But in practice, nothing of the kind is likely to happen. First of all, American corporations are not likely to bring back to this country the full sum of their return investment. To do so would be foolish, since under present law each dollar repatriated as profits will be taxed by the United States. Hence, corporations are inclined, as experience has already shown, to let their foreign profits stay abroad.

Second, even if the returns do pour back into corporate hands in full force, such an accumulation at the top does not necessarily mean that there will be a drip down to the lower layers. The 2 percent of the population which owns about 80 percent of the privately held shares in corporations can never constitute the mass purchasing base for a viable economy. Hence, concentration of income in the hands of the rentiers will not provide jobs to the rest of the nation either directly by work in the establishments of the rentiers or indirectly, by stimulating a massive domestic demand.

But what about other places for employment of those displaced in manufacturing such as in building and construction, wholesaling and retailing, civil service, hotels, restaurants and travel? The argument runs that the 20 million employed in manufacturing are only about one quarter of the total labor force. If the other three quarters expand, they will be able to absorb those who fall out of manufacturing jobs. It is further argued that manufacturing has been a shrinking percentage of the labor force for several decades now, with offsetting employment growth in the expanding nonmanufacturing section of the economy.

What these calculations omit, however, is the key and decisive role of manufacturing in making it possible for the other sectors of the economy to grow. Stepped up factory productivity in the automation following World War II made it possible for a relatively smaller percentage of the labor force in manufacturing to flood the nation with tangible wealth. With this wealth, the nation was able to afford homes and hotels, bars and restaurants, public and private schools and an expensive system of advertising, merchandising, transporting, wholesaling, retailing, and packaging.

Eliminate manufacturing and you eliminate the foundation on which many other sectors of the economy are based. The construction industry depends on manufacturing to build plants and on factory employees to buy homes. The entertainment, restaurant, travel, and sports industries depend on workers whose income is drawn from the makers of tangible commodities. Teachers, police, firemen, sanitation workers, forest rangers, and government weathermen depend on taxes paid by the producers of products.

In short, if manufacturing shrinks, so will virtually every other sector of the economy, except, of course, that elite segment busily engaged in collecting dividends on overseas investments. A rentier economy would make our indivisible nation into two: one living in gentlemanly leisure on its income from foreign investments and the other wallowing in unemployment and poverty.

All this is rarely, if ever, discussed by the devotees of the rentier system. All they see is a way to arrive at a neatly balanced international flow of money. The United States will lose on the balance of trade (more imports than exports) but will gain on the balance of payments (more interest on investments coming in than going out). The question that goes unanswered because it goes unasked is: who in the United States gains and who loses? Under the rentier system, workers lose and rentiers gain; income is redistributed upward to those at the top.

THE BRITISH PRECEDENT: A LESSON FOR AMERICA

In examining this ruinous trend in the United States, Krause notes that our evolution is not without precedent. America "may well be on the road to becoming a mature creditor country," he notes, "not unlike Great Britain, France and the Netherlands in earlier historical periods." His historical reference is particularly poignant at this moment as it applies to the British experience. Recently the former Prime Minister of Great Britain, Harold Wilson, told his ailing nation that Britain's prime need is manufacturing.

What happened to Britain? In the nineteenth century, Britain was the great free-trade advocate in the world. She had nothing to fear from foreign manufacturing, since Britain could beat everyone at the game with her superior ken and capacity. The imports that came into Britain were welcomed by her capitalists because they consisted of cheap raw materials for her mills and cheap foodstuffs for her workers.

Sizable investment by English capitalists in overseas ventures were all to the good. "Investment was largely directed into the development of communications abroad (particularly railroads) and of foodstuffs and raw materials which were highly complementary in nature to British export and domestic industries," states Peggy B. Musgrave in a study for the Senate Foreign Relations Committee. By the end of the nineteenth century, Britain was investing about half her national savings outside England, with minimal detriment to the overall economy.

In the early decades of the twentieth century, however, things began to change. Other nations were now in a position to compete with Britain in manufacturing and were no longer satisfied merely to be suppliers of cheap materials and foodstuffs to England. Instead of putting more money into British manufacturing, British capital began to pour funds into foreign industry. "An increasing proportion of this foreign investment began to move into manufacturing industries such as jute, cotton, iron, steel, paper, tobacco and engineering," records Musgrave. By World War I, Britain was investing 80 to 90 percent of her total capital formation abroad. Britain turned from a manufacturing to a rentier economy.

The British economy felt the impact almost immediately, but at first the decline was slight. In time, however, the slight decline became much steeper and the downturn in trade became a tumble, so that today the once bustling Britain is a dying economy.

If the United States chooses to go the way of the rentier, it is likely to fall into ruin even faster than Britain. Most of the money Britain invested outside its borders was in portfolio form rather than in their own businesses overseas. Hence, they did little of what American multinationals have been doing in recent years, namely, closing plants in the United States while opening them elsewhere. Secondly, British capital did not make a major business of exporting technology. But for American multinationals, the export of technology is as important as the export of capital.

Another difference between the British and the American experience is that the United Kingdom was able to run its rentier system during a century when the sun never set on the British Empire. Hence, they could, when necessary, rush in to secure their investments with armed authority. "Can anyone really believe," asked Paul A. Samuelson, writing in the Morgan Guaranty Survey, "that in the last three decades of the twentieth century the rest of the world can be confidently counted on to permit the continuing flow of dividends, repatriation of earnings and royalties to large corporations owned here?"

14

Multinational Corporations, Employment, and Labor Relations in Western Europe

HANS GÜNTER

IMPACT OF MULTINATIONALS ON EMPLOYMENT

In contrast to the situation in the United States, where real and alleged job exports of MNCs have become a public issue, the considerable foreign investments undertaken, especially in the 1950s and 1960s (mainly by U. S. -based MNCs) appear to have made Western Europe a net beneficiary of employment generation as suggested in several studies.[1] A French white paper concludes, for instance, that considerable employment has been stimulated through foreign investment. Likewise in Belgium 70 percent of the workplaces resulting from new investments between 1964 and 1968 were created by multinational firms.[2]

Whether or not such sporadic evidence of job creation by MNCs represents a general trend, Europe clearly has not needed to rely on foreign MNCs for generating employment. Most Western European countries during the major part of the post-World War II period experienced unprecedented economic growth, and equally unprecedented high employment levels. Influenced by this growth performance, two major convictions developed in influential labor circles and were reflected in their attitudes towards MNCs. The ultimate economic decision-making prerogative of management needed to be preserved in market economies in the interest of efficiency, and the main responsibility for economic growth and employment had to be vested in the national governments.

Adjustments through changes in jobs, skills and location of workers and correlated retraining came to be accepted as a norm for labor and greater mobility of workers became a widely shared goal. As the masses of workers in Europe benefited visibly, even rapid economic and technological change was accepted by virtually all major unions, with the possible exception of the more hesitant British unions. The main union concern was compensation and adjustment assistance for workers affected by change.

Influenced by union requests, instruments for the compensation of workers and their reemployment became a legal requirement in various countries, and collective agreements for the protection of workers against rationalization policies were concluded. At the same time the concept of an active labor market policy was developed in several Western European countries under much union pressure, particularly Sweden.[3]

The positive attitude of unions towards adjustments in employment was helped in some countries by a centralized union organization such as West Germany and Sweden, allowing the unions to develop a broader view of the national interest. Where the trade union movement is more decentralized as in the United States, union leadership is often compelled to take a harder line on job losses through commodity imports and capital exports as a condition for survival. Positive union attitudes towards economic change in small European countries (such as the Benelux countries) may also reflect the heavy dependence of these countries on world markets and international capital movement.[4]

Structural labor force changes as a result of mergers and takeovers frequently engineered by MNCs were recognized as disquieting labor market factors. But as long as the economy produced sufficient and improved employment alternatives, structural changes were generally considered a positive development by all parties involved. In generating employment in economically weak regions in particular there are a number of examples of successful interaction between government schemes seeking to implant new industries and investments by MNCs.[5]

The impact of MNCs has not, however, been invariably beneficial to economically depressed regions. In Germany, for example, a recent study concludes that the growth industries in which MNCs dominate are usually implanted in the areas of heavy economic concentration and not in economically backward regions. The proportion of new foreign investments in economically depressed areas is only half that of the comparable domestic firms. In Great Britain too, foreign investments seem to have made less of a contribution to employment in the underdeveloped regions than they have to employment in the "industrially congested areas".[6]

Similarly, the constant increase of labor migration mainly from southern Europe to highly industrialized countries, such as France, Germany and Switzerland (at least until the present recession) suggests that MNCs have also reinforced international inequality in employment distribution. In the recipient countries of migration, foreign workers are concentrated in areas and industries in which both foreign and domestic MNCs are prominently represented.[7] This discounts the theory that international direct investment necessarily brings jobs to workers.

Other structural employment problems connected with the operations of MNCs in Europe include the mix of job skills, closed labor markets within MNCs, mergers and takeover policies, and the transfer of production to low wage countries. The British unions especially have expressed concern over the possibilities of a lower skill mix in the subsidiaries of foreign firms in Great Britain. Different types of evidence suggest, however, that possible disparities of that nature are not too pronounced.[8] A study by the International Labour Office of a sample of European-based multinational firms in the metal trades, for example, suggests that parent companies do not necessarily have a higher proportion of managerial and technical staff than their subsidiaries.[9]

The closed labor market thesis maintains that the labor force of MNCs will be specially trained and maintained by these firms, with a reduced multiplier effect on the economy as a whole. Closely connected is the "dual labor market theory" which argues that MNCs reinforce a trend toward segregating "established labor" in well remunerated and relatively secure employment from "social marginals" in substandard, precarious employment.[10] Such labor market effects are likely to be more pronounced in developing countries than in Western Europe where competitive domestic enterprises, offering comparable workplaces to those in MNCs, and developed public labor market policies exist.

Both grassroots pressure and a new evaluation of the changed economic situation have helped to spread the opinion in European union circles that labor cannot remain the main adjusting variable in the process of structural change in the present recessionary period. Under union pressure, the protection of workers in cases of mergers, takeovers and shop closures has thus become a special concern of labor legislation in European countries in the last couple of years, and "job bargaining" has been introduced more and more in collective agreements.[11] At the same time resistance of workers to shop closures, including spontaneous strikes and factory occupation, has brought with it new problems for union action and control.

Earlier instances of sporadic resistance of workers to plant closures signaled a change in the "progressive" adjustment ideology. The Akzo case, of successful resistance of Dutch and German workers to labor force cuts demonstrated that border-crossing worker solidarity can, under certain circumstances, counteract employment decisions of multinational management. *

---

*For a detailed account of the Akzo case according to a union perspective, see P. Hoffmann and A. Langwieler, Noch sind wir da!

Problems connected with mergers and takeovers have stimulated social policy initiatives at the level of the ECs. The Akzo case, debated in the European Parliament, accelerated the adoption by the Council of Ministers of a directive requesting improved and harmonized legislation in EC member countries for the protection of workers in case of collective dismissals. Similarly, a directive providing for full protection of acquired rights and privileges of workers in the case of mergers and takeovers has been adopted.

Shifts of complete production units to low wage countries are, thus far, relatively rare events in Western Europe. Western Europe seems likely to remain for some time a preferred "transit station" for multinational business.[12] One prominent exception is the transfer of two-thirds of the production of the German camera producer, Zeiss Ikon, to an Asian country where only ten percent of the West German wages had to be paid, a step which nonetheless failed to improve significantly the firm's competitive position.[13]

Complete transfers of production lines meet many economic and social obstacles in Western Europe. Mass layoffs as a consequence of such transfers are simply not tolerated by governments, unions and public opinion alike in a good number of countries.[14] The more frequent and easier practice for MNCs is, therefore, the expansion of production or the creation of new plants outside Europe, while maintaining more or less the level of activities in the existing European plants. But some German firms have been accused recently of having justified reduced domestic investments during the present recession by a lack of profit while investing heavily abroad.[15]

The whole issue of production transfers by MNCs is interlinked with the broader question of optimal international allocation of investment, production and employment and more specifically with the problems of the so-called declining industries. The labor intensive industries of textiles and leather are such declining industries in Europe. A heavy competition on world markets from both other industrialized as well as developing countries makes certain production lines no longer profitable even in modern European plants. Where heavy competition is coupled with slack demand, MNCs may not transfer produc-

---

Arbeiter im multinationalen Konzern, (Reinbek: Rowohlt Taschenbuch Verlag, October 1974). A critical analysis of the international union involvement in connection with the Akzo case is found in H.R. Northrup and R.L. Ronan, "Multinational Collective Bargaining Activity: The Factual Record in Chemical, Glass and Rubber Tires", Columbia Journal of World Business IX, no. 1 Spring 1974, pp. 112-24, and Summer 1974, pp. 49-63.

tion but simply curtail capacity. This is presently the case for the British textile MNC Courtaulds, which plans to close several plants in the United Kingdom, including a very modern one in Skelmersdale constructed only in 1968.[16]

Other big international fiber producers such as Hoechst (Germany), Rhone-Polence (France) and Montefibre (Italy) have recently resorted to production cuts and shorter working hours. Protective measures are being sought by the industry from the EC Commission, claiming that what is at stake is whether Europe "wants or should have a textile industry".[17] European as well as global planning and phasing of changes in the international division of work seems thus a long-term necessity if major economic and social disruptions are to be avoided and is certainly a necessary prerequisite of any realistic "new international economic order".

Generally speaking, the shift of production from Europe to low wage developing countries by MNCs in Europe is leading to a gradual change in the international distribution employment. An overwhelming proportion of the total work force of the MNCs will, however, remain in the industrialized countries for years to come.* These shifts do contribute in the long-run in Europe as in the United States to the "post-industrial" expansion of the service sector. How much that sector can absorb indefinitely labor displaced from industry is a much debated question.[18]

INDUSTRIAL RELATIONS

In most Western European countries industrial relations practices of MNCs are affected by a variety of internal and external factors such as management response to local situations, existing labor law and regulations, union power, and integration of the firm in respective national industrial relations settings.[19] Western European countries display considerable resistance to transnational influences,[20] and it is not surprising that the position of workers and their representatives in MNCs is often not basically different from that of workers in exclusively national firms.[21]

Much of the behavioral integration of MNCs results from the decentralization of their personnel and industrial relations functions. While U.S. enterprises tend to centralize industrial relations functions to a greater extent than do enterprises of European origin, North

---

*Some data in support of this conclusion are found in the ILO Social and Labour study of the metal trades.

American firms also tend to adjust their home country practices to local conditions. MNCs of European origin on the other hand seem to take over local practices much easier than U. S. enterprises.[22] Since industrial relations practices within Europe more generally resemble each other, this leads to a greater environmental compatibility of European MNCs on their continent.[23]

Irrespective of the degree of decentralization of industrial relations functions in normal circumstances, the foreign headquarters of MNCs tend to come more actively into the picture in crisis situations, for example, when the productivity of the whole enterprise is menaced as a result of certain labor practices in a host country or because of a major labor dispute in an important plant. Hence, industrial relations in MNCs, although normally decentralized and largely integrated in the local setting of Western Europe are "latently transnational."[24]

A substantial degree of integration of MNCs in the local setting is found in the area of collective bargaining and wage policy.[25] Cases in which foreign subsidiaries opt to stay outside employer organizations (more frequently with U. S. than with European MNCs) or to defy an established practice of industry-wide collective bargaining appear to be the exception rather than the rule in Western Europe. This also largely explains why actual wages and labor conditions in MNCs in Europe generally resemble those in comparable local enterprises, although their benefit and training programs seem to be superior.[26] Adaptation to local wage levels in Europe is also clearly cost-saving to U. S. MNCs. These findings definitely contradict the frequent assumption of a worldwide factor cost and wage equalization effect of MNCs.

Similarity between MNCs and local firms in Europe is also found in union recognition problems.[27] This problem has, nevertheless, led to serious concern of unions in some countries, particularly Great Britain, as it touches directly on their interest representation function. Unions feel that they have to again fight battles won long ago.[28]

Most differences in industrial relations techniques of multinational management are minor, although these may cause irritations for the unions (for example, personnel practices and management styles). Even more substantial initiatives of foreign MNCs—for instanc the introduction of productivity bargaining in the early 1960s in Great Britain (a major industrial relations innovation for that country)—have met with union acceptance or at least tolerance. Such initiatives have also found wide emulation in local enterprises, as factors toward improving efficiency or labor management cooperation.

MNCs have taken a leading role in the last couple of years in introducing new forms of work organization such as job enrichment and group production methods. The motive for these initiatives is usually economic—to improve productivity, reduce absenteeism, make unpleasant jobs more attractive, or achieve greater flexibility of production. However, improvements of work conditions go hand in hand with these measures so that they can frequently be considered as a step towards the greater "humanization" of the workplace.

In various European trade union circles the new forms of work organization are considered a potential menace because they may lead to greater worker identification with their employers to the detriment of labor solidarity.[29] On the other hand, the Scandinavian and Italian experiences demonstrate that such managerial initiatives can be used to strengthen the union position by acquiring new influence and participation rights as a condition for their acceptance.[30]

There is little doubt that the more far-reaching impact of MNCs in Western Europe is not caused by direct management initiatives but relates to changes generated by the firms as a result of their economic size, organizational character, and general business strategies. Because of their size MNCs have reinforced an existing trend towards more formal and informal plant level bargaining. Economic size also explains why MNCs may remain outside or withdraw from employers' associations.[31] Yet in countries such as Sweden or West Germany, an opposite tendency can be observed. In the latter country practically all major MNCs are now members of a relevant employers' association contrary to the situation some years ago.

MNCs have on the other hand retarded, if not reversed, the trend toward boardroom participation of workers. (Boardroom participation is otherwise an increasing trend in Western Europe. Such participation arrangements exist in various forms and sectors in Denmark, France, Federal Republic of Germany, Luxembourg, Sweden and the United Kingdom.) In the Netherlands, subsidiaries of MNCs are exempted from the 1971 participation law under certain circumstances and a special regulation exists for the holding companies of international groups having a majority of their employees abroad.[32] In the Federal Republic of Germany, the extension of codetermination was attacked on the grounds that it was contrary to the obligations of the government towards U.S. investments, although it was nevertheless enacted in July 1976. Perhaps more importantly, the right of workers to participate in economic decision-making, where it exists, has become eroded because the final decision-making power of a foreign multinational is far removed at its international headquarters.

Special problems arise with MNCs also in the field of information and consultation. A rather general union complaint in Europe about MNCs is "inadequate information."[33] The complex corporate structure of MNCs certainly is an important factor here. It is significant that many international trade secretariats consider the collection of information on MNCs and its dissemination to their members a high priority task.

Information and consultation requirements take a prominent place in the discussions about standards of conduct for MNCs. The OECD guidelines for multinational enterprises adopted in June 1976 for instance, request the provision of information to employee representatives for meaningful negotiations on conditions of employment. Furthermore, reasonable notice to employee representatives in case of collective layoffs and cooperation with them and governments to mitigate adverse employment effects are called for.[34]

In sum, MNCs in Western Europe and elsewhere are both disruptive and positive influences on industrial relations.[35] Both influences are likely to be greater in small countries—such as Belgium and the Netherlands, where MNCs account for an important part of the growth industries—than in the larger European countries.[36] Employment problems, decision-making of MNCs and related questions of workers' influence, rights, and compensation are the key factors in industrial relations in MNCs and the perceptions and strategies of unions towards the multinationals.

UNION PERCEPTIONS AND STRATEGIES TOWARD MNCS

International and regional union movements headquartered in Europe have been much more affected by the growth of MNCs than have national union organizations. In the MNCs, a considerable proportion of the international trade union movement has found a new concrete purpose and legitimation for activities going beyond traditional functions of information exchange and manifestation of solidarity.

This is particularly true for the free trade unions organized in the ICFTU and the associated International Trade Secretariats (ITSs), and to a somewhat smaller extent for the World Confederation of Labor (WCL), the Christian international union federation. Both cooperate and both consider the growth of MNCs a new challenge for organized labor. The Communist-led World Federation of Trade Unions (WFTU) is less articulate in this respect as it considers the MNC an integral aspect of the general development of capitalism and its contradictions. Cooperation of Communist-led unions is usually not solicited by the other international organizations in dealing with MNCs. It is thus evident that the phenomenon of MNCs has not been a unifying factor for the international labor movement as a whole but rather that it has provided an occasion for confirming existing ideological divisions.*

---

*E. Piehl foresees the possibility of future union cooperation versus MNCs across ideological positions. See his Multinationale Konzerne and internationale Gewerkschaftsbewegung, (Frankfurt am Main: Europaeishe Verlaganstadt, 1974), p. 212.

The ITSs (especially those for the chemical, metal, and food industries) and their European counterparts, of which the European Metal Workers' Federation (EMF) is the most active, see their main tasks as information gathering, assistance to local unions, intervention at company headquarters, and the coordination or initiation of concrete transnational action of various types. One major structural innovation is the creation of world councils for a number of MNCs, mainly European-based corporations. The world councils seek to facilitate information exchange and consultation among unionists in the various units of the corporations. They could eventually become a platform for more specific action, although at present most of them are still rather weak organizations.[37] Most of the successful cases of international union action versus MNCs (such as St. Gobain, Ford, and Akzo) and the talks (especially by EMF) with MNC headquarters (e.g. Philips, Fokker-VFW, AEG-Telefunken) have taken place in Western Europe.[38]

The ETUC has been much concerned with the problems of MNCs since it was founded in 1973. It has called for cooperation of governments of the EC and EFTA member states to achieve greater control of MNCs. It has also asked for worker representation on the boards of such enterprises. The ETUC plans to initiate an action program regarding MNCs in line with the ICFTU charter on MNCs, adopted in Mexico.[39] Many of these ideas would imply changes in company legislation. The ETUC will have to evolve close working relations with the ECs which are concerned with harmonization of company legislation and have prepared an optional European company statute for multinational enterprises in the EC.* The EC's amended draft statute includes, for instance, provisions for a European works council as well as a one-third representation of workers on the supervisory board.[40]

International bargaining in Europe centered on MNCs is still way ahead. Border-crossing union activities relating to MNCs are spreading only very slowly, a fact which can be attributed to existing legal barriers, differences in union organization, and bargaining patterns, ideological splits and entrenched national practices.[41] But the motivation of national unions for international action which might entail a loss of some of their present functions is also questionable.[42] The powerful national unions in Europe have not yet found their representation role and their capacity to press successfully for social change seriously

---

*This section on the ETUC follows the analysis by B.C. Roberts and Bruno Liebhaberg, "The European Trade Union Confederation: Influence of Regionalism, Detente, and Multinationals," British Journal of Industrial Relations, 14, no. 3 (November 1976), pp. 201-243.

challenged by the operations of MNCs.[43] Such important matters as recognition problems, job security and wages and working conditions seem to be not so much dependent on the national or international character of a firm as on the overall strength of a national labor movement.[44]

In countries such as the Netherlands, and more particularly West Germany, the extension of codetermination is, in the eyes of many unionists, an essential part of such a strengthening of the labor movement. It is expected to give workers and unions a definite influence on international investment-employment decisions, at least in home-based MNCs.[45] Another specific aspect of this increase in union strength is the spread of "job bargaining" which was referred to earlier. The long debate over the establishment of a Volkswagen plant in the United States, which was possible only after assurance by management that no negative employment effects would occur in the German plants, is a good illustration.

European union attitudes towards industrial decision-making by management, largely determined up to now by a "progressive" adjustment ideology, are in a state of reorientation as a result of reduced growth prospects and changing views of the role of multinational corporations. Although the protection of labor against the consequences of economic change has improved greatly in recent years under the pressure of the unions, MNCs are recognized as forces likely to limit further improvement.

The pressure for more national and international controls over MNCs has therefore been maintained and has resulted in greater transnational union cooperation in Europe against MNCs. A particular European response to these questions is seen by many unionists in the spread of participation and codetermination at the enterprise, the national, and the supranational levels.

The experience of European labor with MNCs has contrasted in many ways with that of American workers. The result is that there are some basic differences in the approaches of European and American unions toward multinationals. The achievement of fair wage standards everywhere MNCs operate, widely considered in U.S. union circles as the most effective response to the competition of cheap labor overseas, is much less stressed in Europe.[46] In Europe more concern is expressed over a possible transfer of production to countries with restricted union freedom, in particular where strikes are not allowed.

The unions in Eurpoe, with exceptions of emergency situations such as those that have existed in Britain, have not asked for protective trade and investment legislation of the Burke-Hartke type to reduce the impact of MNCs on domestic employment.[47] Rather they have pushed governments to improve the already advanced measures of adjustment assistance, an orientation which may now also gain some ground in the United States. The importance placed on institutionalized participation in company decision-making through codetermination is a distinctive feature of the European labor acene which finds no parallel in North America and which may lead to more striking trans-Atlantic differences in union relationships with MNCs in the years ahead.

NOTES

1. Arnold R. Weber, "Bargaining with Boundaries: Industrial Relations and the Multinational Firm", in Robert J. Flanagan and Arnold R. Weber (eds.), Bargaining without boundaries: The Multinational Corporations and International Labor Relations (Chicago and London: University of Chicago Press, 1974), p. 239. For an examination of conditions specific to Western Europe which bear up labor's position toward MNCs, see Hans Günter, "Labor and Multinational Corporations in Western Europe: Some Problems and Prospects", in Duane Kujawa (ed.), International Labor and the Multinational Enterprise (New York: Praeger Publishers, 1975), pp. 147-48.

2. Delegation a l'amenagement du territoire it a l'action regionale, Investissements etrangers et amenagement du territoire (Paris: Livre blanc, 1974); "Les enterprises multinationales dans le contexte des reglements communautaires", Revue trimestrielle de droit europeen, November-December 1973, Annex II, p. 661.

3. This analysis follows Hans Günter, "Trade Unions and Industrial Policy in Western Europe", in S. J. Warnecke and E. Suleiman (eds.), Industrial Policies in Western Europe (New York: Praeger Publishers, 1975), pp. 93-117.

4. Gerald B. J. Bomers, Multinational Corporations and Industrial Relations: A Comparative Study of West Germany and the Netherlands (Amsterdam: Van Gorkum, Assenn, 1976), p. 27. Bomers refers to a hypothesis made by R. W. Cox, in "Labor and Transnational Relations", in Robert Keohane and Joseph S. Nye (eds.), Transnational Relations and World Politics (Cambridge: Harvard University Press, 1973), p. 217.

5. See, for example, J. van Ginderachter, "Les entreprises multinationales et la politique regionale dans la CEE", Revue des sciences economiques 48 (June 1973), pp. 59-76; Bruno Liebhaberg, Strategies et tactiques syndicales face aux entreprises multinationales (Brussels: Free University of Brussels, Academic Year 1974-75, mimeo.), p. 16; and International Labour Office, Social and Labour Practices of Some European-based Multinational Enterprises in the Metal Trades (Geneva: ILO, 1976), pp. 32-33.

6. Gerd Junne, et al., Die Regionalverteilung ausländischer Investitionen in der Bundesrepublic Deutschland (Konstanz, August 1975 mimeographed), p. 176; Michael Hodges, Multinational Corporations and National Governments: A Case Study of the United Kingdom's Experience, 1964-1970 (Saxon House, 1974), p. 44.

7. For some illustrative evidence, see the 1976 ILO study of the metal trades, op. cit., p. 29.

8. Nigel McCrea, Report on Research Findings Relating to Great Britain (prepared for a meeting of the International Institute for Labour Studies, Geneva, on research findings in the area of multinational corporations and labor, December 1973), IILS/IEME Document No. 4131, p. 6; J. Gennard and M.D. Steuer, "The Industrial Relations of Foreign Subsidiaries in the U.K.," British Journal of Industrial Relations, 9 no. 2 (July 1971), pp. 143-59.

9. ILO study of metal trades, op. cit., p. 18.

10. See R. W. Cox, "Labor and the Multinationals", Foreign Affairs 54, no. 2, (January 1976), pp. 351-352.

11. Lloyd Ulman, "Multinational Unionism: Incentives, Barriers and Alternatives", Industrial Relations, 14, no. 1 (February 1975), pp. 20-27; Bomers, loc. cit., p. 17.

12. Raymond Vernon, "America is Still Ahead", Vision, (June 1973), p. 128. No large-scale transfers are reported in the 1976 ILO study of the metal traders, loc. cit., p. 33.

13. Liebhaberg, loc. cit., p. 20.

14. Bomers, loc. cit., p. 180.

15. Fritz Rath, The Internationalisation of Capitalistic Production and the Labour Movement (paper prepared for the CSE Annual Conference, Coventry, 1976, mimeo.), p. 4.

16. "Courtaulds to Shut at Skelmersdale", The Financial Times, October 28, 1976.

17. "An Industry Fights for its Survival", The Financial Times, October 28, 1976.

18. See, for instance, Hans Joachim Pohl, "Kritik der Drei-Sektoren theorie", Quintessenzen aus der Arbeitsmarkt und Berufsforschung, 1968-1971, (Erlangen: Federal Institute for Labour, 1972), p. 60.

19. Hans Günter, "Erosion of Trade Union Power through Multinational Enterprises?", Vanderbilt Journal of Transnational Law 9, no. 4 (Fall 1976), pp. 771-791.

20. For a further development of the idea of permeability to transnational influences, see Jeffrey Harrod, "Transnational Power", The Year Book of World Affairs, (London, The London Institute of World Affairs 1976, vol. 30), pp. 110-111

21. See, for instance, Malcolm Warner, et al., "The Comparative Measurement of Industrial Relations in Multinational Firms", in

Kurt Tudyka (ed.), Multinational Corporations and Labour Unions (Nijmegen, SUN, 1973), pp. 147-149.

22. Ricardo Peccei and Malcolm Warner, Centralisation and Decentralisation of Industrial Relations Decision in a Large Multi-Plant Business Organisation: An Analysis of Sub-Structural Autonomy, (paper prepared for the European Behavioural Research in Industrial Relations Conference, Milan, April 1976 mimeo.), p. 17; B. C. Roberts and Jonathan May, "The Response of Multinational Enterprises to International Trade Union Pressure", British Journal of Industrial Relations XII, no. 3 November 1974, pp. 403-408; and Bomers, loc. cit., pp. 128, 182.

23. Everett Kassalow, Multinational Corporations and their Impact on Industrial Relations (paper prepared for the International Conference on Trends in Industrial and Labour Relations, Montreal, May 1976, mimeo.), p. 6.

24. Hans Günter, "An Overview of Some Recent Research on Multinational Corporations and Labour", International Institute for Labour Studies Bulletin, no. 12, n.d., p. 42.

25. Some more recent information confirming this view can be found in International Labour Office, Multinationals in Western Europe: The Industrial Relations Experience, (Geneva: ILO, 1976), pp. 10, 32.

26. Organisation internationale des employeurs, "Les enterprises multinationales: leur politique et pratique reelle dans le domaine sociale" (Geneva, The Organization, 1974), p. 16.

27. See, for instance, Gennard and Steuer, loc. cit., pp. 143-59.

28. David Blake, "The Internationalization of Industrial Relations", Journal of International Business Studies (Fall 1972), p. 20.

29. See Yves Delamotte, "The Attitudes of French and Italian Trade Unions to the 'Humanisation' of Work," Labour and Society, 1, no. 1 (January 1976), pp. 49-62.

30. Matteo Rollier, "The Organisation of Work and Industrial Relations in the Italian Engineering Industry," Labour and Society, 1, no. 2 (April 1976), pp. 81-94.

31. John Gennard, "The Impact of Foreign-Owned Subsidiaries on Host Country Labor Relations: The Case of the United Kingdom," in Robert J. Flanagan and Arnold R. Weber (eds.), loc. cit., p. 90.

32. Commission of the European Communities, "Employee Participation and Company Structure" (green paper), Bulletin of European Communities, Supplement 8/75, p. 90.

33. International Labour Office, Multinationals in Western Europe, op. cit., p. 66.

34. Organisation for Economic Co-operation and Development, Press Release A(76), 20, (Paris: OECD, June 21, 1976), p. 7.

35. Gennard, op. cit., p. 77.

36. Kassalow, loc. cit., p. 4.

37. Tom Etty and Kurt P. Tudyka, Konflikte in der Arbeitswelt, (paper prepared for a scientific symposium on the theme of multinational enterprises and interest representation of wage labor, Hannover, October 1-3, 1975), pp. 26, 31-35.

38. For more details see Gunter Kopke, "Union Responses in Continental Europe," in Robert J. Flanagan and Arnold R. Weber (eds.), loc. cit., pp. 203-222.

39. International Confederation of Free Trade Unions, Multinational Charter (the charter of trade union demands for the legislative control of multinational companies, adopted by the 11th ICFTU World Congress, Mexico, October 17-25, 1971), Brussels, November 1975.

40. Commission of the European Communities, "Statute for European Companies: Amended Proposal for a Regulation," Bulletin of the European Communities, April 1975 (Supplement).

41. See in particular K. W. Wedderburn, "Multinational Enterprises and National Labour Law", The Industrial Law Journal, 1, no. 1 (November 1972) pp. 12-19. See also Paul Malles, "The Multinational Corporations and Industrial Relations: The European Approach," Industrial Relations, 26, no. 1 (January 1971), p. 79. For instance, Rath, loc. cit.

43. Günter, "Erosion of Trade Union Power Through Multinational Enterprises?", loc. cit.

44. Rath, loc. cit., p. 10.

45. Bomers, loc. cit., p. 142-43.

46. Carl Gershman, "The Foreign Policy of American Labor," AFL/CIO Free Trade Union News, (April 1976), p. 4.

47. Where they are supported by the employers, see "CBI and TUC List Imports They Feel Should Be Cut," The Financial Times, (October 14, 1976).

PART III

LABOR STANDARDS, COLLECTIVE BARGAINING, AND THE REGULATIONS OF MULTINATIONALS

15

U.S. Labor Standards and Conditions in International Perspective

EVERETT M. KASSALOW

UNIONIZATION AND INDUSTRIAL CONFLICT

Any international comparison of labor standards and practices runs the risk of misinterpretation because of differences between countries in the methods of data collection as well as differences in definitions of occupations, earnings and other labor series.[1] Notwithstanding these limitations, some comparisons are possible and they yield data which can have a significant impact on corporate decisions to invest and trade. The comparisons are also useful in helping to evaluate where the United States stands when comparing key labor standards with other countries.

With some 23 million members the U.S. labor movement is way ahead of any other industrialized market economy country in total trade union membership, as indicated in Table 15.1. The countries closest to the United States in total membership are Japan with 12.6 members, Great Britain with 11.9 million and West Germany with approximately 7.6 million. When trade union density, that is, the percentage of the wage and salary workers who are union members in a country, is calculated, the ranking of countries changes considerably. By this criterion Sweden with a unionization rate of over 80 percent is at the top. (Israel would also show a very high unionization rate, but inasmuch as comparable data for Israel were lacking for a number of the other tables included in this study, union membership data have not been included.) The United States at around 30 percent is next to last, with only France having a lower percentage.

This low rate of unionization in the United States is crucial in both influencing and comparing labor standards. For example, since fringe benefits such as paid vacations and holidays in the private sector in the United States are largely dependent upon union-

TABLE 15.1

Total Union Membership and Percent Unionization of All Wage and Salary Employees (Non-Agricultural) in Selected Industrialized Countries

Country	Trade Union Membership (Approximate, in millions)	Approximate Percentage of Unionization
Australia	2.80	55
Austria	1.60	69
Belgium	2.20	70
Canada	2.90	37
Denmark	1.40	65
Finland	1.30	78
France	3.80	23
Great Britain	12.40	52
Italy	6.00	42
Japan	12.60	35
Netherlands	1.40	39-40
Norway	.86	62-63
Sweden	2.90	82-83
Switzerland	.96	37
United States	22.50	28-29
West Germany	8.80	38-39

Note: Definitions as to what constitutes fully paid up union membership and how to estimate employment vary somewhat among countries, so that very small differences between countries should not be given too much weight. In a few countries there are unions of agricultural workers with moderate size membership, but most of these are quite small. (These unions are included in the membership figures.) Reliable union membership figures for France and Italy comparable to most of the other countries are difficult to compile, and those presented here are rough estimates. For the United States union membership figures include those employee associations, such as the National Education Association, which the U.S. Bureau of Labor Statistics includes in its directory of national unions and employee associations. The union membership data are generally based on 1975 and 1976 reports from various sources.

Source: Compiled by author.

management agreements, the low rate of unionization means that some millions of U.S. workers do not receive such fringe benefits since they are not organized. In Western Europe where rates of unionization are generally higher, the practice of negotiating industry-wide agreements extends benefits to nearly all large and middle size plants and shops as well as many small operations.

It is also common in Western Europe to provide for forms of worker representation at the plant level by legislation, and this offers at least a minimum due process for nearly all wage and salary earners. One of the greatest strengths of the U.S. union movement is its representation power at the plant or shop level, and in this respect it generally exceeds European labor movements. But by the same token, the relatively lower rate of unionization means that millions of U.S. employees enjoy virtually no rights of due process vis-a-vis managements at the work place such as the right to appeal a discharge or downgrading of position to some impartial machinery.

The gap between rate of unionization in the United States and most other OECD countries has widened considerably in the past two decades. The unionization rate in the United States was over 35 percent in the mid-1950s but has declined or stagnated in most years since then. In most European countries the rate of unionization has increased gradually throughout the postwar period. A major reason for the relatively low rate in the United States is employer resistance to unionism, entwined with community resistance in some areas. This resistance is typically much deeper and more widespread in the United States than in most other industrialized countries.* The continental European system in which employers extend union recognition almost automatically by accepting membership in employers' associations, such membership being a virtual necessity in many countries, contrasts sharply with the U.S. system.

Even though U.S. unions devote more effort and resources to organizing than do their European counterparts, U.S. unionization still lags far behind. Employer resistance appears to be the crucial

---

*The Director of Organization of the AFL-CIO calls attention to the drop in the percentage of unionization between 1956 and 1974. Eliminating supervisors and executives from the workforce, he estimates the rate of unionization at 42 percent in 1956 and 32 percent in 1974 (excluding association membership from the union count—if they are included he puts the 1974 unionization figure at "36 percent of the organizable workforce"). See Alan Kistler and Charles McDonald, "The Continuing Challenge of Organizing," AFL-CIO American Federation, 83, no. 11 (November 1976). Kistler also sees fierce employer opposition as the major barrier to unionization in the United States.

TABLE 15.2

Industrial Disputes: International Comparisons among Industrialized Countries
(Days lost per 1,000 people employed)

Country	1965	1967	1970	1972	1973	1974	Average for 5 yrs 1965-1969	Average for 5 yrs 1970-1974	Average for 10 yrs 1965-1974
Australia	410	320	1,040	840	1,030	2,510	482	1,344	913
Belgium	40	90	830	180	500	330	156	512	334
Canada	790	1,200	2,190	1,420	1,650	2,600	1,556	1,732	1,644
Denmark[a]	400	20	170	40	4,020	300	110	912	511
Finland	20	410	270	530	2,500	470	206	1,414	810
France	100	430	180	300	330	250	242[c]	300	274[c]
Ireland	1,720	520	490	600	420	1,260	1,348	688	1,018
Italy	540	580	1,730	1,670	2,470	1,800	1,584	1,746	1,66.5
Japan	360	100	200	270	210	450	198	288	243
Netherlands	30	—	140	70	330	—	12	118	65
New Zealand	50	320	470	300	530	360	242	402	322
Norway	—	10	70	—	10	490	4	116	60
Sweden[b]	—	—	40	10	—	30	28	64	46
Switzerland	—	—	—	—	—	—	—	2	1
United Kingdom	220	220	740	2,160	570	1,270	300	1,186	743
United States	860	1,430	2,210	860	750	1,480	1,230	1,380	1,305
West Germany	—	30	10	—	40	60	10	90	50

[a]Manufacturing only.

[b]All industries included until 1971.

[c]1968 figures not included in percentages.

Note: Where no figure is given the number of days lost per 1,000 employed is less than five.

Source: International Labour Office and Department of Employment Gazette (Great Britain) December, 1975. Data are generally based on manufacturing, construction and transport industries, although local utilities are included in a few countries. Statistical collections vary from country to country and small differences may not be significant. Strikes and lockouts are included.

barrier. This has been vividly demonstrated by the history of the federal government in the past fifteen years. Once the government made it clear it was giving a go-ahead signal to unionization of federal employees (Executive Order 10988 in 1961, and subsequent actions), unionism literally leapt ahead. There is no real reason to believe that U.S. workers are less union prone than their counterparts in Europe, if the path is facilitated.

Employer resistance over many decades has created an industrial relations setting in the United States characterized by conflict. It is paradoxical that in the United States where the trade union movement has generally been willing to accept capitalism, there tends to be a much higher rate of industrial conflict as measured by strikes and lockouts than is true in such European countries as Sweden, Norway, West Germany and Austria where the labor movements are predominantly socialistic and presumably dedicated to replacing capitalism.

Table 15.2 shows that the United States has ranked at or near the top among industrial countries in days lost because of industrial disputes in the past ten years. High levels of industrial conflict represent something of an Anglo-Saxon syndrome, with Australia, Canada, Great Britain and the United States consistently ranking high.

The strong and traditional socialist ties and involvement of some of the Western European union movements, curiously enough, may help account for their lower strike levels. In countries like Sweden, Norway or Austria, where the unions look to legislation to provide many benefits, there are less immediate grounds for labor-management conflict, unlike the United States where health insurance, a large part of workers' pensions, and other important fringe benefits are negotiated as part of collective bargaining agreements. The labor-management stakes thus tend to be higher in collective bargaining in the United States than Europe where some of the potential labor-management conflict is transferred to the political arena.

UNEMPLOYMENT RATES AND COMPENSATION AND PRICE TRENDS

In the past two decades the United States has experienced higher rates of unemployment in comparison to most other industrialized nations (outside of Canada which is linked closely to the U.S. economy). This is true in years of relatively high economic activity such as 1969 and in recession-depression years such as 1976, as Table 15.3 indicates. In 1969 for example, when U.S. unemployment was only 3.5 percent, exceptionally low for the United States, unemployment in Japan, France, West Germany and Sweden was under 2.5 percent. In 1973, a relatively prosperous year in the United States,

TABLE 15.3

Unemployment Rates in Eight Countries, Adjusted to U.S. Concepts, 1969-1976 (percent)

Year	United States	Canada	Japan	France	West Germany	Italy	Sweden	Great Britain
1969	3.5	4.7	1.1	2.4	0.8	3.7	1.9	3.0
1970	4.9	5.7	1.2	2.7	0.5	3.5	1.5	3.0
1971	5.9	6.2	1.3	3.0	0.7	3.5	2.6	3.8
1972	5.6	6.3	1.4	3.0	0.9	4.0	2.7	4.2
1973	4.9	5.6	1.3	2.9	1.0	3.8	2.5	2.9
1974	5.6	5.4	1.4	3.1	2.1	3.1	2.0	2.9
1975	8.5	6.9	1.9	4.3	3.8	3.7	1.6	4.7
1976	7.7	7.1	2.1	4.7	3.8	4.0	1.6	6.4

Source: Bureau of Labor Statistics, U.S. Department of Labor.

TABLE 15.4

Average Annual Rate of Growth in the Civilian Labor Force[a] and Teenage Labor Force Growth, 1960-1974[b] (percent)

Country	Annual Increase in Civilian Labor Force	Annual Growth of Teenage Labor Force
Australia	2.6	0.4
Canada	3.0	4.3
France	1.1	3.4
Italy	0.5	4.0
Japan	1.3	6.0
Sweden	0.8	2.2
United Kingdom	0.2	N.A.
United States	2.0	4.4
West Germany	0.0	2.6

[a]Australia 1964-74, Sweden 1961-74.

[b]These dates vary slightly, country to country.

N.A. = not available

Source: Organization for Economic Cooperation and Development, based on a study prepared by Constance Sorrentino, U.S. Bureau of Labor Statistics.

TABLE 15.5

Females as Percentage of Civilian Labor Force

Country	1960	1970	1974	Female Labor Force, Growth Rate, 1960-1974
Australia	28.5	32.1	34.1	4.4
Canada	25.8	32.1	34.4	5.1
France	36.4	37.9	38.8	1.7
Italy	29.3	27.2	28.0	0.7
Japan	40.2	39.0	37.6	0.7
Sweden	35.2	39.9	42.1	2.3
United Kingdom	35.0	37.6	40.0	1.3
United States	33.4	38.1	39.4	3.1
West Germany	37.5	36.5	36.1	0.2

Source: Organization for Economic Cooperation and Development.

unemployment averaged 4.9 percent, while it was 3.1 percent in Great Britain, 2.5 in Sweden, 1.3 in Japan, 2.9 in France and only 1.0 in West Germany.

Unemployment is a sensitive indicator of worker welfare and standards and therefore an important economic, social and political issue. The relatively high U.S. rate of unemployment has been the subject of a number of studies,[2] though no entirely satisfactory explanation has been provided as yet. However, some additional labor force statistics do shed light on the problem. As Table 15.4 shows, the U.S. labor force has grown more rapidly than has been the case in most other comparable countries. Labor force growth in Canada, the other high unemployment country, has been even higher than the United States. On the other hand, in Australia where labor force growth has also been high, unemployment has been quite low (well below 2 percent, on the average, from 1964 to 1974, although it did rise sharply in 1976).

Further complicating the employment/unemployment problem in the United States has been the high growth rate of the teenage labor force. During the 1960-1974 period, teenage labor force growth in the United States was 4.4 percent annually, compared to the substantial declines recorded in Table 15.4 in France, Italy, West Germany, Japan and Sweden. The teenage group in most countries runs a higher unemployment rate than the rest of the labor force.

TABLE 15.6

Gross National Product Per Capita[a] in Selected Industrialized Countries
(In U.S. dollars)

Country	1955	1960	1965	1970	1971[b]	1972[b]	1973[b]	1974[b]	1975[b,c]
United States	2,407	2,800	3,541	4,794	5,137	5,609	6,209	6,640	7,018
Canada	1,750	2,010	2,450	3,750	4,280	4,700	5,370	6,340	6,750
Japan	270	415	865	1,900	2,450	3,160	3,810	4,110	5,010
European Community	880	1,150	1,680	2,480	3,000	3,520	4,110	4,500	5,100
United Kingdom	1,050	1,350	1,820	2,170	2,620	2,710	3,120	3,380	3,990
France	1,120	1,270	1,910	2,910	3,450	4,210	4,850	5,180	6,360
West Germany	870	1,320	1,900	3,030	3,790	4,630	5,620	6,200	6,610
Italy	500	640	1,100	1,740	2,000	2,250	2,520	2,720	2,940

[a] Current prices.

[b] Based on average monthly rates of exchange.

[c] Estimate.

Source: U.S. Department of Commerce, and International Economic Report of the President.

TABLE 15.7

Consumer Price Changes, 1962-1976
(In Percentages)

Country	Average Annual Change 1962-1972	Changes in Prices			
		1973	1974	1975	1976
Canada	3.3	7.6	10.9	10.8	7.5
U.S.A.	3.3	6.2	11.0	7.0	5.8
Japan	5.7	11.7	24.5	11.8	9.3
France	4.4	7.3	13.7	11.7	9.6
West Germany	3.2	6.9	7.0	6.0	4.5
Italy	4.3	10.8	19.1	17.0	16.5
Great Britain	4.9	9.2	16.0	24.3	16.6
Belgium	3.8	7.0	12.7	12.7	9.4
Netherlands	5.4	8.0	9.6	10.2	8.8
Denmark	6.0	9.3	15.3	9.6	9.0
Austria	3.9	7.6	9.5	10.7	7.3
Norway	5.1	7.5	9.4	11.7	9.1
Sweden	4.7	6.7	10.1	9.7	10.3
Switzerland	4.0	8.7	9.8	6.7	N.A.

Source: Organization for Economic Cooperation and Development, 1962-1975; U.S. Bureau of Labor Statistics, 1976.

N.A. = not available.

Female participation in the labor force has also increased more rapidly in the United States than in most other industrialized countries, and females generally have a higher unemployment rate than do males. From 1960 to 1974, females increased their proportion in the labor force from 33.4 percent to 39.4 percent, a growth rate of 3.1 percent annually. In the same period, as Table 15.5 indicates, the female labor force participation rates were growing only very moderately in France, West Germany, Italy, Japan and United Kingdom, although Sweden, with consistently low unemployment rates, had a higher proportion of females in the labor force than the United States over this entire period.

While the United States has encountered some difficult problems in absorbing new entrants into the labor force, the evidence is by no means sufficient to explain all of the differences in unemployment rates with other industrialized countries. European countries generally have kept unemployment at a lower level by consistently insuring

TABLE 15.8

Unemployment Insurance Systems in Eight Industrialized Nations, Mid 1975

Country	Percent of Labor Force Covered[a]	Required Weeks Employed Preceding Unemployment	Waiting Period (days)	Maximum Duration of Benefits (weeks)
United States	82	b	7	65
Canada	89	8/52[c]	14	51
Japan	45	26/52	7	15-50[d]
France	60	13/52	0	15-104[d]
West Germany	77	26/156	0	52
Great Britain	80	26/52	3[e]	52[e]
Italy	51	52/104	7	26
Sweden[f]	100	20/52	5	60-90[d]

Notes:

[a]Coverage in 1974.

[b]Eligibility requirements vary widely by state.

[c]For minimum benefits, 20 weeks of employment in the preceding year are required for maximum benefits.

[d]Maximum duration for earnings-related benefits depends upon age of claimant, with duration rising with age.

[e]Figures shown relate to flat rate benefits. For earnings-related supplements, waiting period is 14 days and maximum duration of benefits is 26 weeks.

[f]The trade union system covers about two-thirds of the labor force and the labor market support program covers the remainder, including new entrants; other figures are for trade union system.

Source: U.S. Bureau of Labor Statistics.

TABLE 15.9

Unemployment Benefit as a Percent of Average Earnings, Manufacturing Workers in Eight Nations, Mid 1975

Country	Single Worker	Married Worker with 2 Children: Unemployment Benefits	Married Worker with 2 Children: Unemployment Benefits and Family Allowances
United States[a]	50	50	50
Canada	63	63	68
Japan	60	62	62
France			
Regular system			
First 3 months	56	63	69-77[b]
Subsequent months	50	57	63-71[b]
Supplementary benefits system[c]	90	90	96-104[b]
West Germany	60	60	66
Great Britain			
First 6 months[d]	38	60	63
Next 6 months[d]	19	41	44
Italy			
Flat-rate benefits	9	22	22
Earnings-related scheme[e]	67	80	80
Sweden[f]	62-72	62-72	67-79

Notes:

[a]Figures shown are representative of the majority of states.

[b]Lower figures relate to family allowance payable to family with more than 1 wage earner, higher figure includes single wage earner allowance.

[c]For workers under age 60 laid off for cyclical or structural reasons.

[d]Means-tested public assistance payments can substantially raise these ratios.

[e]Industrial sector employee at the same enterprise for 3 months.

[f]Trade union system. Numerical ranges due to trade union funds.

Source: U.S. Bureau of Labor Statistics.

TABLE 15.10

Manufacturing Productivity, Hourly Compensation, and Labor Costs, in Seven Industrial Nations, 1965–1974 (All Employees)

	United States	Canada	France	West Germany	Italy	Japan	Great Britain
1965							
Hourly compensation	100%	68%	42%	37%	37%	15%	36%
Output per man-hour	100	80	56	68	42	26	33
Unit labor cost	100	85	74	55	88	57	107
Hourly compensation in U.S.$	$3.65	$2.45	$1.52	$1.35	$1.34	$0.54	$1.30
1970							
Hourly compensation	100	75	42	46	43	22	33
Output per man-hour	100	88	70	79	49	44	35
Unit labor cost	100	85	60	58	88	51	94
Hourly compensation in U.S.$	$4.96	$3.73	$2.09	$2.26	$2.12	$1.10	$1.65
1973							
Hourly compensation	100	82	62	75	66	41	42
Output per man-hour	100	85	70	79	52	49	35
Unit labor cost	100	96	88	95	126	84	120
Hourly compensation in U.S.$	$5.97	$4.91	$3.70	$4.49	$3.93	$2.43	$2.49
1974 (preliminary estimates)							
Hourly compensation	100	86	61	80	67	46	42
Output per man-hour	100	87	73	82	53	51	35
Unit labor cost	100	99	83	99	126	91	122
Hourly compensation in U.S.$	$6.53	$5.64	$3.96	$5.25	$4.35	$3.01	$2.77

Notes: National-currency data on compensation were converted into U.S. dollars at the New York Federal Reserve Bank's average noon buying rates for each of the years shown. Output levels were derived from estimated gross product originating in manufacturing at factor cost, in 1970 prices: in this case, conversion into U.S. dollars was made at constant 1974 exchange rates. All percentages rounded. Covers all employees, including white-collar workers.

Source: First National City Bank, Monthly Economic Letter, April, 1975.

strong levels of demand (at least until the 1974-1975 recession) and by discouraging employers from casual and short-term layoffs.

In contrast to its characteristically higher rate of unemployment (Table 15.3) and lower rate of gross national product growth (Table 15.6), the United States has recorded consistently slower changes in consumer prices than most of the other industrialized market countries, as shown in Table 15.7. From 1962 to 1972, for example, consumer price changes in the United States averaged 3.3 percent per year, while in most West European nations, as well as Japan, these prices increased 4, 5 and even 6 percent annually. This better price performance may have reflected some natural advantages the United States enjoys (its GNP is less dependent on world trade flows), but it also doubtless reflects the greater tendency in the United States to choose price stability over growth, with resulting higher unemployment, when there is a danger of inflation.

It has become fashionable in some circles to lay the blame for high U.S. unemployment rates on our unemployment benefit system which, according to these critics, encourages higher unemployment than in other countries. Tables 15.8 and 15.9 indicate that there is not much to choose in terms of generosity of unemployment benefits or coverage of labor force when the United States is compared, for example, with West Germany and Sweden, two highly industrialized countries which have had unemployment records very superior to that of the United States in most years.

The U.S. unemployment insurance system covers 82 percent of the work force compared to 77 percent in West Germany and 100 percent in Sweden. Unemployment benefits for a single worker average around 50 percent of average earnings in the United States, and 60 percent and 62-72 percent in Germany and Sweden respectively. For married workers the U.S. unemployment compensation benefits tend to be lower than in most West European countries. With provision of a maximum duration of 65 weeks of benefits, the U.S. system is comparatively generous. But the French system allows from 52 to 104 weeks, and the Swedish system, from 60 to 90 weeks depending upon the age of the claimant.[3]

HOURLY COMPENSATION AND LABOR COSTS

During the past ten to fifteen years workers in other industrialized countries closed the gap in hourly compensation (direct wages plus employer-paid fringe benefits) between themselves and U.S. workers, but the United States wage earner in manufacturing is still at or near the top. Table 15.10 shows that as recently as 1965 hourly compensation for West German or French employees in manufacturing was

TABLE 15.11

Hourly Compensation Per Man-Hour for Production and Maintenance Workers in Manufacturing Industries, Mid 1975
(Includes cost of fringes, social security taxes paid by employer, etc., adjusted to 1975 exchange rates)

Country	All Manufacturing	Primary Metals	Motor Vehicles and Parts	Chemicals	Electrical Equipment	Textile Mill Products	Apparel
United States	$6.22	$8.60	$9.29	$7.15	$6.14	$4.09	$3.88
Sweden	7.12	8.01	7.24	7.05	6.78	6.31	5.67
West Germany	6.19	6.75	7.94	6.94	5.82	5.10	4.56
Canada	6.20	7.27	7.76	6.61	5.75	4.39	3.85
Great Britain	3.20	3.63	3.77	3.72	3.05	2.78	2.03
France	4.57	5.20	4.92	5.38	4.34	3.88	3.30
Italy	4.52	5.63	4.99	5.44	4.36	4.01	3.38
Japan	3.10	4.57	3.61	4.23	2.79	2.09	1.59
Belgium	6.46	N.A.	N.A.	N.A.	N.A.	N.A.	N.A.
Netherlands	5.98	N.A.	N.A.	N.A.	N.A.	N.A.	N.A.

Notes: N.A. = Not Available.

Production workers include production and maintenance (generally all manual or blue collar) but not white collar workers.

Source: U.S. Bureau of Labor Statistics.

TABLE 15.12

Ratios of Hourly Compensation, Production Workers in All Manufacturing, Motor Vehicles, Primary Metals, Textiles and Apparel, Mid-1975
(In percent)

Country	All Manufacturing	Motor Vehicles	Primary Metals	Textiles	Apparel
United States	100	149	138	66	62
Sweden	100	102	113	89	80
West Germany	100	128	109	82	74
Canada	100	125	117	71	62
Great Britain	100	118	113	87	63
France	100	108	114	85	72
Italy	100	110	125	89	75
Japan	100	116	147	67	51

Source: U.S. Bureau of Labor Statistics.

only 37 percent and 42 percent of U.S. levels, but by 1974 these ratios stood at 80 and 61 percent respectively. Other countries also gained on the United States, but were still well behind in 1974.

Of critical importance in any international comparison of employee compensation expenses are productivity and unit labor cost trends, since these are what many companies compare when making plant location and production decisions. Table 15.7 reveals how much the West European-U.S. gap in unit labor costs has closed in the past decade.

A recent survey by the U.S. Bureau of Labor Statistics compares productivity in manufacturing between the United States and two of its important industrial trading partners, Canada and Japan. Tentative results put Canadian manufacturing output per hour at from 76 to 81 percent of the U.S. level and Japanese output at from 65 to 76 percent of the United States. But in some industries such as basic steel, Japanese productivity is ahead of that in the United States.[4] When that is coupled with the much lower compensation rates in Japan, it is easy to see why a number of U.S. unions feel the competitive pressure of Japanese manufactured goods so keenly.

Despite further compensation gains by most other countries in 1975, the United States still remained at or near the top for all manufacturing industry production and maintenance workers, as Table 15.11 shows. But the West German production worker was close to

TABLE 15.13

Comparing Purchasing Power: Work Time Required to Purchase Selected Products in Eight Countries

Product	Austria	West Germany	France	Great Britain	Sweden	Switzerland	U.S.A.	Japan
Automobile	27 weeks	22 weeks	35 weeks	29 weeks	31 weeks	26 weeks	19 weeks	19 weeks
Washing machine	190 hr	95 hr	173 hr	100 hr	109 hr	141 hr	58 hr	54 hr
Television (black and white)	82 hr	60 hr	122 hr	72 hr	63 hr	88 hr	29 hr	39 hr
Man's suit	35 hr	30 hr	52 hr	32 hr	27.5 hr	33.5 hr	18.5 hr	49.5 hr
Man's shoes	6.5 hr	8 hr	12 hr	8 hr	8 hr	9 hr	6 hr	10 hr
Cleaning	91 min	58 min	2 hr	50 min	1.5 hr	1.5 hr	28 min	47 min
0.7 litre of whisky	2.5 hr	1.5 hr	3 hr	3 hr	3.5 hr	2.5 hr	1 hr	3.5 hr
6 bottles of beer	34 min	28 min	30 min	32 min	36 min	30 min	20 min	46 min
1 package of cigarettes	13 min	14 min	11 min	18 min	21 min	10 min	7 min	6 min
½ kg of butter	32 min	24 min	39 min	16 min	18 min	32 min	12 min	34 min
12 eggs	24 min	18 min	26 min	19 min	16 min	17 min	9 min	18 min
1 litre of milk	6 min	6 min	8 min	6 min	4 min	6 min	5 min	12 min
5 kg potatoes	21 min	16 min	26 min	36 min	30 min	18 min	25 min	40 min
½ kg bread	4.5 min	6 min	8 min	8 min	8 min	6 min	5 min	8 min

Source: Trend (Austria, 1976). This survey concludes that the U.S. workers' purchasing power is 30 percent greater than in the other countries.

the U.S. worker, while hourly compensation for manufacturing production workers in Belgium and Sweden actually exceeded that in the United States by mid-1975. In specific industries such as motor vehicles and primary metals, the U.S. worker was way in advance of other countries. At the other end of the manufacturing spectrum, the hourly compensation of U.S. textile and apparel workers trailed Sweden and West Germany and were not too much ahead of France and Italy.

Generally speaking the spread between high compensation industries (motor vehicles and basic metals) and lower paying manufacturing industries such as textiles was greater in the United States than West European countries, as shown in Table 15.12. Thus, primary metals stand at 138 percent and textiles at 66 percent of the all-manufacturing figure in mid-1975 for the United States while in Sweden, the ratios were 113 percent for primary metals and 89 percent for textiles.

The higher general levels of unionization and the broad systems of negotiating for entire industries have had the tendency in Western Europe to narrow the gap in industry wage levels. The deliberate policy of the Swedish Federation of Labor (LO) in seeking to reduce differentials (the so-called solidarity wage policy) helps account for the fairly narrow range between low and higher paid industries in that country.[5]

FACTORS AFFECTING LIVING STANDARDS AND THE QUALITY OF LIFE OF WORKERS

When it comes to comparing workers' actual living standards, virtually all comparisons tend to put the United States in a favorable light. An Austrian study reported in Table 15.13 takes twelve important consumption items in eight industrialized countries and concludes that on the basis of the working time necessary to purchase these goods, the American worker enjoys a 30 percent advantage over his counterparts. The purchase of an automobile, for example, takes 19 weeks of work in the United States, 35 weeks in France, and 22 weeks in West Germany.

Income and other direct taxes generally take a larger bite of European workers' pay as compared to the United States, as Table 15.14 indicates. When an average married worker in the United States receives a 10 percent wage increase, he will pay out 28 percent of that increase for new taxes. A British worker would pay 34 percent, a Norwegian 42 percent and a Swede as much as 62 percent of the increase in taxes. But tax rates are lower in several other countries such as France and Japan.

TABLE 15.14

Rate of Taxation of Ten Percent Salary Increase
in Selected Industrialized Countries
(Percentage of increase paid in taxes)

Country	Single Worker	Married Worker with 2 Children
West Germany	38	26
Australia	35	33
Austria	35	23
Belgium	29	24
Canada	29	27
Denmark	61	54
United States	34	28
Finland	45	38
France	21	14
Greece	15	13
Ireland	26	26
Italy	24	23
Japan	21	18
Luxembourg	39	24
Norway	47	42
Netherlands	43	35
New Zealand	32	31
Great Britain	35	34
Sweden	62	62
Switzerland	28	28

Source: Organization for Economic Cooperation and Development, 1974-75.

While high rates of taxation concern all wage earners, the distribution of the revenue collected also helps determine levels of living and welfare of workers. In the social security expenditures reported in Table 15.15, the United States lags behind most other industrialized countries. Lower social security outlays help account for less comprehensive health, pension and temporary disability benefits in the United States when compared to Western Europe. To some extent employer payments for private company pension and health and disability insurance plans fill a part of this gap.

TABLE 15.15

Social Security Expenditures as Percentage of Gross National Product, 1967 and 1971

Country	1967	1971
Belgium	18.22%	18.33%
Canada	12.86	18.61
France	19.84	18.65
West Germany	19.43	18.73
Japan	5.57	5.93
Netherlands	19.05	21.75
Sweden	16.27	21.75
Great Britain	13.72	12.45
U.S.A.	8.47	10.81

Source: U.S. Social Security Administration and International Labour Office, 1974.

It is difficult to determine national patterns of paid vacation and holiday benefits for employees in the private sector in the United States, since these vary with collective agreements or unilateral action by individual employers. Such evidence, as we have, suggests that these benefits are generally lower than most European countries except Japan and perhaps Great Britain.

In continental Western Europe the four-week paid vacation for every employee with a year's service has become the general standard (with several countries now moving to five weeks), as Table 15.16 shows, and it is usually established by legislation which covers the entire work force. For the United States one can roughly estimate that where employees enjoy paid vacations these average close to two and a half weeks.[6] For many years the United States was the leader insofar as the adoption of the 40-hour work week is concerned, but as Table 15.16 also shows, most West European countries have now realized the regular 40-hour work week, although in a few of them actual practice includes the regular scheduling of overtime hours in a number of industries.

It is also difficult to compare factors affecting the quality of workers' lives such as job security. Yet it appears that U.S. workers suffer from employers' attitudes toward short term layoffs. Trimming payrolls for several weeks to handle inventory excesses is typical in many large U.S. manufacturing corporations but much less known in

TABLE 15.16

Standard Hours of Work, Paid Vacations and Paid Holidays in Eleven Industrial Nations
(Data based on a 1972 OECD survey, but many revisions have been made where later data could be found or estimated.)

Country	Work Week**	Annual Paid Vacations	Paid Holidays
France	44	4 weeks*	8-10*
Japan	40-44	6 days	10
Netherlands	40	16-17 days*	7*
Belgium	40	4 weeks*	10*
Norway	40	4 weeks*	10*
Austria	40	4-5 weeks*	10*
Italy	40	3 weeks	17
Great Britain	40	2-3 weeks	6
Denmark	40	4 weeks*	9*
Sweden	40	4-5 weeks*	9-11*
West Germany	40	4-5 weeks*	10-13*

*Largely provided by legislation. Workers with one year of service receive these benefits. Those who work less than this usually receive pro-rata benefits. Vacations in the U.S.A. are difficult to estimate. In the private sector they often depend on collective agreements (union-management contracts), and thus vary widely. They also vary widely with workers' seniority, under these agreements. A substantial number of U.S. workers in private industry not covered by collective agreements may earn no paid vacations at all.

**These work week figures must be used with caution, inasmuch as in a number of European countries, as, for example, Great Britain or France, overtime is regularly scheduled, and the work week regularly exceeds 40 hours by several hours.

Western Europe. Legislation also places greater restrictions on employers' layoff practices in Western Europe.

The broader coverage of social security systems, including health insurance, may also provide a greater security network for European workers and their families. On the other hand, the more open character of U.S. society, compared to most West European countries, including wider educational opportunities, cannot be overlooked when comparing living standards and quality of life.

INTERNATIONAL INFLUENCES ON LABOR STANDARDS

It has been the fashion in the past to minimize the influence of international forces and agencies on labor standards.[7] Of course a country's labor system will reflect its own basic social, economic and political conditions. But in many countries today, especially in the developing world, labor systems also show the influence of a number of extranational forces. Included are the International Labour Office, the international union movements, bilateral country relationships, the multinational corporation and other transnational forces. These forces have been discussed extensively elsewhere in this volume; the following comments deal with aspects not covered elsewhere.

Bilateral forces acting on labor standards involve situations in which one country's labor institutions influence another's by virtue of the former's colonial administration or through more recent economic aid programs. The most pervasive of these influences are found in the former British and French colonies in Africa and Asia. Most ex-French colonies today have labor systems structured around tripartite national arrangements in which commissions representing government, employers and unions establish broad norms for wages and conditions, such as was the case in France in the decade after World War II. Collective bargaining as it is known in the United States is a relatively rare phenomenon.

On the other hand, innumerable examples of collective bargaining and union-management agreements are found in ex-British colonies in Asia, Africa and the Caribbean area. When one considers the modest levels of economic development in these countries, the level of union-management relations in many industries is striking.

Comparable effects exist in countries with close U.S. association in the postwar period, such as the Philippines, Turkey, South Korea, and Japan.[8] The active union-management system at the enterprise level with its emphasis on bargaining for economic benefits in Japan, for example, could hardly have come about without the enormous influence of the U.S. Occupation after World War II.

The impact of these influences becomes evident in looking comparatively at the situation in Latin America. Union movements are far more politically colored and syndicalistic in character, reflecting the Latin heritage of these countries. While large politically, U.S. influence in the field has been small. The prevailing styles of labor relations in Latin America and Francophone Africa are a reminder of how relatively exotic collective bargaining Anglo-American style is.

The impact on developing countries of more recent bilateral activities such as the various regional labor institutes conducted by AFL-CIO with substantial assistance from the U.S. government's economic aid program or the work of the West German Friedrich Ebert Foundation of the German Federation of Trade Unions (DGB) are harder to estimate. But it should be emphasized that these countries are devising their own labor systems, in which bilateral foreign influences play a marginal rather than central role.

Much more pervasive in its impact on developing countries has been the International Labour Office. The ILO Conventions 87 ("Freedom of Association and Protection of the Right to Organise") and 98 ("Right to Organise and to Bargain Collectively") set the basic pattern for labor relations in many countries achieving independence after World War II. (The language and tone of these conventions reflect to a considerable extent Anglo-American conceptions of labor relations. ILO Convention 87, adopted in 1948, has some uniquely American phrases from the unionizing period of the 1930s as it speaks of employees' rights "to join unions of their own choosing.") The impact of these and other ILO conventions was reinforced by ILO's extensive role in the 1950s and 1960s in helping new countries in writing their labor-relations, safety and social security laws which generally reflected Western conceptions of labor administration.

Although the ILO's ability to influence totalitarian and authoritarian governments is small, it continues to be an important force in those countries which still have even "some" aspects of a free labor system. The ILO's own staff system of reviewing member countries' labor practices to determine if these conform to important ILO conventions reinforces the struggle to advance free labor principles in the world. This system, aided by a panel of outside, high level experts, is still regarded as one of the organization's best operations. Another notable ILO achievement in the late sixties involved helping to reorient the thinking about economic development in most of the world's international agencies and in many developing countries toward giving higher priority to job creation and better income distribution.[9]

The U.S. government and the AFL-CIO have been weighing their own future relationships to ILO in light of excessive politicalization of many of the organization's meetings and threats to its tripartite structure. As they make their reconsideration, one must hope that they will also think about improving their own effectiveness in ILO's work. The lack of sufficient U.S. attention and input of resources has led to missed opportunities to improve the work of the ILO in recent years.

Hardly any country can make a serious move against its own unions today without being subjected to considerable public relations pressures from the ICFTU, the WCL and, albeit more selectively, the WFTU. Even in their somewhat weakened present condition international trade unions compare favorably with their pre-World

War II precursors in influence. The ICFTU, for instance, played a significant role in assisting many of the African labor movements and nations in ending colonial rule in the decades following World War II. When it works effectively, the ICFTU can still fill a major role in mobilizing pressure within the ILO on behalf of beleaguered workers in many countries. Such was the case recently on behalf of oppressed workers in Chile, and a few years ago, in South Africa.

While the power of international union organizations like the ICFTU has waned somewhat in the past decade, the ITSs have tended to increase in importance. The growth in the secretariats can be explained, in part, by the great emphasis now placed upon the industrial actions of trade unions in so many countries. The ITSs have also generally been more able to steer clear of the political controversies plaguing other international union bodies like the ICFTU. This has strengthened their economic and labor relations activities and also enabled most of them to retain many American union affiliates, with resulting financial and organizational strength. The growing importance of the MNC in world labor relations has also given added significance to the work of some of the secretariats.

Despite its enlarged role, an ITS today may still find that its ties to a particular national union affiliate and country are very slender. In democratic industrialized countries the services some ITSs can render to strong national unions may not be many. Much of the concern for ITS relationships with that country may lie in the hands of a very small number of the top officers and staff of one national affiliate. To say the least, this can be a vulnerable situation for an ITS.

In the countries of Western Europe, where labor relations systems, unions and employers' associations have long been established, the enormous expansion of multinational companies in the postwar period has had only limited impact. In their labor practices these companies have been compelled to conform, for the most part, to the national labor systems. This has been especially true in a country like Germany where so much of labor practice is laid down by law, or in Sweden where the strength of the labor unions and the employers' associations is so great that even powerful multinationals must adapt to local labor practices. In a country such as England, however, where the labor system is more "voluntary" in character, U.S. multinationals have had some influence by bringing their own practices and wage systems, particularly in industries like automobiles where U.S. producers play such a large role. Moreover, a few companies like IBM or Texas Instruments have attempted to export their U.S. policies of nonrecognition of unions to several West European countries. The French tire producer Michelin has also exported its anti-union policies from North America.[10]

When they move to less developed countries, especially in Asia and Africa, the multinationals can have even a wider influence. Here they are often large islands of modern labor practice, and their introduction of personnel practices such as pretesting for hiring, job evaluation, some company fringe benefit programs, company training, counselling and human relations programs may serve as something of a model, over a period of time, for less experienced local entrepreneurs. In several Asian countries unions have indicated that it usually is easier to obtain recognition from most multinational subsidiaries than it is from local enterprises.* On the other hand in Latin America some multinationals have bitterly resisted and fought union recognition, and in South Africa their record in dealing with black workers has been poor.

The spread of the MNC has led to a direct response from the trade union secretariats. The ITSs have established worldwide company councils to bring together unions from multinational subsidiaries across the world, to exchange information, and to support one another dealing with these companies. A few multinationals have even come to accept the ITS' call for union-company meetings on an inter-country basis. Such meetings have usually been limited to consultation rather than negotiations, but the transnationalizing influence of multinationals on labor standards is likely to be considerable in years to come.

The EC (the Common Market) has had some far-reaching, transnationalizing effects on labor standards within its member countries. During its earlier years, the EC exercised an upward levelling influence on social security standards. For a decade and more, wage levels, too, tended to draw closer together, but fluctuations in exchange rates, differences in inflation and varying economic growth rates in recent years seem to have brought that wage levelling to a halt. EC influence has also been felt in such areas as workers' participation in management, with much of the impetus coming from the DGB and the German system of codetermination (equal representation for workers and shareholders on the top management supervisory board) in the coal and steel industry.[11]

The EC has drafted a program to help control multinational company development in its member countries, including protection of "employees in the case of the take-over of companies."[12] The OECD has also been active in trying to set guidelines for multinational companies, including labor relations.[13]

---

*I have dealt with the impact of multinational companies on labor systems in selected Asian countries in a study which will appear in the <u>International Labour Review</u> in 1978.

Finally, mention should also be made of U.S. efforts to develop a system of international fair labor standards in world trade. Largely under the pressure of the AFL-CIO (aided, at times by the International Metalworkers' Federation), proposals have been made to insert into GATT—as well as in our own trade negotiations—conditions to upgrade labor standards of products entering into world trade. The Trade Act of 1974 instructs the President to take action to bring about "the adoption of international fair labor standards" as well as to enforce such standards by inserting "procedures in the GATT."[14]

Some of the transnational influences on labor standards have been exercised with conscious purpose, while others have come as incidental to other developments. All of these influences have been enhanced in the decades following World War II by the enormous expansion of world trade and investment. Unless there is a very sharp reversal in the flows of international trade and investment, transnational forces operating on labor standards are likely to become even more important in the years ahead.

NOTES

1. See for example Malcolm Fisher, Measurement of Labour Disputes and Their Economic Effects (Paris: Organisation for Economic Co-operation and Development, 1973), especially appendix to Chap. 2.

2. One of the most recent, and in some ways the most useful, is that by Constance Sorrentino of the U.S. Bureau of Labor Statistics (Paris: 1975, Dec. 8, mimeographed), "Methodological and Conceptual Problems of Measuring Unemployment in O.E.C.D. Countries" (Paris: Organisation for Economic Co-operation and Development, December 1975, mimeo.).

3. See Constance Sorrentino, "Unemployment Compensation in Eight Industrial Nations," Monthly Labor Review, July 1976.

4. See Jerome A. Mark, Comparative Growth in Manufacturing and Labor Costs in Selected Industrialized Countries, (mimeographed), (prepared for the European Association of National Productivity Centers Workshop on Recent Progress in Productivity Measurement and Prospects, Copenhagen, October 27, 1976, mimeo.), especially pp. 19, 21. The range in figures presented for each of these countries is explained by differences which result from using U.S. price weights on the one hand (these yield the higher figures in both cases) or Canadian or Japanese price weights on the other.

5. For interesting data on the effects of the LO's solidarity wage policy in narrowing differentials between men and women, skilled and unskilled workers, and low and high wage industries see

Rudolph Meidner, Co-Ordination and Solidarity: An Approach to Wages Policy (Stockholm: 1974, LO and Prisma Publishers).

6. See scattered data in U.S. Bureau of Labor Statistics, Employee Compensation in the Private Non-farm Economy (Washington, D.C.: U.S. Government Printing Office, 1975), Bulletin 1873, p. 16, Table 7; ibid., Characteristics of Major Collective Bargaining Agreements, July 1, 1974 (Washington, D.C.: U.S. Government Printing Office, 1975), Bulletin 1888, p. 58, Table 5.4 and p. 60, Table 5.6. Some European data are given in an Organisation for Economic Co-operation and Development survey in 1972.

7. For early discussions of this question of "foreign influences" on new countries' labor systems see Charles A. Myers, "The American System of Industrial Relations: Is it Exportable?" in Industrial Relations Research Association (IRRA), Proceedings of the Fifteenth Annual Meeting (Pittsburgh, December 1962), pp. 2, 14, and the papers by John P. Windmuller, S. Kannappan and Elliot J. Berg on the influence of model industrial relations systems, in IRRA, Proceedings of the Sixteenth Annual Meeting (Boston, December 1963), pp. 60-101.

8. U.S. influence on labor in the Philippines and Turkey is discussed in David Wurfel, "Trade Union Development and Labor Relations Policy in the Philippines," Industrial and Labor Relations Review, 12, no. 4 (July 1959), and Bruce Millen, "Factions of the Turkish Labor Movement Differ on Political Role," Monthly Labor Review, June, 1969.

9. See International Labour Office, The World Employment Programme, Report of the Director General to the International Labour Conference, 1969 (Geneva: ILO). Some of the subsequent ILO work on this program has been more controversial and, as yet at least, less influential on development theory and planning.

10. For more detailed description, see the monograph which I prepared for the ILO, entitled Multinationals in Western Europe: The Industrial Relations Experience (Geneva: ILO, 1976), and "Multinational Corporations and Their Impact on Industrial Relations," The Labour Gazette (Canada Department of Labour), 76, no. 11 (November 1976).

11. See "Employee Participation and Company Structure," Bulletin of the European Communities (August, 1975).

12. See Commission of the European Economic Communities, Protection of Workers in the Event of Individual Dismissals in the Member States of the European Communities (Proposed Report of the Commission to the Council of Ministers, 1975). On multinationals and the EC, see "Multinational Undertakings and the Community," Bulletin of the European Economic Communities, no. 15 (1973), p. 17. This same bulletin also sees the need for a "trade union counterweight" to offset some of the power of multinational companies (p. 10).

13. Organisation for Economic Cooperation and Development, _International Investment and Multinational Enterprises_ (Paris: OECD, 1976), pp. 16-17.

14. _Public Law 93-618, 93rd Congress, H.R. 10710, January 3, 1975_. See 121, p. 9.

16

An International Approach to Labor Standards

HERIBERT MAIER

THE CONTINUING NEED FOR INTERNATIONAL LABOR STANDARDS

Labor standards, whether introduced by international trade union organizations or bodies such as the ILO, are intended to harmonize the economic and social conditions of workers in different countries in order to prevent one or more countries from gaining an unfair competitive position over the others. They are sometimes intended to establish minimum conditions for labor legislation, labor contracts or collective bargaining agreements. At other times they are intended to set goals that legislators and trade union negotiators should strive to fulfil. In the case of multinational companies the international trade union movement has set its own labor standards to prevent companies from exploiting international labor cost differentials.

International labor standards adopted by the ILO become legally binding on ratification by national governments and are then subject to international supervision by a tripartite body. Standards proposed by the international trade union movement will not normally become legally binding except when they are incorporated in national legislation by democratic processes or where they are part of labor contracts or collective bargaining agreements. They can only be effectively implemented by the actions of affiliated national trade unions. A prerequisite for the effectiveness of these actions is full respect for trade union and other basic human rights.

The International Working Men's Association, at its first meeting 110 years ago, formulated the principles that underlie the standard-setting efforts of the free international trade union movement today. The AFL's Congress in Philadelphia, 62 years ago, adopted a resolution calling for ". . . a meeting of representatives of organized labor of the different nations to meet at the same time and place" as the general Peace Congress to be held at the end of World War I. The result was the Commission on International Labour Legislation, which, under the chairmanship of AFL President Samuel Gompers, established the International Labour Office in 1919.

In 1919 one of the main preoccupations of the unions in the industrialized countries was to insure freedom of association and, in particular, the "right to organize" which due to the exigencies of war had been threatened in some countries and had never been fully accepted in others. Another of their principal goals was the introduction of the 48-hour week without which it would be difficult to maintain employment in a situation characterized by rapid technological change and increased participation by women in the work-force brought about by the war. It would obviously be difficult to convince either governments or businessmen in any country to agree to reduce working hours unless their main competitors agreed to take similar measures.

International trade union solidarity combined with motives of national self-interest made it imperative for trade unions everywhere to work toward a system of internationally binding labor standards, but the underlying issues were much broader. They are well expressed in the preamble to the constitution of the ILO.

> . . . whereas conditions of labour exist involving such injustice, hardship and privation to large numbers of people as to produce unrest so great that the peace and harmony of the world are imperilled; and an improvement of those conditions is urgently required: as, for example, by the regulation of the hours of work, including the establishment of a maximum working day and week, the regulation of the labour supply, the prevention of unemployment, the provision of an adequate living wage, the protection of the worker against sickness, disease and injury arising out of his employment, the protection of children, young persons and women, provision for old age and injury, protection of the interests of workers when employed in countries other than their own, recognition of the principle of equal remuneration for work of equal value, recognition of the principle of freedom of association, the organisation of vocational and technical education and other measures; . . .

Some of the problems mentioned in the preamble have since been solved in a large number of countries, but the solutions to others—for example, the principle of equal remuneration for work of equal value, the problems of migrant workers, unemployment and even recognition of the principle of freedom of association—are still unresolved in many countries. Hence the situation today is not markedly different from the situation after the First World War. The dimensions of the problems have changed, but the need for international labor standards is as strong as ever. Political, social and economic developments, including the consequences of the rapid growth of new technologies and the greatly increased number of nation states in the world today, have changed the priority areas. But a change of emphasis does not imply a change of principle.

It has been argued that under present world conditions many serious problems cannot be solved through the standard-setting activities of intergovernmental organizations as presently constituted. In the field of labor standards, even the tripartite structure of the ILO is unable to cope effectively with many burning problems posed by multinational enterprises, totalitarian regimes and outdated economic policies. This, however, does not absolve the trade union movement from the duty of using these organizations to the greatest possible extent to make union views widely known at the international level.

Nor does it mean that the free and democratic international trade union organizations should not be engaged in drawing up better and more comprehensive labor standards than the ILO. The International Federation of Commercial, Clerical and Technical Employees (FIET) is in fact doing just that in the belief that our ideas about the problems today will provide the basis for their solution tomorrow. I believe that the international trade union secretariats, whose membership covers trade unions in countries at all stages of development, have a more sensitive finger on the pulse of international labor problems than most other types of bodies. They are therefore among the best qualified to determine the effectiveness of international labor standards, particularly in the fields of development, multinational enterprises and protection of trade union rights, which are all problems concerning both trade unions and the tripartite ILO.

The FIET World Action Program, for example, lays down basic standards for all of our six million members in all parts of the world. These standards, which were adopted by the FIET World Congress in Helsinki in August 1976, are based on regional demands elaborated during the previous three years by FIET's regional structures for Europe, Asia, Africa and North and South America. By combining these regionally elaborated demands into a world program, we have given an example of the contribution decentralized trade union work can make to the setting of universally applicable standards.

STANDARD SETTING AND TECHNICAL ASSISTANCE BY THE ILO

The ILO through its regional structures must continue to follow a similar approach, since regional or double ILO standards would certainly destroy thc organization. The tripartite structure of the ILO (governments, employers and workers) is another element of strength in the setting of realistic standards. The first Director General of the ILO, Albert Thomas, once likened the ILO's tripartite structure to an automobile in which the trade unions had their foot on the accelerator, the employers had their hand on the brake and the governments had to keep the car on the road.

Unfortunately, the ILO has experienced some difficulties in synchronizing these three essential control organs over particular stretches of road in the last two decades. There are several reasons why this state of affairs has been brought about. Sometimes it has been due to a confusion of roles by members of the workers', employers' and government groups who have put regional or similar concerns before adherence to the traditional tripartite group structure of the organization.

This tendency has been particularly marked when attempts have been made to treat the ILO's "new" technical cooperation activities as something quite separate from the organization's so-called "traditional" activities, especially standard setting. It is understandable that developing countries are interested in receiving as much technical assistance as possible. But it is both unrealistic and counterproductive to suggest that technical assistance can be increased by cutting back on the ILO's work in the field of labor standards. The two types of activity cannot be divided. The object of technical cooperation should be to help lay the foundation on which higher social standards can be built. Alternatively, technical cooperation projects can directly or indirectly help implement international labor standards in specific countries or regions.

In the early history of the ILO we find examples of technical assistance being closely linked with labor standards in countries which in some cases were economically poles apart. In 1930, for example, Greece asked for and received advice on a social insurance scheme, and in 1936 the United States received technical assistance in the field of social security.

Today, the ILO has adopted some 300 conventions and recommendations. There is hardly a technical cooperation project in a developing country which does not in some way owe its existence to an international labor standard. It is, unfortunately, also a fact that not all technical cooperation projects are linked to the implementation of these same standards.

We in the trade union movement know that the line between the economic necessity often pleaded in these cases and the political expediency which too often seems to be the underlying motive is very fine. It is discouraging to note that a growing number of countries want to "modernize" the ILO by turning it into yet another international agency for dispensing aid at the expense of its standard-setting activities. It is even more discouraging that these same countries often appear to be the least concerned with implementing the principles expressed in the ILO constitution and the Declaration of Philadelphia, particularly the proposition in the former that "freedom of expression and of association are essential to sustained progress."

This is no new problem. But it has been intensified since Omar Becu, the former General Secretary of the ICFTU stated at the 1966 International Labour Conference that "if the ILO ever attempted to adjust its structure and activities to conditions as they exist in certain Member countries ruled by totalitarian regimes, which completely neglect the foundation upon which the ILO has been built—its tripartite structure and principles such as freedom of association—this oldest organisation in the family of the UN would fail to live up to its objectives and purposes, for the achievement of which it had been created." Ten years later, in 1976, trade union representatives at the ILO still maintain this position.

PROBLEMS IN FORMULATION AND ACCEPTANCE OF ILO STANDARDS

ILO labor standards are certainly not always ideal from a trade union point of view. From the very first preparatory stages of an ILO convention or recommendation through the discussions in the International Labour Conference committees, the tripartite structure of the ILO turns them into negotiated compromise solutions. Often—some trade unionists will say "too often"—the final text which must be adopted by a two-thirds majority vote by the Conference Plenary Session, represents the lowest common denominator of possible agreement. On top of this there are no guarantees that a convention will be ratified or a recommendation implemented by Member States, and even when an instrument is endorsed there are often certain clauses which allow for the standards not to be applied at once or to be applied in stages.

The ILO's machinery for supervision of its labor standards, furthermore, is not a particularly efficient method of enforcement, to say the least. The system introduced under Article 19 of the Standing Orders in 1948, which gave the Governing Body of the ILO powers to require governments to report on the legal position and actual practice concerning unratified conventions, was diluted recently for reasons of economy. Governments are allowed quite a lot of leeway when it comes to actually applying international labor standards.

Given that leeway, it is strange to find that the spokesmen for some countries have recently been advocating two kinds of ILO labor standards: one kind for industrialized countries and another, sometimes referred to as "regional," for developing countries. Taken to its logical conclusion this would seem to imply that the ILO would have two categories of members as well. The very idea is abhorrent to any person believing in democratic principles and is against both the letter and the spirit of the Constitution of the ILO.

The late Director-General of the ILO, Wilfred Jenks, who was also one of the authors of the Declaration of Philadelphia, puts this very clearly when he states that "sub-standards for sub-humans have no place in the ILO."[1] In making this statement, Mr. Jenks clearly reflected the feeling of the ILO Workers' Group when in 1919 a number of countries pleaded that they were unable to apply the 48-hour week proposals. Opposing one of the countries asking for exception, the spokesman for the Workers' Group, Leon Jouhaux, later Vice President of the International Federation of Trade Unions (predecessor of the ICFTU) and winner of the Nobel Peace Prize, remarked at the 1919 Labour Conference that "having called the nations to the defence of liberty and higher civilisation, we have no right to let them crouch under cover of a lower state of civilisation."

The trade unions have therefore demanded of most International Labour Conferences since the Second World War that the ILO machinery for ratification and application of conventions and recommendations should be improved and that acceptance of the services rendered by the organization such as technical assistance should entail acceptance of its standards. The emphasis here is on "acceptance" of standards rather than on ratification and application. The word was used advisedly, for no one who believes in the high ideals expressed in the constitution of the ILO could dream of imposing standards on a developing country that would genuinely restrict its further social and economic development.

It would be unthinkable that the free democratic trade union group would require ratification from countries which, in conformity with ILO reporting procedures, satisfactorily explain why the law of the land or the custom and practices adhered to by fraternal unions make it impossible to ratify or legislate on specific matters. But the ILO should insist that international labor standards be accepted before any services are rendered in countries where there is systematic violation of basic human rights, as spelled out by the constitution and key conventions of the ILO and the charter of the United Nations.

THE IMPORTANCE OF ILO LABOR STANDARDS

ILO labor standards are vitally important to trade unions around the world today for several reasons. The fact is that most governments and employers' organizations like to be regarded as "progressive," particularly in an international forum. This has meant that in certain international labor standards, mainly recommendations which are not legally binding, it has been possible to include references to social issues which were or are important in specific countries. In other cases, and there are many, the pressure of international opinion exerted through the ILO has induced governments to introduce much needed social legislation on the basis of ratification of legally binding, even if basically unenforceable, ILO conventions.

In discussing ILO's problems it is easy to forget that the ILO has managed to do a very good job in many important social spheres. Its conventions on child labor, accommodation of crews (maritime), accident compensation, labor inspection and guarding of machinery are good examples. These and similar conventions have worked reasonably well, and ILO supervision of such purely social international labor standards is generally satisfactory.

With respect to legally binding standards, problems mainly arise in practice only where questions of basic human rights are involved. For example, ILO conventions No. 87 and No. 98 dealing respectively with "freedom of association" and "the right to organise and collective bargaining" have been ratified by more than two-thirds of member states. Yet it is a known fact that many of the ratifying countries do not apply these conventions or violate them in a manner that defies detection. This is hardly new. At the 1968 International Labour Conference the then General-Secretary of the ICFTU, Harm Buiter stated:

> It seems to me axiomatic that ILO activities should be expected to contribute to the ILO aims and ideals. They should, in fact, help to create conditions favourable for economic and social progress and for the promotion of safeguarding human rights in particular. It is an unfortunate fact that quite a number of countries in the world pay scant attention to ILO principles on freedom of association and collective bargaining. It goes without saying that ILO technical assistance should be withheld from governments which do not attempt to recognise those aims and ideals in practice and which persistently refuse to abide by international standards. In other words, technical assistance should be given a social content if it is to have any real meaning for this organisation.

Where nation states treat the ILO with contempt, all the ILO can do is to publish the facts. Trade unions that genuinely support the principles of the ILO can go a little further by making direct proposals and by using their influence in free and democratic societies to bring others around to their point of view.

If correctly researched and formulated, international labor standards can provide better conditions for workers in all countries, regardless of their stage of development. The Workers' Group at ILO Conferences should be united in seeking these standards. Unfortunately, some of the workers' delegates have dual loyalties, giving (or being coerced to give) first priority to the instructions they receive from their governments, which do not permit independent employers' and workers' organizations.

RECOGNITION OF HUMAN AND TRADE UNION RIGHTS BY THE ILO

More recently, additional problems have arisen by convening meetings of special groups of countries within the ILO. Lord Collison, the workers' delegate of Great Britain, as early as 1964 expressed to the International Labour Conference his concern with this practice:

> I have noted with increasing concern the tendency in recent years for groups of people to come together in this Conference, not, as in the past, on the basis of membership of the Government, Employers' and Workers' Groups, but as persons having the same geographical or racial origin, without regard to the traditional groups to which we all belong. There is always value in consultation, but I hope that we in the Workers' Group will always remember that we are workers first and Europeans, Asians, Africans or Latin Americans second . . . I felt that the tendency should be recognised early and as far as possible resisted.

Respect for basic human and trade union rights is indispensable to the enforcement of the standards set by the ILO or the international trade union movement. The key convention is the Freedom of Association Convention No. 87 of 1948. It stipulates that all workers shall have the right to establish and join organizations of their own choice without obtaining permission, to draw up their own rules, to select their own leaders and to formulate their own programs. "The public authorities shall refrain from any interference which would restrict this right," it asserts. The Right to Orgainze and Collective Bargaining Convention No. 98 of 1949 complements Convention No. 87.

These Conventions are very specific about the rights of trade unions. They do not admit of varying interpretations. It is sometimes said, for example, that trade unions have different functions under different social systems. The 1966 ILO report, "Industrialisation and Labour," for instance, remarks that in centrally planned economies management has been largely taken over by the state and that "trade unions accordingly have a different role in labour relations, being concerned mainly with achieving production targets, etc."

It may be true that workers' organizations take over some of these activities in certain countries, but that is no reason why they should not be independent institutions performing, among other things, the essential representative functions of trade unions. The two conventions are plain and unambiguous; their provisions cannot be circumvented, or "interpreted" out of existence. To insist that they be honored, especially by governments that have ratified them, is not to challenge a people's right to create a social system different from our own. It is to affirm simply that freedom of association must be a feature of their system. Many of the founders of the ILO wanted to change the social system and devoted their lives to that end, but they did not see any need to "interpret" freedom as non-freedom.

Apart from the procedures for the application of ILO conventions, special machinery exists for considering complaints alleging infringement of trade union rights. Complaints must be submitted by a national organization directly concerned or by international trade union bodies directly related to the case or having consultative status with the ILO. They are considered by the tripartite Governing Body Committee on Freedom of Association. The committee was formed in 1951 and has dealt with more than 800 complaints, often with significant impact. If a complaint is found to have substance, the Governing Body normally draws the attention of the government to the facts and invites the government to put matters right.

Where a complaint calls for on-the-spot inquiries, the Governing Body may refer the case to the Fact-Finding and Conciliation Commission on Freedom of Association, a body formed in 1950 in consultation with the UN Economic and Social Council. The permission of the government is necessary before the commission can visit a country.

The Committee on Freedom of Association has taken a great number of decisions which go beyond the standards set in the conventions, and the International Labour Conference has repeatedly adopted resolutions which amplify the protection provided by the standards. Two of these resolutions are of particular importance—the resolution concerning the "Independence of the Trade Union Movement" (1952) and the resolution concerning "Trade Union Rights and their Relation to Civil Liberties" (1970).

The 1952 resolution emphasizes that "the trade unions also have an important role to perform in co-operation with other elements in promoting social and economic development and the advancement of the community as a whole in each country" and "to these ends it is essential for the trade union movement in each country to preserve its freedom and independence so as to be in a position to carry forward its economic and social mission."

The 1970 resolution concerning "Trade Union Rights and their Relation to Civil Liberties" was adopted following a detailed discussion in a tripartite Conference Committee of the issues concerned. In the resolution, the Conference:

> Recognises that the rights conferred upon workers' and employers' organisations must be based on respect for those civil liberties which have been enunciated in particular in the Universal Declaration of Human Rights and in the International Covenants on Civil and Political Rights and that the absence of these civil liberties removes all

> meaning from the concept of trade union rights; places special emphasis on the following civil liberties, as defined in the Universal Declaration of Human Rights, which are essential for the normal exercise of trade union rights: (a) the right to freedom and security of person and freedom from arbitrary arrest and detention; (b) freedom of opinion and expression and in particular freedom to hold opinions without interference and to seek, receive, and impart information and ideas through any media and regardless of frontiers; (c) freedom of assembly; (d) the right to a fair trial by an independent and impartial tribunal; (e) the right to protection of the property of trade union organisations. Reaffirms the ILO's specific competence—within the United Nations system—in the field of freedom of association and trade union rights (principles, standards, supervisory machinery) and of related civil liberties; emphasises the responsibility of the United Nations for protecting and promoting human rights in general political freedoms and civil liberties throughout the world. Expresses its deep concern about and condemns the repeated violations of trade union rights and other human rights.

The resolution, furthermore, calls on the ILO to consider "further action to ensure full and universal respect for trade union rights in their broadest sense" and for this purpose asks that particular attention should be given to such questions as:

- right of trade unions to negotiate wages and all other conditions of work;
- right to strike;
- right to participate fully in national and international trade union activities;
- right to protection of trade union funds and assets against intervention by the public authorities;
- right to protection against any discrimination in matters of affiliation and trade union activities;
- right to workers' education and further training.

The resolution also invites the ILO Governing Body to place on the agenda of a forthcoming session of the International Labour Conference "one or more questions which could be the subject of new instruments with a view to enlarging trade union rights, taking into account those civil liberties which are a prerequisite for their exercise."

MULTINATIONALS AND INTERNATIONAL TRADE UNION SECRETARIATS

On the issue of multinational companies the international trade union movement is engaged in a bitter struggle for recognition. Trade unions, recognized in the industrial relations systems at the national level after long years of sacrifice and struggle, now see their position jeopardized by the nature and behavior of the multinationals. Even strong national trade union organizations can often find it difficult to give effective help, particularly if the multinational enterprise brings with it new technologies hitherto unknown in the locality. In cases like this, there will often be no established wage, manning or safety standards that apply to the production or services in question.

The problem becomes particularly acute when multinational enterprises move into a developing country where the government is willing to give any foreign investor preferential treatment, sometimes to the extent of guaranteeing that trade unions will not be permitted to organize. This is often the case even for governments which in general do not infringe on the principles of trade union freedom. ILO labor standards can only be of limited assistance in these cases because no standards specifically exist designed to handle the problems of the multinationals. The combined efforts of the employers' group and investment-seeking governments have insured that so far all attempts to elaborate standards for the multinationals have failed.

The international trade union secretariats have long been aware of this problem and have drawn the only possible conclusion. If international standards are needed but have not been drawn up by any other responsible organization, then we will have to draw them up ourselves. Thus FIET has established basic demands for our members throughout the world, in the form of the FIET World Action Program, in which one of the standards is the recognition, by multinational companies, of free and democratic trade unions for their employees in the countries where such companies have their head offices, subsidiaries or national affiliates.

Another international trade secretariat, the International Transport Workers' Federation (ITF), has long been active in establishing minimum standards for seafarers. Shipping was in fact the first industry for which it was recognized that international standards were needed.

Seamen have always been able to compare notes in ports all over the globe, but the workers in other industries are prevented from doing so by physical distance and national boundaries, though the industries themselves are becoming increasingly international in character. Fortunately, their trade unions are able to minimize this handicap by using their international organizations. This development has in many cases changed the role of the international trade union organizations from information centres and drafting committees for the trade unions' standard setting activities in other organizations, into standard setting bodies in their own right.

THE FIET WORLD ACTION PROGRAM

The program adopted by FIET at its Eighteenth World Congress clearly states at the beginning that "FIET pledges all its resources to the attainment of the standards set forth in this statement."[2] Not so many years ago similar program statements talked more vaguely about the "furthering of aims and improvement of the living and working conditions of the members." These sentiments obviously still underlie the work of the international trade union secretariats but when we talk now, we talk about standards, standards set by us, by the combined efforts of our membership.

Standards are only of use if they become effective, and they can only become effective where there exists the kind of democratic environment indispensable for the work of free trade unions. Trade unions cannot function properly without democracy. Democracy, in turn, needs free and democratic trade unions. The FIET World Action Program therefore starts by stipulating the conditions necessary to achieve the global social and economic conditions necessary for their effective implementation.

The program emphasizes that many of the standards it sets cannot "be attained outside the framework of an enlightened and democratic social and economic system," and asserts that it often takes both governmental and intergovernmental action to achieve this. It goes on to stress the importance of full employment policies. Such policies should respect democratic freedoms and should include short-, medium- and long-term manpower planning; maintenance of consumer demand by fiscal and other means, particularly by maintaining an adequate level of wages; the encouragement of new industries and services beneficial to the community, if necessary by investment incentives; and the correction of regional discrepancies by reallocation of industries, rural improvement programs and revised regional, national, and international marketing procedures.

Governments must accept, the program states, that economic crises caused by inflation or balance of payments difficulties cannot be countered by tolerating, let alone creating, unemployment, nor by reducing the workers' real wages or social conditions. As proof of their commitment to a policy of full and freely chosen employment, the program declares that every government should apply ILO Convention and Recommendation No. 122 concerning employment policy. This specific reference to ILO standards is significant. It stresses FIET's belief that labor standards proposed by the free and democratic trade union movement are designed to complement and improve existing labor standards, not to replace them.

To prevent forces outside the control of national governments from frustrating their efforts, the FIET program states that governments should promote the establishment of regional and international institutions dedicated to achieving the objectives mentioned. These institutions should provide public control over multinational companies and regulate international trade, capital movements, exchange rates and migration of labor. One of their major concerns should be the so-called "North-South problem," that is, they should endeavor to redress the imbalance between the more developed and less developed regions of the world. They should diminish the profit of transferring employment to areas where labor is cheap and bring to an end the exploitation of nation by nation in all its forms.

Governments must insure that there is democratic control of the nation's economy including, if possible, the spheres of domestic and foreign investment. This should help insure a fair distribution of the national income and promote full and freely chosen employment.

Many countries today are legitimately striving to achieve the New International Economic Order called for by the Sixth and Seventh Special Sessions of the UN General Assembly of the United Nations. FIET's program points out that "the new economic order must also be a new social order, in which democratic rights and freedoms are sustained and amplified, and in which the voice of labour is clearly heard." Otherwise, the more intensive the effort to boost production and the more numerous and competitive the agencies which become involved in the task, be it at world or national level, the greater becomes the danger that the interests of working people and their families will be overlooked. In no country, rich or poor, should the promotion of human dignity and the acceptance of democratic values be regarded as obstacles to national progress or sacrificed to false notions of economic efficiency.

The FIET World Action Program states that the new world order must be founded on two inviolable and indivisible principles. First, the world's resources are not for the benefit of a handful of nations. Second, within the nation, human and social progress must not be compromised by concepts which benefit only a handful of individuals.

Alliances between multinational companies and authoritarian governments, which deny the labor force basic trade union rights, must be opposed by every constitutional means, in the interests of the general democratic development of society and of workers everywhere. The growing numbers of such alliances imperil the living standards and the freedoms of workers in other countries seeking to attract international capital, as well as those of workers already employed, in whatever country, by the companies in question.

To meet the challenge of trade union recognition by MNCs and to insure the introduction of democratic decision-making processes and controls over the international financial transactions of MNCs and associated sources of finance, FIET is strengthening research into the structure and operations of these companies. FIET is also continuing to form regional and international company councils with a view eventually of negotiating international collective agreements. At the same time FIET will pursue its policy of seeking international institutional control of these companies and cooperate with other international trade secretariats, the ICFTU and the Trade Union Advisory Committee of the OECD to insure that the activities of these stateless giants shall serve the interests of the people.

FIET's standard-setting activities obviously do not stop at general human rights and measures of control over the operation of multinational companies. The majority of FIET standards relate to immediate and concrete issues of direct concern to the members of its affiliated trade unions such as part-time work, overtime, annual leave and public holidays, unemployment and job security, retirement, education and training, occupational safety and health, and many more.

THE FUTURE OF THE ILO

The application of international labor standards requires the help of free and democratic trade unions, which can insure that governments and employers implement and maintain them. In this critical task, the ILO has a vital role to play. Trade unions have regarded the ILO from its inception in 1919 as a traditional ally in the struggle for the continuous improvement of working and living conditions, in the defense of trade union rights and freedoms and in the promotion of worldwide social justice and economic equality.

It is a great pity that an agency like the ILO should be divided by political discord, which diverts it from its essential task of establishing labor standards. Obviously the free and democratic trade union movement is bound to be concerned, more than any other element within the ILO, with the continued validity of the organization's tripartite structure. Our movement has in fact expressed its concern at these developments over a considerable period of time and made concerted efforts to redress the situation.

With the emergence in the years to come of a new pattern of world economic relations, intensified international effort will be needed to protect and strengthen basic human rights and social justice. On the basis of its constitutional responsibilities, the ILO is the organization within the UN family best equipped to assist in this effort.

Notwithstanding the admitted difficulties, the ILO remains the only UN body in whose work the trade union movement participates as a matter of constitutional right. To weaken it would be to blunt one of the sharpest weapons in our international struggle for the respect of the standards which are set by the ILO and by the international trade union movement itself. Trade unions, therefore, must be united in efforts to preserve the organization to continue to serve the goals for which it was established.

NOTES

1. Wilfred Jenks, Human Rights and International Labor Standards by C. W. Jenks, London: Steven & Sons Limited.
2. International Federation of Commercial, Clerical, and Technical Employees (FIET), World Action Programme, adopted by the Eighteenth FIET World Congress, Helsinki, 1976.

17

The Limits to International Fair Labor Standards

JOHN P. WINDMULLER

LABOR'S SEARCH FOR CONSENSUS ON INTERNATIONAL ECONOMIC POLICY

In shifting from a pro-free trade position in the early 1960s to a quasi-protectionist policy today, the AFL-CIO has not proceeded by means of head counting or cost-benefit analysis. Instead it has done what federated organizations generally must do in situations of this kind. It has shifted direction in response to the persistent pressures of influential affiliates, facing grave harm to their institutional interests, even if other affiliates, directly or indirectly, would be the beneficiaries of liberal trade policies.

The case against a restrictive U.S. trade policy in the postwar period has rested on two principal sets of arguments: economic and political. The economic defense has, of course, relied on the theory of comparative advantage, although not exclusively, and has been "consumer"-oriented. The political case has relied on the free world's confrontation with communism and America's leadership role in that confrontation. Until the early 1960s, organized labor with some exceptions and some qualifications subscribed to both sets of arguments.[1] The main policy line, especially as expressed at AFL-CIO federation headquarters, was optimistically pro-free trade.[2]

In the intervening years, organized labor's position on trade has undergone a significant change, although the political considerations which formerly served to justify a liberal trade policy have scarcely altered. The underlying cause of the shift has been economic: the search by a powerful group of unions for protection against the adverse employment effects of foreign competition. For within a body as diffuse as a labor federation, the concentrated hurt inflicted on a segment of constituents by import competition can easily become more compelling as a guide to policy than the diffuse benefits which all constituents would derive from free trade.

In seeking to defend the jobs and the terms of employment of their members, American unions can choose from a range of possible actions. At one end, there is the oldest and perhaps still the most effective remedy: political pressure on appropriate public agencies at home to secure protection and relief, and if necessary to secure it by unilateral action. But aside from inviting retaliation, such action tends to draw resentment and hostility in many different quarters, including fraternal unions abroad. Consequently labor prefers to achieve its aims by agreement among all affected parties. The problem, however, is that the parties are numerous and dispersed and their interests highly divergent. Thus, while negotiated and agreed multilateral solutions to the problem as perceived by American labor will be more acceptable politically, such solutions are also infinitely more difficult to bring about.

The difficult search for consensus at the national level operates as well at the international level where labor's interests are even more divergent. Take, for example, the idea of international fair labor standards. For well over two decades (perhaps even as far back as 1943 according to one authority), American labor has advocated the promulgation of international fair labor standards as a means of equitably regulating competition in international product markets by mutual agreement.

As long ago as 1956, when labor was still supporting trade liberalization, the then AFL-CIO research director told a congressional committee that "American workers and employers have the right to be assured that they will not be faced with unfair foreign competition. Failure to maintain fair labor standards in the competing export industries of other countries would certainly be an important evidence of unfair competition."[3] There have been many similar statements from other authoritative labor spokesmen since that time. Indeed, one encounters them in almost every policy paper on foreign trade issued by the AFL-CIO and its affiliates.

What is the object? Although rarely defined in precise terms, it is presumably the establishment "through appropriate international channels" of certain minimum employment conditions under which goods must be produced in order to qualify for entry into the American market and perhaps other markets as well. One of the most sophisticated discussions of this idea took place in Paris in March 1960 when a group of European and American trade union economists met "to discuss the potentials of introducing fair labor standards in international trade."[4] From a detailed report of the discussion, I conclude that the participants were unable to arrive at a consensus because they represented different economic interests and aimed at different objectives.

OBSTACLES TO MULTINATIONAL NEGOTIATIONS ON LABOR STANDARDS

There are at least three problems with the idea of international fair labor standards which seem to me to defy solution under conditions of multinational negotiations. What are to be the criteria to determine fair standards? Who is entitled to participate in defining them? And by what means are they to be enforced?

The components of fair standards would presumably consist of "fair" wages, "fair" hours, and "fair" working conditions. But what criteria are to be used in determining what is fair? Surely, American standards are not usable as guides, nor Swedish or West German ones. Nor does it help much to suggest that "fair" ought to be defined in terms of an exporting country's own average standards because these are often likely to be too low to have the restrictive and protective effects desired by American labor.

The question of participation in the drawing up of standards is an even more vexing one. For the standards to have any kind of international acceptability at all, countries with low standards cannot be excluded from multilateral negotiations. But to include them would virtually mean abandoning any realistic opportunity of defining standards that are meaningful to American unions since it would hardly be in the interest of the lesser developed nations to participate in developing measures that would put severe restrictions on their export industries.

Little help should be expected in this endeavor from the trade unions of the developing countries. Singapore may serve as an example. The leaders of its trade unions happen to be on friendly terms with their American counterparts for reasons well known to anyone who is informed about the current state of international trade unionism. Yet earlier this year the General Secretary of the Singapore Trades Union Congress in an official report to his constituents called on the AFL-CIO to modify its restrictive stand on U.S.-foreign trade and overseas investment policies and to adopt policies that would not prejudice the interests of workers in developing countries.[5]

Nor should one expect the ILO or the GATT to do the job on international fair labor standards that American labor wants done. These organizations are able to do only what their constituents allow them do to do, assuming they can reach agreement. Their composition is on balance weighted against the construction of anything more than nominal international fair labor standards. Not even the ILO would claim, I believe, that its existing body of international labor standards corresponds to a level that American labor would regard as fair and equitable. Its most recent publication on this subject,[6] which is not excessively modest in describing the ILO's achievements in standard setting emphasizes the impact of ILO international instruments on human rights, social policy and development policy. While it would be an error to underestimate the long-term importance of these areas, it is also possible to overstate their current significance, especially when one takes into account the inevitable shortcomings in the enforcement of the standards as applied to the less developed countries. And as regards the countries in the Soviet sphere of influence, close monitoring of adherence to ILO standards would encounter just as much resistance as proposals for international inspection of the terms of nuclear arms control agreements.

Finally, there is no way at all at present to develop an international implementation or enforcement procedure for the monitoring of fair labor standards, even if such standards could be agreed upon. This is not to say that the United States, acting unilaterally, is unable to police such standards through its own administrative agencies. On the contrary, that should not be an especially difficult task. But I do not see the possibility of having an international agency in effective control of such a procedure, whether it be the ILO, GATT, or some yet-to-be-created organization. The political constraints that would surely govern the operation of such an agency would most probably result in enforcement policies wholly unsatisfactory to American labor and probably equally unsatisfactory to American business firms in import-competitive sectors.

The idea of international fair labor standards as a genuinely international or multinational venture is still, therefore, an unrealistic one. The only feasible way for the United States at present to inject criteria of labor standards into trade policy is either through bilateral negotiations or through unilateral action. In stating this conclusion I am not suggesting that I consider it to be a way of strengthening relations with our allies or promoting the growth of less developed countries, or for that matter of benefiting the American consumer. In fact, it is more likely to lead to contrary results.

NOTES

1. For an articulate but very moderate expression of labor's producer concerns in the early 1960s, see Solomon Barkin, "Labor's Position on Tariff Reductions," Industrial Relations 1, no. 3 (May 1962), pp. 49-63. For an apt summary of the political argument, see Fred C. Bergsten, "Crisis in U.S. Trade Policy," Foreign Affairs 24, no. 4 (July 1971), p. 621.

2. See, for example, the verbatim text of the AFL-CIO Labor News Conference, Program No. 42, for release on February 12, 1962.

Labor's political analysis of the case for free trade was well articulated by George Meany in an address to the first Conference on World Trade organized by the International Association of Machinists (IAM) in 1961; see news release from the AFL-CIO, November 29, 1961, p. 3. A similar political defense of free trade with Japan was made by A. I. Hayes, president of the IAM, in his "Remarks at the Industrial Management Club" (Port Chester, New York, May 18, 1960), pp. 6-7.

3. Statement of Stanley Ruttenberg before the Subcommittee on Customs, Tariffs and Reciprocal Trade Agreements of the House Ways and Means Committee, September 26, 1956.

4. Joseph Mintzes, "Union Views on Fair Labor Standards in Foreign Trade," Monthly Labor Review 83, no. 10 (October 1960), pp. 1028-30. See also Stanley Ruttenberg, "The Union View of Multinationals: An Interpretation," in Robert J. Flanagan and Arnold R. Weber, Bargaining Without Boundaries (Chicago: University of Chicago Press, 1974), pp. 190-191.

5. Tomorrow: The Peril and the Promise (Report by the Secretary General to the 2nd Triennial Delegates Conference of the Singapore National Trades Union Congress, 1976), p. xv.

6. ILO, The Impact of International Labour Conventions and Recommendations (Geneva: ILO, 1976).

18

The ILO and International Labor Standards: Achievements and Problems

BERT SEIDMAN

LIMITS AND POSSIBILITIES FOR INTERNATIONAL LABOR COOPERATION

It is important to be realistic in considering what can be accomplished through international cooperation among labor organizations. Since World War II, some efforts have been made to inject the idea of international fair labor standards into machinery regulating international trade by attempting to tie wage levels in exporting industries to relative productivity levels in exporting and importing countries. These efforts have been unsuccessful because they were misdirected toward a set of larger issues too much subject to the unilateral actions of national governments to be susceptible to solution through international labor cooperation.

The impact which differing wage levels has on international trade is so much affected by other policies of national governments such as tariff and nontariff barriers to imports from other countries and subsidies for exports that the response of labor must necessarily come in the first instance at the national level. This has been the experience of the AFL-CIO in the postwar period, as it has sought to advance the welfare of American workers in a changing world economy.

Thus the policies of the AFL-CIO on foreign trade have changed in the past decade in a rational response to changing conditions in order to protect the collective interests of American workers. In the 1960s when organized labor supported the Kennedy liberal trade policy, the AFL-CIO was under pressure by the relatively small group of unions already deeply affected by imports to reverse our position. We did not do so because <u>then</u> it was not in the general interest of workers to do so. But as one industry after another, from sophisticated hard goods to soft goods, fell victim to the rising tide of imports, the AFL-CIO had to adopt a policy of calling for import controls to safeguard the jobs and labor standards of millions of workers. As a matter of fact, some of the most pro-free trade labor movements in Western Europe have in recent years adopted similar policies when their members have been hurt by the rising influx of imports.

This question is particularly difficult when it comes to trade with developing countries. The AFL-CIO is in favor of doing everything possible to assist the developing countries and in fact has done much through its own activities to support the development of free and effective trade unions. But the surest way to curtail drastically American aid to developing countries is to permit uncontrolled imports from them to destroy large sectors of American industry.

On the other hand, much can be achieved in areas where meaningful international agreement is possible. Nowhere is this better illustrated than in the work of the International Labour Organization on labor standards. With all its limitations, this activity of the ILO has been a remarkable development of which too few Americans, even American trade unionists, are aware.

THE ACHIEVEMENTS OF THE ILO

The founders of the ILO felt a strong desire, adhered to ever since, to use the ILO to prevent cutthroat competition at the expense of workers. This concern has centered on the idea of developing international fair labor standards. Efforts to inject this idea into regulation of international trade by establishing wage levels in different countries have been unsuccessful for reasons already noted. But the ILO has sought with considerable success to define norms of conduct in the form of international conventions and recommendations for governments and employers in their actions affecting the jobs and lives of workers in just about every field except the establishment of wage levels per se. Even in the wage field, the ILO does have international standards for setting up minimum wage machinery, although it has not sought to specify what the level of the minimum wages should be.

ILO conventions and recommendations run across the board in the labor standards field. Areas covered include occupational health and safety; conditions in specific industries such as maritime, road-building and plantations; various forms of social insurance; protection of groups especially subject to exploitation such as migrants, women, and children; removal of discrimination based on race, sex, national origin or political beliefs; vocational training; and fundamental worker rights such as prohibition of forced labor, safeguard of freedom of association, and the right to organize.

The tripartite representation in the ILO of governments, employers and workers on an international scale made possible a degree of consensus which promised viability to the standards and even to the machinery the ILO has set up to supervise the application of the standards. ILO recommendations and conventions must be adopted by a two-thirds vote of the delegates to the annual conference after discussion and consideration in two successive years. Thus the several hundred ILO conventions and recommendations have achieved a wide degree of international acceptability.

The ILO has not, furthermore, been content to adopt international labor standards. Unique among the UN and its specialized agencies, it has established machinery for supervising their application. This machinery amazingly has had a considerable effect on conditions in ILO member countries although by no means invariably, certainly not with 100 percent effectiveness or, lamentably, evenly and without discrimination. Still, it frequently comes as a surprise to newcomers to the ILO to learn that its Committee of Experts and Conference Committee on the Application of Standards year after year test the law and practice of member countries in labor fields against the requirements of ILO standards to which they have committed themselves and do not hesitate to tell such countries when they fail to observe their obligations. Still more amazingly, many countries to a greater or lesser extent have responded to these admonitions. Some grudgingly take only half measures to correct their deficiencies and some, notably the Communist countries, have ignored the ILO comments altogether. But looked at as a whole, it is remarkable that this machinery has been as effective as it has been in influencing the policies and practices of member countries in the wide field of labor conditions and worker rights to which ILO standards apply.

It is regrettable, in this regard, that the United States has ratified only a handful of ILO conventions. While it is true that acceptance of ILO standards in practice is more important than formal ratification of ILO conventions, the stance of the United States in the ILO in defending ILO principles and in safeguarding ILO procedures would be strengthened if we were to ratify more ILO conventions. Moreover, even though in most important respects the United States already conforms to ILO standards as expressed in its international instruments, this is not true in all fields. Analysis of differences between ILO standards and those in our legislation and practices looking toward ratification of ILO conventions might lead us to make improvements which would advance the welfare of American workers. Indeed this is exactly what has happened in Canada which in recent years has made a deliberate and successful effort to ratify a number of ILO conventions by conforming, where they differ, their national and even provincial laws to ILO standards.

It has sometimes been claimed that ILO standards have no relevance for the developing countries which are now its dominant element. In my judgement this claim is not valid. There is no evidence of flagging interest in the need for new ILO standards and improving old ones on the part of worker delegates who increasingly come from developing countries. To the contrary, because labor legislation and administration is often rudimentary and relatively primitive in most of those countries, trade unionists from developing countries look to ILO standards to bolster their own efforts to improve workers' conditions.

PROBLEMS STILL UNRESOLVED

It is most unfortunate that ILO officials all too often ignore ILO standards in ILO technical cooperation programs aimed at assisting developing countries. The Workers Group in the ILO has insisted year after year that the ILO's labor standards should provide the guidelines for its activities in the developing countries. While the ILO secretariat has paid lip service to this principle, it has seldom been observed in actual practice.

Some have said that whatever need for ILO standards there may have been in the past, that need is past and the ILO should concentrate in other areas. I strongly disagree with this idea. There is no dearth of subjects appropriate for ILO labor standards which are relevant for workers in today's world both in developed and developing countries. Every year when the ILO Governing Body considers the agenda for the International Labour Conference, there are far more issues for consideration for international labor standards than can be fitted into the program. This is clear indication that this most important phase of the ILO's activity must be continued and, if possible, strengthened.

But international labor standards, no matter how much good they do, will not survive unless the ILO faces up to the problem of the double standard. Not only do some member countries ignore ILO standards in actual practice, but the ILO itself discriminates in the treatment of countries violating the obligations which they have freely assumed in ratifying ILO conventions. Nowhere is the unequal treatment by the ILO in discharging such commitments more blatant than between Third World countries, on the one hand, and the Soviet Bloc, on the other, especially with respect to the ILO's conventions on human rights.

The USSR is apparently prepared to sink the entire standard-setting function of the ILO, and especially its supervisory machinery, if there is official ILO criticism of its violation of fundamental human rights, such as forced labor and denial of freedom of association required by ILO conventions which the USSR and the other Soviet Bloc countries have ratified. Unfortunately, themselves often targets of similar ILO criticisms, many governments of developing countries seem ready to support the USSR in its assault on ILO machinery and procedures for safeguarding basic human rights without discrimination among member countries.

There can be only one answer to this onslaught against the basic principles on which the ILO was founded. There can be no double standard. The ILO constitution calls for equal treatment of member countries. If this basic principle is weakened or destroyed, ILO standards, however valuable they may be intrinsically, are meaningless. Are the democratic forces in the ILO prepared to face up to that challenge? The signs are mixed but the very existence of the ILO may depend on their response.

19

Labor's Approach to Multinationals

HERMAN REBHAN

THE DYNAMIC GROWTH OF MULTINATIONALS

Multinational companies are a fully integrated part of our modern industrialized society. Their development is a corollary of mass production and mass consumption. They are often the initiators of large scale rationalization in a search for high and secure profits. Their policies and management methods not only provide for constant changes in the field of production, affecting employment and living conditions of workers, but also greatly influence the living environment of persons everywhere. Multinationals can be a rich source of goods and capital. This wealth must be put to the benefit of society and the world economy as a whole, if serious conflicts are to be avoided.

To aspire to social justice is a fundamental human instinct. The production potential must, therefore, serve basic needs and the constant improvement of living conditions for everybody. This is the main area of the conflict between the multinationals and the trade unions. Multinationals represent economic power. Their policies are largely an attempt to determine—independent from other interests—the lowest possible production costs and the maximum possible prices and accordingly to take unilateral decisions on the location of production, on employment and on their social obligations to the workers. This growing power is largely derived from an expanding multinational structure. The trade union movement is engaged in building up the necessary counterforce to these companies of necessity emphasizing international coordination and solidarity.

Through everyday activities and long term programs, we aim at protecting and defending workers in these companies and in societies where these companies play an important role. Trade unions have done a tremendous amount of grassroots work and have obtained positive results in the social field in their struggles with the multinational corporations, but there is much more which needs to be done.

The MNC phenomenon is particularly prevalent in the metal industry. General Motors has a world sales figure the size of the GNP of several developing countries taken together or of a rich industrialized country like Switzerland. Whole sectors of the metal industry worldwide are in the hands of a few multinationals.

In the auto industry, a dozen multinationals dominate the scene, taking about three-quarters of the world market share, even including the Communist countries. In a basic metal industry like aluminium, important for further new technology, six multinationals account for practically the whole production in the non-Communist world, and in nickel, a metal with one of the largest consumption growths, only three multinationals really matter. The situation is no different in other industries such as agricultural implements, electrical goods and electronics, each of which is dominated by a handful of MNCs.

The mushrooming of components parts production of the MNCs in the developing countries is particularly significant, as is the transfer of modern technology abroad without its adaptation to the needs of the recipient countries. These countries essentially provide a home for low cost production with underpaid labor of component parts which are then exported to other MNC production units to be incorporated in goods sold primarily in industrialized country markets.

Multinationals in the metal industry employ workers in many lands. General Motors, with operations on all continents, alone employs almost 700,000 workers, half of them outside the United States. A European multinational like Philips employs altogether 406,000 workers, half of them in overseas subsidiaries.

The dynamic growth of MNCs is remarkable. ITT, for example, increased its worldwide sales figure, through market expansion and acquisition of new plants, five and a half times over eight years. The Japanese multinational Sony doubled its sales in three years, and the European company IG Telefunken did the same in five years.

Multinational companies, the giants of private capitalism, are joining hands more and more frequently in an unholy alliance with state capitalists of Communist countries through technical cooperation, licensing agreements and investment assistance. Such cooperation agreements with Eastern European countries are not merely an attempt to capture an export market in those countries. They involve wholesale transfers of technology and clearly represent displacement of production in Western countries, particularly when guarantees are given that part of the licensed production will be sent back to be absorbed by the Western market.

A striking example in this field is an agreement of General Motors with the State Planning Authorities in Poland to establish in that country, with the help of the British subsidiary Vauxhall, a whole factory for the production of light trucks and vans. General Motors will not enter into any capital participation with this new Polish venture but will receive compensation for its transfer of technology through deliveries from the Polish production. The light trucks and vans from Poland will be sold through the distribution network of General Motors on the European market, as General Motors has promised not to export these products to the United States. Under these conditions, the American Export-Import Bank has provided General Motors with interest-free loans to cover the whole deal.

It is a pertinent question to ask whether these loans could not have been put to a better use in the developing countries in the framework of national development planning, instead of being given to General Motors to make deals (entirely to their own advantage) to transfer technology, production and marketing wherever they please. Such company decisions, with considerable employment repercussions on countries where production is being displaced, are taken without the workers and the trade unions of the affected plants ever having been informed. Unless trade unions force the MNCs to give explanations, there will never be any negotiations over the welfare of the workers.

Agreements, such as that with General Motors in Poland, are being concluded by governments in Communist countries in their own political interest. It would be like a fairy story to believe that the trade unions in these countries would, or could, pursue any solidarity action with trade union organizations representing workers of the same companies in the non-Communist world. The trade unions in Communist countries are tools of the government and are fully integrated into state planning and operation of production. Strikes are excluded.

THE QUEST FOR BETTER WAGES, JOB SECURITY, AND WORKING CONDITIONS

For all these multinationals, whether their parent company is in the United States or in Europe, the manpower force abroad, particularly in developing countries, is growing much faster than in the plants of the home country. This rapid growth and the expansion of operations throughout the world create constant shifts in employment. Whatever multinational management might say, low wage costs are an important factor of their policies. The best evidence of this is their continual and stubborn resistance to the trade unions.

The main trade union tasks at international level are the fight for the recognition of trade unions, the necessary guarantees for trade union rights and trade union freedom, enabling them to negotiate collective bargaining agreements which bring about improved wages and provide for substantial social benefits. The struggle for employment security is another main field for international trade union cooperation and solidarity. Through the constant exchange of information, the coordination of policies, and a common position on the social objectives and problems arising in whole sectors of industry and within big multinational groups, the trade unions can resist attempts by multinationals to transfer employment or counter threats of plant closures.

The danger of workers in one country being played off against workers in another country has never been greater than it is now. International capital flows, technological cooperation agreements and other different kinds of production or marketing links all create possibilities for shifts of production, of which trade unions must be aware in order to defend and promote employment and social progress.

There is a dispute between MNCs and unions over the wages and working conditions in these companies. The MNCs consider themselves the best employers and try to prove it with figures. The trade unions maintain the opposite and submit facts and figures to show that the typical attitude of MNC management is one of achieving the highest possible profits with the lowest possible total wage costs.

Trade unions have reached a high degree of unionization in many multinational companies, and the possibility of organizing workers is often better in large companies than in medium and small shops. This has had its effect on the MNCs. There are multinationals, or companies within a multinational group, which do provide appreciably good wages and working conditions. Of course, such conditions should be expected and should be further improved, taking into account the high profit potential of these corporate giants.

A study recently undertaken by the International Labour Office, Social and Labour Practices of Some European-based Multinationals in the Metal Trades (Geneva: ILO, 1976), shows the high degree of unionization existing in many plants of MNCs even here and there in the subsidiaries in developing countries. There are, of course, multinationals, including the United States, which pursue their anti-union policies to a point where they resist by all kinds of management tactics any trade unions. In such cases, specific groups of workers considered to be especially valuable for maintaining production may get a relatively high wage (but without any contract guarantees) in order to prevent unionization in the plant, while other groups of workers, frequently unskilled, are miserably paid.

The ILO study just mentioned comes clearly to the conclusion that multinational corporations largely disregard any obligation for employment security. Flexibility of employment—in Europe, for instance, to the detriment of the migrant workers—is an important factor in exploiting any opportunity for increased profits and achieving rapid cost cutbacks in the case of reduced demands. MNCs similarly try to evade any obligation which would hinder the transfer of production from one region or country to another.

This all points to the necessity for the trade unions to expand their collective bargaining to new areas of employment guarantees and standard setting in order to extend shop level trade union rights and to demand trade union representation at all levels of an MNC. Such reforms can best be obtained by building upon what has already been achieved. Trade union rights at company, industry and national levels must be guaranteed and further improved through the achievement of the same and additional rights at international level. Local, regional and national trade union structures must be further strengthened by extending their framework at world level. The IMF World Councils on Multinational Companies and the Council for Multinationals in the Electro and Electronics Industry are important new initiatives in this whole endeavor.

In building up the trade union counterweight to multinationals, a first priority is to develop effective and strong solidarity in collective bargaining in order to secure employment and improve wages, working and social conditions, leading toward improved living standards for all workers employed in these companies throughout the world.

There has been a lot of talk about worldwide collective bargaining. Such ambitions are a long way off. Negotiations at the regional level where the economic and social conditions of a group of countries are more or less comparable would be needed first. At present, however, the bargaining autonomy within the trade union movement lies with the national organizations and, within their own structure, with regional representatives and bargaining teams.

It will be hard to achieve progress because employers fiercely resist any kind of international collective bargaining. It is unlikely, therefore, that industry-wide agreements, which are predominant in Europe, will be supplemented by international agreements. But one day breakthroughs will be achieved by agreements that will rather cover several companies in an international region of one multinational company.

The most realistic item for rapid international progress, which is urgently needed, is health and safety. All workers in all countries have the same right to the protection of their health and welfare. Within multinational companies, some concrete progress can be make by providing the same health and safety standards in their plants throughout the world.

Other items can be working hours and conditions at the workplace and on assembly lines. Wages and social benefits are a much more difficult matter for international bargaining. It is even difficult to achieve uniform expiration dates for collective bargaining contracts so that trade union pressure could be brought to bear worldwide in one round of bargaining for different contracts. Many companies and plants within multinational corporations are covered in many countries by national industry-wide agreements or by regional settlements.

COORDINATED INTERNATIONAL ACTION IN COLLECTIVE BARGAINING

There are great possibilities for strengthening collective bargaining with multinational companies through continuous efforts by competent international organizations of workers. The first step is compiling information, comparing working conditions and setting up action programs to attain well defined goals. This is being done by the IMF World Councils for Multinational Companies. Contacts are thus established among responsible trade union representatives with various plants in different countries, all belonging to the same multinational group. This permits rapid action for mutual assistance wherever bargaining occurs and in the case of some labor conflicts.

A special task for IMF is strengthening trade unions in subsidiaries set up by MNCs in the developing countries. This first requires knowledge about the subsidiaries of each multinational company throughout the world so that, through affiliated organizations in developing countries, support can be given to organizing campaigns and to initial collective bargaining.

The IMF has successfully assisted such new unions in their negotiations through the preparation of collective bargaining arguments. This material for bargaining is derived from an analysis of the economic, financial and technological facts concerning both the multinational group and the specific company with which a round of collective bargaining is about to start. This is practical, down-to-earth international trade union work bringing substantial benefits to the workers in multinational companies, especially in developing countries. On occasion trade union experts with collective bargaining experience with the parent company have been sent to developing countries to assist on the spot in negotiations. At the same time they participated in seminar workshops which deal with the problem of collective bargaining experienced by those particular members.

Trade union representation from plants of the same company in other parts of the world has been present when collective bargaining started with the parent company in the United States. They attended, as part of the trade union delegation, a number of opening sessions and had contact with the American trade union negotiating team and some rank and file members in order to create an awareness of the overall union struggle with the company concerned. Such contacts at the outset of collective bargaining have taken place in the case of Caterpillar, John Deere and International Harvester. These kinds of initiatives are not international collective bargaining but rather reflect coordinated international union action in collective bargaining.

INDUSTRIAL DEMOCRACY

A second priority for international action is more effective representation of the workers' interests and aspirations through the trade unions at all levels of multinational corporations. Trade unions advance different concepts of democratization, all according to the traditional political, cultural and economic development in their respective countries. These serve a common purpose of expanding and guaranteeing workers' trade union rights. There is great need for democratization in multinational companies, particularly because management decisions affecting the daily life of the worker are made at the top of international management in headquarters far away, often across the ocean. MNCs, furthermore, are often highly secretive about their international operations, and they do not release important basic facts indispensable to trade unions whenever they have to defend the workers' jobs and negotiate contract improvements.

In many plants of multinational companies the defense of the worker's rights at his workplace is an especially hard-fought issue. Work environment, wage systems and work organization methods are all issues which make it necessary for each individual worker to be able, in any plant of an MNC throughout the world, to get recognition of his demands. Metal unions have obtained the introduction of democratization schemes, which tackle these problems of shop-level and company-wide trade union representation. Some of the schemes in Europe have provided for trade union representation on supervisory boards and for setting up central works councils, in which the workers from the various plants, even across national borders, meet with management.

The IMF is looking closely into these various systems and is studying trade union proposals for democratization. It seeks to promote an exchange of experience and knowledge which can help in achieving further progress at national level and guide action in the international field. With this in mind, a special meeting took place some time ago in IMF to consider democratization in the multinational automotive companies.

IMF has also had some contacts with the international management level of MNCs and has recently made a new breakthrough with one of the biggest multinationals in the mechanical engineering industry. The discussion with top management served the purpose of coming to grips with employment and related social problems arising from the worldwide reorganization of this multinational group. Full consideration was given to the trade union demands in the individual plants for the protection of workers. Specific situations were then examined on the basis of national and plant level reports, so that urgent and important trade union concerns on the shop floor were brought to the attention of the top decision-making center of the whole multinational corporation.

CODES OF CONDUCT AND OTHER CONTROLS OF MNCS

A third priority of international trade union action is related to social and economic controls on multinational companies. Because of the predominance of multinationals in the metal industry, the IMF has been a leader of trade union efforts in this field, seeking the establishment of concrete programs. An ICFTU/ITS Working Party on Multinational Companies presented to the ICFTU Congress in September 1975 in Mexico a charter of trade union demands for the legislative control of multinational companies. These efforts were instrumental in getting basic trade union demands recognized in the guidelines on multinational companies recently adopted by the OECD, the first instrument to set up moral commitments to be observed by MNCs.

The OECD includes commitments regarding the right to organize, the right to bargain, trade union representation, access to information for negotiations, training and upgrading of the local labor force and advance notice in the case of changes in operations. There are three specific voluntary obligations which respond to basic trade union concerns. The first is that subsidiaries of multinational companies should observe standards of employment and industrial relations no less favorable than those obtained by comparable employees in the host countries. Second, multinationals should abstain from threats to transfer the whole or part of an operating unit from the country concerned in order to influence unfairly collective bargaining negotiations or to hinder the exercise of the right to organize. The third clause asserts that multinationals should accept negotiations on collective bargaining on labor management issues with representatives of management who are authorized to take decisions on the matter under negotiation, including the international management of the firm.

It is regrettable that this voluntary OECD code does not commit multinationals to public accountability, on a country-by-country basis, of their operations across the world. A special committee of the United Nations charged with working out international rules for MNCs has, however, gone much further. It calls for detailed accounting by multinational companies, which should provide essential financial data on the group as a whole, the parent company, and its subsidiaries.

IMF, together with the entire democratic trade union movement, considers the OECD voluntary guidelines merely a first step. They are to be followed by an early revision, with a view to laying down comprehensive objectives to be made binding by an OECD convention. In the meantime, IMF has alerted its affiliates to press multinational companies to adhere strictly to the stipulations of the OECD code. They are called upon to report any infringement of the principles of this code and to submit such cases to the OECD Surveillance Committee in order to seek remedial action through this international body.

IMF, again along with the free democratic trade union movement, is pressing the International Labour Office to develop and apply legally binding conventions to multinational enterprises. For this purpose the question of multinational enterprises and social policy should be brought before the International Labour Conference at the earliest possible date. IMF has been directly engaged in negotiations at ILO, which led to the agreement for a tripartite declaration of principles concerning multinational enterprises and social policy to be formulated rapidly.

The content of the ILO declaration is to be submitted in a suitable form to the United Nations for inclusion in the UN code of conduct. IMF believes that the United Nations' code on MNCs should be legally binding and cover all political, economic and social aspects of their operations and that the trade union demands be fully embodied in it.

The trade union interest in control of multinational companies goes beyond employment-related issues. The trade unions are vitally concerned about the general behavior of multinational companies and the effect of their policies on the economy and society as a whole. For these reasons the IMF, along with the free and democratic trade union movement, believes that MNCs must be obligated to provide systematic information on the structure and operations of multinational corporations, the degree of their market predominance, and their investment policies.

Stringent rules must also be established with regard to public accountability of multinational companies. With their worldwide operations, MNCs can evade the reporting requirements imposed on national companies and cover up financial data through transfer pricing and bookkeeping procedures which consolidate certain accounts only at the international level. MNCs must be required to provide a full picture about all their locations and report for the whole group, the parent company and each subsidiary, the full profits, the cash flow, investment expenditure, projects, capital loans, capital participation, taxes, employment, and wage costs. There should, in addition, be stringent rules on bribery, and financial reporting must give the assurance that such practices are not being used.

The trade unions demand a reporting system to the national banks and governments on the financial transactions of multinational companies. There should also be a careful analysis of the international character and consequences of the multinational banking system and its links with multinational operations in industry. Unions seek a revision of the OECD code for the liberalization of capital movements. This code should contain social obligations in connection with international investment. The free movement of capital and investment guarantees should be based on the obligation to recognize trade unions and to accept collective bargaining and international labor standards. The trade unions propose the setting up of a tripartite commission to ensure compliance with these objectives.

Last, but by no means least, the trade unions insist on a revision of tax systems as they affect MNCs. They urge intergovernmental cooperation in the field of tax information in order to close loopholes in reporting profits, capital movements and internal pricing practices and to elucidate information on the operations of subsidiaries in tax havens.

It is obvious that all these measures to control multinational companies, whether social, economic or financial, cannot be taken at just one level. The elaboration of stringent and effective rules by competent international bodies will take a long time and will need to be implemented by corresponding laws in each country. The trade union struggle, therefore, extends to all these fronts. The combined effort of trade unions at the local, national and international level is the best way to build up the counterforce to MNCs, to strengthen democratic societies, and to advance the welfare of workers throughout the world.

20

Obstacles to Effective International Collective Bargaining

BEN SHARMAN

THE NEED FOR BETTER INTERNATIONAL COORDINATION BY UNIONS AGAINST MULTINATIONALS

The expansion of MNCs in the last twenty years has made the international free trade unions aware of the need for much closer cooperation. They have been desperately trying to come up with an effective program to counteract the enormous power of MNCs. All the major international trade secretariats have, with differing degrees of success, tried to formulate programs to deal with this problem by promoting exchanges of information between unions dealing with branches of the same corporation and in some isolated instances coordinating programs of solidarity.

To many of labor's academic friends the problem is a simple one and the proposed remedy is to implement a program of international collective bargaining and international solidarity during disputes. Although the long-term aim of the trade union movement is to formulate closer coordination in the collective bargaining field, I believe that any meaningful program for effectively dealing with multinational corporations at an international level is a long way off.

Like many other familiar terms, international collective bargaining has many definitions. It could mean, for example, international negotiations for either minimum or maximum wages and working conditions for all General Motors-owned plants throughout the world, or it could be defined as negotiating for an agreement with the same company on a regional basis, such as within the EC. It could also mean negotiating for an agreement with unions dealing with the same company in two or more countries, such as the United States and Canada.

If we are dealing with the latter, there is a possibility of some success, and even at the regional level I would expect over a period of time that progress could be made in some areas. But when dealing with the problem on an overall or global basis as defined in my first example, I cannot foresee international collective bargaining on a worldwide basis being achieved in my lifetime, if ever. I do, however, see the possibility of much closer coordination between unions in different countries during negotiations. I also believe that certain conditions, such as safety and health, for example, could be negotiated and applied on an international level.

COORDINATED BARGAINING WITHIN THE UNITED STATES

In order to emphasize some of the problems of bargaining at the international level, it is useful to look at some of the problems involved in coordinated bargaining in the United States. A union like the International Association of Machinists and Aerospace Workers (IAM) has a long history of local autonomy and it is still common to negotiate agreements at the plant level. A company, therefore, with five different plants in different parts of the United States could be covered by five different agreements, including different expiration dates. Wages could vary according to regional patterns and fringe benefits could be different, based on the needs of the workers in the different locations.

Unless serious problems occur, it is difficult to assure our members that they should be covered by one agreement. This problem obviously would be magnified greatly on an international scale. Workers in California, for example, are not enthusiastic about workers from another location, whether Michigan or Germany, deciding whether they should or should not strike.

Another problem in the metal fabricating industry is that most of the companies make a variety of products and, therefore, different plants can have different job classifications and wage systems. This becomes an even worse problem when dealing with the diverse products manufactured by conglomerates.

We do have examples of successful coordinated bargaining in the American Can Company, the Continental Can Company and in our airline agreements which are national in scope. One of the necessary requirements for any effective coordinated program is common agreement expiration dates, but these are very difficult to obtain.

There have also been many examples of successful coordinated bargaining programs with the Industrial Union Department of the AFL-CIO, but when a number of unions with different structures and traditions are involved, problems become even greater. In these instances autonomy can become a major obstacle, and seeking the cooperation of workers engaged in manufacturing different products is even more difficult.

In spite of these obstacles, trade unions in the United States realize the value of the coordinated bargaining approach and continue learning to work in this direction by trial and error. Often, a union having a major problem with a corporation is the first to call for a form of coordinated bargaining, but when the members have obtained satisfaction, both interest and cooperation quickly wanes.

Coordinated bargaining can also suffer when, as in a McDonnell-Douglas dispute last year, the members of the United Auto Workers in California accepted an offer by the company and returned to work. IAM members in St. Louis refused the same offer and stayed out on strike for several weeks. Similar events have occurred during railroad strikes when unions not satisfied with the general agreement have chosen to strike for further gains. With this background, it is easy to see that all problems like this would be further exaggerated at the international level.

PROBLEMS IN DEVELOPING COUNTRIES

Some of the major obstacles to overcome in the developing countries are the incentives and pressures from governments which are desperately seeking investment and employment possibilities. In practically all the developing countries it is considered necessary to offer tax and other incentives. There is a constant fear that when tax holidays are over and wage levels have been raised, the multinational corporations will leave for more fertile areas where they can become even more profitable. MNCs are, therefore, in an excellent bargaining position and can even insist on legislation imposing controls and conditions on trade union activity.

In Malaysia, for example, there is still a ban on organizing workers in the electronic industry in the Penang area although a large number of the 15,000 workers have indicated a desire to become organized. The union has tried to process this particular case through the courts but has met with little success. They claim that the MNCs have threatened the Malaysian government that they will move out if workers in that area are allowed to become organized. Where such conditions exist, there is no possibility of formulating any kind of coordinating bargaining or trade union solidarity.

Another problem confronting unions, in dealing with companies they have organized in other parts of the world, is that parent companies like Texas Instruments, Motorola, IBM and Eastman Kodak are not organized in the United States. Assistance from unions elsewhere is, therefore, likely to be limited.

A few years ago, for example, Texas Instruments went into production in Curacao, an island in the Caribbean. After a long and bitter struggle, which included a strike supported by the IMF, the union which obtained recognition from the Curacao government also received recognition from the company. A few months ago, after a lengthy court case processed by the union on behalf of workers who were illegally fired was won, the company closed its operations in Curacao and moved to Haiti, where it can operate without any danger of trade union interference. The big weakness exposed in this case is that unless a corporation is organized on a worldwide basis, there is little chance of an effective coordinated bargaining approach.

Another example of difficulties encountered in the less developed countries is that of the Honda Company operating in Indonesia. In this instance the company was paying its workers the equivalent of 35 cents a day which was about one-third the rate other multinational corporations were paying. Workers were hired on one or two year individual contracts and if the workers' performance and behavior were not satisfactory, contracts were not renewed. This company last year was refusing to renew contracts for workers engaged in trade union activities.

Trade unions in Indonesia are very weak and as some of their meagre finances come from the Indonesian government, they are not able to operate independently. In such countries there is little semblance of collective bargaining and small possibility of strikes being tolerated by the governments for any reason.

These examples, which could be repeated many times, show what an enormous amount of work has to be done in order to form an effective trade union organization in many of the countries of the less developed areas of the world. Until this is done there can be no effective collective bargaining at the national level, without even considering the possibility of international collective bargaining.

THE SITUATION IN TOTALITARIAN COUNTRIES

MNCs do not hesitate to move their operations to dictatorship or Communist countries when it is profitable to do so. This raises a whole series of new problems which thwart a worldwide coordinated bargaining goal. Most of the plants in Communist countries are built by MNCs and taken over after completion by the government involved. The MNC is then paid back by products which have to be marketed in the Western world.

FIAT, International Harvester and General Tire Company have all entered into these types of agreements. A representative from a metalworker's union in Europe, recently in Russia, was asked about the possibility of support from their so-called unions in the event that a dispute with one of these corporations arose in any of the Western

European countries. The Russian, of course, explained that all corporations in that country are owned by the state and, therefore, the people, eliminating all such problems.

The union representative then asked if the shipment of products manufactured for an MNC could be stopped during a strike against the same company in a European country. He was solemnly told that all agreements with MNCs stipulate that products will be provided without hindrance. Any work stoppage would be a breach of contract and, therefore, no strike would ever be tolerated. With this attitude it is not surprising that during the coal strike in Britain, the British Mineworkers' Union, which has a strong Communist influence on its executive board, was turned down when it appealed to the Polish mineworkers to stop producing coal for Britain.

In my opinion there is no possibility of any meaningful cooperation between trade unions in the Western world and the government-dominated workers' organizations existing in Communist-bloc countries, where workers are denied basic trade union freedoms and the right to strike. Any coordinated solidarity action would be severely hampered if during a strike supported by unions in several Western countries there was a free flow of the same products coming from Communist-bloc countries.

In right-wing dictatorship countries the same problems exist. Conditions such as those which existed in Franco's Spain, where trade unions were brutally suppressed for many years, attract a large number of MNCs. Some of these corporations in Spain even included army generals on their boards of directors in order to stay in favor with the regime. During this time, workers were arrested and jailed for belonging to a trade union organization having any connection with the international trade secretariats. Once again, a large proportion of the products manufactured in Spain were, by agreement with the corporations, for export to other parts of Europe and the United States. Joint action by the free trade unions of the world would have been seriously jeopardized by uninterrupted production from Spain, and in this instance there could have been no possibility of any form of international bargaining which could have included Spanish operations.

Spain is only used as an example. There are many areas of the world presently under right-wing dictatorship governments which offer the same haven from trade union activity for multinational corporations.

THE OUTLOOK IN INDUSTRIALIZED COUNTRIES

In the industrialized countries, particularly in Western Europe, there has been closer coordination between trade unions through the international trade secretariats, and a great deal of progress has been made in closing the gap between wage levels and fringe benefits. Even in this area, we are faced with many problems in dealing with multinational conglomerates. Often workers are represented by trade unions affiliated to several different international trade secretariats because of the different types of products manufactured. Up until now the international trade secretariats have been working to implement programs with their own affiliates, but dealing with conglomerates would entail a joint program with the participation of several of the relevant international trade secretariats.

The European EC would seem to be an ideal place to start an effective coordinated bargaining program, but even here there are many obstacles. Labor legislation varies from country to country and covers many fringe benefits which in the United States would be considered in the realm of collective bargaining. Vacations, retirement age, restrictions on overtime, holidays and other items are all determined by legislation and generally differ between countries. The different national unions have failed to agree on their basic goals, with few organizations willing, for example, to go the same codetermination route as the Germans. National agreements by industry which are common in Europe would be difficult to get changed so as to allow international bargaining by company.

It would be difficult to imagine the German trade unions that have an entirely different structure and seldom strike to go out in support of a petty grievance in Great Britain. By the same token, it does not seem feasible that the British unions would be willing to change their legislation to conform with other standards set by European unions. In Great Britain, for example, contract negotiations can be opened at any time as there is no set duration of an agreement. Under this system strikes are therefore possible at any time and are often implemented to solve simple grievances that would be resolved in the United States through our grievance and arbitration procedures, with no thought of a work stoppage.

The differences in power structures from one country to another also have to be considered. In the German unions, most of the power is concentrated in the top level of the national unions. Under the British structure the shop stewards' committees, often with representation from several different unions, wield a great deal of influence and would have to be convinced of the need for international cooperation before giving up this authority. Even if in Europe bargaining for the same wage agreements within multinational corporations eventually proves possible, government policies during economic difficulties when income restraints, wage freezes and devaluation are put into effect would cause further complications and eliminate uniformity.

In France, Italy, Portugal and Spain, Communists presently dominate the largest trade union organizations, and these unions would also have to be included in an effective international bargaining agreement. I cannot imagine democratic unions, working within their international trade secretariats, getting involved in political strikes with organizations largely financed by Moscow nor would American unions be willing to work in cooperation with them. In my opinion, this situation does impose an impossible hurdle to overcome in trying to achieve true international collective bargaining.

In most countries different emphasis has been placed on various fringe benefits. It would be very hard to get a worldwide consensus on what should be given priority. In Germany, codetermination has been promoted, and in Scandinavia there has been emphasis on a different form of worker participation in management. In the United States we have stayed away from this approach and concentrate on more pragmatic goals.

In Japan, trade unions bargain for housing allowances, company-supported canteens, one extra month's pay per year and extra wages based on seniority. The idea of lifetime employment is also prevalent in Japan, and there is strong opposition to plant closings and layoffs. Even in the LDCs workers are strongly opposed to layoffs and plant closings, while we in the United States accept the company's prerogative to lay workers off or terminate operations. If any form of international collective bargaining were implemented, all these differences would still have to be settled by local supplemental agreements, with the likelihood that only minimum standards could be bargained internationally.

One of the most obvious areas for international coordinated bargaining is with the international airlines which are multinational in scope, having employees under trade union agreements in many different countries. Even in this area there has been little progress made, although there have been incidents of effective international solidarity action during times of dispute.

One of the more publicized examples of worldwide cooperation was when the Airline Pilots' Association called for a one day strike against hijacking. This was far from successful as many pilots, including a great many in the United States, went to work under threats of legal retaliation by employers. The IAM has fought a long series of court cases because of this incident as our members stayed out in support of the strike. This incident raises the whole question of how effective solidarity action could be on a worldwide scale without legislative changes in most countries.

During the recent strike against the rubber companies, worldwide support was called for by the International Chemical Workers' Federation. Although there were many incidents of solidarity action, it was far from effective and did not prevent a lengthy work stoppage.

THE ROLE OF INTERNATIONAL ORGANIZATION

The international trade union movement has been working to get codes of conduct for MNCs adopted by the OECD, the International Labour Office and the United Nations. These would, if recognized by governments, set the stage for more meaningful future cooperation. The codes by themselves, however, would have little impact in areas of the world where trade unions are weak or under government control. Since these codes have to be accepted by labor, employers and government, it is doubtful that they would be more than weak instruments useful only with the most flagrant abuses by MNCs.

It would also be difficult to envisage the governments of the less developed countries of the world abiding by an ILO convention imposing restrictions on MNCs if by so doing they would jeopardize their chances of much needed investment. By the same token international institutions have given no indication of a change in their policies toward the double standard applied to Communist-bloc countries in dealing with freedom of association, the right to bargain collectively and other necessary requirements for trade union freedom that international collective bargaining would require. Codes of conduct are a necessary first step toward more international uniformity in legislation controlling MNCs but their likely impact has been greatly exaggerated.

OTHER FORMS OF INTERNATIONAL COOPERATION AMONG UNIONS

These are a few of the many problems involved in establishing a framework for international collective bargaining. I believe, however, that much has been done and much more can be done to implement programs of cooperation between the trade unions of the free world in dealing with MNCs. In the IMF we have started a very effective program of exchanging information for collective bargaining purposes, and there have been several incidents of solidarity action among unions in different countries.

The IMF Secretariat has supported collective bargaining educational programs in the LDCs, and this effort, combined with the collection and dissemination of pertinent information, has helped trade unions considerably during contract negotiations. Exchange of information has also helped the European unions to close the gap in wage differentials and fringe benefits over the years and has made trade unions throughout the world aware of new developments in such areas as job enrichment, codetermination, supplemental unemployment benefits, and lifetime employment. It is only natural that trade unions throughout the world with more cooperation will eventually pick out the best aspects of collective bargaining achievements in other countries and use them for their own collective bargaining goals.

International trade secretariat meetings have also been arranged to exchange experiences with unions representing workers in the same corporations operating in different countries. These meetings have already resulted in a more uniform approach to tackling some of the major problems confronting unions in dealing with MNCs.

The entire MNC problem, however, has to be handled phase by phase on a long-term basis. Quick results through any form of coordinated bargaining are only likely to emerge in a few special instances where the right circumstances prevail. On the positive side, international cooperation among free trade unions is increasing. Unless the MNCs change their ways, this will give the international labor movement the inducement to create even stronger and more binding ties.

21

A Multinational's Response to Its Needs and the Welfare of Its Workers

JEROME JACOBSON

THE IMPERATIVES FOR GOING MULTINATIONAL

MNCs are large, complex and varied enterprises, and they no doubt behave in different ways toward the welfare of their workers. Rather than deal with these issues abstractly, I shall describe the policies and experience of one specific MNC. Whether the Bendix Corporation fits the prevailing patterns of behavior often imputed to MNCs, I leave to others to decide.

The reason for the Bendix Corporation's presence in every country in which they are located is evident. If we were not there through local manufacture or license, we could not save our markets by exporting from the United States. Usually, our chief competitors abroad are firms which are owned by host country nationals or other MNCs. If we did not have a piece of the local action, they would simply have bigger pieces of it. Our exports are not diminished by our foreign investments. Most of our products must be produced locally or we could not sell them.

For example, we simply cannot economically ship our braking systems, brake linings, electrical and electronic automotive engine controls to France, Brazil or Japan. Local producers would beat us in the marketplace. For many of our products, moreover, supply lines must be short and very responsive. Because of the intimate contacts required between our engineers and the engineers of firms using our products, we have to be right on hand.

Granted, we do export replacement parts for certain products, particularly highly technical, low volume items. Yet when the overseas market gets to be big and when overseas producers get the hang of the technology, it is inevitable for production to start overseas. If Bendix does not produce in these countries, someone else will. Tariff walls and other "inducements" and local cost advantages will see to that.

Our best hope for competing in the export business is to produce higher technology products—to offset local advantages by exporting technically superior products. We must keep up on R & D and on technology, financing it in part by exporting technologically superior products. This is how we bolster new product development which, in turn, increases our exports.

We have limited experience with the so-called runaway industries—the Taiwans, Mexicos and others—but in several cases the need was obvious. Local producers had gotten the hang of producing our products more cheaply than we could in the United States. Either we went out of the business lines altogether or we produced overseas to export to the United States and elsewhere. Runaways are certainly not always successful. For example, we have liquidated our plant in Taiwan. Our Mexican operation faces stiff competition in sales in the United States from producers in Japan and elsewhere.

We have not curbed domestic investments because of our overseas investments. We have been able to finance all the activities we feel we should be in at home. And our overseas investments contribute to the cash flow and earnings to support both overseas and domestic investments.

What about transfer pricing—the so-called shifting of profits abroad to escape U.S. taxation? U.S. laws are very strict about such matters. I have yet to see a decision made in the Bendix Corporation on the presumption that we could use a "cute" pricing formula to hide profits earned abroad.

THE IMPACT OF MULTINATIONAL OPERATIONS ON LABOR

Some MNCs are accused of shuttling production between countries to weaken labor's bargaining position. We do not do that. Granted, we may use dual sources to meet local customers' needs and to provide assured supplies. In a few cases, we rely on one affiliate to supply another. Again, the reason we do this is because it would be stupid economics not to. If we failed to do it, others would beat us out in both markets.

Bendix has done virtually <u>no</u> exporting from our affiliates abroad to our plants in the United States. Maybe we should do more but we cannot make the economics come out right. That says that at the margin, each of us, at home and abroad, is doing just the right thing. On the contrary, we are exporting to some of our affiliates—equipment to get them started, components to help early production and companion products to round out product lines.

Bendix does not fit the nefarious image that MNCs are supposed to have. For other MNCs, the product mix and levels of technology may cause them to act differently than we do. But if they respond to hard market realities as we do, if they produce locally because local markets require it and exports cannot do the job, then some of them will act as Bendix does.

Understandably, labor is concerned about the impact of MNCs at home and abroad. Are MNCs inherently any less good citizens, here or there? Are they any more hostile to local labor than are local interests? At Bendix we respect local labor laws. We recognize unions, though we are troubled when they allow political considerations to dominate their behavior. Codetermining does not bother us provided we can continue to manage effectively.

Our views toward wages, benefits and the like are not dictated by the fact that we have plants in several countries. Almost every one of our situations is dictated by purely local considerations. In any case, labor's concern should be with the entire industry in a country. Is it really satisfactory to focus only on an MNC in France when the MNC's main rival there is a French company? If labor manages to unify its approach, it should confront an entire industry, not just the MNC. Indeed, trade union officials concerned with international coordination in dealing with MNCs recognize that local laws, policies, culture, and related matters stand in the way of a unified international approach by labor towards employees.

The effects upon labor in the United States of crazy-quilt inducements abroad to attract MNCs are minimal as far as Bendix is concerned. We did not and do not encourage trade barriers abroad. We cannot, of course, be blamed for these and other arrangements that distort factor flows. But we do not rely upon them, for we can be trapped by reversible crazy-quilts—advantages withdrawn or preferences granted one company as against another.

Bendix is not the labor-busting, country-jumping MNC frequently described by labor officials. We have acted as the market and local circumstances have forced us to act. If we did not become an MNC, our overseas profits would be smaller and our domestic market and exports would be smaller. We would be worse off and labor in the United States would be no better off.

MNCs are generally a rational response to market forces and to the realities of national laws. Restraints on the flow of capital and technologies in the name of saving jobs at home would lead to lower efficiency and lower overall production worldwide. Labor opportunities abroad, and to some extent at home, would be worsened, and consumers here and abroad would certainly suffer.

The great push to economic development, to job opportunities, to the upgrading of technology and to the creation of industries of viable size brought about by many MNCs should not be overlooked. None of these considerations, of course, is an argument against the efforts of trade unions to advance the welfare of their members who are employed by MNCs. Workers should indeed strive to upgrade their strength to deal with management.

We have no problem at all dealing with responsible labor unions not dominated by political considerations and in meeting, and sometimes leading in, wages and other conditions of labor. It is wrong to believe that we are hostile simply because we are an MNC and have assets deployed around the world. Unfortunately, that attitude is often imputed toward MNCs. Bendix behaves, and intends to continue to behave, in a responsible way to the ethics, the practices and the environments in which we work, in whatever part of the world that may be.

PART IV

ENERGY, RAW MATERIALS, AND THE WELFARE OF WORKERS WORLDWIDE

22

Protecting the Welfare of Workers in North-South Relations

SHRIDATH S. RAMPHAL

AMERICAN LABOR AND WORLD POVERTY

The 1976 AFL-CIO platform proposals to both the Democratic and Republican parties reaffirm American labor's long-standing commitment to an active and constructive U. S. role in seeking a more just world order. In the postwar era, this began three decades ago with vigorous trade union support of the Marshall Plan and Point IV. Today it is expressed in these words by the AFL-CIO:

> America's foreign aid program, conceived in compassion and humanitarianism, continues to serve a vital need. So long as hunger, pestilence, human deprivation and illiteracy persist, there can be no stable world peace. The needs of other nations for economic progress and social justice are so compelling that America should dedicate an adequate percentage of its annual GNP to continue foreign aid.

That assessment of global instability as the concomitant of worldwide poverty is inescapable; American labor's response to it is worthy of its deep concern. But, although it may be a major need, increased aid is not the priority demand of the countries of the Third World. Like workers everywhere, while they need to survive, they know that in work, not in "welfare," in fair wages, not in the dole, lies the key to real survival. They would prefer not handouts but equality of opportunity to produce and to exchange for a fair return. In a changing world economy they seek assurance of that equality through structural change—through a new order, founded on a new ethos, of international economic relations.

The response of the United States to the call for a new international economic order is critical because its economic strength is such that abstention becomes a veto. But my emphasis is not selective. My exhortations, and sometimes my criticisms, apply with at least equal force to some of the other industrialized nations that are America's friends and partners in world politics and world trade.

And they are directed also, albeit naturally in a different context, to the industrialized Socialist countries which have not so far made a response commensurate with their assertions of concern or with their capability to assist employment and growth in the developing world. Nevertheless, the failure of some to make a satisfactory response cannot be a legitimate reason for inertia by others, least of all the United States.

America's responsibilities for peaceful progress in the world are reinforced by the high standards of idealism that Americans, despite a facade of hardheaded self-interest, have always held to. Great deprivation within this nation, deep division between a minority of super-rich and a majority worse than poor, would be an affront to American decency and a threat to American peace.

How much greater, then, must be the affront offered by the obscene disparities of wealth and poverty on a global scale that now threaten international harmony—threats that we know must be tempered not by the weapons of war but the instruments of peace, not by swords but by ploughshares, not by compulsions but by consensus.

International poverty speaks of the needs of the poorest of this earth: of the 1200 million who live in absolute poverty, uncertain of their next meal, certain only of a joyless life and premature death. They are, for the greater part, the people who lived for generations in the shadow of colonialism. Political colonialism is now almost dead, save in a few painful cases. But the economic structures of colonialism live on, structures of dependency which shackle the human creativity of their peoples. These people cry out for change. The world of poverty, the Third World, seeks what American workers have sought and won and remain vigilant to protect—an equitable sharing of the fruits of man's labor, a sharing whose benefits are felt in a new security for all.

The problems facing the Third World are immense; the human condition within it is desperate and steadily worsening. In 1975, one billion people in the poorest developing countries earned an average income of $105, that is, less than 30 cents a day. In the industrialized countries, the average was $3000 per year, almost 30 times as high. What is more, income inequality between nations has been accelerating. World Bank projections indicate that the increase in incomes which the industrialized countries can expect over the next decade will be 86 times as high as those for the poorest countries. By 1985 per capita income in the industrialized countries will be 45 times that in the poorest countries. This is what the present order has generated—more income inequality than at any previous time in mankind's history.

ECONOMIC AND SOCIAL REFORM AT HOME AND ABROAD

Not surprisingly, the developing countries urge changes in arrangements which constantly reduce their export incomes and which keep 40 percent of their labor force wholly or substantially without work throughout the year. They know and accept that the burden of development rests primarily on themselves. The achievement of the goals to which they aspire—basic goals such as freedom from hunger and the assurance that every head of household is able to earn enough to purchase, for himself and his family, two meals a day and a minimum of clothing—requires the introduction of far-reaching structural changes within their own countries, changes in the ownership and control of production, in social provisions, and in the distribution of wealth. All this they know and accept.

But the introduction of these necessary internal changes is more readily achieved in the context of a reasonable rate of growth. Redistribution which merely equalizes poverty is not a solution. This point, so often so misrepresented, requires emphasis. It forms no part of the demands of the Third World, as reflected in the demand for a New International Economic Order, that the poor in the rich countries should help the rich in the poor countries to become richer. Improved international economic arrangements are no substitute for economic and social reform within the developing countries themselves. But the truth is that the present international economic system actually works to make internal reform, including desirable political evolution, harder in developing nations. Bastions of democracy cannot be constructed on the quicksands of poverty.

By analogy with domestic welfare programs, the poorest among the developing countries ask for increased flows of concessional finance on a predictable basis, free from the vagaries of national economic management. Some seek temporary relief from the crushing burden of debt service which now imposes intolerable strains on their limited foreign exchange budgets and makes long-term planning highly precarious. But these needs for aid and debt relief are transitional problems which the developing countries are determined to overcome through earning the foreign exchange to pay for their essential imports.

All developing countries seek a predictable and remunerative price for their primary commodities. They urge the removal of artificial barriers that prevent their exports entering the markets of the industrialized countries and the end of a system under which a transfer of incomes actually takes place from the poor to the rich countries. They want a system of international credit which will have due regard for their needs and which will be truly international both in scope and management.

COMMODITIES, MULTINATIONALS AND THE NEEDS OF WORKERS WORLDWIDE

On prices, the developing countries as a group have had to endure a long-term deterioration in the purchasing power of their commodity exports—40 percent over the last 20 years. For some countries, like Sri Lanka in tea, the experience has actually been worse. This is how Sri Lanka's Prime Minister, Mrs. Bandaranaike, explained her country's experience at the thirty-first session of the UN General Assembly in September 1976:

> Tea accounts for more than 50 percent of Sri Lanka's export earnings. We have increased our production of tea, and systematically improved its quality over the years, and in the 14 years since 1962 we have watched its real price, in terms of the prices we pay for our imports, plummet by more than 70 percent. That represents a loss for Sri Lanka today of $500 million per annum, which, expressed in our national currency, amounts roughly to 6 billion rupees. That is almost the entire budget of my country for one whole year. How long and how far can modern human society, even parts of it, expect to prosper or even survive with such an economic system?

Superimposed on this long-term decline has been a marked volatility in commodity prices. Is it any wonder that levels of investment in certain critical commodities are considered by many to be inadequate to supply the long-term demand of both the developed and the developing countries? Some have urged that these inadequate levels of investment suggest a greater role for transnational enterprises in raw material production in the developing countries. But if we are to be realistic, can the government of any country, developed or developing, fail to heed the demands of its population for the exercise of greater control over the exploitation of the national patrimony and a greater share in the benefits?

If there is one concern which the governments of developing countries and the representatives of American labor hold in common it is over the activities of the multinational corporation, wherever its country of origin. Consider this statement:

> Although they are a relatively new phenomenon, multinational corporations already span the globe. They know no homeland and have no loyalties to nations or people. Concerned almost entirely with the bottom line on the ledger book, the multinationals too often disrupt economic life, undermine political stability and the social fabric of the nations in which they operate.

This quotation is not from a resolution of the Group of 77 developing nations but from a policy resolution of the AFL-CIO. This is an area where there is scope for dialogue, where the requirements of developing countries for the transfer of technology can usefully be discussed, along with the anxieties of U.S. labor about the export of jobs.

For it is only in such a dialogue that common goals can be identified, along with short-term conflicts of interests. I am convinced that, in the long-term, the interests both of American labor and the wretched of the world will be advanced by pursuing the same comprehensive goals—goals for the pursuit of mutual interest, obviating the need for charity. Many people in the industrialized countries, including some American workers, fear that the emergence of the Third World out of poverty can be achieved only through a reduction in the hard-earned standards of living of workers in these countries. I submit that not only is this view incorrect but that the reverse is true.

It is my case that, over the long-term, the improvement of worker standards in the developing countries is not only consistent with, but necessary for, the preservation of high standards of living and continuing improvements in the quality of life in the developed world. Moreover, if America, or the industrialized nations of whatever ideological persuasion, seek through a continuation of present policies to confine the developing countries to their current state of poverty and degradation, they will be putting at risk the very standards which they seek to safeguard and improve.

Nor should this be strange to American labor. Early leaders of the American trade union movement convinced owners of capital and the government in this country that the way to larger profits, higher incomes and greater social and political stability lay through satisfying the basic needs and legitimate demands of the American worker. It now falls to American labor to recognize, by an extension of the same principle, that in the context of growing interdependence in the world, the improvement of the standards of living of the American worker will depend increasingly on improving the standard of living of the workers in the developing nations, thereby protecting and advancing the welfare of workers worldwide. This is the challenge, and the opportunity which the New International Economic Order presents to American labor.

Almost 75 percent of the population of the world, excluding the Socialist states, live in the developing countries. In 1975, they earned less than 20 percent of its income. Their purchasing power is therefore low and the markets which they create for the manufactured goods which American labor can produce is smaller than it could be, impressive though it already is. The increases in the incomes which the developing countries would earn from the dismantling of trade barriers and other obstacles and from a sustained expansion of their export income from primary commodities and from manufactures would be spent on imports from the industrialized countries.

This thesis is based on fact, not conjecture. The developing countries have shown a high propensity to spend their export earnings. The growth in their absorption of American exports has more than compensated for the declining rate of increase of these exports to the industrialized countries. Moreover, this expansion in import demand has been concentrated, by and large, on those types of exports which are high generators of jobs in the American economy.

AMERICAN LABOR'S STAKE IN THE ECONOMIC GROWTH OF THE THIRD WORLD

Between 1972 and 1975, total American merchandise exports increased from just under $48 billion to just over $103 billion. The importance of such exports is growing rapidly, and they are providing an increasing and dynamic component to growth in the American economy. The share of American exports going to the industrialized countries, which was 66 percent in 1972, fell to under 58 percent in 1975. On the other hand, the share of American merchandise exports going to the developing countries increased from over 28 percent in 1972 to over 35 percent in 1975.*

Besides, the composition of this increasing share of exports going to the developing countries is even more significant for employment generation in the United States. In manufactured goods, 29 percent of U. S. exports went to developing countries in 1972; this rose to over 37 percent in 1975. The share of motor vehicle exports going to developing countries increased from over 18 percent in 1972 to nearly 29 percent in 1975. A similar picture emerges in engineering exports, where the share of U. S. exports going to the developing countries increased from just over 31 percent in 1972 to almost 41 percent in 1975.

In other words, out of every dollar increase in U. S. exports between 1972 and 1975, 42 cents came from the developing countries. Out of every dollar increase of exports of manufactured goods, more than 45 cents came from the developing countries. Out of every dollar increase of exports of motor vehicles, 38 cents came from the developing countries. Out of every dollar increase of export earnings from engineering products, almost 49 cents came from the developing

---

*The data in this and subsequent paragraphs are drawn from the GATT publications for the relevant years: International Trade (Annual) General Agreement on Tariffs and Trade, GATT, Geneva.

countries. All this occurred despite the low income levels and low growth in the developing countries!

But there is a further dimension of the importance of developing countries to U.S. trade, not reflected in the trade statistics. A substantial proportion of U.S. exports to other industrialized countries, in the form of capital equipment and materials, is employed to produce goods which the developing countries buy.

American labor, therefore, has an increasing stake in expanding the import capability of the developing countries in view of its obvious capacity to supply precisely the kinds of goods for which the economic development of the developing countries will generate demand. The benefits to the United States are immediate and direct.

The fastest growing trade between the industrialized and the developing countries, moreover, is not in goods but in services. And it is in the services sector that the major addition to jobs in the United States has emerged over the last few decades. Exports of technology to the developing countries are increasing by 20 percent a year and export earnings from this source are projected to exceed $9 billion in the very near future—a massive and growing source of jobs for the exporters of technology among whom the United States stands preeminent.

The overall threat to U.S. jobs represented by U.S. imports of manufactured goods from the developing countries is greatly exaggerated. Such imports increased by about two-thirds in value terms between 1972 and 1975, to reach a total of $9.68 billion. But this is far below the level and rate of increase in U.S. exports of manufactured goods to the developing countries, which over the same period increased by 170 percent—almost three times as fast—to reach $26.1 billion—almost three times as high.

How, one must ask, will the developing countries be able to purchase from the United States unless they are also able to export to the U.S. manufactures which would allow them to employ their millions of unemployed and under-employed workers?

IMPACT OF DEVELOPING COUNTRIES ON U.S. EMPLOYMENT

Viewed in this light, the developing countries cannot see justification for the continuous escalation in barriers against their exports of manufactured goods, the latest being on sugar. They are disappointed that the limited concessions wrung from the industrialized countries in the form of the GSP are so ringed with conditions, exceptions, and safeguard clauses as to make long-term planning for increased production hazardous and to frustrate the emergence of economic integration among developing countries for which the industrialized countries profess active support. It is unfortunate, as it is unjust, that the response which the United States feels impelled to make, to meet assumed threats from export subsidies—dumping and other trade destabilizing measures adopted by other developed countries—should also apply, often apply solely, to the developing countries which are least able to counter them.

Not surprisingly, many are convinced that positive steps are needed to bring about a more equitable international distribution of labor, with the industrialized countries concentrating on those industries and those parts of industries which make use of their tremendous capability, technology, and their enormous stock of capital—transferring to the developing countries those industries and parts of industries which utilize the one advantage the developing countries have, a vast pool of labor. It is in this context that a Commonwealth Group of Experts, drawn from developed and developing countries, urged upon the industrialized world the need "to accept, and provide for the consequences of, the fact that the relocation of some industries or parts of industries to developing countries is an essential, inevitable, continuous and desirable element in a new economic order, and one which is in the long-term interest of developing and developed countries alike."[1] This cannot take place overnight, but the process must be started.

The historical process by which the American trade unions moved toward higher levels of efficiency within the United States must now be applied to international economic relations between the United States and developing countries. The consequences of such a movement must also be provided for, and quite correctly, American labor has demanded the introduction of policies to accelerate the changing structure of the labor force along the lines which it has followed over the past century, that is, a labor force equipped with greater sophistication, more capital and higher capabilities in technology. These kinds of adjustments are not new; they are an inevitable outcome of functional and productive interpendence which, within national economics, wrought enormous improvements in worker standards.

What the Third World is seeking should not be seen as a redistribution in its favor of a static world income. The higher incomes sought by the poor, through commodity arrangements as well as through better access to rich country markets, would automatically create increased demands for the exports of the industrialized countries. This would generate an expansion in the economies of these latter countries and an increase in their incomes, and signal significant growth in world economic activity with the poor nations sharing—more equitably than before—in the increment to world income created by such activity.

There would be a quickening symbiotic relationship between development in the poor countries and continued growth in the rich. Traditional economics has tended to emphasize the one-way flow from the developed to the developing. I submit that the reverse flow is equally important for sustaining employment levels in the United States and that it is becoming more so.

CONFLICT AND COOPERATION IN NORTH-SOUTH RELATIONS

Yet there are those on both sides of the debate who see the nature of economic relations between developed and developing countries in terms of inevitable conflict of interests and confrontation. AFL-CIO resolutions speak of "threats of cartelization" and of nations producing bauxite, copper and iron exploring the possibilities of limiting the supply and/or raising the price of their exports through cartel-like action. This, if I may say so, is language akin to the abuse heaped on early trade unionists who fought attempts to cut the wages of workers when the price of food was rising. Developing countries are merely seeking to reverse the trend by which they are obliged to produce more and more sugar or sisal or tea or copper to buy the same tractor.

The analogy between the pioneering efforts of the world's poor to secure a better deal through collective effort and the early struggles of American labor is close indeed. When sometimes American trade unionists feel impelled to be critical or impatient with the Third World, using labels such as 'spoilers' or 'blackmailers,' I urge them to look back upon the beginnings of their own movement. Such reflection might encourage them to bring to bear upon the world's poor a measure of the understanding which men like Walter Lippmann showed for the American labor movement in earlier days. In a piece he wrote as long ago as 1914 when this movement stood greatly in need of understanding within the society it was seeking to make more just, Lippmann urged Americans to recognize that:

> The unions are struggling where life is nakedly brutal, where the dealings of men have not been raised even to the level of discussion which we find in politics. There is almost as little civil procedure in industry as there is in Mexico, or as there was on the American Frontier. To expect unionists then to talk with velvet language and act with the deliberation of a college faculty is to be a tenderfoot, a victim of your class tradition. The virtues of labour today are frontier virtues, its struggles are for rights and privileges that the rest of us inherited from

> our unrefined ancestors. Men are fighting for the beginnings of industrial self-government. If the world were wise that fight would be made easier for them.[2]

The world's poor stand today in need of such understanding and the world itself of such wisdom.

Pulling down the shutters on the developing countries will therefore not only blot out the prospect of a profitable two-way process of global development. It will also create an area of darkness far wider than is now believed, with all its attendant consequences for international peace. It will be an abnegation of the principle of labor solidarity which the American worker from his early days has actively espoused. It cannot, therefore, be an option which American labor can support either in its own domestic interest or in its wider international role.

Of course there are costs, as there are benefits, accruing to labor in the industrialized countries in making a positive response to developing country demands for a fairer deal. There will be transitional problems and localized difficulties. But the world economy will be larger, more diversified and more complementary, and better able to cushion the boom-bust cycles that afflict nations from time to time.

The choice, therefore, is before American labor. It can react to short-term considerations and respond solely to immediate and localized problems. It can support restrictive conditions of access to markets, an inadequate supply of credit for the developing countries and an exploitative system for trade in primary commodities. It can press for the pursuit of autarchic policies which can only result in higher costs at home while frustrating the emergence of the Third World.

But there is an alternative—to support an early transition in the international distribution of labor and of production facilities and a furthering of meaningful and highly productive interdependence with countries of the Third World. Such a transition will call for appropriate policies at the level of firms, labor unions and governments, policies which are more readily introduced if the processes of change are orderly and are part of a global bargain. In human terms, in economic terms, in national terms and in international terms, I suggest that the benefits of the second alternative far outweigh the costs.

The new contract which the Third World seeks with the First World and the Second is not aid-oriented. It does not rest on the concept of charity or even the valid one of humanitarianism. It rests firmly and securely on the premise that the dependent relationships of the past have served the world badly, that isolationism is not an option open to even the most powerful of countries and that interdependence is the only road along which the world can travel. In this planetary bargain, its short-term problems notwithstanding, there are no losers.

The idea of change in the world economy, the conception of a new economic order, may prove to be the greatest challenge of our times. It is a challenge that must be met but which could so easily be missed. Its prospect brings to mind those haunting lines of T. S. Eliot:

Between the idea
And the reality
Between the motion
And the act
Falls the shadow.

Between the conception
And the creation
Between the emotion
And the response
Falls the shadow.[3]

As the response of the United States evolves to this challenge to mankind's common future on our planet, workers throughout the world will expect American labor to insure that no shadow be cast upon the creation of a new and more just economic order.

NOTES

1. Commonwealth Group of Experts, Towards a New International Economic Order (London: Commonwealth Secretariat, 1977).

2. Walter Lippmann, "The Strike at General Motors, Today and Tomorrow," New York Herald Tribune, January 7, 1937 quoted in Rossiter & Lare, The Essential Lippmann: A Political Philosophy for Liberal Democracy (New York: Random House, 1963).

3. T.S. Eliot, "The Hollow Men," Collected Poems 1909-1962. Reprinted by permission of the publisher, Harcourt, Brace, Jovanovich, Inc.

23

Equality and Justice in a Lopsided World: How the Rich Can Help the Poor

ROBERT LEKACHMAN

THE GLOOMY PROSPECTS FOR GROWTH WITH EQUITY

In its October 1976 report on The Future of the World Economy, a distinguished UN group of economists headed by Nobel Laureate Wassily Leontieff reached two conclusions of great import. The first concerned the gloomy prospect in the near future for narrowing the gap between poor and rich countries. (In the interests of honesty in language, I shall continue to say rich and poor rather than developed and developing, industrializing and industrialized, or any other pair of euphemisms which soften reality.) Here is the way the 1980s and 1990s look in the absence of substantial changes in the policies of rich and poor societies:

> Target rates of growth of gross product in the developing nations, set by the International Development Strategy for the Second United Nations Development Decade, are not sufficient to start closing the income gap between the developing and the developed countries. Higher growth rates in developing countries in the 1980s and 1990s, coupled with slightly lower rates in the developed countries (as compared to their long-term trends) are needed to reduce, at least by half, the average income gap by 2000.[1]

The UN projection accords unhappily with the conclusions of seasoned observers about what has already occurred since the end of World War II. Out of his experience in the World Bank, Hollis Chenery identified a general "tendency for the benefits of growth to be concentrated in the early stages and spread only slowly thereafter." The vast majority who are poor suffer from "specific disabilities that can be summed up as lack of physical and human capital and lack of access."[2] Policies calculated to share the benefits of growth more equally are difficult to introduce and administer. Elites, as in Brazil and Chile, yield readily to tactics of repression rather than redistribution. Torture in the short run seems an efficient substitute for social justice. Thus, concludes Chenery, only Tanzania, Taiwan, Yugoslavia, Korea, Costa Rica and Israel can plausibly claim effectively to have combined growth with redistribution in the direction of equality. Of Tanzania, Chenery concludes:

> From 1967 to 1973, wage/salary inequality sharply fell, large-scale landlord holdings experienced a total takeover . . . the retailer profit margin reversed and broadening of rural/urban gap halted.

And even here a note of caution was advisable, for the actual distribution of income was "only marginally better in 1973 than in 1967." However, "the trend appears to be positive and built on programs which should sustain it and allow the growth needed to finance it."[3]

Is there no hope? Are the obstacles to equitable development completely intractable? It is worth citing here the second major conclusion of the UN study:

> The principal limits to sustained economic growth and accelerated development are political, social and institutional in character rather than physical. No insurmountable physical barriers exist within the 20th century to the accelerated development of the developing regions.[4]

The UN rejection of the limits of growth argument advanced by the first report of the Club of Rome and popularized in the work of Robert Heilbroner[5] amounts to a statement of possibility. How likely poor nations are to grasp available developing strategies depends above all on their politics, institutions and sociology. Recent events in India, Yugoslavia and Latin America speak discouragingly about the immediate future of development within an egalitarian context.

It is no wonder that, again to cite Chenery, "more than a decade of rapid growth in underdeveloped countries has been of little or no benefit to perhaps a third of the population," for "although the average per capita income of the Third World has increased by 50 percent since 1960, this growth has been very unequally distributed among countries, regions within countries, and socioeconomic groups."[6]

To put the matter more bluntly, alliances in the Third World between authoritarian governments and huge multinational conglomerates have promoted historical tendencies toward enclave industrialization. Ill-balanced industrialization has enriched small indigenous elites of entrepreneurs and stockholders of global corporations, but done distressingly little for the impoverished masses. Unbalanced development has promoted monoculture and turned food exporters into food importers, as Geoffrey Barraclough among others has noted. Premature urbanization has created vast miserably sheltered, unemployed or underemployed hosts of migrants from the land. Ill-advised, wholesale importation of Western modes of crop culture have created a dependence upon petroleum-based fertilizers the costs of which have soared in the wake of the OPEC cartel. Indeed the major victims of that cartel have not been the rich countries of the Western hemisphere but poor nations without oil of their own in Africa, Asia and Latin America, although OPEC has had one perverse but potentially beneficial consequence for the poor nations by jolting political leadership in the West into giving more serious attention to North-South relations.

JUSTICE AND REDISTRIBUTION

Within societies and among societies, the overriding issue of the last half of this century has been, and very likely will continue to be, equality. The UN has become a forum in which huge Third World majorities annually present their bill to the rich West plus Japan. The items on the bill vary. They include commodity agreements which stabilize at high levels the raw materials which often are all that the poorest nations have to export. Other items are loans on concessionary terms or actual grants, easy access to Western technology and acceptance by the multinationals of terms of operation favorable to host nations. Even Americans complacent about the merits of American policy and economic behavior tend to become uneasy when Third World advocates point out that Americans, some four percent of the population of the globe, gobble up more than a third of the raw materials extracted each year the world over.

It is hard for someone who believes as I do, that American income and wealth ought to be less unequally distributed among Americans, to deny the justice of claims by poor nations upon their luckier neighbors. A good Rawlsian ought to be willing to apply his master's difference principle[7] to relations among nations as well as among groups and individuals within a given political entity.

Alas, as in most matters of real consequence, justice is not easily and simply served by transfers from rich to poor countries. When in 1975 the Group of 77 presented at the UN its set of reparations claims, it won from the United States and other Western countries a set of pledges to investigate stabilization of export income in the developing societies, to seek ways of alleviating the crushing burdens of international debt, to provide the Group of 77 with a larger (and louder) voice in the International Monetary Fund and to increase aid in support of industrialization by liberalizing access to established capital markets.

General and unspecific as they were, these promises marked a small advance in the responses of the rich to their impoverished brethren. Fifteen years ago twenty-five tons of natural rubber bought six tractors, but in 1975 only two. So has it gone in trade between raw material suppliers and exporters of finished goods and the artifacts of high technology, until vast OPEC success and substantial gains by bauxite producers. At that the United States, although voting for the 1975 UN resolution, objected to any tampering via indexation or commodity agreements with what the Ford administration laughingly insisted on calling free markets. Nor did the United States promise to increase the proportion of its GNP devoted to foreign aid or, for that matter, promise to diminish the percentage of existing aid wasted on armaments.

The Group of 77 had a case, based on the extensive history of trading and investment between rich and poor nations, against the West. Nevertheless, the UN resolution, a simplistic demand by the poor for more from the rich, barely scratched the surface of the issues of economic justice which are entangled in serious rectification of institutional arrangements among and within nations. Here are some of the more important complications sketchily stated as a series of queries.

> Since the burden of OPEC pricing policy has afflicted most dangerously the poorest communities of the globe, upon whom ought the burden of aiding India, Bangladesh, Pakistan, and nations similarly circumstanced, be placed? OPEC? The West? International agencies essentially funded by the West? If on two or more, in what proportions? Is the cause of justice served by shifting resources collected by unfair, regressive taxes on low- and moderate-income workers in rich countries for the benefit of small, wealthy elites of politicians, landowners, and speculators in poor countries? Specifically, ought Murray Finley's clothing workers pay higher taxes to enrich the elites of oil-poor countries?
>
> If growth in the West is likely for a variety of reasons to slow down, is it fair to ask ordinary citizens to surrender what prospect of improved living standards may remain for the benefit of foreigners, even if the foreigners are much poorer?

Such questions invite counter-questions. How much time should OPEC nations have to learn how to be international patrons of the poor, their plea being they are new to the game? Is there substance to the claim of some of them that they already exceed the dismal U.S. performance in aid as a percentage of GNP? Should they do more because domestic demands on their suddenly swollen resources are less? Avoiding Carlos Diaz Alejandro's trap[8] and remembering that the poor countries have no monopoly on political elites and other parasitic classes, is it any better for Murray Finley's clothing workers to subsidize the rich at home which they in effect do when the big enchiladas exploit all the gimmicks in the Internal Revenue Code and end up paying little or no tax on huge incomes? Is it fair to ask the poor in the poor countries to underwrite the standard of living of most of us in rich countries through cheap agricultural exports?

But the hard underlying questions remain and with them three inextricably entwined issues of equity:

Justice as redistribution between rich and poor societies.

Justice in the treatment of the average citizen of the rich society.

Justice in the treatment of the average citizen of the poor society.

In other words, there is no escape from the realization that the private investment in poor nations, and public aid to those nations from international agencies and developed countries (which is likely simultaneously to benefit poor and working class residents in countries receiving investment and aid, and to attract the continuing support of electorates in rich countries for foreign aid) is inextricably entangled in the politics of rich industrialized nations, the more affluent OPEC members, and the less fortunate portions of the Third World without oil.

In what follows, I shall attempt to sketch the major lines of policy which offer the prospect of realizing the goals of the UN Commission—sufficiently more rapid economic growth in poor than in rich countries to visibly narrow the gap between them.

POLICY FOR THE RICH

Alone among wealthy societies, Sweden has persistently exceeded the target contribution to foreign aid set by the UN. Why has the Swedish public supported the transfer of something more than one percent annually of their GNP to less fortunate neighbors? Why have other Western countries and especially the United States been considerably less generous and why have their voters often responded to political assaults upon aid programs?

Consider for the moment the leading characteristics of Sweden's economy and public policy. During the 1973-75 world mini-depression, Swedish unemployment never rose as high as two percent. In spite of the fact that as a small country exporting a very large percentage of its industrial output Sweden is extremely sensitive to fluctuations in world commodity prices, Swedish inflation was moderate by Western European standards. Swedish social services are extensive. Swedish labor market policy responds sensitively to local erosions of employment. Swedish taxes are genuinely redistributive. By some measures, the Swedish standard of life is higher than the American. Within this climate of social protection and egalitarian pressure, Swedish business flourishes.

Although for the first time in 44 years, a coalition of centrist parties is now in office, they won power largely on the inevitable accumulation of grievances by the electorate against a party so long in power and on the adventitious issue of nuclear power and its potential threat to an environment that Swedes properly cherish. The shift in popular vote from the previous election was a trifle over one percent, and the first thing the new government did in interpreting its mandate from the electorate was to make clear that it had no intention of dismantling the structure of extensive social services and supporting economic policies.

More to the point, even Swedish business opinion is resigned to a continuation of the policies of the momentarily displaced Swedish Democrats. In the immediate wake of the Swedish election, the Federation of Swedish Industries uttered these prudent words:

> Nobody in the business world expected that a right-wing victory . . . should lead to a drastic revision of economic policy—at least not on a short-term basis. In the development of the economic policy of recent decades, the main factor has been compromise. The fight for the middle voter seems to have given a very small margin for defining economic policy. . . . Experience from neighboring countries in Europe shows that periods of right-wing government have not led to any diminution in demand for socialisation or national economic planning.[9]

Sweden is distinguishable from utopia. Its homogeneous population of 8 million, about that of New York City, is scarcely comparable to the 225-odd million Americans who occupy much of a continent. There is a moral for Americans all the same, indeed a familiar cliche: it is the rich who can afford to be generous. Slightly to amend the cliche, in democratic societies generosity to foreigners is likely to be premised, war-time alliances aside, upon the prosperity and the security of ordinary working families, earning median incomes and paying what they regard as no more than their fair share of taxes for public services which they generally esteem.

Generosity abroad begins with justice at home. Hence liberals, social democrats and socialists, even intelligent conservatives ought to begin with a serious commitment to full employment. Full employment is the engine of advance to equality on the part of the poor, black, female, young, and urban—the categories manifestly overlap. In the United States as elsewhere full employment requires at least intermittent job creation and job training by government. The Humphrey-Hawkins Full Employment Bill, much amended in its course in Congress, was reintroduced right after Congress reassembled in January 1977.

One great barrier to effective action against unemployment in the United States has been fear of inflation, a fear that has been fed by learned talk from economists of so-called Phillips curve trade-offs between unemployment rates and price increases. Much empirical evidence casts this asserted relationship in serious doubt. There is indeed a connection between rising prosperity and price escalation, but it is connected not with the tendency of unions to push wages up so rapidly that corporations perforce hike their prices, set off a new round of wage claims, and set in motion a wage-price spiral. The culprits of recent experience have been large corporations which in pursuit of high profits even during recessions stubbornly hike prices even though the customers sulk.* During the so-called recovery from the 1973-75 mini-depression, the steel companies, operating substantially below capacity, several times raised their prices in an effort to widen profit margins.

The record contains the message that the necessary complement to national commitment to full employment and federal job creation programs is mandatory controls over the prices set in concentrated industries. The labor movement has with good reason opposed controls on the ground that Congress will inevitably impose them upon both prices (ineffectively) and wages (effectively). So it was during the Phase Two period, and so, union leaders fear, it will be again. But the unions should make the effective case open to them that in the 1970s inflation started with prices and profits, and that unions, as even business media have often conceded, behaved so responsibly that in real terms average factory earnings have declined, not risen. It is highly unlikely that effective full employment policies will long be followed or even initiated unless they are accompanied by credible measures against inflation.

---

*For new car sales, 1974 and 1975 were two of the worst years since the 1950s. They were also years in which General Motors and its friendly rivals raised sticker prices $1000 per vehicle on the average. Assuming that demand was inelastic and aiming at a decent return on investment, GM simply decided to sell fewer vehicles at higher prices rather than more vehicles at lower prices. It is not the sort of choice that garment manufacturers on Seventh Avenue are free to make.

The Swedish solution for the United States requires as a third element effective tax reform—at last. There are many routes to reform and I am no tax expert, but here is one possibility.

1. Dismantle our present Rube Goldberg tax code, discard all existing exemptions and deductions.

2. Tax all income from every source at gently progressive rates somewhat lower than present rates.

3. Substitute for present inheritance levies Lester Thurow's suggested wealth acquisition tax which would limit the sums an individual during his lifetime might inherit.

4. Turn the social security tax into a progressive levy on total earnings.

It is not my intention to sketch a total domestic program, which must necessarily encompass issues such as health, land use, environment, and housing policy. My point is single and simple: a worried population is likely to devote little thought and scant sympathy to people in distant lands.

Let me shift to another aspect of relations between rich and poor societies. One of the standing irritations between the rich and poor focuses on the role of the multinationals. What is badly needed among the richer societies is formulation of an appropriate and enforceable code of conduct for these mobile corporate and financial giants which currently all too often play regions and governments off against each other, slip between the crevices of variegated legal systems and shift resources from high wage unionized countries to low wage nonunion alternatives. More than once multinationals have defeated public policy both in the countries where they are chartered and those in which they operate.

For the United States a minimum program includes federal chartering of large corporations (a Ralph Nader revival of an old approach), licensing and justification of capital exports (an old UAW scheme), assessment of social and environmental impact (both in the United States and abroad) of technology exports, repeal of unfair tax advantages, prohibition of participation in boycotts of nations friendly to the United States, and use of antitrust statutes to inhibit further growth by acquisitions.

Finally if morality, rather than realpolitik is to guide Western policy, aid should be focused upon governments which treat their own citizens responsibly and withheld from the tragically numerous regimes which oppress their own poor. *

---

*Almost immediately after Allende was overthrown and the Pinochet regime took power in Chile, we resumed aid. The lesson was not lost on the Third World.

POLICY FOR THE POOR

Obstacles to growth in poor countries are numerous. Countries like Bangladesh and Egypt stagger under the burden of a very high ratio of population to arable land. In these countries and much of Latin America, Africa, and Asia rapid population growth consumes the fruits of improvement in agricultural methods. Generalizing about such lands and others in which resources are plentiful relative to numbers of inhabitants is rash but unavoidable. Here are several considerations.

1. As democrats we naturally prefer growth to take place within the context of representative government. As realists we must perforce settle for governance by elites which at least show reasonable concern for the prosperity of their constituents. We should not exclude Pakistan and Egypt by this criterion. We ought to exclude countries like Brazil and Chile where deliberate policy has worsened the condition of working men and women.

2. There is indeed a recrudescence of Malthusian population problems, in some instances accentuated by public health triumphs in controlling malaria and other infectious diseases. For westerners it is convenient to urge population control upon poor nations as the prerequisite to growth. It is more realistic to recall that birth rates in the West began sharply to drop <u>after</u> improvement in living standards became reasonably general.

3. Tax reform and improved tax administration are more badly needed in poor countries than even in the United States where most people pay their taxes more or less voluntarily.

4. Future economic development must pay more attention to agriculture, particularly of a variety which emphasizes decent diet for urban and rural residents and employs some of the intermediate technologies for which E. F. Schumacher argued so elegantly in <u>Small is Beautiful</u>.[10]

5. It seems futile to say so, but wastage of scarce resources on military and nuclear equipment ought to be minimized. The prospects of such limitation are obviously better in situations of detente between the superpowers and still better when the United States ceases to press expensive military toys on potential buyers all around the world.

6. If the connection described above between growth and declining population rates is correct, then genuine land reform, and encouragement of unions and other democratic institutions should be recognized not only as equitable but as offering the rewards in the near future which will lead parents voluntarily to limit the size of their families.

One pillar of justice then, between the rich and the poor, is the equity with which the poor distribute the little that they possess.

POLICY FOR THE NOUVEAUX RICHES: THE CASE OF OPEC

Here it is difficult to be cheerful, at least about the Middle Eastern members of the oil cartel.* In the Middle East an ominous arms race is in progress. During the 1975 fiscal year ending June 30, 1975, the Pentagon exported $9.5 billion worth of armaments, compared to a mere $3.9 billion in 1973. Among them Iran, Kuwait and Saudi Arabia purchased nearly half of this huge total. Latin American countries in the last three years have vastly expanded military acquisitions from the United States and elsewhere. Arms races can absorb even OPEC's billions and slow economic development to a walk.

Thus far their oil bonanzas have done desperately little for poor Iranians and Saudis. In Algeria, major oil fields already are approaching exhaustion and that country's balance of payments has turned into deficit before substantial improvement in the daily life of the Algerian peasant or proletariat has even begun.

OPEC needs desperately to distribute more fairly its resources among its citizens. It should participate systematically in aid programs addressed to the needs of poorer nations without oil. It is unlikely to do either until present emphases on armaments are altered.

JUSTICE, EQUALITY AND AID

Aid and international investments are inseparable from the politics of resource transfer from the rich to the poor among nations. But this international redistribution can only become politically feasible when the several difficult preconditions already briefly noted have been approximated.

Within advanced nations full employment and social equity are necessary but not fully sufficient conditions for more generosity abroad. Popular resistance to foreign aid initiatives will be great and decisive unless such help is seen to assist human beings poorer than most blue- and white-collar families in the West. I am inclined to go further and say that trade union, liberal and radical opposition to foreign aid is appropriate so long as the aid flows to closed groups of foreign politicians, military leaders and well-connected entrepreneurs. It is especially appropriate when unions are outlawed and

---

*Venezuela, a member of OPEC, is engaged in genuine efforts at social reform. It is not embroiled in the anti-Israel politics of its Arab colleagues.

political opponents languish in prison. The time has long since passed for us to take a hard look at past aid programs and see how they can be redesigned to enhance autonomy and equity rather than perpetuate dependence and inequality.

One can do no more than hope that these parallel advances toward economic justice in the component parts of the non-Communist world are feasible. One can do no more than to press for such policies in one's own country and urge such pressure as this country can bring to bear upon the policies of other countries.

Of one thing I fear it is possible to be almost certain. If such advances are long delayed, the alternative is likely to be Robert Heilbroner's grim vision of wars of redistribution, urban violence and replacement of democratic institutions by authoritarian regimes.

As matters stand, the only important human groups capable of promoting either humane capitalism or democratic socialism here and elsewhere are trade unionists, liberal intellectuals and the political parties which they influence. I hope we are enough.

NOTES

1. The New York Times, October 14, 1976, p. 14.

2. See, passim, Hollis Chenery, Redistribution with Growth: Policies to Improve Income Distribution in Developing Countries in the Context of Economic Growth, (New York: Oxford, 1974).

3. Ibid.

4. New York Times, op. cit.

5. See Robert Heilbroner, Business Civilization in Decline, (New York: Norton, 1976), as well as his earlier An Inquiry into the Human Prospect, (New York: Norton, 1975).

6. Chenery, op. cit.

7. See John Rawls, A Theory of Justice (Cambridge: Harvard University Press, 1971). Starting from the presumption that equality of income and wealth is a natural state among human beings, Rawls argues that the only justifiable departure in the direction of inequality is one which results in the improvement of all members of the community. Where income and wealth already are unequally divided, movement toward still further inequality can be justified by benefits which flow to the least advantaged members of the group.

8. Carlos F. Diaz-Alejandro, "Unshackled or Unhinged? On Delinking North and South," (paper prepared for the 1980s Project, Council on Foreign Relations, New York, December 1976), p. 68. Diaz observes that "only the Third World has elites: the First World has 'leaders'."

9. See News from the Federation of Swedish Industries, No. 6, October, 1976, p. 1.

10. E. F. Schumacher, Small is Beautiful (New York: Harper and Row, 1973).

24

OPEC, Minerals, and American Energy Policy in North-South Relations

DANKWART A. RUSTOW

THE OPEC REVOLUTION

The price increases in petroleum decreed by OPEC in October and December 1973 marked an epoch in economic and political relations between the Third World and the advanced industrial countries. OPEC's action constituted the first dramatic success of a raw materials cartel not of private companies but of governments. It brought about a redistribution of income from North to South that dwarfed all sums previously transferred by way of foreign aid. The increased influence on the international political and economic scene that accrued to Saudi Arabia, Iran, Algeria, Venezuela, Libya and other countries was palpable at once, although individual governments exercised this new influence in various ways and for different purposes.

The OPEC revolution thus added a strong impetus to the ongoing discussion about the future of the international economic order, whether carried on among industrial countries or between them and the less developed ones. The Washington Energy Conference of February 1974, the Sixth Special Session of the United Nations General Assembly which adopted a declaration on the "Establishment of a New International Economic Order" in May 1974, the formation of the International Energy Agency in November 1974, the opening of the Conference on International Economic Cooperation in Paris in December 1975—these were among the more notable events in that broadening discussion.

These developments invite questions about the wider and more lasting implications of the OPEC revolution. How durable will the new oil price structure and the consequent redistribution of global income be? How powerful a precedent will OPEC's action set for the formation of other raw materials cartels in the Third World? What will be the financial and economic impact on the global economy in general and the United States economy in particular? What are some of the implications for long-term employment in the United States?

The new structure imposed by OPEC on the global petroleum economy, in which the pace of production and the level of prices are controlled chiefly by concerted action of the governments of producing countries, is likely to endure at least for a decade or two, and possibly for as long as petroleum remains the major fuel of the industrial world. This implies that confident statements, such as were repeatedly heard in 1974 from U. S. Treasury Secretary William E. Simon, that the question is not whether the price of oil will come down, but when, were based more on wishful thinking than on careful analysis.[1]

OPEC was founded in 1960, but efforts by producing countries to secure tighter control and larger revenues over their hydrocarbon resources date back even farther. The most dramatic confrontation occurred in 1951 when Prime Minister Mohammed Mossadegh decreed the nationalization of the Anglo-Iranian Oil Company, later known as British Petroleum. Yet Mossadegh's move miscarried. Even OPEC, founded in protest against the oil companies' price cuts in the late 1950s of a few cents per barrel, took as much as six years to redress that initial grievance. By 1970 the member states had increased their revenues per barrel by only about 20 percent. As a result, the international public took little note of OPEC for the first thirteen years of its existence.

Behind this placid facade, however, a major shift had in fact occurred, and by 1971 the OPEC governments were beginning to wrest control over production and prices from the multinationals. Mossadegh had confronted a single company that could count on full backing in its stand against nationalization from the six other major international petroleum companies (by their current names Exxon, Shell, Texaco, Standard of California or Socal, Gulf and Mobil). These seven companies at the time controlled from one-half to two-thirds of petroleum production, refining and transport in the non-Communist world. Hence, by stepping up production and exploration elsewhere in the Middle East, they could promptly compensate for the shutdown in Iran—even though that country before 1951 had accounted for nearly one-fifth of all petroleum traded internationally.

After Mossadegh's overthrow, the crisis was resolved by extending to Iran the so-called 50-50 profit sharing formula earlier applied in Venezuela and Saudi Arabia. This implied a doubling or tripling of government revenues per barrel, but the increase took the form of income taxes rather than royalties, so that, under applicable regulations on foreign tax credits, it was borne in effect not by the companies or their ultimate customers but by the Western taxpayers.

Meanwhile, Europe's postwar recovery had vastly expanded the market for petroleum, so that aggregate government revenue in the Middle East and Venezuela under the 50-50 formula rose from about $500 million in 1950 to $4 billion in 1960. The appetite for further revenues thus was thoroughly whetted. Moreover, Libya, where a score of oil companies held various concessions, began to play the companies off against one another. "Independent" companies (that is, American refiners with no previous foreign production) proved especially vulnerable to such pressure. And OPEC as a whole extended the divisive tactic to the seven "majors" by threatening an OPEC-wide embargo against any company failing to comply with the financial conditions imposed by any member state.

Two decades of evolutionary change had led to a neat reversal of the field of forces. Where a closely knit group of companies had once carried the day against a divided set of governments, OPEC, through its newly tested solidarity, began to rule over a divided group of companies. The Tehran agreement of February 14, 1971, concluded between six states on the Persian Gulf and 23 Western companies, marks this gradual shift of control from multinational companies to OPEC governments. In the following two and a half years, the oil revenues of producing governments doubled. The foundations for the OPEC revolution of 1973-74 had been laid.

The oil producing countries' gains of the 1950s had been underwritten by Western taxpayers. Those of the 1960s were absorbed by the companies, which made up by vastly increased volume for what they lost in net income per barrel. (Between 1960 and 1970, European consumption tripled, that in Japan increased sevenfold and the lifting of American import quotas early in 1973 opened a fast growing additional market.) Yet by 1973 the multinational oil companies had come near the end of this twofold avenue of retreat from OPEC pressure. Companies, after all, can write off no more than 100 percent of the taxes that they owe to their home governments on their foreign operations, and customers can switch from coal to oil for no more than 100 percent of their energy demand. This time, therefore, the companies could be expected to protect their profits by passing on to their customers in Europe, Japan, and the United States any additional costs imposed by OPEC. As the chief executive of one of the oil majors put it with some hyperbole, the companies now were playing the role of a vast "tax-collecting agency" for OPEC.[2]

This new company policy of passing OPEC's pressure for added revenues on to the ultimate consumer meant that the OPEC revolution, once fully launched, was likely to result in a direct clash between consumer and producer governments. Among the consumers, the United States by mid 1973 had surpassed Japan as OPEC's leading customer. Its Middle Eastern policies were sharply at variance with Arab aspirations; yet the United States also had a larger domestic production of petroleum and larger hydrocarbon reserves than all other non-Communist industrial countries combined. For these and other reasons, it was logical that, if there was to be such a confrontation, the United

States would become the leader, or at least the main target, on the consumer side.

It should not be inferred that the companies withdrew to a merely passive role or that their newly assumed tax collection function was not handsomely rewarded. In effect, OPEC and the companies have established a quiet partnership of considerable benefit to each—a relationship which OPEC's leading strategist, Sheikh Yamani, foresaw as long ago as 1968. Unlike the classic textbook cartel, OPEC has never set an overall limit to production,* nor has it allocated production shares among its members. It has rather imposed a common tax structure with appropriate quality and transport differentials and has thus in effect set a publicly known floor price. This leaves to the companies the task of setting actual prices and of allocating monthly or daily production shares in the light of changing world demand for OPEC oil at given prices. The division of receipts at the production end between governments and companies is now roughly 97 : 2 in the governments' favor, with the remaining one percent or less representing the physical cost of production.

In return, the companies continue to enjoy guaranteed (and in regard to their competitors without former production concessions, privileged) access to crude oil in whatever quality desired. This explains why the companies have been content to yield on such issues as nationalization and rising taxes without much struggle. In their downstream operations, moreover, the companies now can add their profit margins to a vastly more expensive product. And those companies, including all seven majors which produce both in OPEC countries and in the United States, have been able to raise their domestic prices to OPEC levels—or as close to them as government price controls will allow. These various benefits are reflected on the companies' balance sheets, which typically showed sharply increased net earnings, along with stepped up exploration expenditure, for 1974 and 1975.

---

*The Arab production cutbacks during the Yom Kippur War were a temporary exception. Note that these were applied only by seven of OPEC's thirteen members, and an eighth, Iraq, participated in the embargo but not the cutbacks. Venezuela, Kuwait, Abu Dhabi, and Qatar in recent years have applied production limits, chiefly for conservation reasons. Saudi Arabia and Libya also have decreed limits, to which production has not, however, come up. It still remains true, therefore, that OPEC as a whole has set no aggregate limit, and plans to allocate production shares have never gone beyond the discussion stage.

THE WESTERN RESPONSE TO OPEC

The initial reaction to OPEC's price revolution of 1973, particularly in the United States, was one of consternation and disbelief. At the Washington Energy Conference of February 1974, Secretary Kissinger warned that the industrial countries were faced with the prospect of "a vicious cycle of competition, autarchy, rivalry and depression such as led to the collapse of world order in the thirties," and seven months later President Ford confessed publicly that he found it hard "to discuss the energy problem without lapsing into doomsday language."[3] The conclusion generally was that OPEC's price ascendancy could not or must not endure.

Many observers were confident that OPEC would soon collapse from internal political strains.[4] Other observers looked forward to OPEC's collapse not from political but from economic causes. "The cartel's weak spot is excess capacity," Professor M. A. Adelman insisted. "Every cartel has in time been destroyed by one, then some members chiselling and cheating."[5]

To hasten such a process, Secretary Kissinger, in a speech at the meeting of the International Energy Agency in May 1975, advocated "rigorous conservation [of petroleum] and development of alternatives" that would cause "the producers' market . . . to shrink" and put "individual producers—especially those with ambitious development, defense or other spending programs . . . under pressure to increase sales or, at least, to refuse further production cuts." As another weapon directed at OPEC's presumed weak spot, Professor Adelman proposed a system of oil import tickets for which OPEC governments or their anonymous agents would secretly underbid each other.[6] In a more drastic vein, Secretary Kissinger late in 1974 hinted at the possibility of military invasion if ever future OPEC actions should bring about "some actual strangulation of the industrial world."

These hopeful or bellicose scenarios derive from various misconceptions. Kissinger in mid 1975 proposed that the United States and other IEA partners save a total of 2 million barrels a day (m b/d), thus cutting imports from OPEC to about 24 m b/d. But by merely cutting each country's output to the minimum level of production recorded since the fall of 1973, OPEC could cut aggregate exports to as little as 20 m b/d and still collect revenues roughly six times as large as in 1972—hardly a prospect for acute penury. Moreover, since the middle of 1975 events have moved in the opposite direction. Global economic recovery has led to a steady increase in demand for OPEC oil, and the trend is likely to continue upward at least for some years.

Even in this current upward phase, OPEC production may not rise fast enough to keep pace with the financial commitments or ambitions of many of its individual members. Yet Adelman' chisel-and-cheat scenario overlooks the obvious alternative that OPEC countries will simply raise the price further. This is precisely what some of the money-hungry OPEC countries have tended to do. Time and again, Libya, Indonesia and others have charged more for their oil than their comparative advantage over other OPEC members in quality or location would justify. Generally some months later, these countries (with powerful assistance from Iran and over Saudi resistance) were able to persuade their fellow OPEC members to join them at this higher price level.

It also happens that the money-hungry OPEC countries are already producing at or near their present capacity, whereas those with the largest foreign exchange reserves also have the largest excess productive capacity. Hence a downward price spiral that pushed everyone's production toward the limit would very soon reduce, rather than increase, the revenue of the money-short countries and benefit only those that have sizable surpluses already—a straightforward proposition in arithmetic that can hardly have escaped OPEC analysts.* The position of Saudi Arabia, with one-half of OPEC's spare capacity and one-third of its aggregate petroleum reserves and with the largest foreign exchange reserves of any country in the world, is of course crucial. As Saudi petroleum minister Yamani has recently boasted with uncharacteristic candor: "To ruin the other countries of the OPEC, all we have to do is to produce our full capacity; to ruin the consumer countries we only have to reduce our production."[7]

The invasion scenario implied by Kissinger and elaborated by Professor Robert W. Tucker and others poses few purely military difficulties, the most convenient site presumably being the al-Hasa district on the Saudi Gulf coast.[8] Oil wells destroyed in military action or by sabotage could be restored or replaced in a few weeks or months; restoration of port facilities might take a bit longer. But Soviet intervention would be a strong probability, and a total OPEC-wide embargo against the invader a near certainty. Military occupation would have to last so long as to constitute a colonial regime.

There remains the possibility of seeking to break the close link between OPEC and the major oil companies. Adelman's import ticket

---

*Countries such as Iran, Iraq, and Nigeria would gain at capacity production if the price dropped by 10 percent but lose if the price dropped by 20 percent. In contrast Saudi Arabia and Kuwait would still come out ahead if it dropped by 40 percent, Abu Dhabi if it dropped by half, and Libya if it dropped by 60 percent. For detailed argument and calculations, see Rustow and Mugno, op. cit., pp. 99-103.

proposal aims at this effect. Perhaps U. S. antitrust action could be brought against the seven majors to secure competitive access to OPEC oil for U. S. domestic producers or independent refiners. The desire of some large OPEC producing countries, notably Iran, to handle an increasing share of downstream operations themselves might have the same result of abrogating the privileged position of the majors.

Yet it remains very doubtful whether such a diversification of downstream operations would have the desired effect of price cutting and competition among the OPEC governments at the upstream end. The role of the companies was crucial in allowing OPEC to become an effective cartel; it does not follow that it is equally crucial in perpetuating the existing cartel structure. Maintenance of the cartel requires of OPEC members no more than the pursuit of their enlightened collective self-interest by continued enforcement of their commonly agreed structure of government revenues per barrel. The collective reward for such concerted action has been in the neighborhood of $100 billion a year.

The only effective antidote against OPEC's cartel position would be the development of alternative fuel sources to make the industrial world independent of OPEC imports. Here the major problem is one of time and of the very sizable investments required. Atomic energy has been developed at a much slower pace over the years than its spokesmen have supposed, and no fundamental change seems to be in sight. This would appear to leave as the likeliest alternative the large-scale development of the abundant coal reserves in the United States in conjunction with an equally massive gasification program. It is hard to see how this could be accomplished on the necessary scale before the late 1980s or 1990s.

It should be recalled in this context that the projections for early independence from or reduced dependency on OPEC imports by the U. S. Federal Energy Administration and various international bodies in 1974 have since then been scaled down substantially or abandoned.[9] The most responsible current estimates envisage growing U. S. petroleum imports and continued (though perhaps declining) dependence on imports in Western Europe through the early 1980s.

In sum, OPEC's control of world oil prices is not merely a temporary aberration but rests on solid foundations assembled one by one in the 1960s and early 1970s. Ultimately it is derived from the close integration of the world petroleum market achieved earlier by the multinational companies, from the tenfold increase in global petroleum imports in the last quarter century and from the surrender of Western hegemony in the Middle East and other Third World regions. Although OPEC for a start benefited from its close de facto cooperation with the oil multinationals, by now it could very likely survive without them.

Only alternative fuel sources, perhaps together with a drastic reduction of per capita energy consumption especially in the United States, can break OPEC's current stranglehold. But such sources could not be developed or such energy savings achieved on anything like the scale required before the final years of this century. Hence my estimate is that OPEC's ascendancy is likely to continue for a decade or two and perhaps as long as petroleum remains the world's leading fuel.

OPEC'S FUTURE PROSPECTS

If OPEC, far from being headed for an early demise, may be expected to prosper for the next quarter century or so, it becomes pertinent to ask, first, how much further OPEC can push its current advantage and, second, whether its example will be emulated by the Third World exporters of other minerals.

One front on which the OPEC countries themselves might push ahead is price. Government revenue per barrel of exported petroleum at the time of the 1973 embargo rose from \$1.80 to \$3.05; for the first half of 1974 it was \$9.27; in October 1975 it was set at \$11; and for the first half of 1977 at \$11.50 to \$12. Does this nearly sevenfold jump in only three and a half years indicate that they have gone about as far as they can go?

The optimum price for a monopoly or cartel is that price at which elasticity equals one, that is to say, a price level beyond which any further increase would result in a proportionate or more than proportionate decline in sales, with consumers simply doing without the product or finding substitutes for it. In the real world, that level is not as easy to ascertain as textbook chapters on cartel economics and demand elasticity often seem to presuppose. For one thing, the demand for all sorts of goods reflects not only their price and consumer preferences in the abstract but also the general cycle of boom and slump. An essential commodity such as petroleum (which in 1975 accounted for 68 percent of the value of all non-agricultural raw materials traded in the world) has itself a profound effect on the level of general economic activity. Second, there is a crucial distinction between such substitutes as are readily available and others that take time and investment money to develop so that long-run elasticity of the demand for any given product is certain to exceed elasticity in the short-run.

An empirical approach to this elasticity question is to calculate how much oil OPEC has been able to sell at the various levels of government revenue just cited. On an annual basis, the income of OPEC governments per barrel of exported oil more than doubled from 1970 to 1973 while output rose by about one half. In 1974, with unit income more than quadrupled, output remained virtually unchanged. Only in

1975, as revenue per barrel increased another 15 percent did output begin to decline, by about 11 percent. If it were not for the business cycle factor, this might suggest that the crucial threshold of unit elasticity, and hence of maximum return to the cartel, had been reached at a per barrel income of about $10 in 1975 dollars. But in fact the world's leading economies in 1975 were in the depths of a recession, aggravated but by no means caused by the explosion in oil prices. And as the global economy began to recover, OPEC production once again began to rise, from the 1975 low of 25.3 m b/d to 29.7 m b/d in July 1976, with the general trend continuing upward through the summer and fall.

The record of prices set and revenues obtained since 1974 suggest that the income maximizing strategy for OPEC is to keep prices steady in current dollar terms in times of recession, thus making for a slight decline in real terms, and to increase them in line with or somewhat ahead of global inflation in times of recovery. This indeed describes OPEC's recent conduct rather accurately. For three and a half years from late 1974 to mid 1977, it has held prices steady in current dollar terms, except for a 10 percent increase in October 1975 and a 5 percent to 10 percent increase in January 1977.

Two motives, one specific and one general, are likely to have confirmed OPEC in this cautious strategy. First, Saudi Arabia, which has a foreign exchange reserve larger than all other OPEC members combined, has been working strenuously behind the OPEC scenes since 1974 to keep increases to 10 percent a year or less. Having to keep most of their money in liquid assets rather than spending it on current imports, it is not in their interest to ruin or even slow down the world economy on which the value of those assets depends. Second, it is far easier to maintain cohesion in a cartel when the aggregate revenues are rising than when they begin to decline. Hence it is not advisable for intelligent cartel managers to push their advantage to the limit. In cartel economics as in mountaineering, a false step on the way up merely slows one's ascent; a false step on the way down may well prove fatal.

The prospect of modest continuing price increases changes drastically if we assume that, over the next decade or so, the industrial world will continue to recover from its recent recession and will not substantially benefit from major measures to energy conservation or development of alternatives to petroleum. Demand for oil in the non-Communist world grew at a rate of 8 percent a year in 1965-70 and 3.5 percent a year in 1970-75, the growth rates for OPEC, as the world's marginal supplier, being 11 percent and 4 percent respectively.[10]

OPEC's current aggregate production capacity is estimated at 38 m b/d, from which 5 m b/d should be deducted for countries that have limited production for conservation reasons, and another 1 m b/d representing OPEC's current domestic consumption, leaving an exportable surplus of 32 m b/d, or only 4 m b/d above the 28 m b/d of exports reached in 1976.[11] For the next few years, the growth in world consumption and decline in U. S. (lower 48 states) product will be met from new sources in Alaska, the North Sea and Mexico. Yet, if world demand grows at its 1970-75 rate of 4 percent a year, these additional supplies will soon prove insufficient, and demand for OPEC oil will once again increase, catching up with OPEC's available capacity some time in the mid 1980s.[12]

Variations on this scenario are easy to calculate, pushing the date forward or back by two or three years. But whatever the precise date, as long as world demand for OPEC oil expands faster than does OPEC's productive capacity, the time will inevitably come when there will be a physical shortage of oil in the industrial world, and hence a strong sellers' market. There are two basic ways in which OPEC can cope with such a contingency as it arises—or indeed in anticipation of it.

The first alternative is for those OPEC countries that have large undeveloped reserves, notably Saudi Arabia, to expand their productive capacity. Others with known but still unexplored fields such as Venezuela, might engage in additional exploration and development, and perhaps countries such as Libya and Kuwait might temporarily abandon the conservation measures that have been limiting their production. All this would prevent any physical shortage and would keep the price of petroleum at its customary level, that is, rising with world inflation or a bit faster. For the consumer countries, the total oil import bill would rise in proportion to increased consumption. Among OPEC countries, the additional revenues would go only to those countries able or willing to expand capacity.

The other alternative is for OPEC countries to keep producing at something like their current capacities. This would create a physical shortage, and hence lead to a rise, possibly steep, in prices. The consumers' import bill also would go up but because of higher prices rather than larger consumption. Among OPEC countries, the additional revenues would be fairly evenly distributed, thus benefiting not only the present financial surplus countries but also the "money-hungry" ones such as Iraq, Iran, Indonesia, Algeria, and Nigeria. For OPEC as a whole, this alternative would have the advantage of avoiding any problem of production allocation, whether handled as now by the companies or, as it may be in the future, by OPEC itself. It would have the further psychological advantage of saddling the consumers or their companies, rather than OPEC governments, with the onus of setting what will be sure to seem like exorbitant prices.

In effect, OPEC with this alternative would be shifting its strategy from one of fixing prices to one of limiting production. Each country's production capacity would determine its share of the market. The crucial choice would be that made by Saudi Arabia, and recurrent statements by its leaders indicate that the Saudis will tend to link price moderation to such quid pro quos as American pressure on Israel or plane deliveries to Saudi Arabia.[13] Whichever alternative is followed, OPEC's economic, and hence financial and political, power in the 1980s is likely not to decline but to be substantially enhanced.

A second front on which some OPEC members have been inclined to push ahead is what might be called the game of "chasing the companies downstream." Having established firm control over production and prices, they might turn next to expanding their control over the transportation, processing and distribution of petroleum.

Some of the surplus Arab oil money in recent years, for example, has gone into buying tankers, of which, with the recent stagnation of the oil market, there has been a substantial glut. Some of the economically more advanced OPEC countries, such as Venezuela, Algeria and Iran, have shown themselves eager to refine their crude oil at home and to establish their petrochemical industry and various energy-intensive forms of industry, such as steel-making and aluminum smelting. Nearly half of Venezuela's oil exports already take the form of products rather than crude. Iran also appears to be ambitious in this regard, and its National Iranian Oil Company is concurrently pursuing plans to go into such activities as off-shore drilling in the North Atlantic or even refining and distribution in the United States and other major markets.

For a start, however, an expanded petroleum processing and petroleum using industry in the OPEC countries may be expected to serve mostly the function of import substitution and of supplying regional markets, such as the Indian subcontinent for Iran and Latin America for Venezuela. Also shortage of funds and especially of skilled manpower may be expected to slow down many of the more ambitious schemes or stretch them out over the next decade or two.

Yet if and as the relevant constraints ease, the time may come when OPEC countries will shift from exporting crude petroleum to exporting refined products and to finding domestic or regional uses for their energy production. This would enable OPEC members to capture a substantial "value added" to their product. It would also imply a corresponding shift in employment opportunities from the presently industrialized countries in the Northern hemisphere to OPEC countries, which would be joining the second rank of industrialized nations.

THE OUTLOOK FOR OTHER MINERAL RAW MATERIALS

OPEC's spectacular success raised hopes in the Third World and fears in industrial countries that the steep price rises for petroleum would be followed by similar cartel actions for other raw materials.[14] The situation of some of the non-oil-producing countries of the Third World was indeed precarious. Although they paid for only about 10 percent of OPEC's rising bill, the sums often were staggering for the size of their small deficit economies. Unlike the major industrial countries, they could not expect to receive large import orders or attract investments from expanding OPEC economies, and the aid programs of major OPEC countries, though sizable by previous standards, were highly selective, with fellow Arab and fellow Muslim countries of Asia and Africa the largest recipients.[15] For some of the poorest and neediest countries, the petroleum revolution threatened to wipe out almost overnight the result of decades of foreign aid and development effort. Nothing could be more natural, therefore, than for those among them who exported other mineral raw materials to try to profit from OPEC's own example. Throughout 1974, there was intense activity among representatives of countries producing such commodities as bananas, coffee, copper, iron, tin and zinc.

OPEC's members were ready to support such moves with advice, diplomatic pressure at the United Nations or in other North-South encounters and occasionally even funds. Algeria, for example, emerged as the main spokesman for demands for the creation of a "New Economic Order" both within the UN General Assembly and at the Conference on International Economic Cooperation. By rallying all other Third World nations in the fight against "neocolonialism" and for a "new economic order," the OPEC countries could not only deflect criticism from themselves but also elevate their cause from the level of pecuniary pragmatism to one of rhetorical idealism.

Here and there, this broader attack on the whole raw materials front yielded early results. For example, Jamaica in 1974 steeply raised its export tax on bauxite, and Morocco managed to raise the world price for phosphate rock fourfold between 1974 and 1975. But these remained isolated instances, and some examples of failure (for example, in attempts to coordinate the copper producers or to force a rise in the price of mercury) were just as notable.

Although world trade in foodstuffs and other agricultural materials substantially exceeds the value of trade in nonfuel minerals, the problems in the agricultural field are vastly different. What follows examines only the outlook for an OPEC-type strategy in the world market for metals and other mineral raw materials.

The price movement of mineral raw materials on the world market from 1973 to 1975 indicates that the price rise in crude petroleum in that period has been matched about halfway by the export price for coal. Among nonfuel minerals, the price of natural phosphates has followed, or indeed outpaced, that of petroleum, and the price of silver has risen two and a half times. (These and other statistical data on mineral raw materials are taken or calculated from the relevant OECD, UN and IMF statistics for trade, production and prices respectively.) Yet together phosphates and silver account for less than 10 percent of world trade in those nonfuel minerals for which comparable information is available. Some of the major metals such as iron, zinc, bauxite, manganese, have roughly kept pace with the general movement of export prices. For the remaining items, representing about 40 percent of global trade in nonfuel minerals, the price rise in current dollar terms has been significantly less than overall export prices, so that in real dollar terms there has been an actual decline.

This rather indifferent result becomes understandable if one considers some of the technical and economic features that distinguish the world petroleum trade from that in most other minerals. Even before the price increases of 1970-71, no single mineral loomed as large in world trade as did petroleum, and this relative importance has been accentuated by the price jump of 1973, which pushed the value of petroleum to 63 percent of global mineral trade in 1973 and 68 percent in 1975. By contrast the two leading metals, iron and copper ore, accounted in 1973 for only 13 percent and 5 percent respectively of the value of the crude petroleum trade and for bauxite the proportion is 1.3 percent. This means not only that the potential gains from cartelization of any of these metals are much less than they have been in petroleum, but also that price increases might meet much less consumer resistance. This last was clearly a factor in Jamaica's success in raising the price for bauxite, which represents only a minor fraction of the final cost of aluminum.

The modest export earnings derived from nonfuel minerals directly relate to a further weakness of would-be Third World cartelists. OPEC's dramatic coup of 1973 was preceded by two decades of confrontation and accommodation between the exporting countries and the multinational companies. When the final round of the contest began in 1970, OPEC governments had accumulated very sizable foreign exchange reserves, equivalent to six months of imports for Venezuela, eleven months for Saudi Arabia and Kuwait, and nearly three years for Libya. Between exporting countries with one or more years' storag of money and importing countries with (at the time) one or two months' storage of petroleum, the outcome of any showdown was predictable. None of the leading mineral exporters in the Third World are in a comparable position today. Bolivia's financial reserves would finance its imports for four months, Brazil's for two and a half months, and Morocco's for about six weeks.

Metals can be recycled, and for most of them there is a lively scrap market. The world import bill for iron, copper and aluminum scrap in 1973 came to about one-third of that for the new metals; for other metals, the typical proportion is between one-fourth and one fifth. The industrial countries, such as the United States, France and West Germany (even after satisfying a large domestic demand) dominate this market for scrap metals. Repeated use of the so-called "precious" metals, such as gold, silver, and platinum, is so common as to make the term "scrap" sound inappropriate. But mineral fuels cannot be recycled; "scrap petroleum" becomes air pollution. Other nonmetal minerals, such as phosphate, potash and sulphur, also cannot be reused, a circumstance that may have favored Morocco's success in raising the price of phosphate rock.

Other factors such as storage, substitution, and alternative sources of supply also sharply limit the prospects of OPEC-type cartels emerging in other mineral raw materials. Petroleum is a flammable liquid that must be stored in bulky and expensive steel containers. Metals, by contrast, can be stored cheaply and conveniently. In many industrial uses one metal can substitute for another, and sometimes a petroleum-based plastic for either, on fairly short notice. The possibility of substitution for petroleum by coal, uranium or other energy sources remains the major potential limitation on OPEC's market power, but it is a limitation far in the future and receding farther with every year that the United States or other major consumer nations delay initiating the necessary investments in substitutes.

Geographic factors reinforce this technical contrast between petroleum and other minerals. Untapped alternative sources of abundant supply not controlled by any potential cartel exist for several minerals. The so-called manganese nodules strewn over a vast area of the Pacific Ocean floor contain large amounts of other metals, including copper and nickel. The technology for pumping them to the surface is being perfected, the major obstacles being unsettled questions of international law.

Through the accidents of geology, three-fourths of the world's known petroleum reserves are located in the Third World, mostly around the Persian Gulf, so that the Third World produces almost 60 percent of all world petroleum accounting for over 90 percent of total exports. In contrast, most other minerals including coal and the nonfuels are found in substantial amounts in the world's industrialized countries. On the list of major producers of individual nonfuel minerals, the United States appears 13 times and the Soviet Union 12 times, followed by Canada (7) and Australia (5). The only Third World country that appears more than once is Brazil. Sizable proportions of the most important metals and minerals are thus used in the industrial countries where the raw material is mined.

The Third World as a whole thus plays a minor role in the nonfuel minerals trade, accounting for 27 percent of the total if scrap metals are included and 31 percent if they are excluded. There are individual exceptions, such as tin, where the Third World accounts for 88 percent of global exports, bauxite (65 percent), chromium (59 percent) and manganese (49 percent) and where neither the United States nor other industrialized member countries of the OECD show substantial production. In addition, Niger in 1973 supplied 67 percent of OECD's uranium imports, but this amount was dwarfed by the United States domestic production, which accounts for 58 percent of the world total. Not surprisingly, efforts to coordinate Third World producers have been most intense among some of these minerals.

It is sometimes suggested that nonpetroleum cartels would have difficulty getting launched because (in contrast to OPEC with its Arab and Middle Eastern center of gravity) they would have to bring together countries as diverse and distant as Chile, Zambia, and the Philippines for copper or Malaysia and Bolivia for tin. I would tend to discount this factor. OPEC was formed at Venezuela's initiative after some years of intensive courting of Iran and the Arab producers. Among Middle Eastern OPEC members, political tensions are rife. OPEC's strength has derived from coordinating the members' petroleum policies despite such tensions to the handsome benefit of all. Whenever the economic factors promise solid financial gains, cartels will form and succeed. When those factors are unfavorable, cartels are likely to fail.

OPEC's demonstration effect has not led to a whole procession of Third World cartels because the same lesson could only rarely be applied. The industrial world does not depend heavily on imports for its nonfuel raw materials, and even less on imports from the Third World. Third World producers, commanding only a minor share of most mineral markets, are in competition with the domestic production and the stockpiles in consumer countries, potentially with the producers of many other metals, and in the future with deep seabed mining. Nor do they possess the vast financial reserves that enabled OPEC in the early 1970s to stare down the oil companies or the integrated market structure by which those same companies have smoothly passed OPEC's price increases on to the consumer.

THE IMPACT OF THE OPEC REVOLUTION ON THE U.S. ECONOMY

The OPEC revolution has brought about a sizable redistribution of income in favor of the petroleum exporting countries of the South, mostly at the expense of the industrial countries of the North. That part of OPEC's mounting export earnings—almost exactly one-half as of 1975—which is spent on current imports represents an immediate transfer of wealth from oil customers to oil producers. The other half, which is invested or held in liquid assets, represents a claim on such transfers in the future. Just under two percent of the total has been donated by OPEC members by way of foreign aid to non-oil-producing countries of the Third World, either directly or through international institutions.

The economy of the industrial countries did receive a major jolt. Yet early apprehensions such as Secretary Kissinger's prediction of a collapse of world order or President Ford's doomsday fantasies have proved groundless. As Hollis Chenery of the World Bank has pointed out, the current transfers are of a magnitude no larger than those involved in the Marshall Plan a generation earlier.[16] The international banking and monetary systems have handled the resulting problems quite smoothly, one reason being that the problems of "petrodollar recycling" which so intensely preoccupied international bankers and financiers in 1974 arise mostly among the advanced industrial countries.[17]

This transfer of wealth initiated late in 1973 is likely to continue for most of the next generation. The United States in particular will pay a growing share of OPEC's bill. Oil production in all the states but Alaska is continuing to decline, oil consumption continues to rise, and until the formulation of President Carter's ill-fated energy program of 1977, no major effort to reduce our import dependence had even been formulated. In fact, U.S. dependence has substantially increased since 1973. At the time of the 1973 embargo, we imported 33 percent of our oil; that ratio for some months of 1977 was up to 50 percent. With a few exceptions such as phosphate rock and bauxite, the OPEC example has not been followed by other Third World producers of raw materials nor is it likely to be. On the other hand, once world demand for petroleum imports catches up with OPEC's capacity some time in the 1980s, there may well be a new round of OPEC price increases. And not only will OPEC, in selling its oil, continue to charge what the traffic will bear; its more advanced members also are likely to develop their petroleum refining and petrochemical industries. In this respect OPEC's example may well be followed by metal producing countries of the Third World, regardless of the prospects for cartelization.

In comparison with other industrial countries, the effects of the petroleum revolution on the United States have been mitigated by a variety of circumstances. First, we still are one of the world's leading oil producers. Having held first place until 1973, we were overtaken by the Soviet Union in 1974, and then dropped to third place as we were also overtaken by Saudi Arabia in March 1976. Yet we still are less dependent on imports for oil than most industrial countries, our position being rivalled only by Canada, Norway and Great Britain.

Second, petroleum has traditionally accounted for less than half of our total energy consumption, the remainder being domestic coal and natural gas (both domestic and imported from Canada). This favored position of the United States became apparent at the time of the Arab oil embargo of 1973-74. Although the embargo was directed chiefly against our support of Israel in the Yom Kippur War, the attendant cutbacks in Arab oil production led to a much more pronounced energy shortage in Europe and Japan which depended on oil imports for 59 percent and 76 percent respectively of their total energy consumption, as against only 17 percent for the United States.[18] With respect to most other mineral raw materials, our position is even stronger. We are among the world's leading producers of iron ore, copper phosphates, lead, uranium and many others. Bauxite is the most important mineral besides oil for which we rely very heavily on Third World imports.

The financial and economic consequences of the petroleum revolution also have been less severe for the United States than for most other major industrial countries. For the part of OPEC's income that is currently expended, the United States competes very favorably for import orders with other industrial suppliers, not as well as West Germany and Japan but far better than other European countries. As OPEC members begin to concentrate on major infrastructure projects such as ports, desalination plants, and roads and on building up their industrial plant, this competitive advantage of the United States is likely to become even more apparent.

For that part of OPEC's fast accumulating riches that is saved up for the future, the United States also is attractive (not as much as West Germany but far more than other OECD countries) as a recipient of investments. We even benefit from OPEC's need for time in formulating its spending plans; OPEC's oil receipts are payable in dollars so that the money stays in dollars until its owners think of a better alternative use.

All these favorable factors are reflected in our trade and international payments statistics. OECD countries as a whole experienced a trade deficit that mounted from $10 billion in 1973 to $40 billion in 1974 and dropped back to $9 billion in 1975. West Germany alone among the major economies showed a continuing trade surplus. The United States had shown a trade deficit for 1971-73, which in 1974 climbed to $9.5 billion, but in 1975 it showed a surplus of $4.3 billion. Similarly, our foreign exchange reserves, which declined fairly steadily from a high of $25 billion in 1957 to a low of $11.9 billion by the end of 1973, had risen back to $17.8 billion by the middle of 1976.[19]

The world's industrial economies are in global competition with each other. Hence the prime effect of a stimulant to the world economic system such as the rise in petroleum prices has been to enhance the strength of such industrialized countries as Germany, Japan, and the United States and to aggravate the weaknesses of others such as Britain and Italy. The impact on the oil-poor Third World countries has been even more pronounced. As William Rhoads points out in his contribution to this volume, the mechanisms of the world economy have transferred much of the burden of the OPEC surplus from the industrialized countries to the weakest members of the international economic system. Even under indifferent economic management with a Republican President deadlocked against a Democratic Congress, our economic position in 1973-77 was solid enough to benefit from this highly differential impact of the OPEC revolution.

There is one further major asset from which the United States stands to benefit as appropriate policies are adopted. Our extravagant consumption of energy leaves much room for long-range conservation, and our abundant domestic energy resources leave much room for development of alternatives to imports from OPEC. Our energy consumption in 1973 was 8.2 tons of oil equivalent per capita, compared with 3.6 for the countries of the EC and 3.1 for Japan.[20] If we could manage to limit our per capita energy consumption to just twice (rather than two and a half times) the European-Japanese average, we could be wholly independent of any foreign oil imports whatever.

On the supply side, our known recoverable reserves of coal amount to 159 billion metric tons, which with current annual production at about 500 million tons gives us a supply sufficient for 300 years.[21] This does not mean that we can achieve freedom from energy imports overnight or easily. The Nixon-Ford administration's "Project Independence," like most crash programs, came crashing down quickly. But it does mean that for us, along only with Canada and Britian among the major industrial nations, energy independence is a goal that we can rationally and steadily pursue, thus further strengthening our future role in the world economy.

OPEC AND U.S. ENERGY POLICY

When examined against this background of U.S. energy consumption and production, the wisdom and the promise of the Carter energy program of 1977 become apparent. It was a comprehensive program, encouraging savings through more efficient gasoline mileage for cars, higher gasoline prices (mostly through the "wellhead tax"), better home insulation, gradual shifts from oil to coal for power stations and other means. It did not rashly promise "energy independence," but it held out the realistic hope of arresting the increase in import dependence and perhaps decreasing it gradually. It was not a "crash program" but the first step in a long-range program that could be supplemented and expanded later.

One specific hope it held out was to reduce significantly our vulnerability to renewed Arab embargoes. The 27 miles per gallon car efficiency standard alone would be likely to save as much as 1.2 m b/d of petroleum, or as much as the increase in our oil imports from Arab sources since 1973. By encouraging similarly vigorous conservation measures in Europe and Japan, the Carter program was intended to reduce overall demand from OPEC to the point of averting a second price explosion for which the industrial world is otherwise headed by the early 1980s. And all this could be done without, for the time being, requiring major adjustments in our way of life or our patterns of employment.

In due course such a program must be supplemented by more drastic reductions in energy consumption and by massive stimulation of new energy production. The sector that raises our energy consumption most steeply above that of other industrial countries is transportation. Passenger cars and airplanes currently account for over 90 percent of passenger miles in intercity traffic, and trucks haul about 33 percent of long-distance freight. Yet rail transport uses only about 20 percent as much fuel per passenger mile as does air travel, and 30 percent as much as does travel by car. Similarly, a freight train uses only one-fourth the amount of fuel per ton-mile as does a truck. Revitalization of our national railway system therefore should have high priority in our future energy policy.

Stimulation of alternative sources of energy production might well cover the entire range from atomic power and coal to shale and newer forms such as solar or geothermal energy. But coal has a number of distinct advantages that would seem to give it a natural priority among these. Unlike petroleum for which our current reserves are less than ten years, coal is superabundant; our present reserves could last us at present rates of consumption for three centuries. Unlike atomic energy with its huge investments, consistently escalating costs and unresolved environmental problems, coal can be developed rapidly and cheaply with existing technology. Coal gasification and "tall stacks" can diminish substantially air pollution, and stringent requirements for restoration of topsoil and vegetation can prevent other environmental damage. All these precautions are sure to add to the cost but should not be allowed to cause any delay.

A large part of our coal reserves, moreover, are on federal lands, so that they can be developed by government enterprise without encroaching on existing commercial operations while effectively competing with them. The principle bottleneck in coal development is that of transportation. Getting this abundant energy to the population centers where the energy is required, whether by rail, slurry pipelines, gas pipelines (for gasified coal), electric transmission or other means yet to be developed will be a major but certainly not insoluble problem.

To implement this kind of energy strategy there is a need for an effective federal railway system and a federal coal development authority. Such initiatives can resolve our energy problems of the late twentieth century much as the federal Tennessee Valley Authority made an essential contribution toward meeting our energy needs of the late 1940s and 1950s. Both parts of such a program will contribute step by step to making us less dependent on foreign imports. If begun soon, they may prevent or alleviate the second petroleum price explosion for which we are otherwise headed in the early 1980s.

ENERGY AND EMPLOYMENT

The international revolution in oil, the more modest changes in the global market structure of other mineral raw materials, the Carter energy program and additional steps toward securing greater energy independence can be expected to have noticeable or even major impacts on industrial employment in the United States. Yet these impacts are not likely to be as sudden as some observers have imagined. And contrary to some ill considered advance estimates, the impacts on balance are likely to be positive rather than negative.

For example, the tendency of oil producing countries to shift from the export of crude petroleum to that of refined products is likely to encounter many delays and counterpressures. Only a few of the OPEC countries, notably Venezuela, Iran and Algeria, have sufficient pools of skilled manpower even to envisage such a shift. Even in those countries, the construction of refineries, petrochemical plants and gas liquefaction installations is certain to compete for scarce talent and scarce capital with other, domestically oriented aspects of industrialization. In population- and talent-starved countries such as Saudi Arabia, Libya and the United Arab Emirates, port construction, road building, schools, hospitals and other infrastructure and social service projects are likely to take priority for some time.

While OPEC countries have some financial incentives for "chasing the oil companies downstream," these are not compelling and the OPEC countries already are in a pretty comfortable position. Production costs of crude oil in OPEC countries in 1974 ranged from about 7 cents a barrel in Kuwait to about 70 cents in Libya,[22] making for a profit margin to OPEC governments of 1600 percent to 16,000 percent! In contrast, the margin between crude oil plus refining costs and the return on refinery products is only two to five percent. This means that even a minute increase in crude oil prices, at which OPEC governments are past masters, would bring far greater returns than the most ambitious efforts in the untried and hence risky downstream field. Hence, refinery expansion programs in OPEC countries are most likely to be scaled to the needs of internal or regional, rather than world, demands.

The actual record of the past few years corroborates such a cautious assessment. The amount of oil refined in all Third World countries rose fairly steadily from 6.7 m b/d in 1965 to 11.4 m b/d in 1973, after which it declined slightly to 10.6 m b/d in 1975. The increase in the 1965-73 period reflected a general expansion of world oil production and consumption, the overall share of the Third World refining among non-Communist countries remaining steady at 24 to 26 percent.[23]

Even if we assume that the future holds a net percentage shift in refining from the industrial world to the Third World, the impact on the total market thus would still be slight. The impact on the United States would be even less. U.S. refining capacity in the 1970s has not kept pace with rapid increases in oil demand, so that a growing proportion of our imports (about 32 percent in 1975, and rising sharply since then) has had to be refined abroad. An expansion of OPEC refinery capacity (if and as it should occur) is more likely to cut into the operations of the entrepot refineries in Aruba, Curacao, the Bahamas, and other Caribbean locations rather than into refinery employment in the continental United States.

OPEC's negative impact on U.S. refinery employment thus seems to be mostly illusory. By contrast, there is a very real employment stimulating effect from the mounting orders for industrial equipment that OPEC countries will continue to place in the United States (along with Japan, West Germany, and a very few other countries). And the recycling of surplus OPEC funds to the United States creates additional capital for domestic investment. There is little doubt that a comprehensive analysis would show the employment effects of the OPEC revolution within the United States to be positive.

Nor are any energy programs so far proposed likely to have any substantial employment effect one way or the other. For example, the "gas guzzler tax" proposed by Carter and other measures to encourage the use of smaller and more economical cars would not put Detroit out of business unless U.S. car manufacturers take the suicidal decision of conceding the entire small car market to European and Japanese imports.

In the longer run oil imports may be reduced further by a concerted development of our coal resources and by a massive shift from automobiles to metropolitan mass transit for short hauls, and from cars and airplanes to railroads for the medium hauls. All this means additional employment as Detroit over the next decade or two diversifies from cars into busses and railway equipment and as the coal mining, mining equipment and coal transportation industries are headed for a singular long-range boom.

Some pertinent figures on the distribution of employment in the United States help to put the employment picture in sharper perspective. In 1974, there were 2.2 million workers engaged in manufacturing motor vehicles, 583,000 in railroad transportation, 275,000 in local and suburban mass transportation, 169,000 in coal mining, 155,000 in petroleum refining, and 52,000 in manufacturing railroad equipment.[24] Let us assume for argument's sake and in the absence of a more detailed econometric study that the various changes mentioned previously (increased "downstream" operations by some OPEC countries, vastly increased machinery orders from the same OPEC countries, some shift away from automobiles, a wholesale revitalization of U.S. railroads, and a massive increase in American coal production) would have employment effects on the following scale:

10% fewer refinery workers	- 15,500	workers
3% more machinery production for export	+ 66,000	"
20% decrease in automobile production	-172,000	"
10% decrease in trucking	- 27,500	"
A doubling of coal mining	+169,000	"
A doubling of railroad equipment orders	+ 52,000	"
50% increase in railroad & mass transportation	+429,000	"
Net total:	+501,000	"

The net effect of all these trends and proposals over a period of 15 to 20 years would be additional employment for half a million American workers. Even if a more detailed examination should change these somewhat arbitrary estimates, their positive trend is clear and unmistakable.

It is also clear that employment shifts of this character and magnitude will cause short-term adjustment problems for some American workers and that these workers should not have to carry more than their fair share of the burden of implementing a national energy program. For these and other reasons we urgently need, along with a long-term energy policy, a comprehensive long-term employment policy. This employment policy should provide effective adjustment assistance within the framework of active labor market, tax, investment and technology development programs, all carefully coordinated with the national energy program. With such programs in place American labor can approach confidently the inevitable changes which must come if our advanced industrial economy is to continue to progress. Nothing is likely to create more employment for the next generation of American workers than a wholesale shift from oil import dependence toward domestic energy production and greater self-sufficiency.

NOTES

1. For Simon's statement, see New York Times, October 13, 1974. The first sections of the above text summarize the main argument of Dankwart A. Rustow and John F. Mugno, OPEC: Success and Prospects (New York: New York University Press for Council on Foreign Relations, 1976). It is a pleasure to acknowledge how much I have benefited from Mr. Mugno's collaboration.

2. Sir Eric Drake, chairman of British Petroleum, as quoted by M. A. Adelman, "Is the Oil Shortage Real?" Foreign Policy, no. 9 (Winter 1972-73), pp. 70 and 78.

3. See New York Times, February 12 and September 24, 1974.

4. See, for example, Louis Kraar, "OPEC is Starting to Feel the Pressure," Fortune, (May 1975), p. 186.

5. M. A. Adelman, Letter to New York Times, October 3, 1974, and "Is the Oil Shortage Real?" op. cit., p. 87.

6. See Adelman's letter just cited and his article "Oil Import Quota Auctions," Challenge 17 (January/February 1976), pp. 17-22.

7. See Yamani's interview with Oriana Fallaci, "A Sheik Who Hates to Gamble," New York Times Magazine, September 14, 1975, p. 19.

8. Robert W. Tucker, "Oil: The Issue of American Intervention," Commentary, (January 1975), pp. 21-31. For a careful and dispassionate assessment of the military, technical and political problems posed by the invasion scenario, see the study of the Congressional Research Service of the Library of Congress, Oil Fields as Military Objectives: A Feasibility Study (Washington: U. S. Government Printing Office, 1975). In view of the damage to oil installations and the prospect of Soviet intervention, the study concludes that an invasion of the oil fields "would combine high costs with high risks . . . with plights of far-reaching political, economic, social, psychological and perhaps military consequence the penalty of failure." (Pp. 75ff.)

9. The scale of investment required to secure United States independence from petroleum imports has been variously estimated as $75 billion or more (Carroll L. Wilson, "A Plan for Energy Inde-

pendence," Foreign Affairs 51, no. 4 (July 1973) pp. 657-75) and in the trillion dollar range (Thomas O. Enders, then Assistant Secretary of State, "OPEC and the Industrial Countries: The Next Ten Years," ibid. 53, no. 4 [July 1975], pp. 625-37). Hence massive public expenditures would seem indispensable. Just as cost estimates have tended to rise, so estimates of additional energy production and of likely effects of conservation measures have gone down. Hence the Organization for Economic Cooperation and Development estimate of needed oil imports for 1985 rose by 72 percent from 1974 to 1977. See Energy Prospects to 1985 (Paris: OECD, 1974) and World Energy Outlook (Paris: OECD, 1977).

10. See BP Statistical Review of the World Oil Industry 1970 (London: British Petroleum Co., 1971) and the same review for 1975.

11. Capacity figures for mid 1976 according to Petroleum Intelligence Weekly. For production limitations in various OPEC countries, see Rustow and Mugno, op. cit., p. 44. n. 61.

12. See OECD, World Energy Outlook, op. cit., and D. A. Rustow, "U. S.-Saudi Relations and the Oil Crises of the 1980s," Foreign Affairs 55, no. 4 (April 1977), pp. 494-516, esp. pp. 509ff.

13. This implies the possibility of a major U. S.-Saudi confrontation; D. A. Rustow, ibid.

14. For an alarmist view of the prospects of Third World minerals cartels, see C. Fred Bergsten, "New Era in World Commodity Markets," Challenge 16 (September/October 1974); "The Threat from the Third World," Foreign Policy, no. 11 (Summer 1973); "The Threat is Real," ibid, no. 18 (Winter 1974-75).

15. See the article by Maurice Williams, "Aid Programs of OPEC Countries," Foreign Affairs 54, no. 2 (January 1976), who calçulates that OPEC is spending 1.8 percent of its GNP on "official development assistance," as against only 0.33 percent spent by OECD members. Mr. Williams is chairman of OECD's Development Assistance Committee.

16. See Hollis B. Chenery, "Restructuring the World Economy," Foreign Affairs 53, no. 2 (January 1975).

17. For a lucid exposition of the technical aspects of recycling, see Gerald A. Pollack, "The Economic Consequences of the Energy Crisis," Foreign Affairs 52, no. 3 (April, 1974).

18. For these figures see Rustow and Mugno, op. cit., p. 42, n. 50, D. A. Rustow, "Who Won the Yom Kippur and Oil Wars?" Foreign Policy, no. 14 (Winter 1974-75).

19. For detailed data, see International Monetary Fund, International Financial Statistics (March 1976) which gives annual figures since 1951, and subsequent issues.

20. Rustow and Mugno, op. cit. p. 42 and Rustow, "Who Won the Yom Kippur and Oil Wars?"

21. Calculated from United Nations Statistical Yearbook 1974 (New York: U.N., 1975), p. 70ff.

22. Rustow and Mugno, op. cit., pp. 133 and 135, has figures for production costs for all OPEC countries.

23. Third World refining figures are calculated from figures for "Refinery Crude Throughputs" in BP Statistical Review of the World Oil Industry 1975, op. cit., p. 31. I have included all amounts for Latin America, Africa, Middle East, South and Southeast Asia. Since BP's "Latin America" includes the entire Caribbean, the entrepot refineries referred to in the text are included in these totals.

24. See Statistical Abstract of the United States 1975, pp. 355-57.

25

Raw Materials, Technology, and Trade with the Third World

STANLEY H. RUTTENBERG
AND JOCELYN GUTCHESS

THE CHANGING INTERNATIONAL ENVIRONMENT FOR INDUSTRIAL RAW MATERIALS

Our perspective on raw materials and trade with the Third World has changed since the early 1970s. No longer are we so concerned that the physical supply of most raw materials is in danger of immediate exhaustion. The Club of Rome syndrome which was so convincing to so many people has given way to the reasoned argument of informed scientists and qualified experts who have assured us that the end of the world is not in sight and that resources are ample for man's needs for some time to come, albeit at an initial higher cost, and in some cases, dependent on new technologies not yet completely developed.

Our concern over the danger of cartels has changed too. Initially, that concern was touched off by the double trauma of the OPEC oil embargo, and the quadrupling of the price of imported oil. In view of the dependence of the United States and most of the other industrialized nations on imports for essential raw materials, the Third World cartel threat appeared to be both imminent and potentially crippling. A half a decade later, although we have seen the formation of several materials cartels, none has been able to exert the same force as OPEC. The potential for disruption of supply nevertheless remains. Even more worrisome, the potential for market manipulation by the handful of super-companies that control the materials industry is just as great today as it ever was.

A new element, however, has been added to our concern about supplies of essential raw materials. This is the gathering strength of the Third World crusade for what its members call the New International Economic Order (NIEO). In addition to the issues raised by potential cartel control of materials, we must consider the meaning of NIEO for the U.S. economy and for U.S. workers.

NIEO has many facets and many interpretations, but the basic goal is to achieve for the developing countries a larger share of the world's wealth, and in so doing, raise the standard of living of Third World peoples. The means for achieving that goal are generally seen as involving various methods by which Third World nations can obtain a greater return for their resources, especially their raw materials.

Achievement of NIEO objectives can have an impact on the U.S. economy and U.S. jobs in several ways. The ability of the Third World nations to restrict supply and raise the price of their raw materials will obviously have an effect on the U.S. economy, the rate of inflation and the standard of living of the average worker. The pace of industrialization in these nations, especially the development of downstream fabricating and manufacturing facilities for advanced processing of the raw materials, will also have an effect. Until now the normal pattern has been for materials to be exported from the producing countries in the form of ore, rather than as refined metal or in the form of primary shapes ready for manufacture into end use products for consumption. As this pattern changes, not only are U.S. jobs directly affected, usually by being eliminated, but the entire structure of U.S. employment is changed as the trend away from a goods producing toward a service oriented economy is accelerated. Yet another area of impact pertains to patterns of international trade, the relationship of U.S. foreign trade to the domestic economy, and the relationship of both to employment.

Fortunately, the United States is richly endowed with many of the basic raw materials necessary to sustain our industrial economy. But there are some which we must import, either wholly or in part to meet the demands of U.S. industry. The Council on International Economic Policy listed fourteen such materials in its study last year on critical materials. [1] The degree of import dependency ranged from only fifteen percent in the case of copper, to 100 percent for chromite and tin. In between were vanadium (27 percent imported), iron ore (28 percent), titanium metal (33 percent), tungsten (44 percent), zinc (51 percent), nickel and bauxite (each 90 percent), cobalt and manganese ore (each 95 percent) and platinum (99 percent).

At least in theory, for all of these commodities the United States might be vulnerable to cartel action in the form of arbitrary supply restriction and price manipulation. A closer look at the list indicates, however, that for many of the materials, domestic supply could be increased or other materials substituted. In addition, for some materials a substantial part of the imports come from Canada or other developed countries, thereby diminishing to some extent the potential for harsh treatment or overly restrictive cartel measures, but, bland reliance on our northern neighbor as a thoroughly reliable backstop to Third World cartel threats may be wishful thinking.

THE CURRENT SITUATION WITH BASIC RAW MATERIALS

Aluminum is made from alumina, a metallic element which in turn is most commonly extracted from bauxite, an ore which is found only in limited quantities in the United States. Alumina can be extracted from other non-bauxite clays, which are found in great quantity in the United States, but only at a higher cost than from the high-grade bauxite now being used. The Caribbean countries of Jamaica, Surinam and Guyana are the primary suppliers of bauxite for the U.S. aluminum industry.

Bauxite is also found in other regions of the world, particularly in West Africa, Australia, Yugoslavia and Greece. In 1974 the bauxite producers led by Jamaica, established the International Bauxite Producers Association. The cartel has followed a double strategy—first, a direct approach of simply increasing the price of bauxite, and second, an indirect approach which involves the establishment of primary aluminum processing facilities and their eventual takeover by the host developing country. Under the leadership of Jamaica the strategy is not only ingeniously articulated, but at the present time seems to be working.

The levy on bauxite has actually been increased 700 percent, a higher increase than OPEC managed on oil, but since the cost of the raw material represents a relatively small proportion of the total cost of the final product (about eight percent), the effect on the U.S. economy has not been anywhere as dramatic as the increase in the price of oil. The increased levy actually translates into an increase of only a penny or two in the cost of producing each pound of aluminum.

Having successfully increased the return on bauxite, some IBA countries have moved to the second stage of their strategy and are currently involved in negotiations with the aluminum companies to reduce the levy in exchange for the establishment of downstream fabricating facilities and a gradually increasing share of the ownership of both the old and new company operations. In addition to the reduction in the bauxite levy, the companies also get long-term guaranteed access to the raw materials supply.

The IBA, which is made up of eleven of the major exporters of aluminum, has not been able to establish or enforce a uniform price to be charged by its members. Australia, although an IBA member, has not increased its price on the bauxite mined there and at this point does not appear likely to. Since Australia has the world's largest bauxite reserves, its unwillingness to go along with the Caribbean countries sets a de facto ceiling on price increases. The availability of substitute sources of alumina also acts as a brake on IBA's efforts to restrict supply and thereby increase prices.

These limitations on IBA effectiveness are offset to some extent by the structure of the aluminum industry itself. Over 70 percent of the whole free world industry is controlled by only six giant multinationals, three of which are the American majors, Alcoa, Reynolds and Kaiser.[2] Since cost increases can be passed on the consumers without fear of effective competition, the aluminum companies' interest is best served by going along with the cartel, particularly if they can gain guaranteed access to supply by so doing.

U. S. import dependence for copper is less than for any of the other basic metals and minerals. In fact, the United States is the largest producer of copper in the free world. Other major producers are Canada, Chile and Peru (principal suppliers of 15 percent of its needs which the United States imports), Zambia, Zaire and South Africa (supplying the European market) and Australia, Philippines and Papua New Guinea (supplying Japan and the Far East).[3]

Four of the copper producing countries, Chile, Peru, Zambia and Zaire, all from the Third World, are members of the Intergovernmental Council of Copper Exporting Countries, known by its French acronym, CIPEC. Within the last year, Indonesia has joined with the first four, and Iran, soon to become a major copper producer, may join. In 1974, the original CIPEC group agreed to restrict production in an effort to maintain the high prices they obtained during the first part of that year. This same period was characterized by aggressive efforts on the part of all four countries to take full control over their copper industries.

The first step was a ten percent cut-back in production. When this proved ineffective, the cut-back was increased to 15 percent, but this too failed to hold the price line. The cut-back proved to be unenforceable, the principal reason being the dependence of the Third World producers on continued large exports of copper to earn the foreign exchange they needed, especially for oil. More important the CIPEC countries do not control enough of the copper market to affect significantly supply over the long term. If the CIPEC countries are joined by other Third World producers so that as much as 50 percent of supply is controlled by a cartel, the story could be different.

Offsetting the cartel threat is the presence of apparently inexhaustible supplies of copper in deep seabed deposits. At the present time, recovery of copper from this source is not economically feasible, but it is only a question of time before the technological problems are solved and the deep sea resources become economically recoverable.

Approximately half of the U. S. zinc requirements are imported, the major suppliers being Canada, Mexico and Peru.[4] Although the United States has substantial reserves of zinc, import dependency has been increasing over the past decade, as domestic mines and refineries have closed down. In addition, zinc imports are increasingly in the form of slab rather than in the form of ore, a direct result of the shift of processing facilities to other countries. The shutdown of American zinc producing facilities has occurred because obsolescence has made many of the American plants non-competitive with newer foreign plants.

The cartel activity in zinc comes from the private sector, not the governments of producing countries. A European producers' group, which includes virtually all West European, Canadian and Australian privately owned producers, has attempted to stabilize world prices by buying and selling zinc through the London Metals Exchange. Both the European producers' group and the American zinc industry, concentrated in only six companies, have been under investigation by the Department of Justice for possible law violations.

Since lead and zinc are often mined from the same ore body, the situation for lead is very similar to that for zinc. Import dependency is about the same for both metals. From two-thirds to three-fourths of U.S. requirements for lead are met from domestic resources. The major sources of U.S. imports are Canada, Australia, Mexico and Peru.[5]

Like the zinc industry, primary production of lead is concentrated among only a few companies. Moreover, when secondary sources such as scrap make up a significant part of the feedstock of the industry and recycling potential is high, as is the case in the lead industry, it becomes more difficult for an international cartel to influence supply and price.

The world's resources of chromite ore, from which chromium is derived, are found in only a limited number of countries. The most important sources are South Africa, Rhodesia, the Philippines, Turkey and the USSR.[6] United States vulnerability to cartel action is very high since not only are we completely dependent on imports, but there is also no good substitute for chromium in its applications in the steel industry. The chromium industry is dominated by one company, Union Carbide, a factor favoring cartelization.

Manganese is essential in the production of steel but is required only in very small quantities, so that, with bauxite, even very sharp price increases would not greatly affect the cost of the final product.

Manganese consumed in the United States, virtually all imported, comes primarily from Gabon and Brazil (50 percent), other important sources being Zaire, South Africa, Australia, Mexico and Ghana.[7] The manganese industry is dominated by a handful of multinationals, notably the steel companies. Both Brazil and Gabon have taken the first steps toward nationalization of their manganese industries.

Manganese is one of the commodities for which UNCTAD has favored the development of a producer association, but as yet no such association has been formed. To be effective, it would have to include Australia and perhaps also South Africa. Another deterrent to cartelization is the abundance of manganese in the deep seabed.

Like manganese, nickel is an integral part of the steel industry. More than 90 percent of the U.S. requirements must be imported. mostly from Canada. The worldwide resource picture is bright, with new reserves in Cuba, Canada, New Caledonia in the Pacific, Greece, Rhodesia, Australia, Indonesia, and the deep seabed.[8] Only two major companies, International Nickel of Canada (INCO) and the French Société Le Nickel (with major nickel holdings in New Caledonia), together control about 70 percent of the world capacity. There is no reason for cartelization when an effective duopoly already exists.

The United States is also almost entirely dependent on imports for its tin supply, primarily from Malaysia, Thailand, Bolivia and Indonesia. Other important producing countries are Australia, Nigeria and Zaire.[9] Tin has been subject to an international commodity agreement for more than twenty years.

The International Tin Agreement (ITA) is an association of both major producers and large consumers which the United States has recently joined. Under this agreement the International Tin Council sets floor and ceiling prices, and its Buffer Stock Manager buys and sells tin on the world markets with the intention of preventing wide swings in world tin prices. The producers make mandatory contributions to the buffer stock and are required to impose export controls if necessary. The consumers may make voluntary financial contributions to the stock, but most, and particularly the United States, have opted not to do so.

Unlike most of the other metals industries the tin industry is not vertically integrated. No super companies are in a position to make it easy for the group of producing countries to exert arbitrary influence on supply and price, although some Third World producers such as Bolivia and Indonesia have moved toward nationalization of their own industries. The diversity of end uses for tin and the lack of vertical integration in the industry make tin an unlikely candidate for additional Third World efforts to establish downstream operations.

An Association of Iron Ore Exporting Countries (AIEC) of seven nations was formed in April 1975, with Algeria, India and Venezuela taking the lead. Brazil, Canada, Liberia and the USSR, all important producers of iron ore, have not joined the AIEC, but Australia and Sweden have. As of now, the Association has limited itself to an advisory and informational role, rather than attempting any kind of direct market intervention.

Although the United States is one of world's major producers of iron ore, we import about 30 percent of our needs, half from Canada, a third from Venezuela, and the rest from Liberia, Brazil and Peru. Any restriction in world supply of this basic raw material, like the OPEC oil embargo, would cause serious trouble for the U.S. economy.

The potential for cartelization of iron ore must be considered serious. Perhaps even more disturbing is the potential for eventual replacement of the U.S. steel industry by new steel industries in some of the AIEC countries. With the continued export of steel technology we can expect further competition from both Third World and even Communist controlled countries, a rising tide of imports and the eventual "withering away" of the U.S. industry.

Producer associations, primarily composed of Third World countries, have been formed in four of the nine essential industrial raw materials discussed here. One, the International Bauxite Association, has achieved notable success in influencing prices. Another, the Tin Council, a producer-consumer organization, was able to stabilize prices in the world market for some time, although in the past year exaggerated shifts in demand have made stabilization difficult. The other two have not been effective in influencing world markets—the copper association because it is not yet sufficiently inclusive, and the iron ore association because it has not yet tried. For the other five minerals no movement toward cartelization has yet taken place, but such action might well be expected soon for both chromium and manganese. Cartelization for either zinc or lead would be fairly difficult because the supply sources are so widely dispersed. The problem in those industries is market control by private interests rather than by producing nations.

If the threat of cartelization is not quite as ominous as it appeared, neither can we ignore it. Rome was not built in a day, nor will the existing pattern of relationships between the developing and the developed countries be changed in a year or so. The fact that there are only four or five producers associations, operating with varying degrees of success two years after the OPEC embargo, does not mean that there will still be only four or five in three, five or ten years. As the Third World movement toward an NIEO continues, as it most certainly will, the United States must be prepared to deal with the new situation.

INDUSTRIALIZATION IN THE THIRD WORLD

Cartelization, like other forms of market intervention, is only a means to an end, not an end in itself. For the Third World nations cartelization is usually a first step in a broader strategy to increase per capita wealth and improve living standards through industrialization. For the developing countries which are raw materials producers, industrialization often takes the form of downstream fabrication of these materials. In the past decade this process has been occurring at an accelerated pace in many developing countries.

Alumina, copper, and zinc refineries in Jamaica, Zaire, Peru, Guinea, and Indonesia and ferromanganese and ferrochrome plants in Turkey and Brazil are all examples of the development of new materials processing industries in the producing countries.

The rationale behind the desire of the Third World countries to accelerate the pace of industrialization within their own nations is easy to understand. At every step of the industrialization process, the value added by the process of manufacturing obtains a greater return on the investment for the processor. For developing countries, therefore, industrialization appears to be a quick solution to the present maldistribution of the world's wealth. However, Third World industrialization raises important issues for both the developing and the developed nations.

In most cases processing plants for the fabrication of raw materials, especially in the metals industry, are highly capital intensive and create very little employment. They are also apt to require a large input of energy, and frequently generate a substantial amount of pollution. The employment created usually is highly skilled, so the new fabricating plants are of little help in alleviating unemployment which in most developing countries is both chronic and severe.

The British economist E. F. Schumacher, whose book Small Is Beautiful (New York: Harper and Row, 1973) captured the imagination, if not converted, many of those who are involved in one way or another, in the development efforts of the Third World, argued that development should be small scale and employment generating. Following that line, the British Intermediate Technology Group is involved in promoting the concept of labor intensive, small scale rural based industry in the developing countries which would utilize intermediate rather than the most advanced capital intensive technology. In the same vein, the United States is currently in the process of establishing, as part of its economic aid program, a semi-public intermediate technology fund to facilitate the development of small businesses in the developing nations.

It is clear that efforts to lead the LDCs into more modest industrialization schemes, however well intentioned, are not going to work everywhere, particularly in the case of those developing countries which are substantial producers of raw materials and which have already achieved a significant degree of development. They will very likely regard overtures under the Small Is Beautiful rubric as a con job designed to keep the rich richer. Intermediate technology proposals which might be very acceptable to the countries of the Sahel would not fit into the development plan of a country like Brazil, which is already moving well down the road of industrialization, or of Algeria or Iran, both of which are moving ahead persistently and aggressively to implement full scale development plans.

Closely related to the issues concerning the degree and pace of industrialization is the issue of technology transfer. There is no question that the Third World countries want the technology of the industrialized nations. In fact, unrestricted technology transfer at no cost to the user is an important item on the agenda of the NIEO. United States corporations operating overseas, with their European and Japanese MNC cousins, seem to be increasingly willing to provide technology, even very advanced technology, to any country willing to take it. There is no good measure of the magnitude of technology transfer since it can take many forms, from replication of a finished product which is exported, to the training of indigenous personnel, which is a natural fallout from the newly emerging service contracts between U.S. and foreign companies or foreign governments.

Technology transfer occurs when a U.S. company licenses its subsidiary or even an unconnected company to manufacture its product, using the U.S. company's methods, processes and sometimes its machinery. It occurs through joint ventures when a U.S. and a foreign company join together in a new operation overseas, pooling the capital costs, R&D, technology and management skills and, of course, ownership. An example is the joint venture between Rumania and Control Data Corporation. A new company was formed to manufacture and market computer equipment and systems. The Rumanian state-controlled company put up most of the capital. Control Data contributed both technology and management skills.

Technology is also sometimes transferred via turnkey operations. Here the MNC provides everything necessary to get a new plant started and then simply turns it over to the developing country government or government-controlled company. An example of such an arrangement is seen in the agreement between the U.S. multinational, General Telephone and Electronics, and the Algerian electronic company, SONELEC. General Telephone has agreed to provide plant construction, manufacturing technology, fully integrated from the raw materials to the manufacture of radio and TV equipment, and training for a full range of technicians and managers.

Or technology transfer can be in the form of a service contract, the vehicle most frequently found in the OPEC countries, which have all the necessary capital and are not anxious or indeed willing to permit U.S. or other foreign nations to own any industrial capacity within their borders. Under the service contract, the U.S. corporation provides technology, process engineering, training and management, for as long as such service is needed or desired.

It used to be thought that only mature, or even obsolete, technology would be transferred from the industrialized nations to the Third World. As these mature industries were moved to the developing nations, so the theory went, they would be supplanted in the developed countries by newer industries, based on newer and more advanced technology. But this no longer seems to be the case. Today there are numerous incidences of international transfer of very advanced technology by U.S. corporations. Often, of course, the transfer is to other developed countries such as Japan or the European EC. But the developing countries are also the recipients of advanced technology, as in the examples of General Telephone and Electronics and Algeria, and Control Data and Rumania indicate. For some corporations this transfer of technology seems to have become the corporation's primary product.

As this occurs and the corporation product itself changes from the production of goods to the implantation of design, engineering and management capabilities, the foundation for future competition is most certainly being laid. Cummins Engine, for example, has decided to ease up on efforts to manufacture and export its most advanced new diesel engine here in the United States and instead to share its technology and a significant portion of the production for this new product with its former Japanese licensee. Another company, Fluor, is involved in the design and construction of several chemical and petroleum processing plants in Iran and Saudi Arabia, plants which eventually will be in competition with the U.S. petrochemical industry.

IMPACT OF THE NEW INTERNATIONAL ECONOMIC ORDER ON THE UNITED STATES AND THE U.S. RESPONSE

As the Third World moves toward realization of the goals envisioned in the NIEO, four areas of major impact can be readily identified. First, as technology is transferred and investment in new plants and equipment and new fabricating facilities are increased, the current trend of the U.S. economy away from the production of goods and toward the provision of service will be accelerated. Twenty-five years ago, only 30 percent of the U.S. GNP was attributable to the service sector of the economy, and almost 60 percent to the goods producing sector. In 1975 the two sectors were about even, at 47 percent, but clearly the service sector has the momentum.[10] Since technology is more readily applied to manufacturing than it is to the provision of services, it is in this area that the greatest improvements can be made in productivity. Without productivity growth there can be no general improvement in the standard of living—a goal which must continue to be of utmost importance to U.S. workers.

Second, as new basic industries are established in the developing countries, especially in those countries which are the producers of essential raw materials, the U.S. share of world trade in those industries is certain to decline. International trade may not be as important to the U.S. economy as to Japan, but U.S. foreign trade is not unsubstantial, and in recent years has been increasing as a share of GNP.

As the Third World develops its own industries, it could become increasingly difficult for U.S. industry to compete. This would be especially so, if, for example, the iron ore and manganese producing nations were to join together in a cartel and restrict U.S. supplies of these materials, either through an embargo or establishment of quotas or by price manipulation. U.S. steel corporations would not necessarily be the losers in the short run, since the largest of these are already operating in the producing countries and therefore could be expected to be involved in the Third World steel industry development. But the U.S. economy most certainly would be the loser, and in the long run, the steel companies also would suffer.

Third, U.S. employment will be affected, both in quantity and quality. Any severe disruption of raw material supply by international cartels, acting with or without the assistance of the MNCs, would of course have immediate impact on employment in those industries dependent on imports of raw materials. But continued export of technology and the shift of fabricating facilities to the Third World will also affect employment. If as a result of such shifts, U.S. industry plants are closed down or become noncompetitive and are forced out of business, U.S. jobs are lost. Even if there is no direct replacement of a U.S. facility by a foreign facility, in the long run the new plants will eventually compete with U.S. industry and U.S. jobs could be lost.

As the shift to the service sector continues, eliminating manufacturing jobs, moreover, there will be a qualitative change in the general structure of employment. Jobs will be either highly technical, requiring advanced education and technical training, or unskilled, requiring little education and no training. Such a polarization of the labor force could prove ruinous to our democratic society.

Fourth, the U.S. standard of living could be threatened. If the Third World countries are able to impose and sustain arbitrary price increases for their materials, the eventual effect could be a reduction in U.S. standard of living. This is most easily seen in the case of the OPEC increase in oil prices, which already has forced a change in the relationship between the various factors of production to the disadvantage of labor. Similar increases in raw materials prices could produce the same result.

The increasing economic interdependence of the world is a fact of life, probably the most significant development of the postwar period. The developing countries know it. The American labor movement knows it. Although the United States and the developing countries may have conflicting goals, there are also common interests which make resolution of these competing goals possible. Both sides need stable markets. The United States benefits from the economic health of its trading partners and therefore wants the developing countries to be healthy. In turn, the developing countries require strong overseas markets for their exports, and thus they must have an interest in the continued growth and prosperity of the industrialized nations. The problem is how the competing goals can be made compatible—a difficult but not an impossible task.

The United States must first do those things which will protect U.S. interests from arbitrary cartel activity. The United States must have assurance of a secure, stable supply of raw materials. Such measures would include:

1. The development of bilateral commodity agreements with the nations which supply the United States with raw materials. The agreements could aim at the establishment of a fixed U.S. supply for a number of years. In return the United States could offer a guaranteed price or a support floor. In addition, the United States could offer to help the producing country obtain the capital and technical assistance necessary to establish processing plants, but over a period of time.

2. Increased federal support of research and development efforts. Because until recently the supplies of raw materials have been both relatively cheap and reasonably accessible and because the materials industries are typically so concentrated that the controlling companies need not fear competition, there has been little incentive for the development of new materials technology which might provide more efficient and less costly methods of extraction or primary processing. Such support, judiciously made, could help to encourage new entrants into these industries. Increased support of R&D could hasten the development of substitute materials, thereby lessening U.S. dependence on imports and serving as an effective counter to cartel threats of supply disruption.

3. Government support of seabed development. Since the seabed offers an almost unlimited supply of manganese, copper, nickel and cobalt, the present exploratory efforts now being conducted solely by private interests should be expanded and accelerated with government support.

4. Establishment of economic stockpiles. Although there is a U.S. stockpile of critical materials, acquired and maintained to meet defense needs in the case of a war, it would be advisable to initiate a stockpile program for a few import-dependent commodities, which would be designed to achieve economic purposes. Such a stockpile would serve as an effective deterrent to both supply disruptions and price manipulation, whether such actions were the result of country cartels or corporate concentration.

The United States must also do those things that encourage and promote worldwide economic prosperity. There must be a recognition that worldwide economic growth is basic to any long-lasting solution. Clearly, a larger economic pie from which the developed and the developing countries alike can take their piece of economic development and well-being is essential to any lasting solutions. Without such growth, development simply cannot take place.

It must also be recognized that worldwide economic growth is dependent on a healthy and growing U.S. economy. The developing world cannot develop, Third World countries cannot industrialize their economies or sell their products on the world market, unless the U.S. economy—the largest and strongest in the world—is also prosperous and growing.

That this must start with full employment should go without saying. Without full employment in the United States, there can be no worldwide growth, and without worldwide growth, serious conflicts of interest will develop. Moreover, if economic progress for the Third World is obliged to take place at the expense of a reduction in the standard of living in the industrialized nations, there is bound to be much opposition and great resistance. But in a full employment economy, U.S. workers would be in the lead, as they have traditionally been, in support of full scale development in the Third World. Without full employment, workers in all of the industrialized nations will be forced to adopt a protective, if not a negative stance.

In developing and implementing a consistent and constructive policy toward the Third World nations, the United States faces a difficult challenge. The Third World drive to improve its economic and social condition will not and should not be thwarted. At the same time, U.S. social and economic goals cannot and should not be abandoned or compromised. That is the challenge before us.

NOTES

1. U.S. Council on International Economic Policy, International Economic Report (Washington, D.C.: The Council, March 1976).
2. U.S. Department of Interior, Bureau of Mines, Minerals Yearbook, 1974 (Washington, D.C.: Government Printing Office, 1974).
3. U.S. Department of Interior, Bureau of Mines, Commodity Data Series, 1976 (Washington, D.C.: Government Printing Office, 1976).
4. Ibid.
5. Ibid.
6. Ibid.

7. Ibid.

8. Ibid.

9. Ibid.

10. U.S. Council of Economic Advisors, Economic Report of the President (Washington, D.C.: The Council, 1976), Appendix B.

26

Diversity in the Developing World, International Trade, and U.S. Policy

WILLIAM G. RHOADS

RESOURCE POSITIONS AND DEVELOPMENT LEVELS IN THE THIRD WORLD

U.S. interests in energy and commodities trade with the Third World are very much affected by resource positions and levels of development. We can make a rough division of the developing countries into three categories—the poorest, the middle income, and the rich OPEC member countries.

At the bottom are some 65 countries, mostly in Asia and Africa, with well over one-third of the world's population and with per capita incomes under $500 in 1975, including two OPEC member countries, Indonesia and Nigeria. These countries not only have the worst problems of poverty and misery, but with some exceptions, they have not been making sufficient progress in overcoming them. They have had the slowest rate of growth in GNP in the world, and in the last few years, many have had little or no economic growth. They take only 8 percent of U.S. exports. While they depend heavily on commodities for their exports, they are also important commodity importers. They are heavily dependent on foreign assistance for their external financing, and since many do not feed themselves, as a group they are heavy grain importers. The United States has a humanitarian interest in helping these countries. It wants to help them grow more food so they will not become an intolerable burden on world food supplies, and it wants to assist them to achieve their goals of economic and social development and not be a source of instability and failure in a world of increasing nuclear proliferation.

The middle income countries—some 50 countries mainly in Latin America, southern Europe, the Middle East and Far East—have a population of some 600 million. They include a number of OPEC member countries. Contrary to the poorer countries, they have enjoyed very high rates of economic growth in the last decade. They are important commodity producers, and a number have become important exporters of manufactured goods. They are important U.S. trading partners, taking over 25 percent of U.S. exports last year. These countries receive little concessional aid, and in recent years have been able to borrow after they became creditworthy in the private financial markets. They were hard hit by increasing petroleum prices and the world recession and have had to borrow heavily to try to keep their economies supplied with imports and growing. Even so, their economies have slowed down, and their imports from the U.S. were one-half billion dollars less in the first nine months of 1976 than they had been a year earlier in the recession year of 1975.

We still retain our humanitarian interest in helping these middle income countries, but more through increased trade and a strong world economy than through concessional assistance. At the same time, they are a very important market for us, and most of them import more from the United States than they export to us. They are also important suppliers of key commodities and raw materials to the United States.

The third group consists of six member countries of OPEC in the Middle East. With very large oil exports their per capita incomes put them in the class of developed or even superdeveloped countries, even though their economies are still undeveloped in many ways. More importantly, these sparsely settled countries have had such great earnings from oil exports that they have not been able to spend them on imports and services, and their total surplus on current account of their balance-of-payments is running at a rate of around $40 billion per year.

The rest of the OPEC countries such as Venezuela, Nigeria, Iraq and Indonesia have benefited from higher prices, but they have used their earnings to increase their imports and step up their rate of development. While we would not have chosen to increase our transfer of resources to these countries, it created no major problems for our economy.

THE IMPACT OF OPEC

It is important to recognize that for both the United States and the rest of the developed countries, and for the non-oil exporting LDCs too, the burden of higher oil prices on our economies has been less than the effects of the huge surpluses run up by a few Middle Eastern OPEC countries that have not spent their increased oil earnings on imports from the rest of the world. The effect of higher oil prices on the U.S. economy since 1973 has been less than 2 percent of our GNP. We transferred that much of our GNP per year to Europe during the Marshall Plan without any major problems. In fact the real resource transfer of the Marshall Plan took the form of increased production, created jobs and helped the U.S. GNP to increase. But the higher oil price was inflationary in a way that the Marshall Plan was not, since it directly raised oil prices. Instead of creating demand for more jobs, like the Marshall Plan did, it decreased the number of jobs since it reduced domestic purchasing power and the newly rich OPEC countries did not spend their new earnings on imports to offset this.

The United States reacted to the simultaneous inflationary effects, deflationary effects and the pressure on our trade balance from higher oil prices by slowing down our economy. From 1973 to 1975, our gross national product fell by 3.5 percent, instead of increasing by about 7 percent as would normally occur. That loss of output (about 10 percent) and jobs (with unemployment rising to 8 percent) was far greater than the direct loss of purchasing power to OPEC, which was only about 2 percent of GNP.

The same thing happened to the petroleum-importing developing countries. The direct increased cost of their petroleum imports, plus the higher petroleum costs passed on in their imports from the developed countries, was about $13 billion per year. But in the depression year of 1975, their increased trade and services deficit was over double that because the recession in the developed countries caused the prices they received for their commodities and other exports and the quantities they sold to drop dramatically. In 1975 the developed countries as a group actually had a surplus on current account. Through their recession, they transferred the entire burden to the resource-poor developing countries of the rich OPEC country surplus.

In 1976 the recovery in the developed countries has resulted in improved commodity prices and increased export earnings for the developing countries, but overall their levels of imports and their internal rates of economic development are still below the trends prior to 1974.

With unemployment still high in the developed countries at the same time as inflation continues at fairly high levels, and the developing countries slowing down their growth because of lack of imports, it is clear that the inflationary-deflationary challenge presented by the oil price increase (and resulting financial surpluses by a few rich OPEC countries) has not yet been met. While this situation is a new one for most of the developed countries, it is one that some of the developing countries individually have had to cope with for the last decade. In some cases they have had considerable success in meeting the challenge, and we in the developed countries might learn from their experience.

If, as seems likely, oil prices will remain high for years, and the rich OPEC member countries will continue to run large current account surpluses, the first need is to adjust the economies of the developed world to this situation in a manner that does not require such high unemployment rates as they now are suffering. Until the United States reduces its own unemployment below the current high levels, it will be difficult to get public agreement on many specific new measures to help the developing countries, except perhaps for more additional concessional assistance for the poorest countries, since this will help both our unemployment and trade adjustment problems. A higher level of economic activity in the United States will also directly benefit the developing countries through stronger markets for their exports and will probably help them more than many of the other proposals now under discussion.

COMMODITY TRADE AND DEVELOPMENT

The history of the last several years has shown that the principal problem with commodities other than oil is instability in prices rather than the establishment of high stable price levels by cartels. Abrupt increases in commodity prices have made already difficult inflationary situations worse in the United States and other developed countries, while abrupt decreases in commodity prices have seriously hurt some of the developing countries when they were already under pressure from higher oil prices. Both developing and developed countries can benefit by greater commodity price stability if this can be achieved.

There are some cartels in commodities (and some commodities), the import of which is crucial to the United States. The U.S. response has been to propose measures that would diversify and increase commodity supplies from the rest of the world. The U.S. proposal at UNCTAD IV for an International Resources Bank is such a proposal. The damage to the United States from recent cartel formation has not been large, and studies indicate that dangers in the future of supply disruption and cartelization are manageable. The three minerals for which supply access problems are most likely are bauxite, chromite and manganese. With the exception of bauxite, it would take an unlikely combination of countries to form an effective cartel. In bauxite, of course, the price has been driven up. According to a study by Charles River Associates for the Labor Department,[1] the maximum cost to the United States of further price increases by the bauxite group would be just over $235 million per year. Contrast this with sugar, where every change of one cent per pound in the price of sugar costs the United States $100 million per year. Sugar prices have fallen from about 60 cents per pound to around 8 cents per pound, and concerted efforts are underway to see if the price can be increased to a higher level, say 12-15 cents per pound. I think the United States has much more at stake in the upcoming domestic and multilateral discussions on sugar price policy than it has from any further actions by a bauxite cartel.

Administration efforts then are properly going into the case-by-case discussions of individual commodity agreements rather than into questions of cartel formation. We have joined the tin agreement and the coffee agreement, would join a more flexible cocoa agreement, will enter into talks on a sugar agreement and will be discussing stabilization of other commodities at UNCTAD and various individual conferences.

Until the United States is able to reduce unemployment and decrease the threat of inflation, it will be difficult to do more than discuss the longer-run adjustments in commodities and trade that the developing countries are asking for. International developments in energy and commodities have adversely affected both the United States and the developing countries. We cannot reverse the situation, but both the United States and the developing countries have a mutual interest in overcoming many of the problems they have created. In doing that, the goal must be increased employment and economic activity in all countries. The most direct effects of higher oil prices and commodity price instability have not been as dangerous and damaging to us and to the developing countries as have their indirect effects on inflation, unemployment and the deceleration in rates of economic growth. We all have much to learn in how to cooperate in achieving this goal.

NOTES

1. Charles River Associates, Inc., Access to Mineral Supplies: Potential Problems and U.S. Trading Leverage (Cambridge, Mass.: CRA, 1975), p. 8.

PART V

LABOR, AID, AND DEVELOPMENT IN THE THIRD WORLD

27

New Directions in Aid and Development, and Their Implications for American Labor

JOHN W. MELLOR

AMERICAN LABOR'S STAKE IN CHANGING PATTERNS OF WORLD INDUSTRIALIZATION

The United States is both a participant and an observer in a continuing drama of worldwide industrialization. The drama commenced in the eighteenth century with the industrial revolution. The first act included massive colonization of the bulk of Asia and Africa by a small proportion of the world's populace residing in northwestern Europe, where the industrial revolution began.

The second act, following World War II, brought rapid decline in colonialism but nevertheless an explosive widening of income disparities in favor of the richer, early industrializing nations and an equally explosive widening of population growth rates to the detriment of the poor, late industrializing nations. We are now in the third act, during which economic and political power of the low income nations of Asia, Africa, and Latin America is commencing to grow, already must be recognized and will later begin collectively to exceed that of the first nations to industrialize.

The industrialization of low income nations has special implications to American labor because of the importance of expanded trade for rapid development of the low income nations, the key role labor-intensive industrial exports play in that trade, the control by low income nations of significant portions of the world's natural resources, and the inevitable use of that control to assist in diversifying their economies. These forces directly affect American labor by their influence on the rate of growth and stability of total U.S. income and wealth as well as on the share of U.S. income received by labor.

Encouragement and facilitation of those forces can foster substantial growth in average and total real income in the United States, both through access to expanding supplies of natural resources and through favorable trade relations. Those same forces may reduce the proportion of total income paid to labor. The net effect on labor will depend on the size and effectiveness of adjustment mechanisms and other policies influencing the domestic distribution of the overall benefits.

The alternative of increasing isolation, not only from the Third World but from the foreign resource-dependent part of the industrial world as well, could have high costs in overall growth. In addition, by placing heavy demands on capital for replacing natural resources such isolation may also reduce the share of income to labor—without the presence of aggregate gains which could facilitate transfer payments to labor. Thus, adjustment to the new forces in the world may be difficult but preferable to the costs of isolation.

Participation in Third World development offers opportunity not only to encourage stable patterns of economic and social change and influence the timing and character of industrialization but also to help solve major world problems of population growth, natural resource depletion, and protection of the environment. For these purposes our effective focus needs to be on the underlying political and economic processes in the developing nations which determine the development strategy and the breadth of participation in that strategy. American labor has a vital stake in how these underlying processes shape the future economic and social character of the Third World.

POLITICS AND ECONOMICS IN U.S.-THIRD WORLD RELATIONS

U.S.-Third World relations have for the past decade focused on immediate political questions in Vietnam, the Middle East and Southern Africa. Concern with long-term economic relationships has dwindled rapidly, reflected in diminished public interest in aid to and development of the Third World. Obscured by these short run preoccupations, major structural changes have occurred almost unnoticed in the Third World-First World relations.

Failure to recognize these changes works to both the short run and long run disadvantage of major American interests. Adaptation to these changes requires a reexamination of objectives in the Third World and development of a clear, feasible strategy for reaching those objectives consistent with the new Third World reality. Although the ultimate objectives and the instruments of current confrontations are political, the bases for both lie in changing economic relationships and power.

Three major categories of change have been occurring, each providing increasing political power to the Third World. First, the sources from which they obtain financing of their growth have been changing, with the United States declining sharply in absolute importance and even more dramatically in relative importance. Second, points of global interaction including natural resource supply, population growth, environment, and trade have grown in importance and are no longer subject to unilateral determination by the United States alone or even in concert with the other industrial nations. Similarly the extent to which even American humanitarian concerns may be pursued unilaterally is rapidly diminishing, even though the concern itself may remain. Third, an increasing number of nations are achieving the accelerated growth that eventually closes economic and power gaps. This accelerated growth is important in and of itself but also portends even more dramatic changes in the future.

In 1965, out of total resource flows to the LDCs of $11.8 billion, the United States provided 44 percent, $3.5 billion in net official bilateral aid and $1.8 billion in private investment. The multilateral agencies contributed a modest 13 percent of the flow, with the United States supplying 40 percent of that. By 1974 with essentially the same definitions and accounting, the flows had nearly quadrupled to $44.8 billion. United States official bilateral aid, still at about the same nominal amount but halved in real terms, had declined to 8 percent of the total. U.S. private investment had tripled, however, bringing the combined U.S. bilateral flow to 13 percent of the total—still less than one-third the proportion of a decade earlier. The multilateral flows had nearly tripled in proportion to comprise 38 percent of the total. But the U.S. share of the multilateral flows had also dropped substantially.[1]

Perhaps most striking, the Euro-currency market had become three times as important as U.S. official bilateral assistance, and OPEC, the World Bank and the International Monetary Fund (IMF) were each individually two-thirds or more as important as United States bilateral aid. The EC is providing on the order of $1 billion a year to African and a few small island countries, compared to under $200 million to these areas in U.S. bilateral assistance. More generally, while the "real" official development assistance of the United States has been cut in half in a decade and a half, the other member countries of the OECD have increased their real development assistance by 25 percent just since 1970. They have maintained the proportion of foreign assistance to GNP at 0.4 percent for the past decade and a half, while the U.S. proportion has dropped from 0.59 percent to 0.24 percent.[2]

The weight of United States aid to the bulk of Third World countries is even less than implied above because it is so heavily concentrated on a few countries in pursuit of short run political objectives. Thus, Egypt, Jordan and Indochina comprise only 8 percent of the population of countries with per capita income less than $500, and yet they received 58 percent of U.S. official development assistance to the low income countries in 1974. Egypt and Jordan have been allocated 46 percent of total AID and PL 480 expenditure to the low income countries in the administration's fiscal year 1977 budget request.[3]

In some respects the point is even more dramatically made by a sample of ten LDCs which all have under $500 per year per capita income.* For this set of countries U.S. bilateral assistance was five percent of the total, only a quarter as important as the Euro-currency market or the IMF, half as important as OPEC and less than half as important as the World Bank.

Whatever views one may have about changing U.S. aid levels and increases from other sources, it is an inescapable conclusion that the diversity of aid sources has grown in the last decade. With that has come a wider set of options to the low income nations, a capacity to bargain more vigorously on the terms and conditions of aid, and the potential to define for themselves their own development strategies in a more autonomous manner. Aid donor policies based on old levels and patterns of aid under current relationships are likely to lead to miscalculation and confrontation.

GROWTH OF GLOBAL INTERDEPENDENCE IN RAW MATERIALS, TRADE AND POPULATION

While U.S. dominance of financial flows to the Third World has been declining, four major points of global interdependence have further reduced the ability of the United States to deal meaningfully with Third World events on a unilateral basis. U.S. dependence, and even more so that of other industrial nations, on raw materials produced in the developing countries has grown substantially while the economic and political basis for direct control has declined. The environment for industrial growth in the West was made particularly favorable by the ability to virtually expand unilaterally raw material supplies as rapidly as demand required without concern for whether or not such action maximized returns to the countries in which the raw materials existed.

---

*The countries are Kenya, Haiti, Honduras, Philippines, Ivory Coast, Senegal, Pakistan, Sri Lanka (Ceylon), India and Tanzania.

Expansion of raw material supplies can still be advantageous to both consumers and producers, but the considerations and negotiations are now much more complex. These facts are more apparent in the resource-poor countries of Europe and Japan than in the United States. The large aid flow and amicable trade terms of the European Community's Lomé Convention with a number of countries in Africa, the Caribbean and the Pacific are evidence of that. But as Europe and Japan develop viable interactions with the Third World, the United States must cooperate in those relations or itself become isolated not only from the Third World but from the bulk of the industrialized world as well.

Third World nations have already become important trading partners of the United States. Non-OPEC LDCs now comprise 30 percent of trade, compared to 17 percent of U.S. trade with the EC. LDCs with annual per capita income under $500 comprise 7 percent of total U.S. trade; thus these very poor countries are already half as important in our trade as the EC. It is particularly notable that LDC exports of manufactures have been growing at a rate of over 13 percent for the past two decades, a rate of growth more than one-quarter greater than that of the industrialized countries.[4]

Trade is a crucial means whereby low income nations obtain technology and capital-intensive imports, the lack of which would considerably retard their growth. It also facilitates expansion in their manufacturing output and employment beyond what their initially thin domestic markets would allow. Facilitation of such economic diversification is likely to become an increasingly explicit basis for negotiation of raw material access. Increased trade also offers major opportunity for the United States to obtain real income benefits which, given the potential size of Third World markets, could be a significant factor in future growth.

The United States, with some 40 percent of total GNP of the market-economy industrialized nations, is a dominant factor in trade with LDCs. For example, the United States receives over 20 times as large a quantity of LDC manufactured exports as does the Soviet Union. Although that trading weight is formidable, even in trade there are growing options. The Soviet Union is a growing trading partner for several low income nations, particularly as an importer of labor-intensive consumer goods in return for exports of technology and capital-intensive goods. The recent explosion of wealth in the Middle East offers large new markets which will eventually provide greater diversification in Third World exports. And new potentials for trade are rising among the rapidly industrializing low income countries themselves. These options, previously not available, leave the United States strong but nevertheless somewhat constrained in striking its trade and raw materials bargains.

The bulk of the world's population growth is occurring in the low and middle income nations of Asia, Africa and Latin America. Reduction in that growth lies primarily with the internal policies of those nations.

The problem of population growth is seen in sharply different ways by rich and poor countries, and hence the relative priority and means of solution vary equally widely. Implicit in the U.S. approach to population as a global problem is our concern with demand which continued rapid growth will make on the share of resources controlled or used by the United States, including capital, technology, natural resources and food. The low income nations recognize the pressure that population growth places on their limited capital and natural resources but also recognize the power that population provides in control of territory. They are more likely to give priority to improving living standards, with reduction in birth rates considered to be a by-product of this improvement.

ACCELERATING DEVELOPMENT OF THE THIRD WORLD

The economic changes occurring in the Third World are reflected in the increasingly common differentiation into low income and middle income nations, the rapidly increasing access of the middle income countries to Western private capital markets, the spread of capacity to create technology indigenously, and the increasing quantity and sophistication of manufactured goods. This reality of actual and incipient economic growth with its implications for political power, natural resource use, and trade will increasingly condition Third World-First World relations.

In viewing Third World countries generally and the lowest income ones specifically, several points about their future condition should be emphasized. First, popular views about triage to the contrary, even the poorest will be on the scene in the indefinite future. Whole nations of people rarely if ever disappear. By their existence, their population size, their location, their problems and their options in dealing with those problems they will exercise influence, and in an increasingly pluralistic world, increasing influence.

Second, Third World leadership is committed to growth, despite the many other pressing demands on resources, including the effect of short run external and internal threats to their own power. Multiplicity of objectives should not give the misleading impression that growth-related objectives are unimportant or not being pursued.

Third, fundamental to understanding the role of development assistance is the fact that development is basically a process of building a massive physical infrastructure and of establishing and integrating a complex set of institutions staffed by trained personnel. While these basic structures are being built, growth is slow. It accelerates when the structure is substantially in place. It is for this reason that for a considerable period of time each developing country appears to the casual observer as a hopeless case saddled with such corruption, inefficiency and bureaucratic bungling that make further development look virtually impossible. As a result, each case of accelerated growth, when it occurs, usually catches such an observer by surprise.

Fourth, as growth accelerates, the weight of these countries in the international economic system will increase greatly. The potential for the United States to influence the basic processes of growth will also diminish rapidly. The opportunity for significant influence on the bases of development may always be modest but even that modest opportunity is a fleeting one because of the arithmetic of growth. The low income nations' commitment to development, and the power of the United States in so many areas that affect development make confrontation over development policies inevitable. But a clear commitment by the United States could provide the basis for playing a constructive and positive role and molding events in a significant manner.

It is hard to argue the case for the inevitable and ultimate growth of low income countries because of the widespread tendency to extrapolate present conditions and trends into the future and to miss key turning points in the development process. Today's poor inevitably appear to be tomorrow's poor as well. Perhaps the mythology of basket cases, triage and lifeboat theories is best laid to rest by reference to the similar, now seemingly unbelievable and conveniently forgotten views about Europe and the "permanent dollar crisis" of the early 1950s, Japan as an "uncreditworthy" country even a few years later, Taiwan and South Korea as countries with well known poor economic prospects even as late as the latter 1950s, and the dramatic, albeit quite differently based, growth of Mexico and Brazil in the last decade. Perceptions of other countries often seem based on a static view of the world economy and rarely recognize the rapidity of turnaround and the multiplicity of forms of such change. In country after country the change from five-six percent growth rates to ten-twelve percent growth has been dramatic and abrupt.

U.S. OBJECTIVES IN THE THIRD WORLD

U.S. objectives in the Third World include traditional political, economic and humanitarian foreign policy concerns and a new set of global interests and interactions which can only be dealt with through negotiation and accommodation of mutual self-interest. Traditional foreign policy objectives encompass encouraging the growth of democracy and institutions compatible with broad U.S. interests. They also encompass military and economic interests—enlarging the sphere of American strategic influence and increasing opportunities for U.S. investment, markets for goods and access to expanding supplies of fairly priced natural resources.

Americans have consistently expressed a humanitarianism rooted in enlightened self-interest and charitable instincts in their foreign policy. Although probably never sufficient in itself to carry foreign aid, it undoubtedly helped support the massive Marshall Plan effort in Europe and also helped to sustain assistance to the low income nations of Asia, Africa and Latin America as a natural follow-up to the Marshall Plan in the 1950s. Cynicism inevitably followed the aid innocence of the early 1960s. In those days, while aid to developing countries was relatively small compared to the Marshall Plan which took 1.7 percent of United States GNP and 9.5 percent of federal government expenditure from 1947 to 1952 (three times foreign aid in the early 1960s), the problems were immense. India alone has more than twice as large a population as that of Western Europe. The pace was slow due to the strangling effect of the previous colonial system on the development of trained personnel and development-oriented institutions, and the burden of sheer poverty itself was enormous. With slow progress came an understandable tendency to want to withdraw from the scene.

But such a posture now appears increasingly incompatible with the new set of U.S. global interests in trade, natural resource use, environmental control and population. Pursuit of these interests requires interaction with Third World countries, as well as the establishment of new institutional frameworks for exchange of information, understanding of one another's perceptions and accommodation between conflicting positions in a context of shifting power relationships. These types of problems may soon be recognized as the most important facing the United States and as lending themselves least well to unilateral intervention. The recent and dramatic changes in the rules of the game for pricing and distribution of raw materials, especially oil, underscore the growing need to establish a global policy and economic system perceived as "fair and just" by all major elements in the world community.

The current period of U.S. economic dominance is one in which the groundwork can be laid for a set of international relationships quite different from those of the present and yet better suited to United States' interests in an increasingly pluralistic world environment. To be successful, that effort will require understanding of the aspirations and demands of the Third World and a search for means of interaction which accommodates the potentially conflicting objectives of the United States and the Third World. Achieving the new objectives of global interaction also requires a long-term approach with a high degree of reliability and consistency which may from time to time conflict with traditional means of meeting short-term objectives.

THE NATURE OF THIRD WORLD DEMANDS

Third World demands on the industrial nations, concentrated on trade, commodity prices and aid, are backed by growing political power but are economic in character and relate to the desire for accelerated economic growth. The demand for improved trade relations is essentially a demand for greater access to markets in industrialized countries for rapidly expanding exports of Third World manufactured or processed goods. These goods tend to be relatively labor intensive. They offer export markets of equivalent value for capital-intensive intermediate products.

The process is essentially one of trading such items as textiles, electronics, machine tools and bicycles, for those such as steel, aluminum, petrochemicals and goods with a high technology component. Because of the complexity and cost of adjustments it is difficult for the United States to respond rapidly to this demand, although in the long run some accommodation will be essential. We can expect increasing emphasis from the Third World on the slogan of the late Marshall Plan days—"trade not aid."

It is a widely held view in the Third World that Western industrial growth has been built on exploitation of raw materials from the developing countries. Certainly the opportunity to develop rapidly low cost raw material sources in the Third World has allowed growing Western demand to be readily met without raising real prices. The problem now facing industrial nations is a situation in which constraints on supply of raw materials may push up their prices more than proportionately to the general price level. Thus from the point of view of the producers, collective action to contain supply and raise prices is profitable. That is happening with oil. It may happen with some other commodities.

For the industrial nations rising raw materials prices increase costs of production, reduce real incomes, raise capital costs for substitutes, and thus depress both aggregate income and the proportion going to labor in their own economies. The solution to this problem lies in assisting the low income nations to diversify their economies so that they have a continuing interest in maintaining significant levels of foreign trade, greater interdependency, and greater capacity to absorb income fluctuations. This relationship has been recognized by the EC with its greatly enlarged aid flow to Africa, the Caribbean and the Pacific through the Lomé Convention.

The Third World demand is for greatly enhanced aid flows on an automatic basis so that control of domestic and foreign affairs by the aid givers is minimized. Aid is seen as inferior to trade and higher commodity prices, because the latter potentially provide vastly larger net resource flows toward the low income nations with virtually no outside control on their use. On the other hand in the complex dynamics of negotiation, the industrial nations, while recognizing the necessity of some accommodation on commodity prices and the mutual advantages from trade, may find that these approaches are so complex and slow that increased aid in the short run is the only feasible means of accelerating economic growth, especially in the low income countries.

Those countries with under $500 per capita income and comprising one-third of the world's population have total incomes so low that aid at politically feasible levels is still substantial in relation to their national income, investments and exports. These countries now receive aid equal to 24 percent of their total investment. For the low income nations aid may be a particularly important and useful form of resource flow which will play a significant role in determining the pace and the pattern of the development process. This is in contrast to the middle income countries (non-OPEC aid receiving countries of over $500 per capita income) for whom concessionary aid is equal to only 2 percent of total investment.

A NEW AID STRATEGY TO MEET CHANGING THIRD WORLD CONDITIONS

It should be clear from the preceding discussion that the United States has an important stake in the Third World and that the day of unilateral determination of policy in areas important to the United States is receding. It is also apparent that in both trade and commodity pricing, complex negotiations will have to be carried on in good faith and that in the meantime substantially increased development assistance is an important basis for demonstrating that good faith. The question remains whether such aid can be used in a manner consistent with U.S. objectives.

The development strategy which best fits U.S. objectives is the one implicit in the "mandate" of Congress and the "new directions" of AID. That is a broadly participatory approach initially emphasizing the rural sector, labor-intensive industry and expanded trade.[5] In contrast to its capital-intensive alternatives, the strategy seeks to produce more of what the poor consume, that is, food and other agricultural products and to accompany that production with employment growth to provide the incomes for purchase of the food. The employment orientation requires rapid expansion of trade so that domestic capital may be spread thinly in widespread creation of jobs and the products of highly capital-intensive industry can be imported.

Because the strategy emphasizes broad participation, it is effective in reducing population growth rates. It is countries such as Taiwan, with high employment growth rates and broad distribution of income, which have experienced rapid decline in birth rates, even while incomes are low, not countries such as Brazil with their higher but more unequally distributed incomes.

The emphasis on mobilizing labor provides low cost consumer goods for high income countries, and large markets in low income countries for capital-intensive intermediate or high technology-related products from high income countries. The broad participation provides the stability which makes political consensus on economic goals likely. The support through such a strategy of humanitarian objectives is obvious.

The concerns for American labor in this strategy are twofold. Although U.S. aggregate income is increased, the imports are "labor-saving" and the exports "capital-using," with resultant shift in proportion of income to owners of capital and away from labor. Further, the dynamics of such growth call for shifting of U.S. employment. Effective compensatory tax and employment policies will be necessary to assure that labor does not bear an unfair share of the burden of implementing this strategy.

The second concern is that elitist regimes in the Third World may prevent their own workers from increasing consumption as productivity rises, thereby continuing to dump labor-intensive goods on the international market with little increase in domestic demand. Foreign-based corporations may have a similar set of preferences or be unwilling or incapable of challenging income distribution policies of Third World governments.

The employment-oriented development strategy not only advances the new U.S. global interests but also offers the basis for reliable alliances in pursuit of traditional foreign policy objectives. Because the benefits of a broadly participatory strategy are long run and the costs short run, foreign assistance can greatly enhance the chances for success of such a strategy.

Most low income nations gained independence with a narrowly based urban elite in power. That group may strengthen its position through alliance with traditional agricultural and large-scale national and international industrial interests. Modest overall growth rates may be translated into rapid increase in incomes and at least short run stability for these small highly leveraged ruling elites. Policies of cheap food for the cities, often at the expense of longer term growth and investment in agriculture, and concentration of investment in large scale public or private industry in major urban centers are quite consistent with the interests of such groups. Poor performance in agriculture and slow growth of employment depress overall growth rates and exclude the bulk of the population from the benefits of growth.

While major military expenditure may reinforce political power through patronage distribution and the use of the military for political repression directly, it has increasingly been demonstrated that such narrowly based regimes are highly vulnerable to displacement by other members of their own elites. These elites may appeal to any number of interest groups outside the power group or by direct mobilization of some proportion of the mass of low income people. The resultant power shifts may suggest major changes in policy positions and thus the temptation to provide short-term foreign assistance to ensure continuity in such regimes may be considerable, even though recognized as ephemeral in nature.

Ruling elites may not opt for broadening of the power base implicit in a broadly participatory strategy of growth because they feel more secure in continuation of traditional appeals and political processes. There are likely to be long time lags between the initiation of substantial expenditures on an alternative strategy and the generation of significant benefits which form a new foundation for political support. The total investment requirements are large and thus severely tax the limited resource base of the lower income countries, and the political risks are correspondingly great.

Foreign assistance to low income countries can assist in transition to more broadly supported regimes if it is sufficiently substantial in size to absorb a significant proportion of the cost of risks and lags in the transition period, and if it is provided within the framework of a clear development strategy which results in more widespread distribution of the returns of such a strategy over the long run.

The United States cannot bargain over something so basic as the underlying strategy of growth of other countries. However, alternatives do exist with sharply different implications for U.S. objectives. Different national groups facing quite different constituencies, costs and objectives may favor alternative strategies which will better serve these objectives and which should be more actively supported. For better or for worse, U.S. policy in its totality does affect the costs and risks associated with development efforts in low income countries, and hence the United States does affect—knowingly or unknowingly, explicitly or implicitly—the outcome of these efforts.

Ultimately the imperatives for United States support of alternative development strategies rest on recognition of the reality of growing Third World strength in the international economic and political system. In the long run there must be mutually advantageous accommodations over trade and commodity access. These accommodations will call for significant adjustment in the composition of U.S. exports and imports. The magnitude of the adjustments will require considerable assistance to those in the U.S. economy most directly involved in making these adjustments. The benefits will be the assurance of continued access to vital raw materials for rich countries, accelerated growth in real incomes in poor countries and a move towards a more balanced prosperity.

In short run, U.S. interests may best be pursued with an aid program of a magnitude seen as adequate by current world standards. This would mean a level of aid expenditure comparable in relative terms to that of the early 1960s and to that of other OECD nations at present. That aid should be directed toward encouraging a broadly participatory strategy of economic growth, which itself would require a high degree of reliability in U.S. aid. Such a strategy must also be supported by reorientation of the full range of U.S. policies toward broadly participatory systems in developing countries.

The emphasis on a strategy of broad participation in the development process, on the one hand, implies widespread mobilization of labor for productive work and on the production of labor-intensive goods. On the other hand, the strategy emphasizes raising the income of poor people with a consequent increase in their demand for food and basic manufactured goods. The more rapidly this process proceeds and the more it is assisted by measures maintaining consumption, the sooner will real wages begin to rise and the sooner will heavy pressure for export of labor-intensive goods decline.

Narrowly based elites are likely to opt out of this strategy by containing the growth in real wages so that increased national income will be used for military supplies or the capital-intensive goods preferred by high income elites. Such regimes may also resort to political repression as a means of keeping the poor either from organizing themselves or being agitated and manipulated by other elite groups. Thus in the long run, the preferred development strategy is more likely to strengthen broadly its democratic forms of government and to advance the cause of economic and social justice and political freedom—a cause long and vigorously supported by the American labor movement at home and abroad.

NOTES

1. Data on resources flows are from Gerald R. Benedick, Changes in Resource Flows to the Developing Countries, AID/PPC/IEA, 10/6/76 (mimeo).

2. Figures on GNP-aid ratios are given in OECD, Development Cooperation, annual reviews 1971 and 1976.

3. Distribution of U.S. foreign aid is given in "Total Dollar and PL 480 Assistance Per Country," AID/PPC/PB, 6/13/75 (mimeo).

4. For exports to developing countries, see International Monetary Fund, Direction of Trade (Washington: IMF, 1975) and on the growth of LDC manufactures, see John W. Mellor, The New Economics of Growth—A Strategy for India and the Developing World: A Twentieth Century Fund Study (Ithaca: Cornell University Press, 1976).

5. For a full elaboration of this strategy, see John W. Mellor, op. cit.

28

Restructuring the World Economic System: Global Collective Bargaining for Greater Social Justice

MAHBUB UL HAQ

INEQUITIES IN THE INTERNATIONAL ECONOMIC SYSTEM

The Third World seeks today what American labor was seeking only fifty years ago. Before the New Deal, the American labor movement was striving for greater equality of opportunity, more participation in making decisions which affected the welfare of workers, and new rules of the game for determining minimum wages, maximum hours, social security, and unemployment benefits. The Third World similarly seeks today to establish new rules of the game to correct the great inequities in the international economic system. It is all very well to suggest that everything is decided by competitive forces in the market, but we all know that the market mechanism works for those who have the purchasing power. Fifty years ago in America, those with purchasing power were a privileged minority in the country's economic system. Today this is true on a global scale; a handful of industrialized countries with a minority of the world's population have most of the purchasing power.

Look at how the international market mechanism works in providing credit. Eighty percent of mankind gets less than four percent of international credit. I do not say that they should get ten or twenty percent or some other fixed proportion of the total. To create economic growth is their own job, but the crucial question is what access they get to international resources. Since the market system favors those who are already credit worthy and excludes the poor majority who are not, the poor are effectively denied access to one of the most important means of stimulating economic growth.

Note: This is essentially a transcript of Mr. Haq's extempore remarks.

Let me take another illustration. Access of goods and services produced by the developing countries to the industrialized-nation markets is sharply restricted. According to World Bank calculations, if all tariff and nontariff barriers in industrialized countries were removed over the next ten years, the developing countries could earn $34 billion a year more than they do today, about three times the foreign assistance now being given to them.

The greatest source of discrimination in the international economic system today, however, is found in barriers to the mobility of people. Look at it domestically. If a designated group of people is denied mobility because of color, creed, or any other characteristic, that group is effectively denied economic opportunity. Americans should appreciate this point because the United States was built on the basis of immigration, of people traveling across national frontiers in search of economic opportunity and political freedom. So were Canada, Australia, and many other lands. But today, a large part of humanity is confined to an international reservation which they cannot leave, because of immigration laws, even if they are willing to work elsewhere.

These inequities affecting a majority of the world's population persist because of the character of international economic decision-making. The Third World is widely criticized in the United States and other industrialized countries for establishing a "tyranny of the majority" in the United Nations. But actions taken there have little impact. All the really important international economic decisions have been made by a handful of industrialized countries—with one major exception, notably, OPEC.

The Third World today is seeking certain structural changes in the international rules of the economic game—not seeking concessions, not trying to live off the charity of the rich—just as American labor was trying to do fifty or seventy-five years ago. In order to negotiate these structural changes, Third World countries are trying to organize themselves into a trade union of poor nations. They realize that individually their bargaining power is extremely limited, and by coming together they are attempting to increase this bargaining power. At the national level, in the United States and other countries, the economic strength of the trade union movement depends on the unity of the workers. Only through such unity have trade unions succeeded in changing the rules of the game to make them more equitable.

RESTRUCTURING ECONOMIC RELATIONSHIPS

If Third World countries deny equality of opportunity domestically, they greatly inhibit their bargaining effectiveness when they claim equality of opportunity internationally. I firmly believe that reforms of international and internal economic orders have to proceed simultaneously. In some ways, in fact, reform of internal orders may be a prerequisite to reform of the international order.

The trade union movement in America in many ways achieved a new relationship with government and business during the 1930s. It took a severe economic depression and the vision and leadership of President Roosevelt to achieve this new relationship. Roosevelt's New Deal ultimately benefited both labor and business because it elevated the working classes to a partnership with management in working together toward greater economic prosperity. But to many business leaders the restructuring of economic relationships during that decade was a rude shock.

Whenever such restructuring is done in the short run, there is always a cost to those in power because they have to share it. Only over the longer term does it become apparent that the restructuring was a necessary condition for the continued viability of the system. If we judge by these standards, the restructuring of economic power in the 1930s in the United States has led to a shared prosperity over a long period of time. It certainly did not bring about the demise of capitalism, as some had predicted. The working classes, who in fact represented the mass market of tomorrow, provided the sustained and broad-based demand for all the consumer goods produced by the economic system and thus fueled the system for the next few decades.

A similar restructuring of economic relationships took place at the international level during the Marshall Plan in the 1950s. Viewed in short-term perspective, the Marshall Plan appeared only to be strengthening the political and economic power of the principal competitors of the United States in Europe. Many of them have, over time, become very vigorous economic competitors of the United States in the international marketplace. Yet, over the long run the Marshall Plan has provided the basis for a shared prosperity among the industrialized countries.

Today, when the Third World presses for greater equality of opportunity in the international marketplace, more international credit, more exports of their products without protectionism, and more resource transfers from the rich through international taxation, a historic process is repeating itself. It is difficult to argue that this is in the immediate interest of those who now hold economic power because it does mean sharing of power and will require adjustments by the industrialized countries which have most of the power. The question is whether this economic restructuring can be the basis for a longer-term partnership between the developing countries, with eighty percent of mankind, and the shrinking minority in the industrialized countries—which today is twenty percent. In another thirty to forty years it will be only ten percent of the world's population.

CHAOTIC CONFRONTATION VS. COOPERATIVE DIALOGUE

In today's world, which is becoming increasingly interdependent in the supply of raw materials and goods, it is impossible for any country to become an island unto itself. The United States may have a greater option of isolation than its allies, but ultimately, if the United States tries to exercise this option, it will be disowned by its own allies in Europe and Japan. The longer-run prospect of such isolation would be worse for the United States than foregoing its short-term option of non-dependence. If we have to live together in one world, then the question is what relationships need to be restructured today to assure a more prosperous future for all and how can they be restructured.

Here, the analogy between trade union movements at the national level and the Third World effort in collective bargaining at the international level breaks down. The Third World does not have the political power that can be created within nations through effective trade union organization because within a political system, instruments for exercising power exist which are not available at the international level. At the latter level, the choices are more limited: either cooperative dialogue, which may change the rules of the game in an enlightened fashion over time, or chaotic confrontation, which may result in severe economic disruption and lead to armed conflict.

When OPEC was set up in 1960, it would have been possible for the industrialized countries to reach agreement on fairly easy terms. The long-term price increase for which OPEC was asking at that time was very modest. OPEC was also willing to negotiate long-term supply agreements. The price of oil was less than $2 a barrel, and what was being contemplated over a longer period of time was at the most an increase to about $3 a barrel. These proposals were summarily turned down. In fact, the response of the major oil consumers was to deliberately lower the price of oil below the level being sought by OPEC in 1960. Because OPEC was a very loose, weak trade union at that time, it could do nothing. The co-chairman of OPEC, who was also the oil minister of Saudi Arabia, lost his job and was chased out of the country in 1961. The process of radicalization of OPEC began as a result.

The OPEC experience demonstrates that justice delayed can be very expensive, often to both sides. For this reason I firmly believe that it is in the interest of both the developed countries and the Third World to create and use avenues through which they can engage in a cooperative dialogue rather than chaotic confrontation.

At the moment it may not seem necessary to take the polemics of this dialogue too seriously. In the initial stages of any trade union organizing effort, a lot of noise is made and a few windows may even be smashed. The workers struggling for recognition want it to be known that they are around and need to be heard. But there comes the next stage of any union organizing effort when representatives of both sides go into the back rooms to hammer out tough and realistic agreements, based on the interests of both parties. So it is not really necessary to take the polemics at their face value and try to counter them directly. A far more productive exercise is to see what progress can be made on specific issues. Here are two examples.

THE POOREST OF THE POOR

The problems of the poorest of the poor, the 1.2 billion people who have a per capita income of less than $100 a year and live mostly in Asia and some countries of Africa, require immediate international action. For these people, the urgent task is not closing the gap between them and those developed countries with incomes of $5,000 per capita, because that will not happen for a very, very long time. But it is essential that their basic human needs be met in as short a period of time as possible. This means providing at least minimum levels of nutrition, shelter, education, and health care.

It should be possible to meet these basic human needs over the course of the next ten to fifteen years. Various studies have been made to show what will be involved. A very different strategy of development will be required in those countries with large numbers of very poor; they will have to give up the pursuit of grandiose development projects such as steel mills and other large capital-intensive industries and focus primarily on food production, population control, intermediate technology, and indigenous methods of generating human skills and creating the proper economic infrastructure oriented toward meeting the needs of the poor. But also involved will be international investment of about $15 billion a year over the next decade, according to World Bank studies.

Here is an opportunity to create another Marshall Plan, but this time with international, not just U.S., financing. A global compact between the rich and the poor nations to eliminate the worst forms of human poverty should define how this task will be undertaken and how the $15 billion required annually should be shared among developed and developing countries. The latter probably should provide one-third to one-half, with the balance coming from the developed countries. The developed countries' share then becomes an obligation, something to be done on a continuing basis for ten or fifteen years and not just an act of periodic generosity. Such a compact can only be achieved at the highest political level through a summit meeting between the leaders of the rich and the poor nations to negotiate the framework for the compact.

A compact along those lines would give a fresh sense of direction and purpose to the entire foreign assistance field. The major criticism today of foreign assistance is that it has no sense of direction and that it is fragmented in too many projects. There is no clear sense of when it will terminate or what will be achieved when it does end. But if it can be shown that over a manageable period of time, such as a decade, instead of landing men on the moon, the basic needs of the vast majority of humanity can be met through a cooperative international effort, the impetus this will give to international cooperation in other areas will be enormous.

CHANGING THE INTERNATIONAL DIVISION OF ECONOMIC ACTIVITY

My second example is more pertinent not to the poorest countries but to those now described as middle-income countries—countries mostly in Latin American or East Asia, which are more involved in the international market system and which have per capita incomes around $500. These countries need access to markets for goods as well as for capital. I have mentioned before that if all tariff and non-tariff barriers were progressively removed in the industrialized nations through orderly planning over the next ten years, these countries would gain additional export earnings of more than $35 billion a year. But whenever it is suggested that the international market system be opened up in this manner, there is a cry of protest in the developed countries because of the specter of unemployment in those countries. Some industries, it is argued, may even wither away.

But should we not look again at this issue in the longer-term perspective and try to plan cooperatively for the changes in international patterns of economic activity which are certain to occur? If economic history is interpreted correctly, those who have resisted change have always suffered at the hands of change. Contrast the experience of the United Kingdom and Japan. In many ways the United Kingdom, and particularly its labor unions, have never come to terms with changed realities such as the loss of colonies and the consequent need for restructuring their industries and developing or absorbing new sources of technology. They have tried to protect Lancashire for textiles and Dundee for jute mills, when they should have moved on to higher technology, more capital-intensive industries. All they have accomplished is to prolong the period during which these industries slowly expire, while the economy as a whole has declined and so have the prospects of British workers.

Now look at the experience of Japan. The Japanese have tried to anticipate which industries would become less attractive for them as their labor was becoming more expensive. They willingly encouraged the decline of those industries. In fact, South Korea based its development largely on those industries which Japan was going to abandon. And the Japanese kept moving ahead into new areas of industrial activity.

If developed countries have to raise high tariff and nontariff barriers against poor developing countries which have ill-trained labor and often poor technology, it shows that their industries are noncompetitive and cannot stand free competition over the long run. The heart of wisdom is to anticipate what is going to happen over time and then to act on that anticipation. Adjustment assistance and active labor market policies will be required. So will incentives to develop higher productivity industries and new technologies. In that way both the developed and developing countries will be better off because the former will have safeguarded their efficiency, while the latter will be able to export and so to earn their keep in the international marketplace.

It is not necessary for all of us to agree on the diagnosis of the world's economic problems or to come to the same conclusions about Third World demands and their impact on the developed countries. What is important is that we should all be thinking today about what kinds of change to expect over the next thirty, forty, or fifty years. Long-term thinking is always very difficult when we are preoccupied with short-term problems. But the forces of historical change go on, irrespective of whether we have analyzed their nature correctly. And change, as I have said before, comes sometimes in a very chaotic form.

The U.S. trade union movement has been in the vanguard of those seeking economic change for greater social justice. The danger now is that the movement will acquire its own inertia and resist further change. All in the American labor movement who are concerned about the future welfare of workers should fight against the emergence of these responses to a rapidly changing world economy. It is impossible for any of us to postpone or resist the historical forces of change.

29

International Aid and the Labor Movement in the Third World

IRVING BROWN

THE CHANGING CHARACTER OF THE THIRD WORLD

The need and support for international aid to the less developed countries is being questioned and reexamined on both sides of the so-called North-South dialogue. Furthermore, the actual effectiveness of traditional forms of aid is being challenged by many national leaders, especially in the developing countries.

Venezuelan President Carlos Andres Perez, speaking at the International Socialist Congress in Geneva on November 28, 1976, is reported to have said that "development aid is 'hypocrisy' because it can never adequately meet the development needs of poor countries. . . . This can only be done by fair and equitable prices for their products." He also stated in the same address that "a new world political order has been created by the negotiating power of developing countries supplying primary products to industrialized nations."[1] This opinion, coming from the head of one of the few remaining democratic nations in Latin America, can only be ignored at our peril.

This skepticism is greatly enhanced by a recently published report which states that most of the American food aid is not really going to the hungriest people and that profit-making and speculation are rife in the handling of these foodstuffs in the recipient nations.

These concerns of the heads of state in the developing countries must be taken into account by the industrialized countries. But it would be a miscalculation to believe that there is a single point of view on the value of development aid. Quite the contrary, many, while sharing Perez's attitude, still seek external aid but have learned that indiscriminate dependence solely on outside sources of capital is not only insufficient but meaningless if there is not the ability and capacity of their people to absorb and put to effective use large amounts of capital investment. Much of the effectiveness of assistance, furthermore, depends on the recipients' conception of international aid as an instrument by which nations can help themselves.

In approaching the problem of international aid and the Third World, let me paraphrase what Bismark once said about Europe: "Whoever speaks of the Third World is wrong." In other words, there is no single common denominator for what is termed the "Third World" but rather a varying, discordant, sometimes bewildering and disunited number of nations (usually referred to as the Group of 77) seeking first and foremost their own national security, whether economic, political, social or military. Against this background, the major considerations of American labor in relationship to the peoples, the unions, and governments of this "Third World" must take into account certain essential facts.

There are those countries with a relatively long history of political independence and sovereignty, especially in Latin America. Such nations, however, are not economically independent since external investors control, dominate or influence the political development of these countries in combination with indigenous entrepreneurs and bankers. Nor can one ignore the vestiges of early colonial domination which remain in the form of those ruling elites who dominate the indigenous population.

Then there are those areas of the world where colonialism has only been cast off in recent years, primarily after World War II, in Africa and most of Asia. Here racial discrimination is almost as important as colonial rule, especially in Black Africa. The problem is most acute in Southern Africa, where colonial and apartheid regimes still hold sway. In these parts of Africa, the struggle for political liberation is still the overriding consideration and determines American labor's basic association with this area.

The levels of economic development are low in all these regions, but there are great differences between and within nations. A wide gap exists between the rich and the poor nations, between the industrial North and the predominantly agricultural South, as well as between the rich and the poor within these nations.

This leads to a necessity for new distinctions between the poor poor-nations and the rich poor-nations, notably the developing OPEC countries where internal capital resources are not lacking. Therefore, there are different rates and levels of economic development or industrial potential among these nations, resulting in differences in their capital investment and financing needs, as well in their ability to absorb and utilize efficiently capital investment.

No matter when independence has come to these nations, their economies still lack in varying degrees the basic infrastructure for industrialization, and monetary stability which permit even relative economic independence to match their recently won political independence. They suffer from the deformities of a superimposed colonial economy or from overdependence on external investments. This means not only the external domination of economic decision-making which accompanies such a system but also exclusion of a large proportion of the population from active participation in the modern sector of the economy.

The consequences are seen in the labor field with large segments of the population not trained or adapted as workers or as consumers in a modern economy. They constitute a majority, or where there has been some progress in economic development a large minority, without the skills, the aptitudes, the customs, the way of life which characterize a modern society based on growing industrialization, a money-exchange economy and increasing urbanization.

NATIONAL LIBERATION AND POST-INDEPENDENCE NATION-BUILDING

In the struggle for political independence and sovereignty, the American labor movement supported the national liberation movements. American labor believed that there could not exist a real labor movement without a free, independent and democratic society, which was not possible under foreign colonial rule.

In those countries where independence had been achieved in the political sphere, support for the labor movement was essential in order to cope with the problems of the economy and to enable their young, inexperienced trade union leaders to deal on some basis of equality with those who commanded the levers of economic power, whether within the country or outside. Labor movements in these societies need international assistance to adjust and develop as do the other sectors of the population, since the weakness of the trade unions is linked to the lack of industrial development, whether before or after independence. Even in Western Europe and the United States, the trade unions did not reach any degree of strength and importance until there was some industrial development.

In the national struggle, labor was part and parcel of the nationalist movements of liberation and often a main stabilizing factor, especially during the periods when political leaders were in exile. Furthermore, many political leaders acquired much of their training and experience in the trade unions under the colonial regime.

The colonial regimes gave birth to elites who not only directed the nationalist movements but became masters of the new nations with many of the qualities necessary for bureaucratic rule, but with no profound attachment to democracy, which requires the sharing of power. In societies where tribalism prevails, such as Africa, this tended to reinforce the concepts of autocratic rule through the one-party system. This tendency was also strengthened during the struggle for national independence when the Western democracies perpetuated colonial regimes long enough to permit the Soviet Union to become an important element in the situation as a champion of anti-colonialism.

Most of these countries are still seeking to become unified nations, since they have become independent states before achieving national unity. Therefore, their major problem in economic development is to overcome their tribal, linguistic and cultural divisions. Only through national economic development, industrialization, monetary stability, and the training of their people to participate in a modern economy can their political independence become completely meaningful for their nation as a whole. This nation-building process must be at the heart of their own development efforts and can be assisted only marginally by external inputs of capital and technical assistance.

International aid must relate to these political aspects of the problem of nation-building. For development aid without consideration of critical political forces can lead, and has led in many cases, to development without social progress and to the creation of repressive political and economic structures which reinforce dictatorial societies.

AMERICAN LABOR'S INTERNATIONAL AID PROGRAMS

The international aid programs of labor have been, therefore, geared to the efforts of nation-building and democratic development through assistance to budding labor movements, no matter what obstacles and restrictions the new regimes have created for these movements. We hope and expect that eventual industrialization will permit evolution toward a freer society than now exists and one in which unions will also be freer and less restricted.

After having been identified with the labor and nationalist movements of these countries in their pre-independence period, the American trade union movement became associated with the post-independence efforts of these nations and their labor movements to develop strong indigenous economies. This meant that the projects which American labor carried out in conjunction with the trade unions of the LDCs were closely integrated with national political aims and economic objectives.

The major emphasis was first on what we could do to help develop technical skills of workers since vocational training is essential in countries where the great mass of people have been excluded from the modern sector of the economy. We have assisted in such fields as construction, mechanics, clothing and textiles, as well as in the training of professional and white-collar workers.

Along with vocational training programs, there have been literacy projects among workers, many of whom come from rural areas and lack formal education. The need for a fuller understanding of language is part of the whole training process in helping them to cope with modern industrial jobs. In these training programs, it is a question of not only developing their manual or professional skills, but also preparing them to work and live in an industrial society.

In addition to developing work skills, great emphasis has been placed upon the development of trade union leadership not only for the needs of the trade unions as such, but to develop basic knowledge of the economic and social problems facing the new national economies. This is essential in order to guarantee that programs of economic development and the investment of external capital from the outside will be utilized in such a way as to avoid a repetition of the exploitation which accompanied early industrialization in Western Europe in the nineteenth century, and which was an integral part of the colonial system.

The need to emphasize the establishment of basic standards for the workers in these new economies is essential not only from a humanitarian point of view but also to achieve the best results in productivity. In fact, it is an economic necessity to have the workers at this stage of development assured of basic standards in order to have some guarantee that international aid will not merely benefit the elite or those seeking to maximize their profits through the exploitation of cheap labor.[2] This applied especially to certain multinationals seeking to escape the labor standards of their own countries. The participation of labor in the process of development and the application of capital investment helps to assure that international aid will not be, as President Perez said, a form of "hypocrisy."

In its assistance to labor movements in less developed countries, great emphasis has been placed by American labor on the development of cooperatives and credit unions, and in some cases labor banks. Trade unionists have been trained in the establishment and operation of cooperatives and credit organizations. The problems facing the countries in the Third World is such that they should be seeking an alternative to socialist and capitalist economic systems and not merely aping the existing industrialized societies. Their greatest hope lies in the direction of the development of a cooperative system, which corresponds more closely to the historical, cultural, and agrarian nature of these nations. It also means that larger numbers of people participate actively in the management of their own affairs, helping them to adjust to the needs and demands of urban industrial society.

Programs have also been inaugurated in the field of health and housing, once again not only for humanitarian needs but also to assure greater productivity of the workers. Only with a proper community environment involving decent housing and health services do workers feel they have a meaningful stake in making investment, whether from internal or external sources, as productive as possible.

Through its three institutes dealing with Africa, Asia and Latin America, American labor's activities have been directed primarily toward achieving some of the objectives stressed in this critical evaluation of the problem of international aid. These institutes conduct programs along the lines described above in working toward six major goals:

1. The need to develop a trained working force so that available capital investment can be absorbed properly and efficiently with due regard for the social priorities of modern economic life.

2. Emphasis on agricultural development since agriculture employs the biggest percentage of population in most developing countries. This development should, first, meet the basic needs of the people, and second, provide a base for further industrial development.

3. Strengthening of the national identity of workers and the building of a national indigenous economy which cuts across religious, tribal, and community lines.

4. Development of trade union leaders capable of directing their own affairs and able to participate in the economic planning of their countries, including the setting of priorities in the administration of international aid.

5. The necessity of capital investment, whether external or internal, which assists in promoting democratic institutions involving both labor and management.

6. The need for international intergovernmental bodies dealing with trade and development to involve labor and management participation in both the industrialized and nonindustrialized countries in implementing the basic resolutions adopted on such key problems as international trade, commodity price stabilization, allocation of technical assistance funds through the UN system, and Third World debts to industrialized countries now reaching the enormous sum of almost $2 billion.[3]

In addition to providing international aid along these lines and directed toward these goals, American labor must give some heed to the demands of the Third World for commodity price stabilization and some form of preferential treatment in international trade. However, this cannot be a one-way street and there must be full and sufficient guarantee for workers in the industrialized countries that they will not bear the burden of any ill effects of such arrangements. Adjustment assistance in the industrialized countries and an effective system of international fair labor standards are required. The ILO and other agencies dealing with trade and development cannot ignore this aspect of the problem when governments engage in the so-called North-South dialogue. At the UNCTAD IV conference in Nairobi in 1976, great emphasis was placed upon such problems as cancellation of Third World debts and changes in international trade patterns but little was said about needs of an international program to prevent the workers of the industrialized countries from having to make the major sacrifices in working out a more equitable international system.

AGRICULTURAL DEVELOPMENT AND EMPLOYMENT

American labor's approach to international aid seeks answers to some of the problems of how such aid can best be applied to the specific nature and characteristics of the developing countries within the framework of promoting economic equality and social justice. And here we must emphasize that in spite of many differences among these nations, one common denominator among them is the overwhelming percentage of their people, 75 percent or more, who are living and working in rural areas. Any attempt to deal with the problem of basic needs and the creation of mass employment in the Third World must give priority to rural areas, for there are still hundreds of millions in the countryside without employment or the minimum food, shelter, and health care necessary for decent human existence. The importance of the agricultural sector was emphasized in my address on behalf of the AFL-CIO at the June 1976 ILO World Employment Conference.

> The agricultural sector holds the potential for the long-term development of jobs and basic food industries, which in turn can not only fuel the development of other more diversified industrial sectors but can serve as the rallying point for the organization of that majority of the world's human population known as the rural poor. It has been the relative neglect of this sector that has contributed not only to droughts and famine, but to the slow pace of job creation.
>
> The problems facing developing economies around the world revolve around capital investment and the training of skilled workers. The absorption of meaningful capital investment is impossible without cadres of trained workers to man productive facilities that such investment foresees. The ILO must establish formulae calling for a specific percentage of capital investment to be devoted to the training of workers for jobs that will be available as a function of that investment, not as the result of unrealistic planning by

> either government or academic technocrats whose vision is impaired by too much theory and too little exposure to the real world. The worst thing we can do is to train workers for unemployment.[4]

The development of agriculture is the springboard for the Third World to achieve a pattern of industrialization geared to their own needs rather than an imitation of the industrialized and super-industrialized states of the world. The ILO must work from this perspective in the worldwide effort but we should not have to improve the present international economic "order" (or "disorder"), nor should we have any pretensions that international aid alone can eliminate mass poverty.

We must be candid with ourselves. The failure of many nations throughout the world in the past thirty years or so to attain meaningful development is due to the tendency to ape certain models of industrialization and ignore or give insufficient priority to their own agricultural development. Food is essential, but more than that, the development of an agricultural industry is necessary to contribute massively to job creation. The right kinds of food and agricultural production schemes will result in jobs for many of the estimated 75 percent of the world's agrarian population and serve as generators of the capital so necessary for higher stages of industrialization.

We should recall that the initial postwar economic conference in 1948, which led to the creation of GATT, was entitled "Trade and Employment." But in succeeding years, employment has somehow disappeared not only from the title but from the agendas of such meetings.

Decisions of international bodies cannot be implemented unless labor and management in industrialized nations are ready to accept them. The "political will" at the national level which all international organizations require to implement their decisions, whether it be on preferential trade treatment, commodity price stabilization, debt cancellation or large-scale capital investment, is based on the active participation and support of those who present the two essentials in the production process, labor and management. The unique character of ILO, encompassing representatives of labor, management and government, can provide an arena for negotiation, not confrontation, in meeting the needs and demands of those who have been exploited for hundreds of years by systems of colonialism and unfair patterns of world trade.

But central to the elimination of this exploitation and the achievement of economic and social justice is a fundamental principle of free trade union movements. That principle is worker participation in basic economic decisions but with the guarantee of free collective bargaining.

This principle has guided the international work of the AFL-CIO for the past 40 years. American labor has been described recently as having turned isolationist in the 1970s. This theory is wrong. The AFL-CIO's continuing participation in programs to help trade unions in developing countries and many other international activities, only a few of which have been described here, provide ample evidence to the contrary. A 1975 study of American labor's international role concluded that the AFL-CIO "has followed a policy of consistent engagement" in world affairs since the 1950s.[5] We shall continue that policy in the future, responding to new challenges and opportunities but always seeking to advance the cause of justice and freedom for workers throughout the world.

NOTES

1. Carlos Andres Perez in an address to the International Socialist Congress in Geneva, International Herald Tribune, November 29, 1976.

2. The necessity for guaranteeing freedom of association in order to achieve economic development and social progress is discussed in Guy Caire, Freedom of Association and Economic Development (Geneva: International Labour Office, 1977).

3. Further information on the current programs of these organizations is given in newsletters and other publications available from the African-American Labor Center (345 East 46th Street, New York, N. Y. 10017), the Asian-American Free Labor Institute (815 16th Street NW, Washington, D.C. 20006), and the American Institute for Free Labor Development (1015 Twentieth Street NW, Washington, D.C. 20006).

4. For the full text of this address, see the AFL-CIO's Free Trade Union News 31, no. 7 (July 1976), pp. 5-7. Subsequent paragraphs have been adapted from the address.

5. Roy Godson, "American Labor's Continuing Involvement in World Affairs," Orbis 19, no. 1 (Spring 1975), p. 93.

30

Trade Unions and Economic Assistance: A Developing Country's Perspective

KIMANI WA NYOIKE

IMPERATIVES FOR INTERNATIONAL AID AND THE AMERICAN RESPONSE

Because of differing economic and political conditions in individual developing countries, there cannot be any single definable "labor position" on the issue of international economic aid from the developed to developing countries. There are almost as many views as there are countries and trade union movements. In a large number of countries, furthermore, it is impossible to isolate "the voice of labor" from the general national chorus because organized labor in those countries is not free and independent. In others, trade unions are married to political parties so that different worker-groups in the same country may have opposing views, depending on their party affiliation and political ideology. Therefore, in discussing international economic aid, we must avoid assuming any consensus between workers and peasants in the developing countries. The comments which follow should also be seen for what they are—the views of one trade unionist in one African country.

Some political theoreticians and practitioners in Africa, Asia and Latin America have claimed that international economic aid is not necessary for development. They view aid as a weapon by the industrialized nations to introduce neo-colonialism and perpetuate economic dependence in the developing world. They depict the donor-recipient relationship as that of master and servant. According to them, international aid is inherently inconsistent with political independence and self-respect for any developing country. These analysts prescribe national discipline and hard work as the only sure cure for underdevelopment. They argue that every country has to pull itself up by its own bootstraps.

Foreign aid by itself cannot transform a primitive economy into a modern industrial system. There is no doubt that in the final analysis internal factors determine responses to external stimuli such as foreign aid or influx of private capital. Hard work, national discipline, ability to save and such other positive traits are all very important for development. Nevertheless, I do not subscribe to the "bootstrap theory." We have to accept international aid as a necessary evil. In addition to hard work and the other catalytic factors mentioned above, some fundamental ingredients for development, including capital and technical skills, are in short supply in developing countries. Such ingredients have to be imported. Under conditions of general scarcity, the cheapest method of importation is unilateral aid from a rich to a poor country.

Historically speaking, furthermore, in modern times, all countries that have industrialized, including Japan before and after World War II, did so with massive importation of foreign capital and skills. The reason is simple. By the very definition of underdevelopment, a country's economic system is sluggish and dormant. Production is low, the population uneducated, and the majority of workers are unskilled. With great determination such a system might develop all by itself but it will take a very long time. Such a socio-economic system needs external stimuli to shake it up, disturb it and quicken its slow rhythm toward takeoff. External aid may not be politically palatable, but it is necessary as a technical catalyst for fast development.

In the context of international power politics, the real purpose of external aid is sometimes played down or ignored altogether. "The purpose of concessional aid is to help the poorer people of the world," states the Development Assistance Committee of the OECD, the club of rich country governments.[1] This is an obvious statement, but one often overlooked both in international discussions and in the way in which aid has been distributed and used.

If the legitimate purpose of international aid is to quicken the pace of development towards self-propelling growth in the recipient countries and not primarily to maximize political influence of donor countries, then the record of American exportation of "money, men and machines" cannot be rated as an unqualified success. U.S. aid over the last 25 years can be indicted mainly on two grounds. First, the composition of that aid has been more military than economic. Admittedly, during that period the United States was involved in two costly wars in Korea and Vietnam. But even taking that into account, there is no reason that military aid should be still predominant.

Second, American foreign aid has been too little. Whether taken as a percentage of gross national product, in terms of actual dollar amounts, or in relation to American per capita income, the aid is disappointingly low. In 1974, for example, American official development assistance (ODA) to developing countries was a mere

0.25 percent of GNP. This was one of the lowest among member countries of the OECD Development Assistance Committee. American ODA was slightly more than Switzerland (0.14 percent of GNP) and Italy (0.15 percent), but far behind Sweden, Netherlands and even small Belgium.[2]

The situation is exacerbated by the fact that the American Congress, suffering from an acute attack of isolationist fever that gripped the United States as an aftermath of Vietnam has been reluctant to approve requests for foreign aid submitted by the President. "But many people maintain that, despite this evidence of public concern about human suffering and poverty, current public opinion polls provide evidence of a swing towards isolationism that seems to parallel the disengagement policies of the U.S. Government. . . ."[3] Further examination of public opinion data shows, however, that while after Vietnam, Americans have been increasingly opposed to political and especially military intervention abroad, they support continued economic cooperation which they understand is essential to the welfare of both the United States and other countries, rich and poor.[4]

Organized labor in the United States, working with other progressive groups, must exert greater pressure on the government and the Congress to increase foreign aid, make it more economic and less military, and insist it benefit those most in need in the developing countries. Increasing aid is not enough; it must help the poor workers and farmers, not the rich landlords, industrialists and government officials. Americans will support more aid if they are convinced that aid really is bringing a fairer deal to ordinary people like themselves who are worse off than they are but willing to work hard to improve their lives.

NEGLECT OF TRADE UNIONS IN ECONOMIC ASSISTANCE

In most aid-receiving countries the trade union movement has not benefited significantly from government-to-government external aid. Such assistance normally goes to government projects or to private business enterprises with government approval. It is important to remember that foreign aid provided by the United States or any other industrialized country is essentially tax money from American workers. I am aware that private corporations and individual businessmen pay taxes also, but as a labor leader, I choose to emphasize another fact often ignored—that all national wealth is created by the workers. It is therefore most disheartening to observe that only negligible amounts of American aid ever reach labor unions in the developing countries or go to projects that would directly benefit workers.

The blame is not entirely that of the United States or other industrialized countries. In most developing countries, labor unions have a very faint voice in their national affairs. It is sad but true that when plans are being formulated to utilize money received through foreign aid, views of organized labor are neither sought nor considered when given. Labor leaders in many developing countries would readily admit that compared with trade unions in the developed countries, our movements are much weaker and consequently we exert minimal influence upon our national governments.

Under the terms of the Lomé Treaty which governs economic relationships, including foreign aid, between the member states of the EC and 46 countries in Africa, the Caribbean and the Pacific, European trade unions have won the right to be heard by the EC. Presently there are some attempts by European labor unions through the EC and through governments of individual member countries to exert diplomatic pressure in favor of sister trade unions in the ACP countries so that unions in those countries should be accorded some consultant status in their own countries while aid demands to the EC are being formulated. European unions have suggested giving preference for aid to those applications that include significant "workers' content" in the proposed projects. The Lomé Convention specifically mentions "micro-projects" which may be proposed by nongovernmental agencies including trade unions.

American labor can also help. The AFL-CIO could, for example, approach the U.S. government to see that the foreign aid projects approved by the United States for funding should include some with direct benefit to labor unions in the aid-receiving countries. Presently it is out of fashion for the aid-giving countries to dictate openly internal policies of aid-receiving countries, but despite civilized public pronouncements to the contrary, the old adage still applies: "he who pays the piper calls the tune." The demand by labor is that when this polite, diplomatic behind the scenes arm-twisting occurs during aid negotiations, worker-oriented projects should be given more emphasis.

THE ROLE OF PRIVATE INVESTMENT

Private foreign investment in developing countries generates more political interest than other forms of capital importation. One aspect of foreign investment which is widely discussed is the role of multinational corporations and their relationship with the weak economies of less developed countries. I shall not dwell on these international giants except to concur with current wisdom that an internationally approved and enforceable code of conduct for regulating the multinationals should be established as soon as possible.

Distribution of foreign private investment among developing countries is significantly uneven. There has to be a "proper climate" for private capital. Theoretically, foreign businessmen should invest in any country with an open market system where private enterprise is allowed to exist. In practice, however, private capital is most attracted by the offer of monopoly benefits and other advantages by the governments concerned. Hence investors from the democratic United States become intimate and cozy with strange bedfellows, among them reactionary right-wing dictatorships and state monopolies in Communist countries.

Private foreign companies are, of course, an important source of capital and technical skills for developing countries. But there are serious dangers associated with investments by such companies. First, when foreign companies are given monopoly positions, they normally distort resource allocation and resource utilization. They encourage inefficiency because of imposed absence of competition, and they also frustrate competitive local enterprises. Some of the distortions may become permanently structured into the system so that the economy may not recover even after the foreign element is removed.

Second, unless there is substantial local participation in the ownership of foreign business enterprises, local political feelings tend to harden over time against these enterprises. A business concern should not only contribute toward national well-being of that country as understood by the majority of the citizens, but it must be seen to do so. In some cases, local opposition to foreign companies tends to spread into general antagonism against all private enterprise. Therefore, for those societies which accept that private enterprise under careful supervision by the government can hasten development, entry of private foreign capital should be allowed only with extreme caution.

Third, private foreign investments from industrialized countries are basically capital intensive. With high levels of unemployment in recipient countries, the need is not only for fast growth through high productivity but for rapid increase in employment. It is in the area of employment creation that foreign private investments are weakest. Their advanced technology was developed under conditions of labor scarcity. To some observers, the American technological genius is most visible in destruction of jobs, with its emphasis on "automation" and "computerization." In the developing world, there is clearly a need for governments to introduce disincentives against foreign companies that insist on using highly capital-intensive production techniques.

There is a general tendency to give foreign companies permission to import capital goods and machinery duty free. This practice introduces factor-price distortions and discourages the use of labor. Such bias in favor of capital-intensity should be rejected and normal chargeable duty be imposed on all machinery. For example, an ILO report on Kenya observes that "there is scope for varying the factor proportions in favour of greater labour intensity in various sectors of the economy. To a large extent, removal of factor price distortions and the introduction of the concept of shadow pricing for project evaluation, especially in the public sector, should result in greater labour absorption . . . factor price distortions now working against labour-intensity should be eliminated, for example, by abolishing investment allowances and by levying differential import tariffs on capital goods, which are at present imported duty-free."[5]

TRADE AND ECONOMIC DEVELOPMENT

International trade is absolutely essential as an instrument of development of the Third World. We know that official foreign aid, even with substantial private investment, cannot be sufficient because development programs require massive imports which generally cannot be fully covered by the present level of exports and foreign aid. Many developing countries therefore experience a perpetual trade deficit. That is why all developing countries are united in seeking trade concessions from the industrialized nations in order to increase exports.

At the beginning of 1975, an important landmark was reached when the Lomé Convention became operative. A group of 46 countries, some of them very small and poor, in Africa, the Caribbean and the Pacific, were allowed to export any of their commodities into the nine industrial countries of the EC free from customs duty and other restrictions. The EC also established a novel fund called STABEX to stabilize export earnings of the developing ACP countries. Furthermore, the EC countries gave up the principle of reciprocity so that ACP countries do not have to give them reciprocal concessions as in the past.

Now, the whole developing world is looking to the United States to open its doors in a similar manner and allow the freer flow of goods from the developing countries. It is clear that the matter is not that easy. Apparently, labor union leaders in America are worried about the unrestricted entry of foreign goods into the U.S. market because of the serious danger of loss of jobs by American workers.

These negotiations will, therefore, be difficult. It is not necessary to discuss various technical issues needing to be resolved. It is enough to request our brothers in the American labor movement, and indeed all American leaders including politicians and industrialists, to start preparing for a gentle dismantling of trade barriers in favor of goods from the developing world. With goodwill and determination, the American economy is so dynamic and diverse that it can accommodate any necessary changes without widespread unemployment among American workers. I am convinced that the political direction being shaped by current international social ethics will push the United States in the direction of considering seriously and eventually introducing some concessions to developing countries along the lines of the Lomé Convention. This is a small world.

THE IMPACT OF ECONOMIC ASSISTANCE

It is difficult to determine with any precision the extent to which foreign aid has benefited the economies of developing countries because external aid is but one of the many factors affecting performance and change in the economic system of developing countries, but some consequences and trends seem apparent. First, external aid does bring valuable scarce ingredients into the economic system of these countries. Whatever the political persuasion of the developing country's leadership, capital and technical skills must be found. All countries need technology.

Second, the effectiveness of external aid, whether in the private or public sector within recipient countries, depends mainly on internal factors. The level of social infrastructure, the political climate, including maintenance of law and order, social attitudes towards work, savings and self-denial, plus a host of other factors, largely determine the degree of success of foreign aid.

The ability of the receiving country to match external aid with local contributions is sometimes taken as an indication of technical worthiness of an aid recipient. The concept of "worthiness" as applied to aid-receiving countries is so sensitive that most commentators prefer to dodge it. If the rich countries are prepared to discontinue the discredited use of foreign aid as an instrument of the Cold War, then the world community should move toward establishing some objective guidelines to be followed by donor countries in determining worthiness among foreign aid recipients. Clearly some countries cannot derive maximum benefit from external aid because of internal constraints. They should be required to put their houses in order first. There are others with such reactionary institutions and leadership that the world conscience should restrain donor countries from assisting them when doing so simply perpetuates injustice. As a trade unionist, I have no moral compunction in suggesting that those developing countries that deny their citizens basic human rights, particularly the right to organize workers into trade unions, should not be given foreign aid.

Trade union movements and cooperative societies in developing countries should benefit directly from foreign aid. I hope that American labor will exert maximum pressure on the government to insure that projects involving labor organizations in recipient countries are included more frequently in lists of "approved projects" under the aid agreements. In those same countries wages are very low partly because labor unions are weak. Therefore, American labor's enlightened self-interest requires that unions should help their counterparts in recipient countries to improve labor's organizing power. With much lower wages in foreign countries, there will always be an incentive for American companies to move jobs away from the United States to lower-wage areas. Aid money can be used to strengthen the labor movement in recipient countries.

TECHNOLOGY, UNEMPLOYMENT, AND THE WELFARE OF WORKERS

Unemployment is a major problem in all developing countries. Foreign aid should be used to support research on labor-intensive industrial techniques. With the character of presently available technology, there is a danger that the introduction of more labor-intensive production methods in factories, in construction, and in services will mean substituting advanced technology with inferior techniques. Most existing know-how in production techniques is capital-intensive. High wages and the scarcity of labor in the developed countries have created a powerful push toward development of advanced technology based on the proposition of substituting workers with machines. Less developed countries cannot therefore import technology appropriate to their needs from the industrialized societies because none exists. It has to be created through research. International agencies such as the United Nations might be used to coordinate an international approach, involving developing countries working together with aid-giving countries.

Indeed, industrialized countries like the United States might find such research useful. There are pockets of undeveloped areas within the United States whose problems are more similar to those of Asia and Africa than the rest of America. There are hundreds of workers who have lost their jobs and who need to be retrained and be given new jobs. In assisting developing countries through research, the United States might learn to meet its own need for reducing unemployment.

Recipient countries should be encouraged to utilize foreign aid to develop a genuine middle class within their own countries. In many countries there are only two antagonistic classes—a very privileged minority and a large starving majority. Organized labor cannot survive as a predominantly workers' movement without a membership that defines itself as a middle class with reasonable possibilities of upward mobility. Governments and political parties tend to equate workers' interests with those of the elderly, the sick, the feeble-minded and the unemployable.

Trade unions, while being concerned with the larger social issues which affect all members of the society, nevertheless should concentrate on and emphasize specific interests of workers. The labor movement should not allow itself to play the role of the government or the church. Our movement must remain partisan and biased, principally for our members. Pressure should therefore be exerted to allocate more resources, foreign as well as national, for labor-oriented economic and social programs. Priority must be given to measures for strengthening organized labor as the most effective instrument for rapid development of a middle class. The American labor movement can help its counterparts in developing countries destroy the social disease of one millionaire for every one million beggars.

NOTES

1. Organisation for Economic Co-operation and Development, Development Assistance Committee, Development Cooperation: 1975 Review (Paris: O.E.C.D., 1976), p. 68.

2. Ibid., p. 194.

3. James W. Howe and John W. Sewell, "Triage and Other Challenges to Helping the Poor Countries Develop," in U.S. and World Development: Agenda for Action, 1975 (Washington: Overseas Development Council, 1976), p. 69.

4. See Bruce Russett, "American Disengagement from World Affairs," World Politics, 1975, pp. 2 and 20.

5. International Labour Office, Employment, Incomes and Equality: A Strategy for Increasing Productive Employment in Kenya (Geneva: ILO, 1972), pp. 15-16 (emphasis supplied).

31

Meeting Basic Human Needs: Third World Demands and American Labor's Response

COLLIN GONZE

THE NEGLECT OF THIRD WORLD AGRICULTURE

Let us take a hypothetical developing country, three-quarters of the population of which are still on the land. The country has been independent for two decades, during which its civil authorities have gradually lost ground to the military. Martial law and suspension of habeas corpus have been in effect for the last two years. Strikes are technically forbidden although they do occur on a small scale from time to time. Wages are set administratively after informal "consultations" with trade union leaders, who count themselves lucky even to have been asked. Wages in the industrial sector are approximately one-tenth of wages for workers in developed countries.

The government has established tax-free zones for overseas companies and tolerates extraordinary returns on investments of up to 30 percent a year, little of which is retained in the country. The casual visitor encounters three very different worlds. The first is that of the rich local entrepreneurs, government leaders and representatives of the overseas corporations that made it all possible. The second is the world on the outskirts of the capital—the industrial zone with its dusty roads and shantytowns occasioned by the presence of mile after mile of foreign-owned assembly and manufacturing plants. And lastly, there is the world outside the capital—the villages and farms, the little plots and fields, the large plantations, a world without adequate schools and health clinics and where the poorest of the poor are agricultural laborers who can scarcely get enough to eat because they are engaged in producing cash crops for export rather than growing the food they need. Our hypothetical country represents a classic case of distorted and unbalanced economic growth, alas not uncommon in the Third World.

In the last 20 years, although 75 percent of the population of most LDCs and 80 percent of the really poor depend on agriculture, less than one-fifth of investments in development have been made in agriculture. The bias of LDC national governments is clearly toward getting as much from agriculture with as little investment as possible. Yet most modern mass-consumption societies were built on the gradual and simultaneous creation of agricultural surpluses of both products and people. Today the real cement in the EC is, of all things, a common agricultural policy. The most significant single sector in U.S. export performance is agricultural products. Aware of the risk of sounding like a pastoral romantic, I submit that, once basic needs are met, rural life can remain for many, no less and perhaps a good deal more satisfying than survival in urban ghettos.

THIRD WORLD CITIES, MULTINATIONALS AND RURAL DEVELOPMENT

Development of provincial and capital cities has drawn the greatest attention and support of national leaders. At first, every piece of flatland is covered with shacks; then these start crawling up the sides of hills, eventually stretching for miles into the countryside. In city after city—Lagos, Manila, Bangkok, Mexico City—the same situation occurs. Three-quarters of the urban population live under bestial conditions, saved from an early death mostly by the softness of the climate. Wrenched from the psychological security of the village and struggling with each other for food, clothing and shelter, these new urban poor constitute a major problem for all Third World governments. People want and call for schools, jobs, food, clean water, clinics, police and they get instead a generous cover of clerks, lawyers and other office workers to administer programs to meet these wants, which rarely deliver much of anything.

It is stunning to watch this implosion, to see a city go from oxcart and bikes to mopeds, vespas and Japanese cars in the wink of an eye. In terms of transportation, Bangkok changed from a U.S. city of the 1880s to one of the 1930s in less than 10 years! To prevent the growth of private transport and to provide adequate public transport in Third World cities calls for a level of governmental effectiveness almost as great as it would to prevent massive migration to the cities in the first place. There is simply no conceivable way in which most Third World governments can meet the expectations of their own city dwellers at present or in the foreseeable future.

The Third World shopping list of greater access to U.S. markets for manufactured goods, generous loans through international financial institutions, direct official assistance without strings and rescheduling of commercial banks debts falls on somewhat deaf ears of American workers—in part because they have their own problems of high unemployment, low or absent economic growth, and inadequate adjustment mechanisms—and in part because they feel betrayed by their own employers, the multinational corporations. When an American corporation closes a plant in this country and opens one making the same product abroad, an intolerable injury is visited on the workers. The sense of being an expendable pawn in a global game of corporate chess being played by unseen manipulators has become widespread among American workers.

When all is said and done, one doubts that developing countries will ever get rich by passively offering themselves as export platforms to multinationals. The first national task of developing countries is to feed themselves adequately. This requires a peasantry of small landowners, free of debt and assured of a profitable return on their labor and land. But the critical question beyond this obvious first step is how to generate the more modest but still necessary foreign exchange to support a development effort which gives priority to food self-sufficiency and other basic needs. A search should be made for a mix of distinctive indigenous economic activities in which the country has enough of a comparative advantage to remain competitive internationally.

Such bootstrap efforts are not going to end the inequitable division of world wealth. The illustration is given principally to demonstrate that workers in industrialized countries will not look with sympathy on special favors to the Third World if multinational corporations are playing a major role in their economies.

BANKS AND FOREIGN AID

Early in the days of the first Nixon administration, the notion that economic aid was rapidly becoming a political dead-weight gained wide acceptance in Washington, and aid levels began to decline substantially. Into the breach conveniently stepped private commercial loans by multinational banks. The sudden injection of OPEC funds into American banks a few years later further increased the volume of loans to certain "acceptable" developing countries. Instead of unprofitable development assistance with its politically damaging stories of waste and corruption, here were sound private investments. And for OPEC, there was a double profit. The first came with the price increase to the Third World, and the second with the interest on funds deposited in American banks.

Many of these private investments were no sounder than they would have been had they originated from the public purse. The risk of losing a loan does not decrease because a private bank instead of a government has made it. Direct foreign exchange assistance has more to say for itself than private loans by multinational banks for at least two reasons.

In the first place, AID is more accountable to us than is Chase Manhattan. Banks are not instruments of public policy but of private gain. Second, AID should more readily be able to call a spade a spade, that is, to know a bad investment when it is made and to call it a grant. AID spreads the risk of assistance to all Americans, where the risk belongs.

THIRD WORLD DEMANDS AND AMERICAN LABOR

The Group of 77's platform of demands has not been exactly calculated to win the endorsement of American trade unionists. In the Charter of Economic Rights and Duties of States adopted by the United Nations at the Third World's insistence, for example, are several paragraphs on the rights and duties of MNCs. The all-too-frequent inducements and hidden promises made by Third World governments to woo MNCs give these words a false ring.

We would have rather seen in that charter a chapter on the rights of workers in developing countries. Although we are aware of the view of some that the task of nation-building must be placed before that of union-building, we do not think that the unionization of Third World urban and plantation workers is an academic question which can be delayed. We believe that "good habits" of trade unionism must be built into developing political economies right from the start and that such implantations will prevent future bitterness, violence and social conflict. To be sure, we do not live in a perfect world; we understand how and why limits are sometimes placed on trade union freedom of action in fragile economies. Nevertheless, Third World governments so bold as to invite MNCs into their lair ought to fear nothing from extending similar invitations to free trade unions.

The Third World demand about which American trade unionists are most sensitive is the call for nonreciprocal decreases in tariffs on manufactured goods. A number of preliminary studies were recently commissioned by the Labor Department to estimate the probable effect of general tariff decreases on U.S. employment. These estimates do not, for the most part, address themselves to the special impact of Third World imports. We need careful analyses of what access under different conditions would mean for the Third World itself, as well as for American workers. At the very least the U.S.-Third World trade in manufactured goods should be roughly balanced.

The question of initiating programs to stabilize selected primary commodities largely exported by the world's poorest countries is a different matter. We should move ahead as rapidly as possible to establish these programs.

American trade unionists are concerned with the total development of Third World economies, not just with the care and feeding of urban elites. Our aid and our attention should be concentrated on evolving programs of broad participation and widespread distribution of the benefits of economic growth. Such assistance should seek to make farming pay and to discourage flight to cancerous cities, as well as to limit ruinous military budgets.

We welcome the rational presentation of economic demands of the Third World. We recognize that the very making of demands is evidence of strength and of awareness of common interests. Bargaining takes place between two extremes. At one extreme, each opponent threatens, "concede or I will injure you," while at the other, opponents present rational, reasonable arguments, granting points with merit, rejecting those without, and in the end, signing stable and renewable agreements. Trade unionists with their extensive experience in bargaining should be much more actively involved in dialogue with the Third World. Only by such involvement can we begin to assume our proper share of responsibility in seeing that the urgent needs of the developing world are met.

ABOUT THE EDITOR AND CONTRIBUTORS

WARD MOREHOUSE is president of the Council on International and Public Affairs, research associate at the Columbia University School of International Affairs, and a Fellow of the Center for International Policy in Washington. He was a visiting professor at the University of Lund in Sweden in 1976-77 and continues his association as Convenor of the Lund Seminar on Science and Technology in the Changing International System. Morehouse has been a Senior Fellow at the East-West Center in Honolulu, visiting professor at the Administrative Staff College in India, and consultant to the Ford Foundation. He was for more than a decade director of the Center for International Programs and Comparative Studies of the University of the State of New York. He is the author and editor of numerous works on development in the Third World and North-South relations, including Science and the Human Condition in India and Pakistan (New York: Rockefeller University Press, 1968), and Science, Technology, and the Global Equity Crisis: New Directions for United States Policy (Muscatine, Iowa: Stanley Foundation, 1978).

JACK N. BEHRMAN is professor of international business at the University of North Carolina at Chapel Hill. An authority on the multinational corporation, he is an advisor to national and international organizations including the National Academy of Science, the U.S. Department of State, and the United Nations. He was assistant secretary of commerce under Presidents Kennedy and Johnson. He is the author of more than 100 articles and several books.

IRVING BROWN is the international representative of the American Federation of Labor and Congress of Industrial Organizations (AFL-CIO) in Europe and represents that organization on the Trade Union Advisory Committee to the Organisation for Economic Co-operation and Development (OECD). He has been actively engaged in Euro-American relations ever since World War II, when he established the present European office of the AFL-CIO. He is also interested in the activities of Eastern European and the Third World, particularly African trade unions.

ARNOLD CANTOR is the assistant director of the AFL-CIO Department of Research. He has been an economist in several U.S. government agencies and the International Labor Organisation (ILO).

He is the author of numerous publications, primarily in areas of public finance and tax policy.

COLLIN GONZE is the coordinator of the World Auto Councils of the International Metalworkers' Federation in Geneva, Switzerland. He was formerly the assistant director in the International Affairs Department of the United Autoworkers of America (UAW) in Washington, D.C.

DONALD L. GUERTIN is a senior advisor on international issues in the public affairs department of Exxon Corporation. He is involved in a variety of industry studies on multinational corporations, including studies concerning the OECD and the United Nations. He is secretary of the USA-Business and Industry Advisory Committee on International Investment and Multinational Enterprise.

HANS GÜNTER is head of the Quality of Working Life and Social Perspectives Sector of the International Institute for Labour Studies of the ILO in Geneva. He is the author of numerous works on social policy, industrial relations, and labor matters connected with multinational enterprises, many of which have been published both in Europe and in the United States. He has recently been appointed ILO advisor on multinational enterprises.

JOCELYN GUTCHESS is currently on leave from her position as senior associate and analyst at Ruttenberg, Friedman, Kilgallon, Gutchess and Associates, Inc., Washington, D.C., to work at the OECD in Paris. She is the author, co-author or contributor of numerous books and articles in the fields of manpower policy and international trade.

MAHBUB UL HAQ is currently director of the policy planning and review department in the World Bank. He has previously served as chief economic advisor to the government of Pakistan. He is the author of several books, the latest being The Poverty Curtain.

PETER HENLE is deputy assistant secretary for policy, evaluation and research, U.S. Department of Labor. In recent years he has been chief economist, Bureau of Labor Statistics, and also senior specialist in labor at the Congressional Research Service, Library of Congress. He has contributed articles to many journals on different aspects of labor economics.

JEROME JACOBSON is senior vice-president of the Bendix Corporation, where he is responsible for long range planning, acquisitions, and divestitures. Formerly he was deputy assistant secretary of state for economic affairs and a consultant to many corporations and governments. He is actively involved in study and discussion groups on international economic affairs.

ELIZABETH R. JAGER has been an economist with the Department of Research of the AFL-CIO since 1955. Her areas of research include international trade, investment issues, and multinational corporations. She has served on the Export-Import Bank advisory committee, the U.N. Commission on Transnational Corporations, and, as chairman, on the foreign labor and trade committee of the Labor Research Advisory Council, Bureau of Labor Statistics.

EVERETT M. KASSALOW is senior specialist in labor, Congressional Research Service, Library of Congress. He has taught labor economics at the University of Wisconsin and held various economic and research positions with the AFL-CIO, including director of research, Industrial Union Department. His publications include books and articles on economic development, industrial relations, multinationals, and other aspects of the labor field.

LANE KIRKLAND is secretary-treasurer of the AFL-CIO.

HAROLD T. LAMAR is staff director of the Subcommittee on Trade, Committee on Ways and Means, U.S. House of Representatives. As professional staff member in charge of trade legislation, he assisted the committee in developing the Trade Act of 1974. An international economist, he has worked with the U.S. Department of Commerce, the U.S. Army Corps of Engineers (Civil Works), and the Legislative Reference Service of the Library of Congress.

ROBERT LEKACHMAN is Distinguished Professor of Economics at Lehman College of the City University of New York. He is the author of _The Age of Keynes_, _A History of Economic Ideas_, _Inflation_, and most recently, _Economists at Bay_. He has contributed to numerous scholarly and general periodicals.

HERIBERT MAIER is general secretary of the International Federation of Commercial, Clerical, and Technical Employees, and a member of the governing body of the ILO. A graduate of the University of Vienna with a doctorate in economics, he formerly held the position of assistant general secretary of the International Confederation of Free Trade Unions.

JOHN W. MELLOR is director of the International Food Policy Research Institute, Washington, D.C. He was formerly chief economist for the U.S. Agency for International Development. Prior to that he was professor of agricultural economics, economics, and Asian studies at Cornell University. He is the author of several books, the most recent of which is The New Economics of Growth: A Strategy for India and the Developing World.

DANIEL J. B. MITCHELL is a Senior Fellow at the Brookings Institution and a professor at the University of California, Los Angeles School of Management. He has written numerous articles in the area of wage determination. Recently, he co-authored, with Arnold R. Weber, The Pay Board's Progress: Wage Controls in Phase II. He is currently working on a Brookings study dealing with the economic effects of collective bargaining.

PEGGY B. MUSGRAVE is currently a visiting professor of economics at the University of California, Berkeley. She was a research associate with the International Tax Program of the Harvard Law School and has served as a consultant with governmental and international agencies. She has written widely on international aspects of public finance and is co-author, with her husband, of the well-known textbook, Public Finance in Theory and Practice.

KIMANI WA NYOIKE is the secretary general of the largest union in Kenya, the Union of Kenya Civil Servants. He is an economist who received his training from Lincoln University in Pennsylvania. He undertook graduate studies in economics at the Massachusetts Institute of Technology. He was administrative secretary of a multi-million dollar state company, the Agricultural Development Corporation of Kenya. He lectures widely in Kenya and elsewhere, on trade union and economic issues.

CLAS-ERIK ODHNER is the head of the research department of the Swedish Trade Union Confederation. He is also active in various international organizations, in particular the trade union advisory committee to the OECD and the European Trade Union Confederation. He has written several books on economic and agricultural policy. He is also one of the co-authors of Wage Formation and the Economy, a book which has played an important part in discussions on wage and prices in Sweden.

SHRIDATH S. RAMPHAL became the first Third World secretary-general of the British Commonwealth in 1975. The period of his stewardship has been one of concern with global issues of political, economic, and social justice. Previously he was foreign and justice minister of Guyana. He is also a member of the Brandt Commission and served on the Joint Economic Committee of the U.S. Congress.

HERMAN REBHAN, general secretary of the International Metalworkers' Federation, was formerly administrative assistant to the late Walter Reuther and director of the UAW International Affairs Department. In 1970 he represented the United States on the ILO Metal Trades Committee, playing a major role in initiating ILO policy on the activities of multinational corporations. In 1978 he was elected to the supervisory board of Ford Motor Company, Germany.

WILLIAM G. RHOADS is economic advisor in the U.S. Agency for International Development (AID) mission in Haiti. He was formerly in the AID Office of Interagency Development Coordination.

DANKWART A. RUSTOW is Distinguished Professor of Political Science at the City University of New York. He previously taught at Columbia and Princeton Universities and served on the senior staff of the Brookings Institution. He served as a vice-president of the American Political Science Association and of the Middle East Studies Association of North America. He has written numerous books and articles, the most recent of which is OPEC: Success and Prospects, with John F. Mugno.

STANLEY H. RUTTENBERG is president of Ruttenberg and Associates, economists and manpower counselors. He was economic adviser to the secretary of labor from 1963 to 1965 and assistant secretary of labor for manpower and manpower administrator, 1965 to 1969. The preceding twenty years he was in various positions with the AFL-CIO, including director, Department of Research, 1955 to 1963.

HOWARD D. SAMUEL is deputy under secretary of labor for international affairs. He was formerly vice-president of the Amalgamated Clothing and Textile Workers Union. He has served as a trustee of the Carnegie Corporation, the Joint Council on Economic Education, and has been a member of several government advisory groups and commissions. He co-authored the books Congress at Work and Government in America.

BERT SEIDMAN is the AFL-CIO social security director. He was formerly AFL-CIO European economic representative. From 1958 to 1976 he was on the U.S. worker delegation to the ILO, serving from 1972 to 1975 as U.S. worker delegate and a member of the ILO governing body. During the 1950s and 1960s he was involved in AFL-CIO activities in international trade and foreign aid.

BEN SHARMAN is the international affairs representative from the International Association of Machinists and Aerospace Workers and serves on the executive committee of the International Metalworkers' Federation. He has spent several years working in the less developed countries for the Peace Corps, the ILO, and the Center for Rural Development. He is author of a number of articles on multinational corporations and trade problems.

GUS TYLER is assistant president of the International Ladies' Garment Workers' Union and director of the union's Department of Politics, Education, and Staff Training. He is a syndicated columnist and has written nine books and hundreds of articles on unionism, politics, crime, minorities, urban affairs, and education. He has taught at several colleges and universities, served on numerous governmental commissions, and lectured before governmental and corporate seminars.

WILLIAM N. WALKER is a member of the law firm of Mudge Rose Gutherie and Alexander, in New York. From 1975 to 1977 he was deputy U.S. special representative for trade negotiations and head of the U.S. delegation to the multilateral trade negotiations in Geneva, Switzerland. Previously he had been general counsel of the Federal Energy Office (1974) and general counsel of the Cost of Living Council (1972-74).

JOHN P. WINDMULLER is professor of industrial and labor relations at Cornell University. He is the author of studies on comparative industrial relations systems, international trade union organizations, U.S. labor's role in American foreign policy, and labor history. At present he is preparing a volume on the international trade union movement.